Israeli Identity

For many years before and after the establishment of the state of Israel, the belief that Israel is a western state remained unchallenged. This belief was founded on the predominantly western composition of the pre-statehood Jewish community known as the *Yishuv*. The relatively homogenous membership of Israeli/Jewish society as it then existed was soon altered with the arrival of hundreds of thousands of Jewish immigrants from Middle Eastern countries during the early years of statehood. Seeking to retain the western character of the Jewish state, the Israeli government initiated a massive acculturation project aimed at westernizing the newcomers.

More recently, scholars and intellectuals began to question the validity and logic of that campaign. With the emergence of new forms of identity, or identities, two central questions emerged: to what extent can we accept the ways in which people define themselves? And on a more fundamental level, what weight should we give to the ways in which people define themselves? This book suggests ways of tackling these questions and provides varying perspectives on identity, put forward by scholars interested in the changing nature of Israeli identity. Their observations and conclusions are not exclusive, but inclusive, suggesting that there cannot be one single Israeli identity, but several.

Tackling the issue of identity, this multidisciplinary approach is an important contribution to existing literature and will be invaluable for scholars and students interested in cultural studies, Israel, and the wider Middle East.

David Tal is the Kahanoff Chair in Israel Studies and a Professor in the Department of History at the University of Calgary, Canada. He is an expert in the history of the Middle East as well as nuclear proliferation and disarmament. His previous publications include *War in Palestine, 1948: Strategy and Diplomacy* (2004), *The 1956 War: Collusion and Rivalry in the Middle East* (2001), *Israel's Conception of Current Security: Origins and Development 1949–1956* (1998), and *The American Nuclear Disarmament Dilemma, 1945–1963* (2008). He is currently working on a history of the strategic arms limitation talks and détente.

Routledge Studies in Middle Eastern Society

This series seeks to examine the various developments and changes in contemporary Middle East society. From a variety of disciplinary approaches it includes books on issues such as globalization, the impact of economic, religious and political change on people's lives, the family, and gender relations in the region.

1. The War in Darfur
Reclaiming Sudanese History
Anders Hastrup

2. Israeli Identity
Between Orient and Occident
Edited by David Tal

Israeli Identity
Between Orient and Occident

Edited by David Tal

LONDON AND NEW YORK

First published 2013 by Routledge

2 Park Square, Milton Park, Abingdon, Oxfordshire OX14 4RN
711 Third Avenue, New York, NY 10017

Routledge is an imprint of the Taylor & Francis Group, an informa business

First issued in paperback 2017

Copyright © 2013 David Tal for selection and editorial matter; individual chapters, the contributors

The right of the editor to be identified as the author of the editorial material, and of the authors for their individual chapters, has been asserted in accordance with sections 77 and 78 of the Copyright, Designs and Patents Act 1988.

All rights reserved. No part of this book may be reprinted or reproduced or utilised in any form or by any electronic, mechanical, or other means, now known or hereafter invented, including photocopying and recording, or in any information storage or retrieval system, without permission in writing from the publishers.

Notice :
Product or corporate names may be trademarks or registered trademarks, and are used only for identification and explanation without intent to infringe.

British Library Cataloguing in Publication Data
A catalogue record for this book is available from the British Library

Library of Congress Cataloging in Publication Data
Israeli identity : between Orient and Occident / edited by David Tal.
    pages cm. – (Routledge studies in Middle Eastern society)
Includes bibliographical references and index.
1. National characteristics, Israeli. 2. Jews – Israel – Identity.
3. Group identity – Israel. I. Tal, David (Historian), editor of compilation.
DS113.3.I873 2013
956.9405–dc23   2012049332

ISBN: 978-0-415-82021-9 (hbk)
ISBN: 978-0-8153-6111-4 (pbk)

Typeset in Times New Roman
by HWA Text and Data Management, London

Contents

List of figures	viii
List of tables	ix
List of contributors	x
Acknowledgements	xii
Israel *in* or *of* the Middle East DAVID TAL	1

PART I
In or out of the Middle East   **13**

1. How it began: Europe vs. the Middle East in the orientation of the first Zionist settlers   15
   ALAN DOWTY

2. Israel and the Middle East: on the unresolved matter of Israel's foreign policy orientation   26
   AHARON KLIEMAN

3. Unfortunate misplacement: Israeli-Jewish public perceptions of Israel in the Middle East   51
   TAMAR HERMANN AND EPHRAIM YAAR-YUCHTMAN

4. The Israeli party system in comparative perspective: a 'unique case' or part of the West European tradition?   65
   CSABA NIKOLENYI

PART II
Contested identities   83

5 Where East meets West   85
   DAVID OHANA

6 The irresolvable geographies of Mediterranean-Israeli music   105
   AMY HOROWITZ

7 The architect and critic Leo Adler and the definition of Tel Aviv as a modern Mediterranean city   118
   YOSSI (JOSEPH) KLEIN

8 Double exclusion and the search for inessential solidarities: the experience of Iraqi Jews as heralding a new concept of identity and belonging   140
   REUVEN SNIR

9 Remote participants: lessons about Israeli identity from the experience of Israeli parents in America   161
   UDI SOMMER AND MICHAL BEN ZVI SOMMER

10 The Israeli triangle: (de)constructing the borders between Israeliness, Jewishness and migrant workers   177
   ROBIN A. HARPER AND HANI ZUBIDA

PART III
Cinema and identity   197

11 Israeli cinema's 'I'm in the East and my heart is in the West'   199
   IGAL BURSZTYN

12 Visions of East and West in contemporary Israeli cinema and television   212
   PAUL KUBICEK

13 MediterEastern blues: new discourses of locality in Israeli cinema   223
   MIRI TALMON

PART IV
Arabs and Jews 237

14 Israeli-Palestinian conflict: the psychosocial and identity
   impact on Arab and Jewish adolescents in Israel 239
   ALEAN AL-KRENAWI

15 Paradoxes of identity: Jewish/Muslim interpenetration in
   Almog Behar and Sayed Kashua 264
   RANEN OMER-SHERMAN

16 Democracy and liberal-democratic values in Religious-Zionist
   discourse: the case of Halakhic Q&A websites 279
   OREN STEINITZ

   Index 293

Figures

3.1	Interest in political regional integration by age groups	56
3.2	Preferences regarding economic regional integration by level of religiosity	57
4.1	The number of parties in Israel	73
4.2	Electoral turnout in Israel since 1949	75
7.1	Architect Leo Adler (1891–1962); picture courtesy of Nurit Arnon	119
7.2	Leo Adler, 'Zur Methodik der Architekturtheorie'; published in: *Wathmus Monatshefte fur Baukunst*, 1–2(1921)	121
7.3	Leo Adler, 'Vom Wesen der Baukunst', Verlag der Asia Major, Leipzig, 1926	122
7.4	Leo Adler, the Blum factory built in Nahalt Yizhak, Tel Aviv, during the 30s; picture courtesy of Nurit Arnon	124
7.5	Leo Adler, Schlagman House built in Tel Aviv during the 30s; picture courtesy of Irmel Kamp Bandau	125
7.6	Leo Adler, 'The Architecture in our country'; published in *Gazith* (8–9)1936	127

Tables

3.1	Attitudes on political, economic and cultural integration into the Middle East	53
3.2	Chances of Israel's integration into the Middle East in the next 20 years	54
3.3	Support for integration into the Middle East (West) by ethnic origin	55
3.4	Regional integration preferences by support-opposition to peace negotiations	58
3.5	Jewish Israelis' estimation of Israel's acceptance in the Middle East if peace prevails	59
3.6	Regional integration preferences of Arab-Israeli citizens	61
3.7	Israeli-Arab citizens' expectations regarding regional political, economic and cultural integration	61
3.8	Arab Israelis' estimation of Israel's acceptance to the Middle East if peace prevails	61
3.9	Logistic regressions	63
4.1	The introduction of PR in Israel and Western Europe	69
4.2	Elections to elected Assembly of the Yishuv	70
4.3	The number of parties in Israel and Western Europe	73
4.4	Electoral turnout in Israel and Western Europe	74
4.5	Cabinet representation of the plurality party in Israel and Western Europe	77
4.6	Cabinet stability in Israel and Western Europe	78
10.1	Distribution of 'legal' migrant workers in Israel	184
10.2	Survey sample characteristics	186
10.3	Identity ranking	188
14.1	Nationality differences on sociodemographic variables	245
14.2	A comparison of Jewish and Palestinian-Israeli participants on political violence and psychological functioning	246
14.3	Pearson product moment correlation coefficients between the research variables	247
14.4	Political violence, nationality, and sociodemographic variables as predictors of psychosocial functioning	248

Contributors

Igal Bursztyn, Adjunct Professor at the Tel Aviv University Film and TV Department.

Alan Dowty, PhD, Professor Emeritus of Political Science, University of Notre Dame, Indiana.

Robin A. Harper, PhD, Assistant Professor of Political Science, York College (CUNY), New York.

Tamar Hermann, PhD, Vice President for Academic Affairs, The Open University of Israel.

Amy Horowitz, PhD, Scholar in Residence, Lecturer at Melton Center for Jewish Studies and International Studies at Ohio State University, Columbus.

Yossi (Joseph) Klein, Architect and Urban Planner, Senior Lecturer at The Bezalel Academy of Art and Design, Jerusalem.

Aharon Klieman, PhD, Dr. Nahum Goldmann Professor Emeritus in Diplomatic Studies, and Founding Director of The Abba Eban Graduate Program in Diplomacy at Tel Aviv University. Senior Editor of *The Israel Journal of Foreign Affairs*.

Alean Al-Krenawi, PhD, President of Achva Academic College and Professor at Spitzer Department of Social Work, Ben-Gurion University of the Negev, Israel.

Paul Kubicek, PhD, Professor of Political Science and Director of Religious Studies at Oakland University in Rochester, Michigan.

Csaba Nikolenyi, Professor and Chair, Department of Political Science, Co-Director, Azrieli Institute of Israel Studies, Concordia University, Quebec.

David Ohana, PhD, The Ben-Gurion Research Institute for the Study of Israel and Zionism, Ben-Gurion University of the Negev, Israel.

Ranen Omer-Sherman, PhD, Professor of English and Jewish Studies, University of Miami.

List of contributors xi

Reuven Snir, PhD, Department of Arabic Language and Literature, University of Haifa, Israel.

Michal Ben Zvi Sommer, Senior Psychologist, Women's Health Project, St. Luke-Roosevelt, New York.

Udi Sommer, PhD, Assistant Professor, Tel Aviv University.

Oren Steinitz, PhD candidate at the University of Calgary's Interdisciplinary Graduate Program, concentrating on Judaism, Islam and the Internet.

David Tal, PhD, Kahanoff Chair in Israel Studies, Professor of History and the Director of Israel Studies Program, University of Calgary, Alberta.

Miri Talmon, PhD, Chair of the Department of Communication and Senior Lecturer at the Nazareth Academic Institute, Israel. She also teaches with the graduate (MA) program at Tel Aviv University, Faculty of Arts, Department of Film and Television.

Ephraim Yaar-Yuchtman, PhD candidate, Head of the Tami Steinmetz Center for Peace Research at Tel Aviv University, and Head of the Evens Program in Mediation and Conflict Resolution, Tel Aviv University.

Hani Zubida, PhD, Assistant Professor, Department of Political Science, The Max Stern Yezreel Valley College, Israel.

Acknowledgements

This book is the result of a workshop hosted by the Israel Studies program at the University of Calgary in October 2010. The authors presented papers, which they turned into articles published in this collection. I would like to thank the authors for the work they put into their presentations and into the articles.

The Kahanoff Foundation, based in Calgary, and Calgary's Jenny and Hy Belzberg financially supported the program, making it possible to have the workshop and the other activities of the Israel Studies program. I would like to thank the Foundation and the Belzbergs for their generous support.

Israel *in* or *of* the Middle East

David Tal

It is commonly held that Israel is a western state – 'the last European nation-state,' as Ran Halevi, the French scholar, calls it.[1] For many years before and after the establishment of the state of Israel, this belief remained unchallenged. It was based on the predominantly western composition of the pre-statehood Jewish community known as the *Yishuv*. The vast majority of the 650,000 Jews living in Israel when it achieved statehood in 1948 were of eastern and central European origin. The relatively homogenous membership of Israeli/Jewish society as it then existed was soon altered with the arrival of hundreds of thousands of Jewish immigrants from Middle Eastern countries during the early years of statehood. Seeking to retain the western character of the Jewish state, the Israeli government initiated a massive acculturation project aimed at westernizing the newcomers.

Only in recent years did scholars and intellectuals begin to question the validity and logic of that campaign. Political interests undoubtedly motivated these questions, as those affected by the acculturation process felt that they were denied their rightful place within Israeli society, economy and culture, but these claims do have merit. Ella Shohat, for example, introduced the term 'Arab-Jew', arguing that the Jewish elite, who were Ashkenazi, 'invented' the Mizrahi in order to separate him from his real environment, which is the Arab environment. Thus, rather than retain their real identity, which was Arab, under the influence of the Zionists, the Jews of Arab origin became Mizrahi and, therefore, part of the Zionist project. In fact, argue Shohat and other Jewish intellectuals of Arab origin who have followed her, Israel is Arabic, as the Arabs within Israel, among whom she counts both Jewish and non-Jewish Arabs, constitute a majority of Israelis.[2]

Shohat and those who followed her did, in a sense, what the Ashkenazi had done: they imposed an identity on people who might not accept that identity. As Yehuda Shenhav admits, his branding of the Mizrahi as Jewish-Arabs was met with great resistance by those affected by his (or, indeed, Shohat's) proposal.[3] Thus the question is: to what extent can we accept the ways in which people define themselves? When someone says that he is a Jewish-Arab, should we 'believe' him? If someone else identifies himself as Occidental in his mindset, should we regard him as such, even if his birthplace is Iraq? In other words, what weight should we give to the ways in which people define themselves?

There seem to be several ways to answer these questions. The first is by allowing people to decide for themselves. If enough people assert that they share common traits and hence constitute a community (or ethnicity or nation), then their claim cannot be ignored.[4] If this is the measure, then it would appear that the proponents of the idea of Jewish-Arabs as the source of identity have failed to garner the support of the 'people'. To date, only a few academics have defined themselves as Jewish-Arabs. The vast majority of the Mizrakhim, the would-be Jewish-Arabs, reject this label; as we can see from the reaction of many of them to a suggestion along these lines that was made during a conference at Tel Aviv University in May 2008 on the integration and culture of Iraqi Jewish immigrants to Israel. According to a news report, 'The stormiest debate arose when most of the lecturers objected to the definition "Arab Jew". This term, commonly used by the members of the Mizrahi Democratic Rainbow Coalition and Sephardic Jewish intellectuals, angered many of the conference participants.'[5]

Another way to address the above questions would be through the creation of objective criteria, as exemplified by Sammy Smooha, one of Israel's prominent sociologists. Suggesting a quantitative approach, Smooha questions what he defines as 'the premise of mainstream sociologists' (who – according to him – constitute the vast majority of sociologists in Israel), which holds that Israel is a western society. This premise is false, argues Smooha. He lists a large number of reasons to support his claim that Israel is not in fact a western state. Because this list includes most of the arguments proffered by scholars on this issue, I will present all of them here: the Israeli democracy is not truly western; Israel does not have a constitution; Israel has been under a constant state of emergency (which has never been lifted) since 1948; the principle of equality has not been explicitly established by law, and inequality under the law exists between Jews and Arabs and between men and women; Israel's borders have been extended by protracted occupation; in western societies all citizens are considered one nation, that is, they constitute a civil nation, whereas in Israel an Israeli nation does not exist, and ideological opposition to the creation of one nation, which would include all citizens, is prevalent; no western state defines itself as belonging to its ethnic majority group and to ethnic people who do not reside within it rather than to its citizens and residents; western societies maintain a *de facto* separation between religion and state, whereas the state of Israel divides its citizens into religious groups, does not allow individuals to leave their group, and determines individual status on the basis of these religious groups; Israel is a developed state with high indexes of human development, but approximately 25 percent of its population are poor, while half of those employed earn wages below the tax threshold – not because of low tax rates but because of the low wages they earn; most of the people in Israel belong to the lower strata or consider themselves underprivileged, including Arabs, Sephardim, the ultra-religious, Russians and Ethiopians; the birthrate in Israel is lower than the average in the west.[6]

A third way to approach the questions posed above would be to concentrate on the *idea* of Orientalism[7] and Occidentalism. The use of a self-proclaimed identity and the checklist method to define Israel's orientation tell only part of the story.

Another important ingredient, which has remained under-discussed but is of major importance in our understanding the meaning of the state of Israel, entails exploration of the meaning of Orientalism and Occidentalism. This approach makes it easier to argue that Israel is a western state, relying not only on its western attributes and the examples presented above, which are in fact seen as reflective of larger phenomena. Israel is western because its core values are western.

The idea of Occidentalism

Military historian Victor D. Hanson poses the question of 'Why the West Has Won'. To answer this question, he begins with the story of the 10,700 Greek warriors who were recruited by Cyrus the Younger to support his claim to the Persian throne. The warriors made the 1,500-mile journey from Greece to north Babylon and crushed an entire wing of the Persian army at the cost of one wounded Greek hoplite, only to find that their services were no longer needed. Unpaid, without supplies and surrounded by many enemies, the 10,000 began their journey back home, a journey described by one of their commanders, Xenophon, in his book *Anabasis* ('The March Up-Country'). 'Surrounded by thousands of enemies, their original generals captured and beheaded, forced to traverse through the contested lands of more than twenty different peoples, caught in snowdrifts, high mountain passes and waterless steppes, suffering frostbite, malnutrition, and frequent sickness, as well as fighting various savage tribesmen,' the Greeks made it back to their destination – the shores of the Black Sea – 'largely intact' less than a year and a half after having left home. 'Five out of six made it out alive, the majority of the dead lost not in battle, but in the high snows of Armenia.'[8]

How did it happen? How could these 10,000 make it against all odds? Their values and culture made it possible, explains Hanson. The soldiers were all free men and felt equal with one another: 'a lowly Arcadian shepherd had the same vote as the aristocratic Xenophon.' Each of them felt that he was in control of his own destiny, and his leaders were those he elected. The Greeks fought with 'a sense of personal freedom, superior discipline, matchless weapons, egalitarian camaraderie, individual initiative, [and] constant tactical adaptation and flexibility.' The Greek way of war was the result of 'consensual government, equality among the middling classes, civilian audit of military affairs, and politics apart from religion, freedom and individualism and rationalism.'[9]

These were the values that would become the values of the western world from ancient to modern times: 'organization, discipline, morale, initiative, flexibility', 'sense of legal freedom' and '[f]ree inquiry and rationalism'. The westerners had 'little to fear from religious fundamentalism, state censors, or stern cultural conservatives.'[10] These values are at the heart of what is termed here 'the Occident', which reached the present western world through modernism.

Modernism marked a dividing line in the history of Europe and divided Europe from the rest of the world. It also provided the other essential component that distinguished the west from the rest of the world and from its own past: secularism. Beginning with the 14th century's Renaissance and continuing through the 17th century's scientific revolution as well as the Enlightenment and the developments that took place during those centuries, Europe changed the course of its and the world's history in a profound way. The shift happened on several fronts, all of which were interrelated. First, the Renaissance's humanism put an emphasis on knowledge that served no religious purposes. While still strongly attached to Christianity, the humanists explored the writings of ancient Greek and Roman scholars, and knowledge became more widely available. This pursuit of knowledge was aimed at benefitting the citizen, not just the believer.[11] That knowledge then laid the foundation for a new way of looking at and understanding the world. It did not aim to serve any purpose other than itself and humanity. The work of individuals, most prominently those of the 17th century, expanded the boundaries of knowledge not only through new revelations but also through the employment of new approaches and methodology that enabled such exploration. The 17th-century scholars no longer referred to the scriptures as a source of knowledge and scientific authority, but to the writings of the ancients. They posed questions about those writings and sought to explore the findings of the ancients while using methods that could provide them with knowledge and data that were not dependent on the scriptures. Furthermore, they rejected the content of the scriptures when their findings contradicted these scriptures. The Renaissance shifted the attention from the God-made world to human beings and the individual. The 17th-century scientists secularized science.[12]

It would be hard to overstate the significance and impact of secularization on European society and, later, on the rest of the world:

> The human sciences are secular, whatever the inadequacies of the dominant account, and in this sense, secularization has occurred. The human sciences are everywhere premised on humanist presumptions – their founding presumption is that the objects of their study are what men (and later women), not gods and spirits, have made and that from these cultural objects we can re-create the human world that produced them. The social sciences are resolutely secular and humanist, even if the humans they study often are not – and nothing illustrates this better than the modern study of religion, which presumes that it is not gods that explain men but men whose needs, fears, and desires are projected onto the gods.[13]

Hence, two western principles emerged at this early stage in the history of modern Europe: first, that human beings should be considered the center of the universe, and second, that science and knowledge should be independent of Church or religion. These two principles, along with individualism, laid the foundation for the creation of a west that became a world power – intellectually, economically, politically and militarily.

The value and impacts of the *idea* of westernism were manifested when the Occident prevailed over the Orient. After millennia of Muslim dominance, the Christian west prevailed over the Muslim Orient. Consequently, the Muslims sought to meet the west on its own terms. The Orient endorsed modernity and technology, and the Ottoman leaders – and later the Arab leaders – armed their forces with modern weaponry and equipped their nations with technology and industry. Science made possible the cannon and the tank. What allowed science to create the tank and the cannon, however, was the dissociation between knowledge and religion. This dissociation did not mean that people could no longer turn to God. It meant that they did not look for truth in the Holy Scriptures. They now looked for the truth around them, in the world surrounding them, in the world they had created – their laboratories and the world of science. Their truths were no longer subject to transcendental truths, nor were they themselves. They could believe in God, but they were at the same time sovereign, free people. They were individuals, standing on their own, subject only to themselves.

This was a distinction that separated the Orient from the Occident. The Muslim forerunners of Arab nationalism attributed the Islamic world's fall from glory and subjugation to western powers to the technological inferiority of the Muslim world. Their solution, however, was not to embrace western ideas and practices, but to call for the revival and reformation of Islam. Indeed, Arab nationalism was based on religion. Muslim intellectuals grappled with the deterioration of Islam, seeking to invent their own brand of modernism, one that would suit the needs of the new world.[14] They did not, however, intend to make fundamental changes in Islamic doctrine that would allow science and people to be free from the shackles of religion, as can be deduced from the statement of Egyptian religious teacher and scholar Muhammad 'Abduh:

> [T]he cure for these ills of Muslim countries is not to be found in multiplication of newschapters, for these have little influence; nor in the introduction of schools modeled after those of Europe, for these can be used, together with the sciences they teach, to foster foreign influence; nor in European education and imitation of foreign customs, for imitation has only succeeded in quenching the spirit of the people and drawing down upon these countries the power of the foreigners whom they imitate. The only cure for these nations is to return to the rules of their religion and the practice of its requirements according to what it was in the beginning, in the days of the early caliphs.[15]

Religion as an impediment to scientific progress is blended with the social rejection of individualism. Individualism as a concept is denounced by the Arab society: 'the Arabic word for "individuality" or "individualism" (*fardiya*) is derived from a root with a mixture of positive and negative connotations.'[16]

Examining Israel's orientation from the perspective of the *idea* of Occidentalism, the conclusion that Israel has been and remains a western state is justifiable. This certainly was how the founding fathers of the state of Israel, most notably David Ben Gurion, saw and envisioned it. While the Israeli leadership was unanimous in its assumption that Israel should be western (as were the leaders themselves; that is, the vast majority of the Israeli elite at the time of the establishment of the state was western), it was Ben Gurion who most frequently voiced his views on this issue. The bottom line of his advocacy on this subject was that Israel was an enclave within a very hostile Middle East. According to Ben Gurion, perpetuating the Occidentalism of the *Yishuv* and, later, of Israel was vital to the existence of the fledgling state in a hostile Middle East. Because of his profound fear regarding the ability of the Jewish state to survive in the Middle East, Ben Gurion regarded westernism and modernism as vital to the survival of the state of Israel. He believed that only a western-oriented Jewish state had a chance of overcoming the existential challenges it faced and of surviving until the day its neighbors accepted it in their midst. The best way for Israel to withstand the existential threat it faced and to survive would be to maintain its western features and excel in its western abilities, especially its scientific and technological advantages. All hopes revolved around this.[17]

Geographically, argued Ben Gurion, Israel was in the Middle East, but by any criteria it was different from its neighbors. It was different in 'its language, the fundamentals of its existence, its spirit and values, in its political and social regime and in its historical destiny.' Israel belonged, 'without doubt', to the group of democratic nations that adhered to the freedom of the individual and respected the freedoms of thought, speech and science.[18] Material modernism and science, however, were not enough. What mattered most, argued Ben Gurion, was not the science and technology, but the man and his spirit. He highly appreciated western and modern qualities such as individualism and independence of thought, and he placed a high value on the sovereignty of the individual.[19]

Ben Gurion's vision of Israel, like his contemporaries', was of a modern, western, democratic state and society: the civilian should be both an active and willing participant in communal and state life, an individual who was free in his thinking. Those two aspects of citizenship were complementary in Ben Gurion's eyes, and he saw them as the essence of a free and democratic society that could flourish precisely because its citizens were part of the state as well as individuals. Ben Gurion drew from the republicanism that had emerged in Europe, which was based on the ability of the individual to shape his life by his own will and power. He was also part of a community, and the authority of the community – the state – was derived from the individual's willingness to waive, of his free will, some of his rights in order to allow the community to accomplish what was also dear to the individual.[20]

To what extent did this idea correspond with reality? While 21st-century Israel seems to diverge significantly from the Israel envisioned by Ben Gurion – unified and struggling toward similar goals, the basic premise that drove him and his contemporaries is still valid. The *idea* of westernism remains a very conspicuous feature of life in Israel and can be found in various venues. Furthermore, as Ephraim Yaar-Yuchtman and Tamar Hermann's chapter reveals, one characteristic unifies Ashkenazi and Mizrahi, religious and non-religious, Jews and Arabs: the desire to see Israel as part of the Occident.

The discussion hitherto has concentrated on what I call the external aspects of identity; that is, identity as seen from the outside. This form of identity does not depend on what people think or feel but is, rather, based on parameters that are external to them. Yet identity also encompasses the way people feel, think and talk about it. A discussion of identity cannot avoid examining it from the inside as well. When viewing identity from this perspective, matters become more complicated because even members of the same community (let alone the same state) can 'choose' different identities, and each is valid. This variety is illustrated in the volume before us, where we can find all the features introduced above: the self-perception, the quantitative approach and the idea of identity.

The first section discusses the place of Israel in the Middle East and addresses the question of the extent to which Israel is part of the Middle East, and the extent to which it only resides there without actually being part of the region. The underlying assumption of the four chapters within this section is that Israel is *in* the Middle East, but not *of* the Middle East, an assumption that is strengthened by the conclusion Ephraim Yaar-Yuchtman and Tamar Hermann draw from their survey, which shows that most Israelis, regardless of their ethnicity – Ashkenazi or Sephardic, Jewish or Arab – and regardless of their religion – from completely secular to orthodox Jews, all want to see Israel associated with the west politically, culturally and economically.

Alan Dowty goes back to the roots, to the arrival of the first Zionist *Aliya* (immigration), and in so doing also addresses the relations between the *idea* of the west and the practice. He shows that while the new arrivals detached themselves from the Europe that had rejected them, and even imitated the attire of the local Arab population, still 'they overwhelmingly clung to their European identity', and they did so because they believed that Europe was superior to the Middle East and that their Europeanism would serve them much better in their colonization of the land of Israel. He depicts the regional forces of integration and separation among the new immigrants and concludes that to this very day the issue remains unresolved.

Aharon Klieman also assumes that Israel is a western state and society, detached from the region – it is *in* the Middle East but not *of* the Middle East – and he suggests that it is in Israel's interest to rectify that state of affairs while still adhering to the *idea* of the west. That is, Klieman emphasizes the geo-strategic necessity for Israel to take measures that would lead to its integration with the region, but Israel should do this without relinquishing its western features. Israel should remove the political obstacles that prevent it from becoming *of* the Middle East, without distancing itself from the west. The *idea* should remain; Israel's foreign policy should change.

As much as the idea is important, it is not enough. Practice must follow in its wake, and this is the theme of Csaba Nikolenyi's chapter comparing the Israeli party system with those of western European states. Adopting a quantitative approach, Nikolenyi establishes that while Israel's political system is unique by Middle Eastern standards, it is not so when compared with those found in western Europe. Csaba Nikolenyi traces the genesis of the Israeli party system and compares it with the political systems of western European party systems. His approach to the study of the Israeli political system is, once again, to refer to the *idea*. Nikolenyi looks 'under the hood' of Israel's political system and compares it with the premises upon which western political systems are based, concluding that the Israeli political system is indeed similar to the western European system. This is hence a quantitative research chapter but one that goes beyond mere data analysis.

The section entitled 'Contested identities' is an example of the complexity of the subject of identity in Israel. The question of identity in this collection is viewed along the east-west axis, but it is not necessarily a dichotomy comprising two distinct options or two ends that cannot meet. Using the model of a triangle defined by idea, practice and demography, the unavoidable conclusion is that the lines dividing Occident and Orient are not impenetrable. The Mediterranean option, introduced and advocated by David Ohana, supports this conclusion. The Mediterranean option brings together Orient and Occident and provides a place for 'permanent dialogue, creative synthesis', where 'it is in their reciprocal difference that each discovers itself.'

One area where the Mediterranean option seems to apply is in the field of music. At a time when the Israeli society was still culturally predominantly Ashkenazi, the first sign of awakening on the part of the Sephardim was through music. Singers and performers of Muslim-state origin performed in clubs in the periphery, and their music was introduced through cheaply produced cassettes that were sold in Tel Aviv's central bus station during the early 1970s. Amy Horowitz has studied the impact of the music that originated from these first endeavors on Israeli society. While challenging the Ashkenazi music, these musicians did not brand their music as Arabic. Then, as today, this genre was called Mediterranean music, thereby avoiding the label 'Arabic', even though Arabic musical themes are evident in the songs. At the same time, Horowitz also shows how, through the use of different musical instruments, Mediterranean music encompasses a wide range of musical styles that stretch from the Occident to the Orient. All of this is illustrated through the career of one of the most successful singers of the Mediterranean style, Zehava Ben, who is also among the very few Israeli-Jewish performers who has never hesitated to sing Arabic music openly. Through Zehava Ben's career, Horowitz shows how the Mediterranean and Arabic tones have infiltrated the Israeli-Jewish mainstream, even at times of deepening tensions along the Israeli-Palestinian front.

The story that Yossi (Joseph) Klein tells is in a sense the opposite of the one told by Horowitz. If the latter described a shift from the margin to the mainstream, the former tells the story of an architect who tried, decades before Zehava Ben, to introduce Oriental elements in a mostly Occidental city and failed. The city is Tel Aviv and the architect is Leo Adler, who wished to integrate Tel Aviv's architecture, which was predominantly western during the 1920s and 1930s, with the region's culture, the 'region of the Mediterranean'. Adler's story is a story of failure, symbolizing the inability and reluctance of the *Yishuv* to become *of* the Middle East, even if only through architecture. Adler's contemporaries represent the very same group that determined the nature of the Jewish *Yishuv* and state for many years to come.

The east-west dichotomy, salient in the chapters discussed hitherto, is challenged by Reuven Snir, who introduces and makes the case for multiple identities. Snir's argument is double-fold: it is up to the individual to 'choose' his identity, and one can have more than one identity. Such is the case with Iraqi Jewry, which indeed represents a more complex phenomenon than the Occident-Orient dichotomy. Identity, argues Snir, is an otherness; that is, more than an intrinsic quality, it is defined by others. Thus, the identity of Iraqi Jews cannot simply be defined along the Orient-Occident axis. It contains a variety elements, some of which are exclusive and some inclusive.

The subject of Snir's inquiry is the person who made the journey from the outside to the inside – from Iraq to Israel. This subject has multiple identities, argues Snir, and he presents some of them. In contrast, the subject of Udi Sommer and Michal Ben Zvi Sommer's chapter took the opposite path – from the inside to the outside – emigrating from Israel to the United States. Here we learn that the emigrant too also has multiple identities. What makes this case interesting, though, is that it also provides an opportunity to see identity at work; that is, identity as an empirical field. Because there is a somewhat 'dictated' element to identity, wherein scholars make definitions and distinctions that presumably apply to the relevant group, the Sommers' chapter provides an opportunity to see objects turned into subjects, as the authors introduce what in their eyes is an Israeli identity. The Sommers' chapter makes it evident that identity is also a matter of resolution: when in Israel, the Israeli would ask, 'What kind of Israeli am I?'. But when he is an émigré, his Israeliness defines him as opposed to his new (possible) identity as (in this case) American.

Immigrants must deal with their identity under changing circumstances and within a new geography. Yet immigrants also effectively present a mirror in the face of the people they have joined because, as Robin A. Harper and Hani Zubida show us, the reaction of the people on the receiving end toward the immigrants reveals a great deal about the way the former view their own identity. That is, immigrants force the absorbing community to review their own identity. Harper and Zubida offer two criteria by which to measure the impact of foreign-labor immigrants on Israeli identity: first, by Israel's treatment of foreign-labor immigrants, and second, by the way in which the immigrants themselves, through their stories, determine the limits and boundaries of Israeli (i.e., Jewish) identity. The authors' conclusion is that from both perspectives, the foreign-labor immigrants have deepened the schism between Israeliness and Jewishness, pushing Israel further away from western democratic values toward segregated and exclusive modes of identity.

Even before Israeli movies became a subject of scholarly attention, it was quite obvious to anyone who watched them that they are loaded with statements pertinent to the east-west divide. Any Israeli (indeed, anyone) who saw films such as *Salah Shabati, Katz and Carasso* or *Casablan* could see the east-west divide in operation, even if the true ramifications and messages of those films were yet to be explored. As Igal Bursztyn observes in the introduction to his chapter, the study of Israeli cinema became a very rich field of research and an important source of our understanding of issues pertaining to Israel's identity and place along the Orient-Occident divide. *Salah Shabati* marked a shift in Israeli cinematography, which 'moved away from Soviet-like heroism to Western-like individualism.' In a process that took several years, Israeli filmmakers began to scrutinize the cultural options available to Israelis, suggesting that neither Orient nor Occident should be ruled out.

Paul Kubicek shows how the Occident-Orient options are set in motion in Israeli cinematography through the study of two films (*Lemon Tree* and *For My Father*) and one TV series (*Arab Labor*). What is new and unique about these three pieces, argues Kubicek, is that they break away from the east-west and Jewish-Arab line of division. The setting is the Arab-Israeli conflict, but the heroes overcome the stereotypes of Jew and (especially) Arab, struggling to reach out toward each other across political divisions while actually being close culturally and socially. With such works of art, concludes Kubicek, Israeli films are no longer 'Eurotropic' but rather much more 'polyphonic'.

The polyphonic voices of Israeli cinematography are also demonstrated by Miri Talmon. Talmon suggests that the Mediterranean option is in fact a place of meeting – and multiculturalism, where various cultural trends are merged. She identifies this feature within Israeli cinematography, which reflects 'a range of cultural and historic phenomena, which construct discourses or narratives about this "place" – as a geo-political, cultural, historic or ethnic site of expression, action and interaction.' The films she analyzes reflect this aspect of Israeli life, which comprises diverse cultural discourses.

The Arab-Israeli conflict seems to be an issue that crosses the Occident-Orient lines of division within Israeli society, at least among Jews. Music that otherwise might be regarded as Arab is dubbed Mediterranean in Israel, and the attempts of Mizrahi activists such as Ella Shohat and Yehuda Shenhav to change the lines of division from Jews (both Mizrahi and Ashkenazi) vs. Arabs to Jews (Ashkenazi) vs. Arabs (Mizrahi and non-Jewish Arabs) were met with resistance by many Mizrahim. The power of the traditional Jewish-Arab line of division is evident in the chapter by Alean Al-Krenawi, who studied the impact of politically motivated violence on Jewish and Arab youths. His findings substantiate the assumption that the conflict is stronger than the cultural and social divisions embedded in the Orient-Occident divide. While acknowledging the diversity and heterogeneity of the Jewish population, Al-Krenawi finds that Jewish adolescents are better able to deal with political violence than Palestinian adolescents. One reason might be the better medical treatment available to Jews, but another explanation might be the cohesiveness of Jewish society and their feeling that their cause is just, and hence the violence easier to handle. The in-group solidarity in this case is stronger than the centrifugal forces that otherwise seem to plague Israeli-Jewish society.

Where Al-Krenawi finds inter-communal division, Ronan Omer-Sherman finds encouraging signs of reconciliation. Al-Krenawi analyzes the Israeli/Jewish-Arab divisions from the perspective of the injured, whereas Omer-Sherman relies on men of words, Jews and Arabs, and finds through their works 'a more hopeful multicultural ethos based on an expansive sense of regional belonging (that transcends national identity).' Analyzing two stories of mixed and hence confused identities, Omer-Sherman sees them as an option for blending rather than continued separation. Identities are mixed, but these mixtures present viable options. Orient and Occident blend together, creating a new and refreshing reality.

One feature at the heart of Occidentalism is modernity and technology. While technology is an obvious hallmark of western society, one should not confuse westernism with modernism. Modernism is a tool that can be transferred across societies – the decisive factor is the idea, the values. This cannot be more evident than in the case presented by Oren Steinitz. While using what is considered practically the frontier of present technology – the internet – its religious users transmit messages and values that are anti-western and anti-liberal. Indeed, as Steinitz observes, 'While it is evident that the democratic nature of the medium has had its impact on the nature of the online Jewish legal discourse, it is not clear whether this influence has extended to content rather than form.' In fact, throughout the chapter Steinitz shows that, essentially, the influence of this modern tool has not permeated the content of the messages transmitted through it. Thus, a modern tool is put in the service of an old mechanism, the Jewish Q&A – *Shut* (in Hebrew: *she'elon u'tshuvot*) – where communities and individuals asked contemporary prominent Jewish scholars questions regarding the *Halacha* (Jewish law). Here, through a survey of internet sites that serve the same purpose – where rabbis provide online answers to questions that were also posed online – Steinitz concludes, 'While some responders seem to have absorbed the Western mindset regarding universal human rights and equality, the majority of scholarly opinions found on the web demonstrate that ideas of cultural exclusivity, and even ethnic superiority, still dominate extensive portions of the Religious-Zionist discourse.'

This conclusion brings us back to where we started: data, checklists and self-identifications are important tools for categorizing identities. Yet the ideas and values upon which people rely are no less important. Sometimes these are the best definer.

Notes

1 Ran Halevi, "The Elusive Idea of the Nation: Israel in the Mirror of Modernity", *Journal of Israeli History*, Vol. 26, No. 2 (2007), 140.
2 Ella Shohat, "Sephardim in Israel: Zionism from the Standpoint of its Jewish Victims", *Social Text*, No. 19/20 (Autumn 1988); Ella Shohat, "The Invention of the Mizrahim", *The Journal of Palestine Studies*, Vol. 29, No. 1 (Autumn 1999); Ella Shohat, "Reflections by an Arab Jew", available at http://www.bintjbeil.com/E/occupation/arab_jew.html (Accessed on July 20, 2010). Yehuda Shenhav, *The Arab-Jews: Nationalism, Religious and Ethnicity* (Tel Aviv: Am Oved, 2003).
3 Shenhav. See also Salim Fattal, *An Idol in the Temple of the Israeli Academy* (Jerusalem: Rubin Mass, 2010).
4 Edwin N. Wilmsen, "Premises of Power in Ethnic Politics", in Edwin N. Wilmsen and Patrick McAllister (eds.), *The Politics of Difference* (Chicago, IL: The University of Chicago Press, 1996), 2.
5 Verel Lee, "Conference asks: Iraqi Israeli, Arab Jew or Mizrahi Jew?" *Haaretz.com*, http://www.haaretz.com/print-edition/features/conference-asks-iraqi-israeli-arab-jew-or-mizrahi-jew-1.246035. (Accessed on July 24, 2011.)
6 Sammi Smooha, "The Israeli Society: Society like any Other or Sui Generis?" *Israeli Sociology* 11, No. 2 (2010), 298–299.

7 I use 'Orientalism' here to mean a place and mindset, rather than the way Edward Said uses it.
8 Victor D. Hanson, *Why the West Has Won* (London: Faber and Faber, 2001), 2.
9 Hanson, *Why the West Has Won*, 2–3.
10 Hanson, *Why the West Has Won*, 21–22.
11 John Merriman, *A History of Modern Europe*, Vol. 1 (New York: W.W. Norton & Company, 2010) (third edition), 56–58.
12 Merriman, *A History of Modern Europe*, Vol. 1, 288–296.
13 Sanjay Seth, book review: "Vincent P. Pecora, Secularization and Cultural Criticism: Religion, Nation, and Modernity", *Modern Philology*, Vol. 107, No. 2 (November 2007), 306.
14 Nissim Rejwan, *Arab Faces the Modern World* (Gainesville, FL: University Press of Florida, 1998), 2–26.
15 Rejwan, *Arab Faces the Modern World*, 19.
16 Brian Whitaker, *What's Really Wrong with the Middle East* (London: Saqi, 2009), 61.
17 David Ben Gurion, *Uniqueness and Destination* (Tel Aviv: Ministry of Defense Publications, 1971), (April 1950), 193, 210, 213–214; ibid. (March 1953), 358.
18 Ben Gurion, *Uniqueness and Destination* (March 1953), 352.
19 Ben Gurion, *Uniqueness and Destination* (November 1948), 43–44; Ben Gurion, *Army and Security* (August 1949), 109–110.
20 Nir Kedar, "Jewish Republicanism", *Journal of Israeli History*, Vol. 26, No. 2 (September 2007), 179–199.

Part I
In or out of the Middle East

1 How it began

Europe vs. the Middle East in the orientation of the first Zionist settlers

Alan Dowty

To what extent did early Zionist pioneers of the first *aliyah* (1882–1905) seek to integrate the Jewish national movement into a Middle Eastern context, and to what extent did they see themselves as bearers of European civilization in a non-Western land? In other words, what patterns did the first quarter century of Jewish settlement set in relations with the existing culture and population of the area? Let us turn to the diaries, letters, and publications of the first Zionists to find answers to these very fundamental questions regarding the orientation of those who set the stage for the subsequent development of the *yishuv* – the Jewish community in *Eretz Yisrael*/Palestine – and ultimately of the state of Israel.

The focus here is on the 'new' *yishuv*: those who arrived in Ottoman Palestine during this period, mainly from Russia. The new *yishuv* initially constituted a minority against the 'old' *yishuv*: the already-established, predominantly orthodox, Jewish community. This first *aliyah*, or wave of immigrants, has also been overshadowed by the second *aliyah*: those who arrived between 1905 and World War I and who captured the high ground in the ideological battle between the generations. For this reason the first *aliyah* has been relatively neglected in Zionist historiography, yielding pride of place and prestige to those who followed it and laid claim to a more decisive role in shaping the ideas and institutions that eventually formed the state of Israel. But at the same time, those who arrived earliest did set the stage for what was to follow, creating a framework that may have influenced their successors in many subtle ways, and for this reason it is important to investigate their stance on critical issues – such as orientation between West and East.

It is also important to understand the initial state of mind with which early Zionists approached these questions, before the press of events and new realities forced changes. This is especially true of issues involving the Arab population, regarding which many of the settlers became more prescient in the course of time and then tended to project this wisdom backward to indicate that they were aware of this problematic relationship from the outset. For this reason, it is preferable whenever possible to rely on contemporary documents from the period surveyed and from the settlers themselves, as in the quotations that follow below.

The international context

Before looking at the settlers, however, we need to emphasize two critical basic facts about the international context of the time. The first fact is the seriousness of threats to the Ottoman Empire – the sovereign power in what others called The Holy Land – and the impact that this had on the Ottoman position in Palestine. Over the previous two centuries, the Ottoman Turks had lost half of their empire to a combination of European imperialism and nationalist uprisings by European-oriented minorities. And as the Turks saw it, the Zionist movement combined both of these threats.

Furthermore, in their remaining territory the European powers were assiduously pursuing their prerogatives under the so-called 'Capitulations', which gave them extensive extraterritorial powers. The Capitulations had originated as agreements under which European states had been granted jurisdiction over their own citizens who happened to be in Ottoman territory, something that was quite consonant with Muslim and Turkish traditions of giving autonomy to non-Muslim minorities. But in the course of time the European states had asserted more extensive jurisdiction over entire categories of non-Muslims, including Ottoman citizens: France emerged as the protector of all Catholic Christians in the Ottoman Empire, Russia assumed the right to intervene on behalf of Orthodox Christians, and so on. Since the right to claim protégés meant the right to intervene within Ottoman territory, and since the powers were engaged in keen rivalry among themselves, there was even intense competition for protégés. For example, when Russia declined the opportunity to protect Russian Jews in Palestine – since they had hardly bothered to protect them in Russia before they fled – Great Britain, which suffered from a lack of constituencies they could claim as their own, stepped in temporarily to claim that role.[1]

In this context, the idea that the Ottoman government would willingly accept the introduction within its territory of a new community, representing yet one more European-oriented minority, was the pinnacle of self-delusion. The Turks closely followed the emergence and development of the Zionist movement, and they made consistent if ineffective efforts to prevent Jewish immigration to Palestine, to forbid land purchases by those who managed to get there, and to withhold building permits on lands that were nevertheless purchased. Why were these measures not more effective? In fact, we do not know how effective they were since we do not know how many Jews would have settled in Ottoman Palestine had the restrictions not existed. But those few thousands who managed to overcome these obstacles were aided by the inefficiency and corruption of Ottoman rule, by various subterfuges used to circumvent the rules, and above all by frequent interventions of European governments, under the Capitulations, to protect their own citizens and force the Ottomans to grant equal rights to non-Muslims (for example, many of the early Zionist settlements, supported by the French Baron Edmund de Rothschild, were protected by frequent French diplomatic intervention).

The second important contextual element was a deep hostility among the indigenous Arab population to all European presence or intrusion. This hostility, dating back to the Crusades (of which it was in part a legacy), has been well documented in contemporary accounts. When European powers were finally allowed to open diplomatic missions in Jerusalem in the 1830s – for the first time since the Crusades! – the first consuls were able to move about only with the protection of armed escorts.² This hostility was not 'nationalist' in the modern sense; as numerous observers have pointed out, there was no Arab nationalist movement of consequence before the early twentieth century. But it clearly represented a collective consciousness of Muslims, of Ottoman subjects, of members of local communities and clans, and perhaps most basically of an indigenous population facing what they saw as the intrusion of an alien presence. For such an instinctive and visceral response, no articulated ideology or fully formed national identity is required.

The bottom line is that both Turks and Arabs saw the early Zionist settlers as Europeans more or less in the same category as non-Jewish Europeans (the comparison to the German Protestant Templers, who settled a few years earlier, is instructive).³ Turkish authorities even saw the influx of Russian Jews as part of a plot by the Tsarist regime to create a pretext for further intervention in Ottoman affairs; this suspicion must be read in light of the intense hostility between the two states, which fought each other in 13 wars over the centuries. In any event the Ottoman government clearly distinguished between *Ashkenazi* (European) Jews and the existing *Sephardi* (Eastern) Jewish community within the Ottoman Empire, which was culturally assimilated and recognized officially – as the *Ashkenazi* community was not. In fact there were tensions, even *before* the rise of Zionism, between the Ottoman government and the *Ashkenazim* of the old *yishuv*, who also tended to remain European and claim the protection of their countries of origin. The early Zionists, in this respect, were fitting into an already existing pattern.

Rejection of Europe?

Let us turn now to the thoughts of these early Zionists about the choice between European and Middle Eastern models. At first, it might seem quite logical that they would have rejected Europe, which had failed them so miserably. For an entire generation, influenced by the *haskalah* or Jewish Enlightenment, Russian Jews had looked to assimilation into a progressive West as the path of the future. Now this vision had been cruelly dashed to pieces by a tidal wave of vicious anti-Semitism that swept Russia following the 1881 assassination of the Liberator Tsar, Alexander II, and the ascension of his reactionary son Alexander III to the imperial throne. To the dismay of young upwardly mobile Jews, even educated Russians had participated in these tragic events or turned a blind eye. The dominant mood was one of bitter disillusionment. To take one typical example, Vladimir (Ze'ev) Dubnow, one of the members of the pioneer settlement group Bilu, wrote to his brother:

> With my own eyes I saw the terrible tragedy in one of the more beautiful and enlightened cities. ... In one flash all my illusions were revealed, and all the beautiful pictures of the future, that I and my friends painted for ourselves, dissipated like smoke. ... There is a source of hope. Eretz Yisrael must become our future land.⁴

And occasionally these expressions did extend to the rejection of Europe as a model. For example, a notable article by one Moshe Aizman appeared a few months after pogroms began in *Hamelitz*, the Hebrew-language weekly published in St. Petersburg that became the main organ of the early Zionists. Aizman wrote:

> The [Jewish] people ... must turn their back to all the luminaries and mighty lords who choose to assimilate Israel among the nations, and must help one another to settle in the land of our fathers, where there is no 'Japhet' and therefore no hatred toward the descendants of 'Shem'; there the enflamed mob will not charge us with the libel that we slaughtered their gods; there no one will dare to say that we are aliens. There we will not be enslaved by the fist of an impure European civilization. There we will spread the wellsprings of the civilization of the Children of Shem among our relatives, the Arab tribes, and the civilization of Shem is – wisdom and morality, love of mankind and peace. Ishmael is our brother, the son of Abraham our father, a believer in the oneness of the creator, and the children of Abraham cannot be predators and plunderers and murderers like the children of Japhet.[5]

An echo of this sentiment can be found in the words of Zalman David Levontin, the main mover behind the first settlement, Rishon Letsion, in 1882. Writing soon after the event, Levontin recounts an encounter with anti-Semites on a Russian train during the first days of the 1881 pogroms. Since the hatred was directed against all sons of Shem, he resolved to return to live among the sons of Shem.[6] Clearly the idea of assimilating to the Middle East was also favored by *Sephardi* Jews who were already living in *Eretz Yisrael*, for example Nissim Malul:

> We must consolidate our Semitic nationality and not obfuscate it with European culture. Through Arabic we can create a true Hebrew culture. But if we introduce European elements into our culture then we will simply be committing suicide.[7]

There were also instances of the superficial adoption of Arab dress or customs among some of the early settlers, as they sought to emphasize their sense of belonging to the reclaimed homeland. For example, when they began organized duty as guards of the settlements, they often imitated the dress and style of the horseback Arab guards whom they had initially hired as protectors. This tendency carried over into the early days of *Hashomer*, the first defense organization founded somewhat later in 1909.

But these were the exceptions.

Affirmation of Europe

The dominant attitude in Zionist circles, both in Europe and among the settlers in *Eretz Yisrael*, was represented by Moshe Leib Lilienblum, one of the leading figures among Russian Zionists, who responded immediately to Aizman's attack on European civilization:

> There are many among us in general who, after the pogroms, let out their fury at the haskala in all its aspects and argue that we have to return to the ways of our fathers in the Dark Ages. It is hardly necessary to say that this is ... so much froth on the ocean.[8]

The *haskalah*, or Jewish Enlightenment, represented the adoption of European culture and ideas, and the first *aliyah* drew disproportionately from the ranks of the *maskilim* (followers of *haskalah*). They had absorbed much of European culture, and while disillusioned by the failure of European societies to practice what they preached, they still believed in the fundamental progressiveness of European civilization. If pressed on this, they probably would have responded that European ideas and ideals were still a model to be emulated and that the Europeans themselves should give them a try.

This was, if anything, even more pronounced among those who actually found themselves outside of Europe, in *Eretz Yisrael*. Finding themselves in a non-European context, they overwhelmingly clung to their European identity as a point of reference and overwhelmingly thought of this identity as a favorable factor in their new and challenging environment. It is striking how often the word 'European' crops up in the earliest writings and expressions of the settlers, whether in reference to European culture, European agriculture, European education, European law and order, European technology, or European ethics – and finally in reference to themselves, in agreement with the way they were perceived by the native population, as Europeans. What happened was similar to the magic by which later immigrants to Israel from English-speaking lands became 'Anglo-Saxons'. The first settlers had not referred to themselves as 'Europeans' while still in Russia, and had good reason to be bitter about their place of origin. But when they arrived in *Eretz Yisrael*, they became Europeans.

This unsurprising shift of identity was occasioned in the first place by the undeniable cultural difference they encountered upon arrival, and it was reinforced by the self-flattering perception of the superiority of European civilization. One admittedly extreme example was Yehuda Leib Bienstock, writing from Jaffa in 1892:

> And in general, Asia has not yet tasted the taste of civilization, and until this day the Biblical way of life continues slowly and in its ancient purity. Naturally Europeans (including our Jews) are a harsh dissonance here.[9]

Coming from this perspective, it was natural to expect that the Arab inhabitants of Palestine would acquiesce in the colonization process, just as other peoples around the world were – in his view – falling into the orbit of European influence. It is important to remember the prevailing assumptions of a period in which European powers were establishing their control over Africa and much of Asia, after having Europeanized the entire Western hemisphere. The spread of European models was considered to be synonymous with the spread of modern civilization.

The same Zalman David Levontin who spoke of living among the sons of Shem also made it clear that the settlers expected to be the senior partner in the relationship:

> And if the colonies are established in bonds of love and peace, then the holy land will be a land of freedom and liberty for them; they will not hear the voice of the gendarme and the oppressor, and the Arabs who people the land will submit to them with the attitude of love and respect they show to all Europeans who work the soil and engage in commerce here ...[10]

In one account, even the animals belonging to the Arabs had learned to regard Europeans with awe and trepidation. When Arab cattle, sheep, or goats were allowed to graze on cultivated Jewish fields, the practice was to round them up and hold them for ransom until compensation for damages was paid. Haim Hisin, another member of the pioneer group Bilu, wrote in his diary that rounding up the animals was not easy because 'the wild beast of the Arab is very fearful of a European.'[11] (However, in another vein, Hisin also admits that the settlers' certainty of European superiority was not always grounded in reality in such areas as agriculture: 'Many, know-it-alls in their own eyes, regarded Arab farming with scorn, and discussed with exaggerated self-confidence European agricultural theory – of which their understanding was extremely murky.'[12])

Be that as it may, the dominant attitude was that Jews coming from Europe had much to teach to and little to learn from the peoples of the Middle East. This was expressed with great clarity a few years later by Joseph Klausner, editor of the influential journal *Hashiloach* (founded by Ahad Ha'am) and leading intellectual:

> But I certainly would not want ... the Jews to imitate the Arabs and the Beduins, that is, to be influenced by a primitive culture. ... We, the Jews, who have dwelt two thousand years and more among cultured peoples, cannot and must not descend again to the cultural level of the semi-barbaric peoples. ... Is the change of center to be only this, that we leave the Exile of Edom for the Exile of Ishmael?[13]

It was only natural, therefore, that Zionist settlers would rely on European protection, clinging to their European passports and invoking the intervention of European diplomatic agents to overcome Turkish resistance to their enterprise. This of course only confirmed in the minds of Ottoman officials that Zionists were in fact simply another agency of European penetration. But the intervention of French, British, Austrian, German, and even Russian Consuls in support of the rights of their nationals was often vital in supporting the Zionist colonies during critical moments. For example, in the new settlement of Petah Tikva, founded in part by Jews with German citizenship, the German Consul not only intervened to forestall demolition of houses built without permits, but even threatened to mobilize the German Protestant Templers from the nearby settlement of Sarona to prevent such action![14] The parallel between Templers and Zionists has already been noted; among other things, both faced similar problems of Turkish and Arab hostility, and both were protected diplomatically by their countries of origin. Despite being competitors in some respects (for available land in particular), the two communities faced similar situations and shared some common interests, as strange as that may appear in retrospect.

The theory of benefits

In sum, early Zionist settlers clung to their European identity for a number of reasons: first, because of the stark reality of very real differences between the world they had left and the new and strange environment into which they had ventured – together with a sense of superiority toward that new setting. Second, this self-perception was confirmed by the fact that Turkish rulers and Arab residents also treated them as Europeans. But perhaps most critically, this difference provided the strongest argument, in their own minds, in defense of the establishment of a new community in the midst of an existing society.

This is a key point and it bears elaboration: *the assumed difference between Europe and the Middle East, and the assumed superiority of the former, provided a key justification in relations with the Arab population.* This view is splendidly illustrated in an example that not only encapsulates the dominant view in stark language, but also condenses into a few days an evolution of thinking that typically took much longer. The exemplar in this case is none other than Eliezer Ben-Yehuda, a legendary figure revered as the father of modern spoken Hebrew but also a key mover in the first *aliyah* who deserves to be remembered for his larger role in early Zionism.

In his account of his arrival at the port of Jaffa in 1881, Ben-Yehuda wrote:

> I must confess that this, my first meeting with our cousins Ishmael, was not a joyous meeting for me. A depressing feeling of fear, as though before a fortified wall, suddenly filled my soul. I felt that they see themselves as citizens of the land that was the land of my fathers, and I, the son of these fathers, I come to this land as a stranger, as a foreigner, as the son of a foreign land, son of a foreign people. ....[15]

But, in the same account, Ben-Yehuda records his feelings a few days later:

> I ... also found a little comfort regarding the general position of the Arabs in Eretz Israel, which I have also managed to observe: that in general it is very lowly, that they are impoverished paupers and total illiterates. This fact ... was for me the first ray of light since the moment that my foot first trod on the land of our fathers.[16]

Discovery of the great gap between Europe and the Middle East of their time, as the first settlers saw it, not only made achievement of Zionist goals more conceivable but also added a new positive dimension to the entire project.

Zionism would bring the benefits of modern civilization to this unenlightened corner of the world and to its untutored people. This 'theory of benefits' would later become the heaviest piece of artillery in the Zionist rhetorical arsenal in debates over the 'Arab question' – as in, for example, Theodor Herzl's famous 1899 letter to Yusuf Zia Al-Khalidi.[17] But the thinkers of the first *aliyah* anticipated this argument and, in the case of Ben-Yehuda, raised it from the very outset of exposure to the issue. A couple of years later, Ben-Yehuda added the argument that being in this position was also highly beneficial for the difficult task of building a new Hebrew nation:

> The nation in whose midst we dwell ... is not an enlightened nation. ... Here too this country is better for us than any other ... because we want to revive our nation ... and how can we succeed in this in a country where ... there is an enlightened nation? ... In such a country the Jews will not be able to be a separate nation in spirit and language even if they want to, because an enlightened nation will not let them do so. ... This is not the case with a non-enlightened nation.[18]

Separatism vs. integration

The framework of European vs. Middle Eastern orientation can be usefully recast along the lines of Yosef Gorny's separatist and integrationist outlooks on the relationship of Zionism to the Arab population of Palestine.[19] These distinct schools of thought, which had emerged by the end of the period under review, largely correspond to the central division under review here: separatists were *de facto* Europeanists since they fell back on the cultural baggage they had brought with them, while integrationists advocated some kind of accommodation to Middle Eastern cultures and realities.

This is not a perfect correlation. There were separatists (Ahad Ha'am, the later Moshe Smilansky) who accepted the need of some kind of accommodation with the local population. There were also integrationists who wanted Arabs to assimilate to Jews, rather than the reverse; this included Rabbi Binyamin (Yehoshua Radler-Feldman) and socialists such as Yitzhak Ben-Zvi who believed that class struggle would override national conflict and provide common ground for the two communities. But basically separatism was associated with a Europcentric outlook, while pursuit of integration implied a more positive attitude toward Arabs and toward the Middle East generally.

In this debate separatists were clearly the dominant voice, for the reasons already cited but also as a result of the historical legacy of Jewish relations with non-Jews. Jews had historically sought to separate themselves from host populations in order to maximize Jewish autonomy and security.[20] Zionism built upon this tradition and in fact took it to its logical conclusion: building a Jewish society that was totally independent and sovereign, no longer subject to the dictates of others but exercising an equal right of self-determination in the family of nations.

This line of thinking led to the corollary that the issue of relations with the Arab population needed no solution *beyond the success of Zionism itself.* There was no need to abandon the course of separate development; in a Jewish Palestine, Arabs would be in the same position as minorities in all other societies – the position that Jews had so often occupied. In this view it was not necessary, or perhaps even advisable, to pursue active programs of integration or accommodation. In a Jewish Palestine, Arabs would enjoy prosperity and humane treatment as individuals, but they would remain separate from the dominant identity and narrative.

Even Ahad Ha'am, a separatist with strong liberal views, did not advocate accommodation with Arabs beyond the need to deal with them fairly. His seminal 1891 article, written on the occasion of his first visit to the new Jewish settlements in *Eretz Yisrael*, is often cited as the first serious Zionist recognition of the Arab question, and Ahad Ha'am himself is accordingly seen as the first dove in debates over the conflict. But a closer look reveals that there are only two passages, in a rather lengthy (and scathing) review of the entire Zionist enterprise, that deal with 'the Arab question'![21] These two passages, quoted endlessly in numerous discussions of the topic, do take a step beyond previous expressions by recognizing a collective Arab dimension and by urging the need to deal in a fair and humane way with Arabs. It was no longer sufficient, given this perspective, to think of the existing population in *Eretz Yisrael* simply as non-Jewish *individuals* who could be left out of the equation.

But on the whole, Ahad Ha'am's article fits into the prevailing theory of benefits: Zionism's very success would, in the end, resolve the issue by creating a Jewish framework to which others would have to adjust. This success would, he reasoned, provoke some hatred by the time that it reached this ultimate goal, but – in a passage much less often quoted – he added that 'this is nothing. ... By this time our brothers would be able to secure their position in Eretz Israel by their large number, their extensive and rich holdings, their unity and their exemplary way of life.'[22]

In other words, even though Ahad Ha'am recognized a collective dimension to the Arab presence in *Eretz Yisrael*, he did not foresee any need to negotiate with Arabs on the collective level, as one people to another (at a later date, he denigrated the idea of publishing a Zionist newspaper in Arabic in order to reach out to the other side[23]). The course of events would make this unnecessary. Nor did he, or others of this period (with minor exceptions), expect that Zionists would need to use force in order to achieve their goals. At this time the idea of Jewish military might was still non-existent as a historical legacy or as a conceivable future option. Again, the success of Zionism in itself would resolve the issue.

Ahad Ha'am was, in the final analysis, the exception that proved the rule.

The second, integrationist, side of the debate was introduced by Yitzhak Epstein, an educator who settled in Rosh Pina in 1886 and was active in the movement to teach Hebrew in Hebrew. Coming at the end of the first *aliyah* period, Epstein provided the first analysis that projected the eventual dimensions of the problem and introduced the full integrationist agenda:

Let us open our public institutions wide to residents of Eretz Yisrael ... let us arrange popular lectures, plays, and musical performances to their taste and in their language; let us give an important place to the Arabic language in our schools and willingly enroll Arab children in them. ... We have a duty to become properly acquainted with the Arab people, their attributes, their inclinations, their aspirations, their language, their literature, and especially to gain a deep understanding of their life, their customs, their sufferings and their torments.[24]

But the separatists were, as noted, the dominant voice. Epstein's article, published in the journal founded by Ahad Ha'am, evoked numerous negative reactions, including one from the writer Nechama Pukhachewsky that appeared in *Hashiloach* itself:

Mr. Epstein said correctly that it is very hard to buy the love of the Arabs; but if so, why should we toil in vain? The more we grovel, the more they hate us, the more we continue to submit, to enslave ourselves, the heavier our yoke. ... So please let us abandon this path of defeat and proceed by a straight track to our rebirth; let us begin to think about ourselves, our existence and our happiness.[25]

At this point, the lines of debate begin to look familiar. Obviously there have been many changes over the years, reflecting new circumstances. But at its core there remains the issue of whether and how the Jewish state could and should integrate into the region.

And the debate began with the prevailing view that it could not and should not.

Notes

1. Isaiah Friedman, "The System of Capitulations and its Effects on Turco-Jewish Relations in Palestine, 1856–1897", in David Kushner (ed.) *Palestine in the Late Ottoman Period: Political, Social, and Economic Transformation*, Jerusalem: Yad Yitzhak Ben-Zvi, 1986, p. 281, and Arnold Blumberg, *Zion Before Zionism*, Syracuse, NY: Syracuse University Press, 1985, pp. 114–15.
2. Blumberg, *op. cit.*, p. 18.
3. On the Templers, see Alex Carmel, "The German Settlers in Palestine and Their Relations with the Local Arab Population and the Jewish Community 1868–1918", in Moshe Maoz (ed.) *Studies in Palestine during the Ottoman Period*, Jerusalem: The Magnes Press, 1975, pp. 442–465, and Mahmoud Yazbak, "Templars as Proto-Zionists? The 'German Colony' in Late Ottoman Haifa", *Journal of Palestine Studies*, 28, No. 4 (Summer 1999): 40–54.
4. "Michtavei haver agudat bilu" [Letters of a Bilu Pioneer], *B'tsaron*, Iyar-Sivan 5719 [April-June, 1959], translated from Russian by L. Shefel. Located in the Kressel Archive, Oxford Centre for Hebrew and Jewish Studies, files by subject, "First Aliyah and Bilu". The letters, clearly those of his brother Vladimir (Ze'ev), were first published in 1915 by the noted historian Simon Dubnow in the Russian-Jewish publication *Yevreiskaya Starina*.
5. Aizman, "P'nei halot halot" [Face of the Covering Shroud], *Hamelitz* 20 (June, 1882): 392.

How it began 25

6. Levontin, *L'eretz avoteinu* [*To the Land of our Fathers*], first edition, Warsaw: n.p., 5644 [1883–1884], pp. 10–14
7. Malul, "Our Position in the Country", *Haherut*, June 1913, quoted in Yosef Gorny, *Zionism and the Arabs 1882–1948: A Study of Ideology*, Oxford: Clarendon Press, 1987, p. 48.
8. Lilienblum, "Ezrat sofrim: michtav lamol" [Authors' Assistance: A Letter to the Publisher], *Hamelitz* 22 (June 8, 1882), 436.
9. Bienstock, letter to Menashe Margalit, June 19, 1892, *M'yamim rishonim* 2, parts 5–6 (October-November 1935), 199.
10. Levontin, letter to Peretz Smolenskin, March 19, 1882, in Shulamit Laskov (ed.) *K'tavim l'toldot hibat-tsion v'yishuv eretz-yisrael* [*Documents on the History of Hibbat-Zion and the Settlement of Eretz Yisrael*], Tel Aviv: Hakibutz Hame'uchad, 1982, pp. 190–91.
11. Hisin, *M'yoman achad habiluim* [*From the Diary of One of the Biluim*], Petah Tikva: Beit Neta, 1967, p. 75.
12. Hisin, *op. cit.*, p. 91.
13. Yosef Klausner, "Hashash" [Foreboding], *Hashiloach* 17 (July-December 1907), 575–76 (the bound volumes of this journal do not specify issue dates).
14. Friedman, *op. cit.*, p. 287.
15. Ben-Yehuda, Eliezer, *Kol kitvei Eliezer Ben-Yehuda* [*Collected Writings of Eliezer Ben-Yehuda*], Vol. I, Jerusalem: Ben Yehuda Press, 1941, p. 26.
16. Ben-Yehuda, *op. cit.*, p. 36.
17. Ernst Pawel, *The Labyrinth of Exile: A Life of Theodor Herzl*, New York: Farrar, Straus & Giroux, 1989, pp. 406–7.
18. *Hahavatselet* 31 (1882–83): 242, quoted in Jack Fellman, *The Revival of a Classical Tongue: Eliezer Ben-Yehuda and the Modern Hebrew Language*, The Hague: Mouton, 1973, pp. 43–44.
19. Gorny, *op. cit.*, pp. 40–57.
20. Alan Dowty, *The Jewish State: A Century Later*, Berkeley, CA: University of California Press, 1998, 2001, chapters 2 and 5.
21. Ahad Ha'am, "Emet m'eretz yisrael" [Truth from Eretz Yisrael], *Hamelitz*, June 19–30, 1891, translated with commentary and notes in Alan Dowty, "Much Ado about Little: Ahad Ha'am's 'Truth from Eretz Yisrael', Zionism, and the Arabs", *Israel Studies* 5, No. 2 (Fall 2000), 154–181.
22. Dowty, "Much Ado", p. 178.
23. Gorny, *op. cit.*, pp. 59–60.
24. Epstein, "She'elah ne'elamah" [A Hidden Question], *Hashiloach*, 17 (July-December, 1907), 193–206, translated with commentary and notes in Alan Dowty, "A Question That Outweighs All Others: Yitzhak Epstein and Zionist Recognition of the Arab Issue", *Israel Studies* 6, No. 1 (Spring 2001), 51, 52.
25. Pukhachewsky, "She'elot galuyot" [Revealed Questions], *Hashiloach* 18 (January-June 1908), 67–68.

2 Israel and the Middle East

On the unresolved matter of Israel's foreign policy orientation

Aharon Klieman

From a strictly geopolitical perspective, where (if anywhere) do Israel's core interests and future prospects lie? Posing the question in this sixth decade of Jewish statehood serves in itself to attest to the unrelieved tenuousness of Israel's foreign policy moorings.

For a country like Israel not to be party to any formal international treaty alliance and neither incorporated within any self-evident regional grouping nor possessing any clear, unambiguous regional identity might perhaps be shrugged off as inconsequential in today's transnational world. Still, the wave of political turbulence in the Arab belt of countries most immediately surrounding Israel during 2011 only further contributes to a sense of disconnectedness. Of not exactly fitting in; and considering the violent and unstable nature of Arab and Middle Eastern politics, perhaps not even wishing to fit in. While at the same time posing once again existential questions: Is the Jewish State fated to be physically *in* the Middle East but never really *of* the Middle East in the fullest sense? And were it the case that Israel is not and will not be intimately of the Middle East, must non-acceptance and non-integration remain of such major concern given the sufficiently wide and infinitely more appealing range of prospective geostrategic alternatives?

Whither Israel?

When confronted by signs of regional and international apartness, Israeli nationalist true believers, in their complacency, may instinctively seek comfort in the prophet Jeremiah's reassuring '*lo alman Yisrael*', wherein Israel – both the eternal people and the contemporary state actor – are never friendless and abandoned, nor ever to be left without survival options. Yet, when viewed geopolitically rather than philosophically, a recent string of temporal diplomatic reversals underscore the abiding impression of conditionality by the Middle Eastern and global communities in acceptance of the State of Israel. Consequently, informing all Israeli decision-making in the realm of '*chutz u'bitachon*' (foreign affairs and security) is a palpable sense of still not quite belonging. Least of all in the midst of today's unpredictable Middle East crosscurrents, with their mixture of both hope and anxiety.

Israel and the Middle East 27

Among the more stinging as well as worrisome recent diplomatic setbacks: a Palestinian-forced United Nations Security Council draft resolution condemning Israeli housing construction in East Jerusalem endorsed by all 15 members save for the United States; nearly universal dismissal of Israel's legal brief for its maritime blockade of Gaza; Turkey's rather abrupt turnabout in its posture of close strategic cooperation towards Israel; mounting boycott initiatives within otherwise friendly countries targeting Israeli manufacturers, academics, generals, sportsmen and visiting public figures; audible censure of Israeli policies regarding both the disputed West Bank territory and the derailed peace process by the United States, the European Union and the UN-backed Middle East Quartet. In the first weeks of 2011 the political sandstorm spreading so rapidly from Tunisia across the entire expansive Arab region, with Egypt at its epicenter, only further heightened Israeli insecurities, offsetting otherwise noteworthy diplomatic triumphs such as burgeoning bilateral ties with India, or accession to the prestigious Organization for Economic Cooperation and Development (OECD).

Normally, states are expected to pursue their national interests initially through direct diplomatic, commercial and cultural contacts within their regional neighborhoods and with immediate neighbors before spreading the net in seeking allies further afield. Yet true regionalism encompasses something far deeper than political convenience in pursuing alignments, or efficiencies of scale when calculating preferred patterns of trade. To be truly 'European' or, for that matter, 'Middle Eastern', implies the sense of a *shared* fate or destiny; of *mutual* security; of a *common* and hence better tomorrow. '*Jointness*', in a word, is what epitomizes strong confederations and regional integration.

Unlike most other countries, however, the proximate Middle East just beyond Israel's borders has been diplomatically off limits for most of its political history. Neither conference rooms nor negotiating tables serve as the principal venue for Israelis meeting Arabs. Instead, countless battlefields straddling both sides of Israel's exposed northern, eastern and southern frontiers mark the principal points of bloody contact.

This geopolitical reality of a foreign policy unanchored in what political geographers refer to as 'propinquity' and 'contiguity' has been a constant of Israeli foreign relations: from admission into the family of nations in 1948–1949 until the present. As a result, the country's bedrock diplomatic orientation, subject, on the one hand, to the ironclad Arab veto on membership in Middle Eastern councils and, on the other hand, to larger global forces beyond the capacity of a small state to control, remains very much fluid. Indeed, in the historical pattern of Israeli foreign affairs and alliance policy the only consistency is its inconsistency.

Is Israel authentically Western and European? Asian? Third World? Middle Eastern? All of the above? None of the above? The resultant inability of successive governments to determine which part of the world commands Israel's closest attention and where national efforts and talents might best be concentrated accounts in large part for two dominant foreign policy images, neither of them particularly reassuring. 'Perfidious Israel': an unprincipled and entirely opportunistic international state actor shifting tack with the wind in a constant search for momentary openings and settling for provisional *ad hoc* partnerships. Alternatively: 'Satellite Israel' – a dependency of the United States, and therefore sovereign in name only.

To which might be appended a third no less unflattering characterization: 'Fortress Israel': a pariah state; withdrawn, defensive, militaristic; closed in on itself, and thereby evoking yet again the all too familiar historical subtext of Jewish ghettoization, only this time more on a vast than localized scale. If an intractable Arab-Israeli conflict and its concomitant of longstanding Arab denial to Israel of a Middle East presence represent the two most formidable barriers to diplomatic normalcy, then Israeli leaders have been singularly unsuccessful at removing them. And, as a result, equally unsuccessful over the last 60-plus years at steering a consistent foreign policy course founded upon a fixed regional affiliation outside and beyond the Middle East.

Anywhere but the Middle East

We begin nonetheless with the Middle Eastern option, which by reason of sheer physical proximity ought to have been the Jewish State's logical orientation, and was in fact its original inclination. State archives amply document initiatives by pre-state Zionist diplomacy aimed at accommodation with moderate Arab nationalism dating back to the January 1919 Weizmann-Feisal agreement, with its proud reference to 'the racial kinship and ancient bonds existing between the Arabs and the Jewish people'. Thereafter, efforts at an understanding branched off into separate negotiations with any number of Arab notables from Cairo to Baghdad, and from Amman and Beirut to Damascus.

Outreach toward this most immediate Arab hinterland was never better articulated than in the Declaration of the Establishment of the State of Israel which in May 1948 solemnly pledged:

> We extend our hand to all *neighboring* states and their peoples in an offer of peace and good neighborliness, and appeal to them to establish bonds of cooperation and mutual help with the sovereign Jewish people settled in its own land. The State of Israel is prepared to do its share in a common effort for the advancement of the *entire Middle East*. [Italics mine]

But this ideal was soon shelved in favor of capsule self-descriptions reflecting the new state's inhospitable geopolitical realities. Already in the 1950s Israel came to be portrayed – and to regard itself – as a 'garrison state', and a veritable 'island' – of stability, of democracy, of anti-communism – with all else being mere commentary. This trope of Middle East encirclement resonates even today in the celebrated reference by Foreign Minister Abba Eban in May-June 1967, quoting the Egyptian newspaper *Al Gumhuriya* on how 'The noose around Israel's neck is tightening'.

When compelled to look out at the world, Israelis overwhelmingly continue to perceive themselves and their country as having the misfortune of being situated physically *in* the Middle East, but certainly not being part *of* the Middle East in any real sense. Israel as an island surrounded by Arab and Muslim enmity thus continues to serve as the unchallenged foundational premise of Israeli foreign and security affairs. More than that, in retrospect the extraordinary 1977 Sadat-Begin peace offensive and the equally dramatic 1993 Oslo initiative only momentarily revived Israeli hopes for regional acceptance and integration.

On the contrary, given their precariousness the disappointingly minimalist 'cold peace' with Egypt and Jordan since 1979 and 1994 respectively remain the solitary deviations from the Arab norm of formal non-recognition. Rather than providing inspiration for renewed efforts for a wider Middle East breakthrough, they only serve at present to arouse deep concern among Israeli publics and officials alike, especially in the context of Iran's regional ascendancy and strides toward nuclear capability, Turkey's *volte face*, Hizbullah's stranglehold over Lebanese politics and the spread of Islamic radicalism, combined with domestic opponents of the peace treaties both in Cairo and Amman stridently demanding their cancellation. Besides which, in world politics such parchment barriers to conflict as legal peace treaties do not necessarily indicate genuine acceptance on the part of former belligerents.

In terms of actual diplomatic practice, therefore, the climate of Arab rejection and hostility into which Israel was born has led over six subsequent decades to pursuit by Israel of the full register of substitute diplomatic frameworks and strategies known to international relations theorists and practitioners. Often short-lived, demonstratively non-Middle Eastern, all of them problematic – these extra-regional attempts at overcoming regional isolation reflect deep-seated and mounting skepticism within the Israeli body politic over any plausible medium-term Israeli prospect for Middle Eastern recognition and alignment.

Unilateralism

In effect an '*ayn breira*' or 'no option' option, this isolationist policy course reinterprets the traditional mindset of the Jewish People being 'A Nation Apart' into modern, contemporary terms as a prescription for Israel's 'going it alone'. Taken as an article of faith and as a political 'given', the proven untrustworthiness of the other nations – particularly those of the Middle East, as seemingly reconfirmed of late by Turkey – would have Israel dig in its heels, entrench behind a defensive wall, and fend for itself by acting even preemptively when deemed necessary (Lebanon, 1982; Lebanon, 2006; Gaza, 2008) on behalf its own narrow interests ... world opinion and the rest of the world be damned.

The objective unfeasibility of so narrow a security-based diplomacy, with its emphasis on self-sufficiency and on retaining the widest degree of latitude for independent action, was perhaps best brought home to policymakers in Jerusalem as early as 1987 by the forced cancellation of the indigenous 'blue & white' *Lavi* fighter aircraft project. Even so, the lesson bears repeating: in an era of growing regionalism, interdependence and globalism, to willfully and consciously forego reliance upon outside sources of aid and reinforcement, whether oil and gas imports or military hardware, is not only unrealistic but an unmitigated march of folly.

Nonalignment

A somewhat more sophisticated variant of the unilateralist approach for assuring independent decision-making was pursued at the outset of statehood. Born into a global Cold War setting and thus unavoidably caught up in the struggle between East and West, the new state's initial preference sought to avoid entanglement through an enunciated posture of evenhanded neutralism. Just how untenable was not committing to either bloc became evident almost immediately as Israel found itself already, by 1950–1951, increasingly gravitating toward the Western camp. Again, given current trends, should the late Professor Samuel Huntington's thesis of a bifurcated clash of civilizations between militant Islam and the '*dar al-harb*' or non-Islamic world tragically eventuate, then – positioned as it is at one of the major cultural fault lines – it would be delusional for Israel once again to seek safety on the sidelines.

Internationalism

Hoping to acquire legitimacy, universal recognition, collective security and peaceful commerce under the aegis of the United Nations Organization proved equally impracticable. Already by the mid- and late-1950s, early Israeli aspirations for being admitted at last into the comity of nations as 'a nation like all others' were deflated under the weight of overwhelming counter-evidence. Appealing to the UN on the basis of international law for the right of innocent passage through the Suez Canal international waterway, denied Israel by Egypt, proved to be an exercise in futile diplomacy; so, too, were calls for condemnation by the UN of violations of the 1949 Armistice Agreements on the part of Egypt, Jordan and Syria. Years before the 1967 victory exposed Israel to the charge of being an occupying power, especially disillusioning was the UN's gradual transformation, from a positive agency recognizing Israel into an instrument for successively criticizing, one-sidedly condemning, isolating and ultimately delegitimizing the Jewish State.

This regression reached one of its all-time low points in November 1975 with the passage of General Assembly Resolution 3379 equating Zionism with racism by a vote of 72 to 5, and 32 abstentions. In sum, neither the UN international body nor its auxiliary agencies like the Human Rights Council or UNESCO have ever really been respected in Jerusalem as offering a credible option for assuring Israel fair play, or for guaranteeing its vital interests.

Minimum winning coalitions

Between the first two poles – defiant disengagement *versus* a broad-gauged outreach policy toward the international community-at-large and any non-Middle Eastern actor willing to establish ties – there are, to be sure, an intermediate and more moderate set of survival strategies best categorized as 'selective engagement'. Here, success, at least in Israel's case, rests on an accurate early reading of global trends and shifts in regional balances of power in order to single out pivotal countries with overlapping interests or concerns, and then actively pursuing close cooperation with them. This approach fully corresponds to accepted theories of alliance- and coalition-building, wherein nations are best advised to negotiate narrow collaborative frameworks with a chance for working smoothly rather than broadly inclusive ones that only encourage discord from within.

The diplomatic record, although incomplete, provides ample evidence of functional cooperation by Israel at different times with an extensive list of outlying target regions and nations. Particularly meaningful in the second and third decades of Israeli foreign relations in dealing with emergent Afro-Asian and Third World countries, whether conducted openly or secretly, formally or tacitly, this expedient for outflanking Arab hostility and Middle Eastern isolation has lost none of its cogency.

Among better known illustrations of strong bilateral associations with smaller or medium-sized powers residing on the perimeter or outside the Arab core of the Middle East: the French connection spanning much of the 1950s and 1960s; the exceptional Israel-German relationship; Iran under the Shah; South Africa; the opening to Red China; the 'Asian dragons' – Singapore, Taiwan and South Korea; expanding commercial, cultural and defense ties with India; and, of course, Turkey until 2010. Inclusion of the latter, despite the recent strained relationship, enables generalizing that without necessarily meeting the test of durability or permanence, each example does meet the two-fold standard of utility *for* Israel and resourcefulness *by* Israel. Taken together, these examples also serve as a useful corrective to the overly simplistic impression of Israeli statecraft fixated wholly and solely on the United States.

The one great power doctrine

This diplomatic school of thought traces back to early political Zionist thinking and pre-state experience, manifested by the successful effort at securing England's endorsement of the Jewish national home enterprise, at least during the initial phase of the British Mandate for Palestine. After 1948, further reinforcement for this policy of placing all of Israel's eggs in one basket, so to speak – of cultivating and then relying upon a single 'Great Power' patron to compensate for Israel's own power deficiencies or diplomatic shortcomings – stemmed historically from the Soviet Union's strong tilt in favor of Arab clients and against Israel. Fortuitously, ruptured relations with the Kremlin were paralleled by initially grudging then increasingly more enthusiastic respect for Israel in the West, but especially in American circles, as an asset in the global containment strategy aimed at preventing Communist encroachment in the Near and Middle East.

This doctrine, as its name suggests, mandates doing everything possible, or necessary, in order to enlist the support of at least one world power with the influence and resources to compensate for Israel's own deficiencies, and with the resolve to deter any challenge to Israel's security or existence. In accordance with this logic, comparable to one-stop shopping, and benefiting from a receptive environment in the United States, the last forty-plus years have seen Israeli diplomatic efforts concentrate primarily upon deepening and widening the 'American connection', upgraded, especially in Israeli eyes, to the level of a 'special' and 'strategic' relationship.

Extra-regional relationships

Israel's map of the world has been depicted only half in jest as showing one pinhead, and one pinhead only: Washington, DC. Not surprisingly, most Israeli commentators, not to mention the general Israeli public, would confidently point with pride at winning America's friendship as the single greatest triumph of Israeli statesmanship. Sustained US aid in excess of $3 billion annually would seem, at least on the surface, to fully vindicate the profound wisdom behind the 'one great power' orientation. Nevertheless, notwithstanding the multiple and cumulative advantages for Israel accruing from such intimate ties with the US superpower, any such unipolar orientation carries with it for Israel a number of real as well as potential disadvantages, some more obvious than others.

Critiquing the relationship has largely been disfavored within the Israeli foreign policy establishment. Still, prudence cautions that trust in the United States carries with it potentially negative longer-range consequences, and to some extent already has. By breeding complacency and a certain conceit on Israel's part as the envy of less favored countries. By tying itself too closely to American foreign policies, or to peacemaking strategies cooked up by headline-seeking competitive Washington think tanks or, in their mix of hubris and desperation, by State Department peace processors. By deflecting attention from other promising areas like Europe, and downgrading or neglecting other prospective bilateral relationships. And by counting far too often on Washington to do Jerusalem's diplomatic work for it: at the United Nations, in other diplomatic forums, and *vis-à-vis* the Middle Eastern countries themselves.

For added measure, excessive reliance on an outside country, and how much more so a forceful superpower, of necessity complicates Israel's own governing and policymaking processes. As seen in the constant need for prior consultation with American counterparts, and by having to factor in America's own definition of a given situation, *its* national interests and *its* policy preferences – thereby compelling Jerusalem to defer to America's wishes, or else to act in defiance of those expressed desires. A telling case in point is the effective veto power Washington has come to hold over Israeli defense exports. Another: heavy pressure upon Israel during 2010 by the Obama Administration in insisting on a total settlement construction freeze. Finally, any such asymmetrical patron-client relationship over time stands to violate an iron principle of world politics: that largesse from a Great Power patron, no matter how altruistic or bountiful or well intentioned, must inevitably bear a price tag.

To complete the spectrum of alternatives to a Middle Eastern orientation, two more deserve mention. The first argues that for Israel there is only one true and constant ally – the Jewish People – and only one special relationship – with *World*

Jewry. Hence, the imperative for Jerusalem, transcending physical and geographic boundaries, is to channel efforts and resources towards strengthening bonds with communities throughout the Jewish Diaspora in the name of Jewish solidarity and Jewish survival. Here, too, however, relations are not immune to strains common to all alliances. These include: miscommunication and misunderstanding; contests over leadership and pride of position; tasking and role performance; agenda prioritization; the proper forums and procedures for debate, decision-making, criticism, dissent and policy review; alienation and threats of defection. Even so, it would be irresponsible for any Israeli diplomacy willfully to neglect or forego its Jewish option.

Left for last in this menu of diplomatic strategies geared to a non-Middle Eastern future is the appeal of closer association with a regional bloc, to be sure, but other than the Arab-dominated Middle East. The prospective alignment most talked about centers on Europe.

The Euro-centric orientation

Linking Israel's national interests to the liberal, industrialized, high-tech European countries has its beginnings in the first decade of statehood, mirrored in the 1952 Reparations Agreement with West Germany and in the 1956 Anglo-French-Israeli agreement. More recently, with enlargement of the 27-member European Union, already now a significant trading partner for Israel with pretentions of becoming in the near future a major influence in world affairs, this favorable view of continental Europe has gained increased cogency as well as a larger and more vocal constituency inside Israel among respected university intellectuals and economic planners.

Some shapers of policy and public opinion project this Euro-centric course of action as a logical trans-Atlantic extension of the US connection. For others, cultivating the Europeans, their separate governments and the European Community might very well prove itself a timely counter against over-dependence upon Washington. A kind of insurance against Israel suddenly finding itself under extreme pressure to make concessions towards the Palestinians or the Arab states in order to consummate a US-brokered peace settlement of the Israeli-Arab conflict. Or worse: no longer safely positioned under a protective American shield.

Hebrew University's Professor Shlomo Avineri, among others, uses the economic, scientific and cultural argument for targeting the EU, citing the sophisticated European market as complementary to Israel's own economy and crucial for its sustained economic growth. Others, like Dr. Uzi Arad, former national security adviser to Prime Minister Binyamin Netanyahu, are leading proponents for Israel's assigning the highest priority to acquiring NATO membership. Undoubtedly, Israel's invitation to join the European-dominated OECD in May 2010 has given a significant boost to those who in an age of globalization and transnationalism would have Israel divorce itself as much as possible from Middle Eastern affairs and better seek its fortunes elsewhere among the more developed, democratic nations having the most to offer Israel.

Worth underlining is that the above orientations need not be mutually exclusive, at least in principle. On the contrary, under favorable circumstances, with the obvious exception of self-imposed isolationism, they actually allow for cultivating one or more relationships simultaneously. With the proviso, of course, that the interplay between them be sensitively monitored in Jerusalem and closely concerted. Thus, for example, the 1970s saw the weaving of an effective coalition and lobby among the United States, world Jewry and Israel on behalf of Soviet Jewry. Likewise, taking the EU, NATO and the OECD more seriously – when pursued as a prudent supplement to the 'one great power' focus – is not inconsistent with close US-Israel relations. Nor, if carefully orchestrated, are low-keyed functional ties with the rising BRIC countries of Brazil, Russia, India and China alongside other interested Asian and African states.

Middle Eastern interventions

The above foreign policy options share a common denominator: each is conceived and promoted as necessary – some might say convenient – external cultural, commercial, diplomatic and security outlets which lie outside of the Middle East arena. They are viewed in Tel-Aviv and Jerusalem as substitutes; as replacement strategies for playing the game of nations without the Arab nations. And by diplomatic hardliners like Prime Minister Binyamin Netanyahu and his decidedly undiplomatic former foreign minister Avigdor Lieberman, as providential instruments for keeping the predatory Middle East at bay.

Nonetheless, at no time in its history has Israel been able to keep the intrusive Middle East off its radar screen. Notwithstanding an unconcealed preference for having as little as possible to do with perfidious Middle Easterners and for cold-shouldering the Middle East as an unstable, violent political arena, Middle East intrigues are a recurrent theme as circumstances have led previous Israeli leaders and successive governments repeatedly to engage in regional deterrence and balancing politics. On average: defensive, tactical and patterned on the principle of 'divide and rule'; also not without a measure of success, albeit ultimately short-lived and uniformly disillusioning.

Under the above-discussed rubric of minimalist bilateral, goal-oriented coalitions, Israel has been party to two particularly meaningful regional pacts. Both of them were conducted covertly, but only one was remarkable for its resilience. Ben-Gurion's 'periphery' or 'minorities' strategy for leaping over the wall of Arab hostility in the fifties and sixties saw an unwritten alliance of convenience – more akin to understandings than a formal pact – among Israel, the two non-Arab Middle Eastern peripheral states of Turkey and Iran, Ethiopia, the Kurds and the Maronites of Lebanon. All of them threatened at the time by the wave of Nasserist revolutionary fervor in calling for violent regime change, by anti-Westernism, by militant Arab unity and by the extension of Soviet influence southward into the Middle East. All of them backed by the United States.

In a category of its own in the annals of Israeli foreign relations is the very special tacit security regime forged by Israel with the Hashemite Kingdom of

Jordan, its most proximate Arab neighbor. Commonly referred to in shorthand as Israel's 'Jordanian option' – but whose mirror image rightfully translates into Jordan's 'Israeli option' – this bilateral relationship with a fellow Middle Eastern country at the very heartland of the Arab world is immensely more complicated as well as truly unique. First, for our purposes, it is the principal exception to the rule of Israel purposively detaching itself from its Middle Eastern moorings. Second, interactions with Jordan have been at once overt and covert, cooperative and conflictual, adversarial and supportive. Third, for all its ups and downs, this mixed relationship of amity and enmity has met the test of alliance-maintenance, surviving countless adversities and crises. Fourth, as a direct result of both sides respecting complicated rules of engagement improvised through trial and error over decades, but above all after the 1967 War, ties with the Hashemites of Transjordan and then Jordan date back to the 1930s. Amazingly enough, no matter how sorely tested at times, this may very well represent Israel's most continuous and lasting relationship with any foreign country. Fifth, what the Amman-Jerusalem axis teaches is that shared threat perceptions, immediate needs and geopolitics can in fact make for strange bedfellows, trumping political and cultural differences. Without making light of the many barriers, both objective and subjective, dividing Arabs from Israelis, the multi-layered and surprisingly durable Israel-Jordan connection speaks to the logic, indeed the imperative for promoting regional links with regional partners whenever possible.

In looking to the future, Israeli policy planners would be irresponsible in discharging their duties were they categorically to rule out, *a priori*, the likelihood of openings presenting themselves for closely monitored functional cooperation with similarly predisposed Arab and Middle East actors. In particular, expectations that the courageous protest in 2011 against decades of arrested social, economic and political development by Arab publics from Tunisia, Libya and Egypt to the west of Israel and Bahrain and Yemen to the east were actually to materialize in substantive domestic reforms. This would have the potential for transforming each country's agenda and priorities away from anti-Israel extremism while conceivably altering the climate of Arab opinion toward reaching an accommodation with Israel. But in order not to fall into the trap of entirely foreclosing on the Middle East as a strategic policy option, Israelis must first critically rethink their own standard arguments before conceding the Middle East.

The case against Middle Eastern engagement

Given the opportunities for transcending one's physical location offered by 21st-century globalization, out-looking worldly Israelis have long since given up entertaining the notion let alone actively pursuing the option of assuming a direct role in Middle Eastern affairs. Their ranks, swelled by countless others on both the political Right and the political Left disillusioned by Israeli-Palestinian-Arab rounds of peace probes and peace negotiation at the disposal of Israel's Middle East rejectionists are an admittedly powerful and initially compelling battery of justifications. A set of rationalizations that permit and indeed encourage clinging steadfastly to the deeply entrenched position that Israel 'punish' the Arab world's own rejectionists by a combination of turning inward ('Fortress Israel') or, conversely, looking elsewhere for more meaningful opportunities, however short-lived ('Perfidious Israel'), and for far more rewarding relationships ('Satellite Israel').

The brief against proactive Middle Eastern engagement reads like a catechism – a rote response and formulaic statement built upon five central arguments. This 'Anywhere but the Middle East' mindset maintains the adjacent region is, successively, unreceptive, undeserving, undesirable, incompatible and, for good measure, expendable.

The Middle East: Unreceptive towards Israel

The first line of defense against placing undue stress on prospective Arab relationships is commonsensical. Ever since 1948 our Arab neighbors have made it patently clear they simply do not want us among them. While possibly differing among themselves over the preferred means for doing so, the strategic goal of the Arabs remains unaltered: liquidation of the Zionist entity through the one state solution, 'Palestine'. So internalized and so socialized by now in Arab and Muslim collective thought is this intransigence Israelis believe to be so deep-seated and widespread, that it all but precludes those profound ideological, theological and psychological adjustments (let alone political and territorial ones) that are the prerequisites for genuine reconciliation and for truly accepting Israel into the Middle East fold. Suffice to imagine Arab world outrage at the very suggestion of having to rename the "League of Arab States" the "Middle East League" or something comparable in order to accommodate Israel's taking a seat at the regional council table between Iran and Iraq on one side and Jordan on the other.

Taking stock, even in the three instances of seeming breakthroughs the experience has been less than inspiring. In fact, disheartening; most of all, for leaders of the Israeli peace camp. Normalization with Egypt – 'Sadat's peace' – rather than filtering throughout the Egyptian society after 1979 has yielded a peace in name only. Normalization with Jordan has encountered deep domestic opposition since 1994 on the part of that country's trade unions, parliamentarians, Islamists and media. Similarly with the Palestinians and the 1993 Oslo Declaration of Principles, normalization has unleashed two *intifada* and an extreme countermovement led by Hamas, whose 1988 charter openly calls for replacing the State of Israel with a Palestinian Islamic state incorporating the area that is now Israel, the West Bank, and the Gaza Strip.

In effect, many Israelis willing to write off any Middle Eastern policy course do so for reason of the seemingly intractable dispute with the Palestinians. On the one hand, there are those convinced that no matter how forthcoming Israeli negotiators might be, and irrespective of how liberal the peace terms offered, extending as far as returning 100 per cent of the disputed West Bank, dividing Jerusalem, yielding any claim to even shared sovereignty over the Temple Mount, and accepting full culpability for the Palestinian refugee problem, nothing Israel is capable of suggesting short of self-extinction would satisfy Arab and Islamic world demands.

On the other hand, no few Israelis are of the opinion that any price to be paid for a tenuous peace and for grudging admission into regional councils and coalitions, even if not so concessionary, is simply not worth Israel's while. Despair among Israelis at prospects for reconciliation and for lasting peace being so rampant, there is the popular perception of an impervious and singularly unreceptive Middle East. And the equally widespread interpretation of the Arab Middle East as simply unworthy of Israel's petitioning for regional membership.

The Middle East: **Undeserving** *of Israel*

Given the professed aim of Arab secular and religious leaders physically to erase Israel from the map of the Middle East, and in light of Arab world pathologies, why would any rational person advocate for Israel's vigorously marketing ties with its neighbors? Even less conscionable, how could any responsible Israeli leader trumpet a foreign policy highlighting membership in a region unwilling to accept it as a member?

Israelis are not in a position to impose themselves upon their neighbors. Besides which, no self-respecting state pushes itself where it is not wanted. Nor is it politically wise for Israel to appear too eager for Middle Eastern association. Suffice to recall the firestorm of Arab scorn greeting the then-Minister of Foreign Affairs Shimon Peres' visionary 1993 appeal for a 'new Middle East' that would incorporate Israel – which was widely misinterpreted as a Zionist stratagem for gaining mastery over its weaker, divided Arab neighbors.

Better – so the argument goes – for Israel to adhere to its original declaratory policy, cited earlier, with but a slight change in wording, structure and nuance to reflect the bitter lessons of 63 years. To be sure, we continue to 'extend our hand to all neighboring states and their peoples in an offer of peace and good neighborliness'. Likewise, the State of Israel '*is* prepared to do its share in a common effort for the advancement of the entire Middle East.' But it no longer deems it either fitting or necessary to 'appeal' to them 'to establish bonds of cooperation and mutual help with the sovereign Jewish people settled in its own land'. Borrowing from the 1917 Balfour Declaration, Israel might passively 'view with favour' regional association, but in its political maturity knows better now to wait for Arab overtures and to then respond, rather than actively to seek Arab openings or to go about creating them.

The Middle East: **Undesirable** *for Israel*

The third link in the chain of arguments underlines the many disincentives in tilting towards the Middle East. Not only is the region unattractive, it's nothing short of detrimental for Israel's purposes. Therefore, rather than moving closer, Israel is advised to distance itself as much as humanly and politically possible. Here the reasoning is three-tiered. First, with its culture of violence and impulse to aggression, compounded by economic underdevelopment, the Middle East is, if anything, the least desirable neighborhood imaginable. For Aaron David Miller it is "one screwed-up region of the world". For Ehud Barak it is a "dysfunctional region", with Israel "a villa in the jungle". For Edward Luttwak, it is "the middle of nowhere … a mostly stagnant region where almost nothing is created in science or the arts".

In which case, secondly, the Middle East as presently constituted – and for the foreseeable future – offers no real appeal for Israel. There do not appear to be any positive incentives overriding the known risks and liabilities; neither in commercial or economic terms, nor culturally. So that, simply put, if there is little Israel stands to gain, why bother? Besides which, thirdly, on the other side of the cost-benefit calculus Israel can expect to be called upon to pay a prohibitively high fee for regional admission, and certainly one incommensurate with the questionable rewards.

Among the anticipated asking price: painful territorial concessions in a peace settlement with the Palestinians *ala* the 2002 Arab Peace Initiative; Egyptian-led demands for Israel to renounce its nuclear option; having to take sides in intraregional rivalries and other forms of political entanglement; being accused of upsetting the traditional Arab balance; being charged with aspiring to become the predominant regional power; Israeli delegates finding themselves repeatedly outvoted in any Middle East forum, and in effect politically isolated.

The Middle East: Incompatible *with Israel*

The anti-Mideast bias goes a step further by insisting that not only does the cost-benefit balance sheet reveal far greater disincentives than positive payoffs, and not only do the Arabs want to keep Israel out, but Israel – on the grounds of incompatibility – has no reason for wanting to be in. Where Israelis are cosmopolitan and outgoing, other Middle Eastern societies, with the exception of the Persian Gulf oil emirates, tend to be more traditional, more tribalist and xenophobic, more insular. And if, as Syrian President Bashar Assad boasts, 'The new Middle East we've started building is a Middle East whose essence is resistance' rather than progress, what business could Israel possibly have with such a benighted region?

Culturally, Israel's tastes in music, literature and the arts tend markedly toward the sophisticated West. Politically, its place is with the progressive democracies. Economically and commercially, its logical trading partners are located among the sophisticated markets and industrialized manufacturing nations of Europe and Asia. The case is similar with reference to health, education and social welfare services; and to other cutting-edge fields like scientific and medical research, computerization and nanotechnology, in which Israel has shown itself to be highly competitive.

To grasp how out of place Israel is in the Middle East, one only has to read *Start-up Nation* by Dan Senor and Saul Singer, subtitled 'The Story of Israel's Economic Miracle', juxtaposing it with the series of five Arab Human Development Reports sponsored and published by the United Nations. Indicative of this enormous developmental disparity between Israel and its Arab neighbors is one small piece of data, chosen arbitrarily from among many: in the period 1980–2000, while Egyptians registered 77 patents in the United States, Saudis 171, Syrians 20, and Jordanians 15, Israelis put their names on 7,652 applications. In short, as far as Israel, its future interests and most promising prospects are concerned, the rough parity and those basic commonalities necessary for Middle East community-building are simply lacking.

Once convinced it is possible to divorce personal and collective national interests from the bonds of geography and they are intimately linked, instead, to the West, to the US and Europe, Israelis can only derive immense satisfaction from statements of reassurance like that of former Spanish Prime Minister José Maria Aznar, who, in June 2010, affirmed 'Israel is the West's best ally in a turbulent region'. A formulation that best underlines the magnetic field in which Israeli statecraft maneuvers – the pull *towards* other parts of the world – and the push *away* from the immediate Middle East.

The Middle East: **Expendable** *for Israel*

Considering Israel's limited resources and overstretched professional diplomatic corps, refocusing upon the Middle East might have to come at the expense of other possible orientations. Particularly when Israeli strategists insist there are more promising ties to be cultivated in a world of multi-polarization, extra-territorial networks and new opportunities over the regional horizon.

From this dynamic geopolitical perspective each of Israel's core scientific, commercial, defense and other needs are to be met through a four-pronged strategy: continuing to nurture relations with the United States; cementing relations with leaders and governments in Western Europe and the EU still understanding of Israeli concerns; cultivating more robust ties with ascendant powers like Brazil, China and India; constantly exploring fresh openings as they present themselves in East Asia, the trans-Caucasus region and the Southern hemisphere. In short: exploiting favorable constellations on a truly global scale rather than looking out at the world from the narrow, *i.e.* wrong, Middle Eastern end of a telescope.

While not categorically ruling out interactions with the Middle East and North Africa, this widescreen diplomatic strategy does implicitly instruct that regional actors be approached with utmost caution, and with modest expectations. That these interactions be viewed through the tapered prism of immediate security concerns. That the only coalitions worth considering are bilateral ones, with secret backchannels giving Arab interlocutors willing to risk dealing with the 'Zionist enemy' room for plausible denial. These exceptions aside, the broader Middle East, at once unwelcoming and unattractive, is best bypassed, at least until further notice.

This leaves the question: what must it take for Israeli policy attitudes toward the region to change? Among those still open-minded enough to entertain so hypothetical and unpopular a question, the most likely response would be: Nothing less than a sea change. But, most adamantly, not on Israel's part; and surely not in Israeli attitudes or policies, like those regarding the terms for peace. Rather, the onus remains – where it has remained since 1948 – squarely on the other, Arab, side. For Israel to re-orientate itself *toward* instead of *away* from its Middle Eastern habitat, a major revolutionary upheaval would be necessary. An upheaval in the established Arab political order; in Arab intellectual, religious and political thought toward the Jewish-Zionist enterprise; in Arab, Iranian and Turkish perceptions of the region and of regional priorities; and in patterns of behavior from zero-sum rivalry to non-zero-sum collaboration with their Israeli neighbor and prospective partner.

But with the possible exception of a new Arab order emerging from the dramatic chain of events in early 2011, because these geopolitical game-changers do not appear on anyone's radar screen, this course of thinking renders any Middle East policy reorientation entirely moot. Indeed, in the context of this paper, the Republic of Turkey's strained relations with the United States and with Israel by the close of 2010 can only be regarded as a crushing blow to Middle Eastern neighborliness. If the vast resources at Ankara's disposal and its web of political contacts make it an excellent prospect for assuming a leadership role in building bridges, in negotiating compromises and in drawing Israel more closely into regional affairs, that scenario, too, has now had to be shelved.

Besides which, it is widely accepted that the proverbial 'key' to both normalization and regionalization resides in closure, once-and-for-all, of the unresolved Palestinian problem. Meaning, only when all outstanding issues subsumed under the 'Israeli-Arab conflict' have been satisfactorily negotiated, and only then, will the front door to the Middle East possibly be unlocked. Except that a deeper knowledge of the true complexity of the peace issues, which continue to defy iterated attempts at a compromise formula at once comprehensive and definitive, provokes skepticism as to whether objectively there does in fact exist a workable peace formula for accommodating Israeli, Palestinian and Arab aspirations. From which it follows that, practically speaking, Israel's door to the wider Middle East remains securely bolted, both from within and without.

It is on these seemingly compelling grounds that the 'anywhere but' approach to the Middle East in Israeli foreign affairs attracts understandably wide public appeal and rests its case. Resolved: the Arab Middle East was, is, and of necessity must remain hazardous. At once alien and alienated, it is therefore an arena best guarded against, advisedly kept under constant watch, and deftly sidestepped in favor of alternative diplomatic relationships and commercial trading partners.

The case for 'Middle Easternism'

In the face of the forceful argument against the Jewish State ever interacting normally within its most immediate geopolitical arena, there are conceptual as well as practical reasons for at least retaining, if nothing else, the original Zionist and later Israeli aspiration. The Middle East, made up of both its Arab and non-Arab components, is and will always remain as it has been: a mixture of both hope and anxiety, promise and peril. The Israeli anxieties are ever-present and there to see, as are the perils of Arab world politics. Where, though, is the hope? Where the sense of promise for Israel in the emergence of a new Arab political order?

Therefore, the counterargument needs to be given expression also. Not for the purpose of casting aside parallel foreign policy initiatives aimed at other countries, regions or multilateral frameworks. Rather, to challenge and combat the tendency toward Israeli groupthink and taking comfort in conventional wisdom. And in order to elevate in Israeli public discourse the notion of 'Middle Easternism'.

Questioning the previous reasoning begins by critiquing each of the pillars of this conventional wisdom. For one thing, the region should not be dismissed as a legitimate arena for diplomacy by Israel because it *cannot* be dismissed. Situated where it is, and sharing a frontier with four Arab countries, as far as Israel is concerned there is no escaping the Middle East. This dysfunctional geopolitical region, even with its many shortcomings, is not so readily displaceable or replaceable. Whether manifested in freedom of navigation, in safe civilian air corridors, in peaceful borders, or in water, oil and natural gas pipelines, when all is said and done, location does still matter in 21st-century international relations. For another thing, the region is nowhere near representing a seamless cloth. It is patently not true that all Arabs and all Middle Eastern countries are of one mind in their denial of the reality of Israel's existence; or of one mind when assessing the country's potential contribution to regional stabilization, security and development.

Geography

While reluctant to admit as much, most Israelis are themselves painfully conscious of the extent to which the Middle East daily presses in on their lives. Black humor serves as one outlet for masking deeper fears and insecurities by retreading old jokes accusing the biblical leader Moses of stuttering 'Canaan' when he really wanted to say 'Canada'. Or, in a variant form: half-seriously blaming him of a major navigational blunder, since he might better have directed the Children of Israel eastward to more promising lands, not to mention the lucrative oil deposits of Arabia, instead of westward to inhospitable and contested Palestine.

Ancient historical antecedents aside, Israel's entire history is a testimony to the fact that it is very much 'in' the Middle East. If nothing else, sheer physical closeness dictates that whatever transpires in the Arab regions of the Middle East has a bearing – direct or indirect – on Israeli chances for stability, security and wellbeing. Indeed, the region imposes itself relentlessly onto the Israeli psyche from all directions. Still fresh in the national memory is how over the course of 18 days the grassroots Egyptian political revolution unfolding in Cairo's *al-Tahrir* Square, a mere one hour's flying time away, riveted the attention of Israelis, heightening concern over possible implications for the 1979 peace treaty and for Israel's military deployment along its shared southern border with Egypt. Apprehensions are stirred up no less over Iran's nuclear shadow and disquieting signs of an Iranian-Syrian-Hizbullah-Hamas axis; over a revanchist Gaza-West Bank Palestinian state emerging to squeeze Israel on its western and eastern flanks as well as over a regime change in Jordan unseating the Hashemite monarchy. Hence the twin imperatives of vigilance and military preparedness, which mandate an early intelligence warning system plus a rapid response capability in order for Israel to be able to meet possible threat situations originating from within the Middle East.

So, too, in the opposite direction, by its very founding and since its establishment, Israel has impacted upon Arab ideological and political trends, with political fortunes of Arab governments rising or falling as an indirect outgrowth of Israeli-Arab fighting. Subsequent to the 1948 *débâcle*, governments were overthrown in Syria and Egypt and Jordan's King Abdullah assassinated on Israel-related issues – the former for mismanaging the war against the Zionists, the latter for secretly negotiating peace terms with the Zionists. The Assad dynasty seized and consolidated power in Syria following 'Black September' in Jordan, when Israel played an instrumental role in defusing the 1970 crisis. The military siege of Beirut in 1982 by the Israeli army and open support for the Maronite Christian community and its leader, Bashir Gemayel, further complicated the Lebanese civil war and Lebanon's political instability. Arguably, Israel's uncharacteristic self-restraint despite the provocation of Iraqi missiles launched against it contributed to the failed attempt by Saddam Hussein to consolidate his annexation of Iraq in 1990–1991.

Thus, even while formally barred from being a direct actor in Middle Eastern affairs, Israel has certainly been a factor in the political fortunes and considerations of the neighboring Arab countries. A perennially divisive issue, how to contend with the Zionist entity represents a major variable in the uneasy balance between the two poles of Arab unity and disunity. So, too, does it factor in the tension among Middle Easterners over *their* orientations and *their* alignments: pro-Western *versus* anti-Western, traditionalists *versus* modernists, militants *versus* moderates, Arab nationalists *versus* pan-Arabists *versus* pan-Islamists.

Ideology

In 1903 the Jewish national movement reached a strategic crossroads when the Sixth Zionist Congress turned down England's offer of chartered territory in East Africa. The principle being that only in the ancient Near Eastern homeland of '*Eretz Yisrael*' could the Jews as a people truly achieve normalcy after nearly two millennia of dispersion and wandering. This fateful choice meant that whatever Jewish society came into being would forever be destined to exist within – and of necessity, coexist with – a predominant Arab and Islamic cultural milieu. However much the restless grandchildren of the modern state's founders might question the biblical site for a Jewish promised land, Zionist ideology joins physical proximity as a second rationale for a closer awareness of the Middle East's potential.

The fateful decision having been taken over a century ago, since then the fortunes of the Zionist enterprise and of the State of Israel have become inseparable from that of the surrounding Arab regions. The Middle East, for better or for worse, is Israel's natural habitat. Their attractiveness notwithstanding, all other regions and associations and policy orientations are in a certain sense auxiliary outlets. In the starkest terms, as the Middle East goes, so goes territorial Israel.

Israel, accordingly, has a vital stake in peace maintenance with its formal treaty partners, Egypt and Jordan, just as it has a vital interest that neither country experience political radicalization or succumbing to Islamist extremism. The sizeable Israeli-Arab community with its network of familial and other ties spreading into the Arab world serves as another cross-border link. Yet another is the dependence of the West Bank upon agricultural exports to the nearby Arab countries. The policy lesson these contact points bring home is that Israeli-style 'splendid isolation' from the backyard of the Middle East is completely unrealistic and impossible to maintain.

Perceptions

Too easily overlooked is a further consideration. Were Israel deliberately to retract whatever regional ties it does retain and voluntarily withdraw from the region, in effect declaring itself a non-Middle Eastern country, it would provide the Arab rejectionist front with an inestimable propaganda coup.

What is the entire thrust of the Arab and Islamic campaign to delegitimize the Jewish State if not to portray it as an alien implant rather than an integral part of the Middle East? Israel's taking itself out of the region is as unacceptable as persistent Arab efforts at airbrushing 'Israel' out of Middle East maps. This is comparable in academia to arguing for incorporating Israel-related courses either as part of a diffuse multicultural or social sciences curriculum, or as a sub-field of specialization within a Jewish studies program, thereby playing into the hands of Israel's opponents who would delight in being able to remove Israel from where it properly belongs academically: as an integral part of contemporary Middle Eastern studies.

Besides which, the image of Israel as un-Middle Eastern and standoffish does it an injustice. Today's young Israelis have come a long way in acclimatizing to the prevailing local milieu. Culturally speaking, their eclectic music and dance forms embrace oriental rhythms alongside Western ones. Linguistically, their Hebrew conversation is sprinkled with choice expressions in Arabic. In the culinary arts, their mixed palate favors spicy native foods prepared according to Eastern Mediterranean recipes no less than traditional Eastern European ones. Likewise in negotiations; their bargaining style comfortably merges bazaar haggling and free-wheeling backgammon with the dry formalism of the chessboard and department store fixed price-tagging. Less complimentary yet no less valid, foreign visitors commonly note sophisticated Israel's other, 'Levantine' side, whether manifested in refuse-strewn sidewalks, unaccommodating drivers bypassing the rules of the road, or the heavy hand of bureaucracy in meeting Middle Eastern standards for inefficiency and red tape.

Necessity

Current regional urgencies present a fourth consideration governing Israel's Middle Easternization, and arguably the most compelling. As a co-inhabitant,

Israel, too, is adversely affected by the long-term trend toward Middle Eastern 'declinism'. This downward trajectory, unless arrested in time through a concerted effort, threatens to deprive all peoples of the region of their global competitiveness and international status.

Whither the Middle East?

Indicative of a Middle East region of walls and barriers, where countries are still motivated by suspicion and self-help in coping with their respective insecurity dilemmas, are definite tell-tale signs pointing to misdirected priorities, to energies wasted and to resources foolishly depleted. First and foremost, there are human resources, with talents untapped and lives callously snuffed out by incessant regional strife and bloodletting. In its closely documented report of January 2009 on the 'Cost of Conflict in the Middle East', for example, the Strategic Foresight Group estimated that violence has cost the region about $12 trillion in forfeited economic growth and development over the last two decades.

So, too, are the region's other prized liquid resources of oil and water being squandered. The World Bank reports that the Middle East and North Africa suffer the world's lowest rate of net renewable water supplies. Without preliminary steps toward a Mideast water regime and the pooling of water resources, desertification is winning in the timeless struggle between the desert and the sown. Today, arid desert covers 60 per cent of Israel, 70 per cent of Syria, 85 per cent of Jordan, and 90 per cent of Egypt. Little wonder, therefore, that in the UN's listing of High, Medium and Low Human Development countries in terms of per-capita income, educational levels, health care and life expectancy, Israel, while topping the list of Middle Eastern states in 2007–08, is ranked only 23nd, followed by Kuwait in 33rd place.

The cumulative weight of statistical and political data points unambiguously to a net deficit region, leading respected Lebanese editorialist Rami Khouri to conclude dolefully in 2009: We Arabs 'have marginalized ourselves as serious players on the global political stage' and 'now assume the role of nagging annoyances and miscreants'. Of late, too many international observers have begun applying this judgment to Israel as well.

The principal cause for this decades-long downturn needs to be stated in full candor. Parochial narrowness has made Middle Easterners oblivious to the true magnitude of the threats on their collective horizon. These range from: social, scientific and educational stagnation; economic underdevelopment and demographic pressures; severe resource depletion and environmental disaster; water scarcity and desertification; internal strife and external intervention; faith-based fanaticism; and relentless conventional arms races now compounded by nuclear proliferation.

Singularly unsuccessful in overcoming its historical and geographical divisions, the Middle East has therefore been one of the world's poorest economic performing regions. Individual state incapacity is leading, in turn, to collective regional disempowerment, warranting the observation that 'never missing an

Israel and the Middle East   45

opportunity to miss an opportunity' is by no means an exclusive Palestinian (or Israeli) monopoly but appears to be a shared Middle Eastern trait. Following the Second World War, the region had begun to recover its lost pride, former economic and geostrategic prominence, and political independence. But in a post-Cold War moment of renewed potential, once again internal shortcomings and shortsightedness combine with world trends, threatening to leave Arabs and Iranians, Israelis and Turks behind the global learning curve.

A regionless regionalism

There is considerable irony in the fact that the very people resident in this geographically broad, indeterminate ecosystem, and destined to live together, have long since adopted the contrived Western 'Orientalist' designation of a 'Middle East': *Shark al-Awsat* in Arabic, *HaMizrach HaTichon* in Hebrew, *Ortadoğu* in Turkish, *Khāvarmiyāneh* in Persian. Yet even when faced by region-wide threats, they are nowhere near actually perceiving themselves, let alone organizing themselves, as 'Middle Easterners'.

When judged by accepted economic criteria for measuring degrees of integration, which include freedom of mobility, unhindered trade and investment flows, an internal market for the subsystem's members, collective measures to standardize legal and financial management regimes, a technical secretariat for cooperation, *etc.*, the Middle East is rightly pronounced 'one of the least "regionalized" regional systems of the world' by Anoushiravan Ehteshami and others. Indeed, leaving aside conventional media and atlas references to *the* Middle East, there is still not a single regional institution which gives expression to this concept of *a* Middle East. In short, an 'imagined community'.

In today's world, when nations are finding it increasingly advisable to pool their sovereignty in order to deal with problems reaching beyond national boundaries, and where regional disunity is an economic, strategic and political liability of colossal proportions, the countries of the Middle East, derided as 'tribes with flags', are an anomaly. This pursuit of unilateralist policies by Middle Easterners – *all* Middle Easterners – is more than merely embarrassing since not going regional contributes a new and depressing layer to the 'culture of defeatism' which has plagued the region for so long and which, unless fought against, has all the potential for sliding the region back into medieval squalor at the margins of global society.

There is no denying the strength of anti-regionalism or the presence of 'spoilers' with a vested interest – economic, political or religious – in thwarting confidence-building and cooperation among the diverse ethnic groups and nation-states of the region. Nevertheless, even in the face of major deterrents, precisely because of the urgency of many issues on the Middle East's agenda, and when so much is at stake, a start has to be made in searching for some minimal common ground leading, in turn, to collective action.

It is precisely because basic intraregional skills for communication, consultation, coordination and coexistence have yet to be acquired that extreme sensitivity and patience are called for on Israel's part. Certainly nothing so grand as 'The New Middle East' outline prematurely sketched by Shimon Peres in the heady days of the 1993 Oslo Accords, with its visionary call for open borders, regional planning, economic integration and the like.

Modest beginnings toward advancing from neighborhood to community can only be based on the authentic needs of the region, while also respecting its special features. With this in mind, as a first step Jerusalem might exercise its prerogative and articulate a set of basic regionalist principles. More specifically, that any regional initiative be:

- indigenous rather than generated or directed from outside
- altogether voluntary
- inclusive and non-discriminatory
- functional in approach and selective in agenda-setting, so as to avoid being overly ambitious
- gradualist, building incrementally upon initial success
- constructive, conferring benefits and rewards upon all parties concerned which also provide additional incentive for undertaking further functional cooperation.

As the post-1945 European experience readily confirms, being able to separate political from apolitical issues by neighboring countries with a long history of enmity and distrust is key to regionalist cooperation. In the instance of Israel and Middle Eastern countries, eleventh-hour steps aimed at achieving minimum shared ground are of no less immediacy than democratization, or sweeping social reforms. Catering to national self-interests rather than dismissing them is the very heart of the functionalist approach. Such intergovernmental and multinational pilot projects as crisis prevention and early warning and rapid response mechanisms as well as for arresting further economic and environmental decline might meet this condition. They are seen as holding out the best prospects for early, readily visible, tangible results while satisfying each participating country's definition of its own enlightened self-interest.

A Middle Eastern horizon for Israeli diplomacy

Rationally accepting Israel's need to be part of a larger regional framework is one thing. Getting from here to there is a different matter, especially when the Jewish State is only one among many countries needed to enlist in the cause of Middle Easternism; and when current realities in the overall Israel-Mideast relationship only give emphasis to how much separates the ultimately desirable from the immediately possible.

For all of its supposed advantages in the Middle East military balance, Israel is unable to coerce its way into Arab and Middle Eastern councils against the express wishes of opposing states and determined would-be spoilers, headed at present by Iran and Hamas. Nonetheless, it does fall within Israel's sovereign capacity to emphasize its Middle Eastern identification and its standing commitment to 'Middle Easternism'.

Authorized spokesmen are encouraged to reiterate this regional commitment publicly and at every opportunity, as well as to assure readiness on Israel's part to consider any serious proposal for cross-border cooperation. In launching this regional orientation government leaders could choose, for instance, to retrieve and recycle archival documents like the statement by Abba Eban before the Ad-Hoc Committee of the United Nations on 1 December 1952, entitled 'Blueprint for Peace', in which he foresaw how 'we could achieve together, each within its own limits and in co-operation with others, a development of the area with its vast human and material resources'. Persistently broadcasting Israel's support for regional engagement – and in Arabic, Turkish and Farsi – can have invaluable psychological merit for the two target audiences that matter most: those at home, and those inhabiting the region. Redefining Israel's image in the eyes of its Middle East neighbors is thus organically linked to Israel's own self-image.

Acknowledging domestic sources of foreign policy, a first item of business must be to combat deeply ingrained Israeli predispositions. Long conditioned to Arab hostility in word and deed, Israeli publics cling to the notion of a monolithic Arab and Islamic world united against them, resulting in the powerful sentiment among Israelis to wash their hands of Khalid Mashal and the Palestinians, Muammar Qadhafi and the Arabs, Recep Tayyip Erdoğan and the Turks, Mahmoud Ahmadinejad and the Iranians; in short, the entire Middle East.

Countering this collective 'groupthink', Arabs and Muslims are in fact often schismatic and 'worlds' apart, sharply at odds among themselves over a full range of issues. And which, incidentally, Israel has been highly effective in exploiting through its anti-Middle Eastern strategy of '*hafrayd umshol*' (Hebrew for '*divide et impera*' or 'divide and rule'). Favored by Israeli strategists and dating back to the pre-state and Ben-Gurion eras, the inclination is to employ divide-and-rule tactics in order to sow dissension and reinforce intra-Arab rivalries, thereby preventing any coalition of Middle Eastern forces from mounting a unified front against Israel. Now the current Middle East situation requires a major reinterpretation of the tactic. The thrust of statesmanship lies in taking a forceful and consistent stand by encouraging a bloc of voices of Middle Eastern moderation and reason: Egyptian democratizers, Palestinian pragmatists, Turkish liberals, Iranian student protesters, Saudi reformers, Arab Emirate entrepreneurs.

So, too, shapers of Israeli public opinion and their domestic audiences would do well to avoid wishful thinking and, instead, to internalize at least two foundational principles of national security and foreign affairs:

- Other geopolitical orientations and associations notwithstanding, history, ideology, politics, geography and necessity nevertheless underpin Israel's inescapable regional connection
- Since Israelis are *in* the Middle East, they are obliged to make the best and the most of it.

It is for the very reason that the Jewish commonwealth has re-established itself in this part of the world for the duration that statesmanlike prudence, patience and persistence must be prized over the long haul. Never can Israelis permit otherwise justifiable feelings of alienation or frustration with the state of Arab affairs to cause them to lose sight of the twin objectives enshrined in the proclamation of statehood: recognition by its direct Middle Eastern neighbors and ultimate regional acceptance.

Israeli policy planners, for their part, might well consider Lord Palmerston's timeless 1848 guide to foreign policy realism:

> We have no eternal allies, and *we have no perpetual enemies*. Our interests are eternal and perpetual, and those interests it is our duty to follow.

One step above the declaratory for demonstrating this renewed regional commitment is to promote the study of Arabic together with modern Middle Eastern history, politics, society and culture within the educational system of Israel from public school through university. The psychological value of such pronouncements and reforms cannot be overestimated. Their main purpose is to disabuse both critical audiences – Israelis and fellow Middle Easterners – of their respective falsehoods. To liberate the former from their 'Masada' or 'siege mentality' while bringing home to the latter that the 'Crusader' mentality toward Israel as a momentary phenomenon lacking staying power is a dangerous misconception. A secondary purpose is to perpetuate the view of the Middle East as a heterogeneous region, respecting and celebrating diversity against all those who would impose an oppressive conformity of dogma and political authority upon its inhabitants.

Middle East-weary resignation on the part of Israelis because of the strident tone of Arab domestic politics and Islamic-supported Palestinian indoctrination for anti-Zionism needs to be combated with all the resources at Israel's disposal. Affirmative 'divide and rule' means persisting in searching patiently for any glimmer of realism in Arab circles toward Israel and the region. It mandates exploring even the smallest openings in order to convey the message of Israel as pro-Middle Eastern, pro-democratic reforms, pro-greater social equality under accelerated economic growth, pro-peaceful coexistence. It means outreach, initially through quiet diplomacy, then progressing to direct, official and open discussion of blueprints for Middle Eastern cooperation. It suggests encouraging those as yet hesitant voices in the region courageous and forward-thinking enough to embrace the idea of including Israel and to speak out publicly on behalf of enlightened, progressive 'Middle Easternism'.

For such voices are to be found, like Egyptian writer Masri Feki who courageously calls for acceptance of Israel 'as a natural and legitimate regional component'. Like Bahrain's Foreign Minister Shaykh Khalid bin Ahmad al-Khalifa who, when speaking from the UN podium in 2008, dared propose creation of an organization to embrace 'all states in the Middle East without exception to discuss longstanding issues openly and frankly'. Or like Ali al-Jarbawi, professor of political science at Birzeit University, appointed Minister of Planning and

Development in The Palestinian National Authority, who, in the spirit of 'Middle Easternism', has written: 'Perhaps it is the clear and present danger of collapsing states that will finally help forge a community, crossing all ethnic and religious boundaries, committed to working together to find solutions to the challenges in our neighborhood'. Voices such as these, if acknowledged by Israel, make it increasingly possible to promote the cause of constructive regionalism and to advance from partisanship to Middle East partnership.

While key to building a growing constituency and operational political lobby in favor of practical cooperation, realistically, mobilizing support for 'Middle Easternism' inside Israel and in progressive Arab circles remains painfully slow. Calls for 'Middle Easternism', rather than hasty or premature, are shamefully overdue. Particularly when considering the supreme urgency for tackling region-threatening problems, time is a luxury the Middle East may not be able to afford. Therefore, the greatest contribution Israel can make is two-fold. Its leaders have it in their capacity to convey to wary neighbors that this strong regional emphasis is not propagandistic, nor merely tactical. Neither is it meant to evade a shared responsibility with the Palestinians for terminating the Israeli-Arab conflict.

As argued here, a strategy of 'Middle Easternism' does not in any way deflect from the peace process or from a permanent resolution of the Palestinian problem on the basis of a mutually hurting compromise. On the contrary, peacemaking is meant to be an integral part of a regional reordering of priorities dictated by larger, no less legitimate and certainly no less pressing shared concerns. What 'Regionalism Now' does posit is that – on both conceptual and realistic grounds – peacemaking and regionalization be conducted *simultaneously* ('peace with regionalism') and not *sequentially* ('peace before regionalism'; 'peace, then regionalism').

So complex and intractable are many of the area's political conflicts that they require considerable patience and diplomatic ingenuity in order to reach ripeness. Logic therefore suggests a commitment by as many parties as possible to tackle their shared regional agenda neither *before* nor *after* conflict resolution but *parallel* with intense, ongoing political negotiation. This formula has the virtue of jump-starting functional cooperation while at the same time actually helping to create an atmosphere conducive for processing peace through collaborative confidence-building measures.

'Peace with Regionalism' is by no means a new or original formula. Offering evidence that a community of interests might still be forged before it is too late are two actual experiments at fostering a consciousness of regionalism as well as a framework for actually promoting it.

The Mediterranean basin.

Now on the table is the option of pursuing a Mediterranean-oriented foreign policy. Israeli observers see considerable promise and untold potential rewards for Israel through actively supporting European initiatives aimed at closer functional cooperation among the 21 countries clustered around the Mediterranean Sea and sharing its long shoreline. Here the logic for Israel is three-fold. By endorsing such initiatives as the Euro-Mediterranean Partnership (1995), also known as the Barcelona Process and the French-sponsored *Union pour la Méditerranée* (2008), Israel creates for itself yet another political configuration and diplomatic orientation even as it assures against the renewed threat of exclusion and isolation. Secondly, not only would Mediterranean frameworks make it easier to turn away from the turbulent arena of Arab politics, it might also serve as an avenue for quietly and progressively integrating Israel more fully into European-supported projects. Lastly, if successful, such multilateral frameworks stand to bring Israel tangible benefits while helping to foster apolitical contacts and professional exchanges with Algerians, Egyptians, Lebanese, Libyans, Moroccans, Syrians and Tunisians sharing common concerns like climate control, promotion of tourism, preservation of archeological sites, pollution of Mediterranean waters and its effects on sea life, illegal immigration and negotiating the lowering of artificial trade barriers.

The Madrid formula

An alternative model is the proto-experiment in Middle Eastern networking instigated in 1991 as part of the Madrid peace initiative. A multilateral track process was inaugurated concurrent with negotiation of outstanding political issues. This two-track approach succeeded in bringing together experts from Israel, regional Arab states and other countries outside the region who met in separate working groups over the course of months to address five key functional issues of common and immediate concern. These Middle East issue areas wisely concentrated on water, environment, arms control, refugees and economic development. Before being suspended indefinitely in November 1993 due to derailment of the Arab-Israeli peace process itself, these collaborative workshops did succeed in breaking new ground. Given the previous levels of distrust and non-communication, having representatives from adversary countries engage each other in serious professional dialogue around a shared table was – even from today's later perspective – in itself no small feat. These multilateral consultative forums thus argue on behalf of the gradualist-functionalist approach.

Nearly two misused decades later, 'Middle Easternism' calls for reconvening these suspended workshops. It is patently in Israel's interest to lend its voice for a return to the Madrid principles and framework since regionalism alone offers residents of the Middle East an alternative reality built on hope rather than fear, cooperation rather than conflict, win-win rather than zero-sum logic, imagination rather than stagnation.

Granted that the Middle East regional subsystem as presently constituted remains an imperfect place, restive, full of resentments and hostile to the Jewish national enterprise. It may be less than appealing for Israelis or complementary for Israeli national goals, but long-term regional coexistence is, for Israel too, still tomorrow's imperative. Were Yehuda Halevi, the 12th-century Spanish Jewish poet, writing in the 21st century he would almost certainly counsel Israeli statesmen: 'My heart may be in the West, but I am in the East' – the Middle East.

3 Unfortunate misplacement

Israeli-Jewish public perceptions of Israel in the Middle East

Tamar Hermann and Ephraim Yaar-Yuchtman

Introduction

The question as to whether it is desirable for Israel, as a country situated in the Middle East, to seek economic, political, and cultural integration among the peoples of the region, or, instead, to continue upholding its long-established 'Western' orientation is often raised, particularly when envisaging a peace reality.[1] It is no secret that from the very beginning of the Zionist movement, which emerged in Europe and followed the footsteps of the European nationalist movements, through the formative pre-state era, as well as in the post-independence years and up to the present, the Western concept of the nation-state, along with its political, economic and cultural traditions, were adopted as a model for the building of the Jewish new society in *Eretz Israel*. In fact, the vast majority of Jewish immigrants to Palestine during the pre-state period were of European origin. This, and the ongoing violent conflict between the Jewish and Palestinian communities, which emerged as a result of the implementation of the Zionist vision and developed into a full-fledged conflict with the entire Arab world, and has not lost momentum until the present day, largely explains the negative sentiments of Israeli Jews toward everything associated with the Middle East (with the notable exception of certain food products of the region, such as *humus* and *falafel*).[2] In fact, as previous studies have pointed out, even Jews of Middle-Eastern origin who were born in Arab countries, as well as their descendents, a social category which could be expected to have stronger motivation to turn eastward, seem not to be very fond of the integration idea.

Over the years, there have been voices challenging this orientation, calling to draw Israel closer to the Middle East and cultivate a close affinity with its Arab neighbors. Early examples of such voices, going back to the 1940s and 1950s, were represented by the Canaanite intellectual circle and the *Ha'Ivrim Ha'Zeiirim* movement, led by poet Yonatan Ratosh, and followed by journalist and politician Uri Avnery's idea of the 'Semitic space' and his small circle, *Eretz Israel Ha'zeiira*. It is worth mentioning that by and large, both endeavors were led and followed by Ashkenazi Israelis. More recently, several Mizrahi intellectuals, like author Shimon Balass,[3] have argued that Israel would be better off by being 'geopolitically' integrated into the countries of the Middle East. Others holding similar views called for closer regional affinity based on the alleged shared grievances of the Arabs and the non-Ashkenazi sectors in Israel, who, in their claim, have been oppressed, humiliated and abused by the Israeli Ashkenazi establishment and elites. Yet, under the leadership of its dominant elites from both Left and Right, Israel as a state and Israeli society as a whole have consistently maintained over the years an unmistakable Western orientation, manifested in three major spheres of activity of state and society – political, economic, and cultural.

Against this background, in this study we address three interrelated questions concerning the hegemony of Israel's Western orientation. First, to what extent is this orientation favored by citizens of Israel? Second, are the public preferences in the choice between East and West consistent across the three spheres? Third, in which ways and to what extent is Israeli society unified in terms of these preferences? For example, are the attitudes of Ashkenazi and Mizrahi – or 'Arab Jews', as the latter have been labeled by certain Mizrahi intellectual/activists[4] – alike, or does the ethnic origin of these and other groups affect their priorities in this regard?

To answer these questions on empirical grounds, we have used data collected in the context of the Peace Index Project (PIP), and mainly the survey of February 1995, as well as a designated survey conducted in May 2010.[5]

Findings

Before even touching on the issue of regional integration, some background information on Jewish Israelis' estrangement from the Middle East is worth keeping in mind. First, according to the 2010 PIP survey, about three-quarters (73.1 per cent) do not read, write or speak Arabic (14.3 per cent speak but do not read nor write, and only 5.8 per cent read, write and speak the most widespread language in the region). Two-thirds (66 per cent) have never visited an Arab country (Jordan, Egypt, Morocco, etc.) and 66 per cent of these say that they are not interested in doing so. This negative attitude seems not to be influenced by the fact two-thirds of those who did visit one or more Arab states stated that they felt comfortable or very comfortable during their visit there. The detachment from the region is further expressed by the fact that from their replies, it appears that an overwhelming majority (84.1 per cent) never watch Arab TV stations, and another 10.5 per cent watch them very rarely. On a different level, the conflict is apparently viewed as unrelated to the Western orientation of Israelis: over two-thirds – 68 per cent – disagreed or strongly disagreed with the hypothetical argument that if the Zionist Jewish immigrants who came to Palestine in the first half of the 20th century had tried to integrate into the Middle East and had maintained less strong relations with the West and their Western characteristics, the Israeli-Arab conflict might not have deteriorated to its present state.

The overall impression created by the above data is that, at least at present, the vast majority of Jewish Israelis are not interested in deepening their roots in the Middle East, nor do they view this as a factor in the development of Israel's unfavorable relations with its neighbors.

Table 3.1 Attitudes on political, economic and cultural integration into the Middle East (% responding positively, Jewish sample)

Sphere:	Political		Economic		Cultural	
	1995	2010	1995	2010	1995	2010
Middle East	29.1	22.6	23.4	12.4	14.4	11.5
Europe/America	50.1	62.6	61.0	70.5	64.1	71.9
Neither (unassisted)	5.4	2.7	1.8	0.9	8.2	4.9
Both (unassisted	6.4	7.8	6.9	14.8	6.2	10.3
Don't know (unassisted)	9.0	4.3	6.9	1.4	7.1	1.5
Total	100.0	100.0	100.0	100.0	100.0	100.0

Regional integration preferences

The main questionnaire item that was used to examine Israelis' preferences for regional integration was formulated as follows: 'In each of the following areas – the political, the economic, and the cultural – are you interested in having Israel integrated into the Middle East or into Europe-America?'. This question was asked in exactly the same wording on two occasions: February 1995 (sample size: 503)[6] and June 2010 (sample size: 513).[7] The findings of these two surveys allow us to address this question by comparing the results of the first poll and the one taken over 15 years later (Table 3.1).[8]

The figures in Table 3.1 reveal the existence of a clear and consistent pattern that can be briefly summarized as follows: First, at both points in time, the Israeli-Jewish public preferred the West over the East with respect to all three spheres of integration. Second, over the years, the Western bias has increased and the interest in the Middle East per se has declined consistently across the political, economic and cultural dimensions. Although a minor option, the interest in a dual integration (the 'Both' option) has increased particularly with reference to the economic and cultural realms. Third, notwithstanding these uniformities, it can be observed that at both points in time, the stronger appeal of the West was not uniform across the three spheres, being most salient in the realm of culture, followed by the economy and polity, in that order.

We took it one step further and moved from the level of attitudes to that of expectations. We therefore asked in 2010: 'In your opinion, what are the chances that Israel will get integrated politically/economically/culturally into the Middle East in the next 20 years?'. Apparently, the majority of the Jewish-Israeli public are not very optimistic in this regard (Table 3.2).

Apparently, Israeli Jews are very skeptical about the chances for political integration (81.8 per cent estimate them as low or very low and 15 per cent as high or very high); second comes cultural integration (69.6 per cent estimate that the chances for this are low or very low and 26 per cent as high or very high); while, as one may expect, economic integration is perceived as more likely (with

Table 3.2 Chances of Israel's integration into the Middle East in the next 20 years (%, 2010 Jewish sample)

	High or very high	Low or very low	Don't know (unassisted)	Total
Politically	15	81.8	3.2	100%
Economically	35.8	61.9	2.3	100%
Culturally	26	69.5	4.5	100%

61.9 per cent estimating the chances for this to happen as low or very low and over a third, 35.8 per cent as high or very high).

An argument can be made that those who do not expect that political, economic and cultural integration will materialize will develop resistance to the very idea, i.e., will say that they are not interested in the Middle East in order to avoid a cognitive dissonance, while those who see integration as a feasible possibility will be more supportive of it. We therefore cross-tabulated the relevant questions. The findings are quite conclusive – among the 'believers' as well as the 'non-believers', the majority is uninterested in regional integration.

Regional integration preferences and socio-demographic characteristics

Since the results of Table 3.1 show that there is still a non-trivial minority of Israeli Jews who do not share the views of the majority, hence suggesting that Israel would prefer the East over the West, it seems pertinent to try and find out if this minority has any unifying features and forms a 'group' in terms of its demographic and social attributes. For this purpose, we performed a series of analyses in two stages: 1. Cross-tabulation and, 2. Regression analysis.

Ethnic origin

It is almost trivial to assume that ethnic descent would serve as a significant factor in determining an individual's position vis-à-vis the question of regional integration. Intuitively, one would assume that Israelis of Mizrahi origin would be more open to the idea that Israel should become integrated into the Middle East. However, the data suggest that this is hardly the case, and that the attitudes in this regard of Mizrahi and Ashkenazi Israeli Jews are not significantly different, and in the present even more so than in the past (Table 3.3).

Although the overall patterns are identical across all ethnic groups – the majority in each of them favors the West over the East – in all realms there are still some differences between them worth noting. In 1995, Mizrahi respondents (first generation, i.e., who were themselves born in the Middle East) were clearly more supportive of the integration idea than all other ethnic groups, including second generation Mizrahi regarding all three spheres, and particularly regarding the political one. In fact, regarding the latter, the plurality of this group favored the Middle East over the West. However, as of now, their support for Israel's

Table 3.3 Support for integration into the Middle East (West) by ethnic origin

	1995					Politically 2010				
	ME	West	Neither	Both	DK	ME	West	Neither	Both	DK
Mizrahi (1st Generation)	46.7	33.3	2.7	12	5.3	28.3	50.0	2.1	15.3	4.3
Ashkenazi (1st Generation)	28.7	51.5	7.9	7.9	4.0	27.6	62.1	1.7	3.4	5.2
Israel	23.5	61.2	4.7	7.1	3.5	21.6	64.7	2.9	6.9	3.9
Mizrahi (2nd Generation)	25.2	51.0	7.3	7.9	8.6	22.1	64.6	3.5	8.0	1.8
Ashkenazi (2nd Generation)	26.4	51.6	9.2	9.9	9.9	26.6	63.8	1.1	4.3	4.3
USSR	–	–	–	–	–	16.3	61.3	3.8	11.3	7.5

	1995					Economically 2010				
	ME	West	Neither	Both	DK	ME	West	Neither	Both	DK
Mizrahi (1st Generation)	36.0	43.0	2.7	8.0	5.3	19.1	57.4	2.1	21.3	–
Ashkenazi (1st Generation)	22.8	61.4	2.0	8.9	5.0	13.3	68.3	–	16.7	1.7
Israel	18.8	74.1	1.2	3.5	2.4	15.8	72.3	1.0	8.9	2.0
Mizrahi (2nd Generation)	21.9	59.6	3.3	5.3	9.9	8.0	77.0	0.9	13.3	0.9
Ashkenazi (2nd Generation)	23.0	60.4	–	7.7	9.9	18.3	68.8	–	11.8	1.1
USSR	–	–	–	–	–	5.1	67.9	1.3	23.1	2.6

	1995					Culturally 2010				
	ME	West	Neither	Both	DK	ME	West	Neither	Both	DK
Mizrahi (1st Generation)	24.0	56.0	6.7	8.0	5.3	19.1	63.8	9.1	14.9	–
Ashkenazi (1st Generation)	19.9	66.3	8.9	7.9	4.0	10.0	73.3	5.0	8.3	3.3
Israel	15.3	69.4	9.4	2.4	3.5	8.8	71.6	3.9	13.7	2.0
Mizrahi (2nd Generation)	15.9	60.9	9.3	6.6	7.3	12.6	71.2	8.1	7.2	0.9
Ashkenazi (2nd Generation)	6.6	69.2	5.5	8.8	9.9	14.0	73.1	4.3	7.5	1.1
USSR	–	–	–	–	–	6.3	75.9	1.3	13.9	2.5

integration into the Middle East, although still somewhat higher than that of the other groups, is of the same pattern. Furthermore, first generation Mizrahi show a much sharper decline in their willingness to see Israel becoming integrated into the Middle East compared to the other groups, and were 'assimilated' in this regard into the general Israeli-Jewish public. The second generation Mizrahi seem to be consistently closer in this regard (in certain cases even supersede them) to the Ashkenazi groups, rather than to their parents' generation.

As for the newcomers from the USSR, in all three spheres they are even less enthusiastic than all other Jewish groups about the idea of Israel's integration into the Middle East.

Age

Unlike other closely related political issues, for example peace talks, regarding which age has turned out empirically to be an inconsequential demographic factor in today's Israeli-Jewish society, it appears that support for political integration into the Middle East is systematically influenced by this independent variable (Figure 3.1). Indeed, all age groups are more in favor of regional integration into Europe-America. However, the younger Jewish Israelis seem to be significantly more reluctant to become part of the Middle East and are much more interested in becoming integrated into the West. This may be part of the global Western orientation, as well as the result of the younger generation's political socialization in times of severe conflict with the Palestinians (first and second Intifadas, second Lebanon War), and the daily manifestations of hostility towards Israel, mainly by Arab, but also by non-Arab Muslim (Iran, and more recently, Turkey) actors in the neighborhood.

A similar distribution was found regarding economic integration. Thus, none of the interviewees of the youngest (18–22) age group was interested in integration into the Middle East, compared to 6.5 per cent of the 22–29 age group, 13.7 per

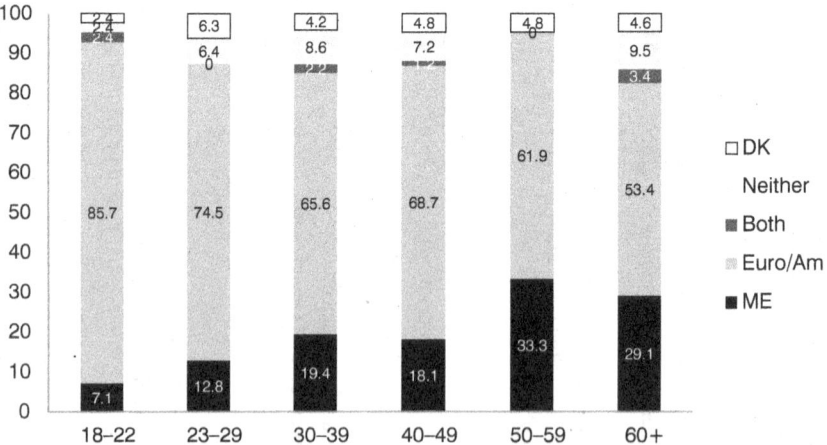

Figure 3.1 Interest in political regional integration by age groups (2010 Jewish sample)

cent of the 30–39 group, 8.3 per cent of the 40–49 group, 19 per cent of the 50–59 group and 19 per cent of the 60 and above group. However, there seems to be no linear correlation between age and desire for cultural integration into the Middle East. Here 9.5 per cent of the 18–22 age group are in favor, and so are 2.1 per cent of the 23–29 group, 14.9 per cent of the 30–39 group, 9.8 per cent of the 40–49 group, 20 per cent of the 50–59 group, and 12.8 per cent of the 60 and above group.

Religiosity

The PIP surveys have indicated numerous times that, in Israel, the individual's level of religious observance is closely correlated with his or her perceptions of peace-related matters. Surprisingly enough, this has not been the case as far as political integration into the region is concerned. Indeed, all groups are more in favor of integrating into the West. In addition, the differences between ultra-orthodox, orthodox, traditional and secular Jews are apparently hardly significant. Hence, while 19.6 per cent of the ultra-orthodox wish to integrate into the Middle East, so do 20 per cent of the orthodox, 24.7 per cent of the traditional and 22.1 per cent of the secular. As for integration into Europe/America, the numbers are also very similar: 65.2 per cent for the ultra-orthodox, 66 per cent – orthodox, 62.1 per cent – traditional and 62.1 per cent – secular.

As far as cultural regional integration is concerned, once more the majority of all groups dislikes the idea of integrating into the Middle East. Moreover, much as in the case of political integration, level of religiosity does not have a systematic influence. Hence, while 20 per cent of the ultra-orthodox are interested in such integration, only 9.8 per cent of the orthodox compared to 13.8 per cent of the traditional and 8.3 per cent of the secular have the same preference.

With reference to economic integration into the Middle East or the West, here the level of religiosity seems to be more influential (Figure 3.2) although again, the majority in all groups prefers that Israel integrate into the West. Beyond that, apparently, the more religious one is, the more one prefers such integration.

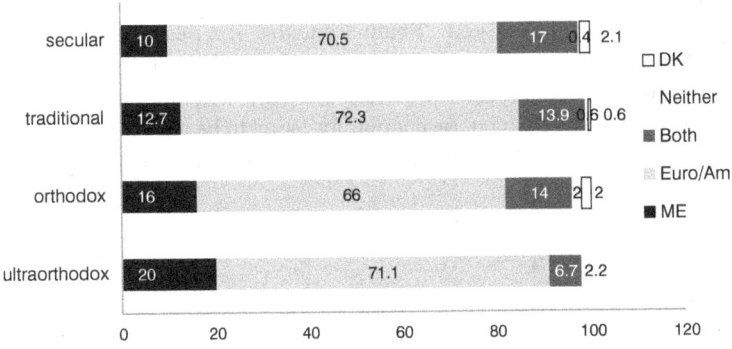

Figure 3.2 Preferences regarding economic regional integration by level of religiosity

Table 3.4 Regional integration preferences by support-opposition to peace negotiations (%, Jewish sample, 2010)

Sphere:	Political		Economic		Cultural	
	Support	Oppose	Support	Oppose	Support	Oppose
Middle East	26.2	13.4	13.3	11.2	15.3	10.1
Europe/America	59.7	69.7	69.3	72.7	68.7	73.5
Neither	2	5	0.6	2.1	0.8	6.0
Both	8.8	5.6	15.5	11.9	14.5	8.5
Don't know	3.3	6.3	1.3	2.1	0.7	1.9
Total	100.0	100.0	100.0	100.0	100.0	100.0

Regional integration preferences and attitudes toward negotiations with the Palestinian Authority

One may assume that attitudes towards the peace process would be correlated in one way or another with regional integration preferences. We therefore cross-tabulated the Jewish public responses to the question: 'What is your position regarding the peace negotiations with the Palestinian Authority?' (Table 3.4).

In all three realms, both the supporters and those in opposition to peace negotiations with the Palestinian National Authority are more enthusiastic about integration into the West than into the Middle East. There are, however, some differences between the two groups, with the most salient being their attitude toward political integration in the region: here, twice as many (26.2 per cent) of the supporters, compared to only 13.4 per cent of those who oppose, favor Israel's integration into the Middle East. The differences between the two groups in relation to economic and cultural integration are smaller. Interestingly, whereas among the supporters the order of preferences regarding integration into the Middle East is economic, cultural and political, among the opponents, the order is cultural, economic and political, as in the overall Jewish population.

We tried to determine whether the respondents saw a necessary correlation between the prevalence of peace and Israel's chances of becoming integrated into the region. We therefore asked: 'Some argue that if a peace treaty between Israel and the Palestinians is signed, a door would open for Israel to become integrated politically/economically/culturally into the Middle East. However, others maintain that this would not be enough for Israel to be admitted politically/economically/culturally into the Middle East. With which of the two opinions do you agree more?' (Table 3.5).

Multiple regression analysis

The results of the cross-tabulation indicate that the differences in the choice between East and West according to demographic and socio-cultural attributes of Jewish respondents are relatively small. Nevertheless, it seems worthwhile to examine the extent to which individual attributes exert significant effects on this

Table 3.5 Jewish Israelis' estimation of Israel's acceptance in the Middle East if peace prevails (%)

	Politically	Economically	Culturally
Admitted	29.0	48.7	28.9
Not admitted	67.2	48.0	64.7
Don't know	3.8	3.3	6.4
Total	100.0	100.0	100.0

choice, and in what direction. Given that the latter is a dichotomous variable, we used logistic regressions for the purpose. The main results of these regressions can be summarized as follows (with detailed outcomes provided in the appendix).

Political integration

Of the six independent variables in the regression analysis, only one variable – age – appears to have a significant influence, with the youngest age group having the strongest Western orientation and the oldest the least. For example, the chance that the youngest age group (18–29) would prefer the West over the East is 2.64 higher than that of the middle age group (30–49) and 5.41 higher than that of the oldest age group (50+).

Economic integration

The impact of the individual attributes in this sphere is more pronounced, with significant effects of religiosity and age and, to a lesser extent, party voting. Accordingly, a higher degree of religiosity and older age reduce the likelihood for a Western preference. As to the last variable, voters for parties on the Left (Labor, Meretz and Rakah, the Israel Communist Party) are somewhat less likely to prefer economic integration into the West.

Cultural integration

The only attribute having a significant influence with regard to the cultural domain is religiosity. As in the case of the economic domain, a higher degree of religiosity is less conducive to cultural affinity with the West.

Taken together, the results of the regressions are generally in agreement with the conclusions derived from the cross-tabular analysis; namely, that the Israeli-Jewish community tends to be relatively homogeneous in its Western orientation with regard to the political, cultural, and economic spheres, with the notable exception of age and religiosity. In fact, even the significant disparities generated by age, religiosity, and party voting were quite limited, given that in each of the categories comprising these variables, the West was preferred over the East across the three spheres. As to the remaining individual attributes – years of schooling, gender, and ethnic origin – the latter is of particular interest since, as noted earlier, one might have expected that the common heritage of the Arab people and of Israeli Jews of Middle-Eastern origin would draw the latter closer to the former, especially in the cultural domain. Yet, their preferences are almost indistinguishable from those of Ashkenazi Jews who immigrated to Israel from European countries.

Israeli-Arab citizens – attitudes towards regional integration

While the prevalent Western orientation of Israeli-Jewish citizens is well known and in fact rather expected against the background of the ongoing Israeli-Arab conflict and other cultural and political inputs mentioned above, it is certainly much less self-evident or expected in the case of Arab citizens of Israel. Yet, our findings suggest that although proportionally less strongly, the Israeli-Arab sector also manifests significantly greater interest in integrating into the West than into the Middle East (Table 3.6).[9]

The data confirm that in all three realms, the Western orientation of the Arab-Israeli public is stronger than toward the Middle East, although as mentioned, the proportions are different – in the Arab case, a plurality, not a majority, prefers the West over the Middle East. The order of preferences is also somewhat different than that of the Jewish-Israeli sector: economic integration comes first (45.6 per cent), then cultural (43.3 per cent) and political (41.2 per cent). The only visible difference perhaps is the second option of the cultural realm – among the Israeli Arabs, the proportion of those interested in integrating into both worlds, West and Middle East (26.7 per cent), is significantly higher than among the Israeli-Jewish population (10.3 per cent).

As for Arab Israelis' expectations regarding the integration of Israel into the Middle East in the next twenty years, again, in the same direction but with lesser intensity, Arab-Israeli citizens are also rather pessimistic. Furthermore, much like their Jewish counterparts, they view economic integration as least unlikely and political integration as most unlikely (Table 3.7).

What, then, in the Arab Israelis' view, is the expected influence of a peace treaty between Israel and the Palestinians as far as Israel's integration into the Middle East is concerned? On this question, Arab-Israeli citizens seem to be significantly more optimistic than their Jewish counterparts. They are not 'unrealistic' in the sense that half of them estimate that even with peace, no door to integration into the Middle East will open for Israel. At the same time, a significant minority does believe in the feasibility of such opportunities if and when peace prevails (Table 3.8).

Concluding remarks

Taking into consideration the extreme fragmentation of Israeli society and the prevailing perception that the 'national consensus' has been critically shaken in the last two decades or so, it is actually amazing to find such substantial similarity, almost unanimity, between Left and Right, Ashkenazi and Mizrahi, old and young, Jews and Arabs, on the topic of regional integration. The most striking finding

Table 3.6 Regional integration preferences of Arab-Israeli citizens (% 2010)

Dimension:	Political	Economic	Cultural
Middle East	30.0	22.2	16.7
Europe/America	41.2	45.6	43.3
Neither	13.3	10.0	10.0
Both	12.2	16.7	26.7
Don't know	3.3	5.6	3.3
Total	100.0	100.0	100.0

Table 3.7 Israeli-Arab citizens' expectations regarding regional political, economic and cultural integration (%)

	High or very high	Low or very low	Don't know	Total
Political	28.9	67.7	3.4	100
Economic	43.3	55.6	1.1	100
Cultural	37.8	60.0	2.2	100

Table 3.8 Arab Israelis' estimation of Israel's acceptance to the Middle East if peace prevails (%, Arab sample 2010)

	Politically	Economically	Culturally
Admitted	48.9	47.8	47.2
Not admitted	50.0	50.0	50.6
Don't know	1.1	2.2	2.2
Total	100.0	100.0	100.0

presented in this article is that the majorities of all these otherwise contending public sectors, which hold rather antithetical views on almost all other political matters, are, in fact, united in their unwillingness to integrate into the Middle East politically, economically and culturally. Nevertheless, there are some significant differences in the level of their respective resistance to such regional integration and in their interest in integrating into the West. Furthermore, their reasons for holding such an attitude (or perhaps sentiment) are by no means identical. However, the bottom line is the same: the majority of Israelis, regardless of ethnic origin, nationality, age or political affiliation, turn their back on the Middle East and look to the West.

Most Israelis are indeed quite skeptical about the possibility of Israel being welcomed by its neighbors in the region politically, economically or culturally. One may well argue that this is the classic 'chicken and the egg' syndrome – as the Israelis feel unwanted in the region, they turn away from this 'club' which they expect will decline to grant them membership. Yet, the data presented here suggest that this is not the case, as the majority, even of those who do believe in the possibilities of political, economic and cultural integration in the foreseeable future, are reluctant. Neither, as we showed, is the willingness, or actually the unwillingness, to integrate into the Middle East a derivative of Israelis' support for or opposition to peace negotiations.

Is this really surprising? On the surface, taking into consideration the bitter disagreements that characterize Israeli society today, the solid consent described above is fairly unexpected. However, beyond that, Israelis seem to be of a very similar opinion to people throughout the world, including many in the third world and even in the Arab world, who would prefer to become individually or collectively part of what they see as the prosperous, modernized, and democratic, although obviously far from perfect, West. This is true, even if it means losing some of their specific traditional identities and increasing the potential for domestic and external conflicts with their immediate environment. Indeed, when patterns of international migration are examined, Western countries are places that people typically try to move into, whereas Middle-Eastern countries are places they tend to wish to move out of.

Will this Western orientation create an impediment to the resolution of the Middle East conflict? Not necessarily. Not only are some convinced that high fences make good neighbors, but also, certain students maintain that this same attraction to the West is quite prevalent among wide circles in Palestinian society who only take refuge in Islamic anti-Western fundamentalism due to the dismal repercussions of the protracted conflict with Israel. If this is the case, peace can expand the common ground of the two peoples and bring them closer together.

Appendix

See Table 3.9.
Coding:
A. Country of origin
Reference category: born in Europe or America
AS-AF: born in Asia or North Africa
USSR: born in the former Soviet Union
IS-IS: respondent and father born in Israel
IS-AS-AF: respondent born in Israel, father born in Asia or North Africa
IS-EU-AM: respondent born in Israel, father born in Europe or America
B. Party voting in the last general elections
Reference category: Kadima party (centrist)
Left (Labor, Meretz, Arab parties)
Floating vote
Right (secular and religious parties on the right)
C. Religiosity
Rank order scale: 1=Ultra-orthodox; 2=Orthodox; 3=Traditional; 4=Secular
D. Age
Reference category: middle age (30–49)
Young: 18–29
Old: 50+
E. Education
Natural scale: years of formal schooling
F. Gender
Reference category: female

Table 3.9 Logistic regressions

		Political integration			Economic integration			Cultural integration		
		B	SE	Sig	Exp (B)	B	SE	Sig	Exp (B)	B	SE	Sig	Exp (B)

		B	SE	Sig	Exp (B)	B	SE	Sig	Exp (B)	B	SE	Sig	Exp (B)
A	AS-AF	−0.840	0.541	0.120	0.432	−1.220	0.694	0.079	0.295	−1.729	0.748	*0.021	0.177
	USSR	0.053	0.514	0.917	1.055	0.342	0.826	0.679	1.408	0.876	0.772	0.257	0.417
	IS-IS	−0.707	0.490	0.149	0.493	−1.315	0.653	*0.044	0.268	0.978	0.752	0.194	0.376
	IS-AS-AF	−0.489	0.482	0.310	0.613	−0.316	0.711	0.656	0.729	−1.261	0.719	0.079	0.283
	IS-EU-AM	−0.387	0.464	0.404	0.679	−1.047	0.621	0.092	0.351	−1.206	0.708	0.089	0.300
B	Left vote	−0.634	0.459	0.168	0.530	−1.109	0.544	0.042	0.330	−0.585	0.579	0.312	0.557
	Floating vote	−0.134	0.399	0.736	0.874	0.499	0.537	0.353	1.647	0.324	0.525	0.538	1.383
	Right vote	0.218	0.407	0.593	1.243	0.419	0.536	0.435	1.520	0.259	0.508	0.610	1.296
C	Religiosity	0.093	0.152	0.540	1.098	0.517	0.191	*0.007	1.677	0.471	0.184	*0.011	1.601
D	Young	0.971	0.439	*0.027	2.641	1.596	0.724	*0.028	4.934	0.878	0.551	0.111	2.407
	Old	−0.717	0.318	*0.024	0.488	−0.921	0.431	*0.033	0.398	−0.137	0.398	0.732	0.872
E	Y's-Education	−0.014	0.046	0.762	0.986	−0.075	0.059	0.205	0.928	0.016	0.057	0.782	1.016
F	Gender	0.159	0.262	0.543	1.173	0.126	0.346	0.717	1.134	0.313	0.329	0.341	1.368
	Constant	1.530	1.077	0.155	4.619	2.037	1.373	0.138	7.671	0.816	1.357	0.548	2.261

*Statistically significant (p<0.05)

Notes

1. For the Western orientation of Israel as far as its foreign policy was concerned, see, e.g., Uri Bailer, *Cross on the Star of David: The Christian world in Israel's foreign policy* (Indiana University Press, 2005). For the Western, mainly American, orientation, see, e.g., Maoz Azaryahu, "McIsrael? On the 'Americanization' of Israel", *Israel Studies*, 5(1), (2000), 41–64; Uzi Rebhun and Chaim I. Waxman, "The 'Americanization' of Israel: A demographic, cultural and political evaluation", *Israel Studies*, 5 (2000); Anat First and Avraham Eli, "Globalization/Americanization and negotiating national dreams: Representations of culture and economy in Israeli advertising", *Israel Studies Forum*, 22(1), (2007), 54–74.
2. In the 'golden days' of the Oslo process, when peace between Israel and the Palestinians seemed to be on the horizon, it seemed as if the completion of the process would entail some significant changes in Israel's political, economic and cultural nature. Some envisaged that it would also result in growing Westernization of the state and society. See, e.g., Sammi Smooha, "The implications of the transition to peace for Israeli society", ANNALS AAPSS 555. Pdf (1998).
3. From statements by Prof. Shimon Blass during a discussion on Avirama Golan's program on Channel 2 of Israeli television, "On a First Reading", 13 December 2003.
4. See Yehuda Shenhav (2003), *The Israeli Arabs* (Tel Aviv: Hakibbutz Hameuhad, 2003, Hebrew).
5. Until 2000, the PIP samples, comprising about 500 interviewees, represented the Jewish population only. Since then, they have also included the adult population of Israel's Palestinian-Arab citizens and the sample size has increased to about 600, with the latter represented according to their share in the population. For the sake of methodological consistency, the numbers in Table 3.1 on both dates refer to the Jewish sample only. Israeli-Arab citizens' attitudes are discussed hereafter.
6. This survey was conducted under the auspices and with the financial support of the Tami Steinmetz Center for Peace Research, Tel Aviv University.
7. This survey was conducted under the auspices and with the financial support of the Evens Program for Mediation and Conflict Resolution, Tel Aviv University and of the Israel Democracy Institute, Jerusalem.
8. Since the 1995 survey did not include the Arab population, the comparisons over time relate to the Jewish sector only.
9. As the Arab sample is small (N=90), we were unable to analyze it by subgroups and reach valid conclusions.

4 The Israeli party system in comparative perspective

A 'unique case' or part of the West European tradition?

Csaba Nikolenyi

In the regional context of the Middle East, where non-competitive political regimes tend to be the norm, the political system of the State of Israel stands out as a unique case. Ever since the inception of the State in 1948, democratically organized elections have decided which political forces will control the legislature and, in turn, form the political executive. Elsewhere in the Middle East, by stark contrast, democratic elections have been by and large absent.[1] Even compared against those new states that were formed after the end of the Second World War in other parts of the world, e.g. India and Pakistan, the stability of Israel's record of democratic credentials and arrangements stand out as a major exception. Although the international identity of the State has been under constant threat since its creation, Israeli politics always remained competitive and participatory, and avoided the path leading toward authoritarianism.

The stability of Israeli democracy is in large part due to the inherent nature of the political institutions that its Founding Fathers designed. The combination of a parliamentary system of government with a proportional electoral system, which provides representation for the widest spectrum of political views and positions in the directly elected legislature, has ensured that no single political force would be able to control and centralize political power in its hands. As such, the political system was built to generate consensus and compromise among the representatives of the different segments of Israeli political life. Indeed, it has been well documented in the literature that other kinds of institutional choices, namely majoritarian electoral laws and/or presidential systems of government, pave the way to fragile and ultimately unstable democracies in other parts of the world.[2]

The institutional choices that the Israeli political leadership made at the time of the creation of the State were clearly based on the model of the stable West European democracies, even though most of the Founding Fathers had been actually socialized in Eastern Europe, where the roots and tradition of democratic politics were extremely weak. Nevertheless, geographical proximity to and the regular interaction with Western Europe, facilitated by the regular meetings of the transnational Zionist Congress, provided a favourable condition for institutional learning and adaptation. Yet, in spite of the inherent Europeanism of the Israeli political system, conventional scholarly wisdom held Israel in a unique category of its own; it was a case like no other, which, due to its uniqueness, defied meaningful comparability.[3]

This conventional view of Israeli uniqueness has been challenged, perhaps most strongly and successfully by scholars of political parties and party systems. It was in this field, more than in any other, that a number of works have been put forward with the explicit purpose of exposing the comparability of the Israeli party system and stressing its relevance for a wider audience. For instance, Emanuel Guttman argued that Israel fit the category of a 'continental European political system' in Gabriel Almond's well-known classification of political systems, and more specifically the subgroup called 'working multi-party system'.[4] A decade later, Arian and Barnes explained the emergence of Israel's multi-party system, dominated by Mapai and then the Alignment, in terms of Maurice Duverger's concept of a dominant party and party system and showed several parallels with the post-war experience of Italy.[5] Similarly, Gregory Luebbert developed a theory of coalition governments that explicitly accounted for the Israeli as well as Western European cases in the same framework, while Dan Avnon cast the emergence of Israel's party laws in the broader context of party legislation in democratic regimes, new and established alike.[6] More recently, Reuven Hazan and Gideon Rahat have shown that the politics of Israel's legislative process, institutional and electoral reform, could be and should be analyzed and assessed in the same framework along with West European cases.[7] Perhaps the single most significant statement of this research agenda is the 2008 publication of a special issue of *Party Politics*, the premier international journal devoted to the study of political parties and party system, on 'Israeli Party Politics: New Approaches, New Perspectives', bringing together five articles – each of which addresses a comparative research question with special focus on the Israeli case.[8] In the same vein, this chapter argues that the development of the Israeli party system ought to be understood and appreciated by placing it in the broader comparative context together with the democratic multi-party systems of Western Europe. Having a parliamentary system of government where elections are conducted under a proportional representation electoral system, Israel shares the same institutional foundation that defines and forms the basis of party competition in almost all West European political systems. As a result, many of the political consequences, in terms of the dynamics of party politics, which follow from the combination of these institutional features, are also more similar than different. In short, the central argument of the chapter is that since the Israeli party system inherited a quintessentially West European 'genetic model' at the time of the birth of the state, its development over the ensuing six decades has also followed a quintessentially West European pattern. Of course, this is not to deny that there are special particular features that also characterize the Israeli party system. However, in this Israel is not unique and different from any other contemporary democracy.

The chapter will develop as follows. The first section provides an overview of the main arguments about the uniqueness of the Israeli case. The second section offers a description of the development of the Israeli electoral and party system. The third section draws explicit comparisons between the Israeli and the West European cases with regard to the politics of electoral systems and party competition.

Is Israel unique?

In his opening essay to the volume dedicated to debunking the notion of Israel as a unique case, Michael Barnett writes that:

> The Israeli case lives an uncomfortable existence in comparative research. The challenge of classifying and categorizing the Israeli experience leads many to question the suitability of the Israeli case. Neither East nor West, developed nor undeveloped, capitalist nor socialist, Third World nor First World, there is relatively little about Israel that automatically reminds us of other countries or their historical experiences. ... Because Israel is unique in many dimensions, it slips through the cracks of social science inquiry into historical peculiarity.[9]

According to Barnett, the main reason for this established wisdom is the paradigm shift that took place in the comparative social sciences. As researchers moved away from deductively oriented cross-national studies, in search of broad and universally applicable causal relationships, and shifted toward historically derived context-specific approaches, Israel fell through the cracks.[10] As long as theory building and testing and the collection of large numbers of empirically observable indicators of political and social processes drove comparative research, Israel could be treated as any other country: a source of additional units and points of observation. However, when context became important, Israel suddenly had to be explained and justified to be a case of the particular variable under investigation. Given the enormous complexities of Israel, this proved to be very difficult, since on so many dimensions the country just could not be categorized or classified as the above quote suggests.

Giovanni Sartori's seminal work on comparative parties and party systems provides a vivid illustration of this attitude.[11] Sartori attempted to provide a two-dimensional taxonomy of party systems based on the number of relevant political parties and the direction of competition amongst them. With regard to the first dimension, he locates Israel in the category of extremely fragmented party systems, defined as those with more than five relevant parties, and in the company of ten other democracies: Chile, Denmark, Finland, Fourth and Fifth Republic France, Italy, the Netherlands, Norway, Switzerland, and the inter-war Weimar Republic.[12] However, on the second dimension Israel appears to be special, because the dynamics and the direction of competition among these parties are more similar to what Sartori finds in the much less fragmented party systems.

According to Sartori, extreme multi-party systems lead to a high degree of polarization (e.g. France, Italy, Chile) unless society is divided into autonomous segments whose representatives share political power in a consociational framework (e.g. the Netherlands, Switzerland). Israel is special because it has neither of these characteristics: it is neither polarized nor segmented. Instead, moderate ideological competition and consensus rather than adversity are the hallmarks of the party system. Furthermore, Sartori refutes the comparability of Israel as a combination of the 'fragmentation and multiconfessionalism of the Netherlands with the polyethnicity of Switzerland'.[13] On the one hand he argues that Israel's religious parties, constituting one of the principal electoral and political blocs in the country, position themselves in a unique manner which renders them completely unlike the confessional parties in Holland: while the latter fit the Left-Right continuum, the former are only concerned with securing additional religious controls over society through the arms of the state. On the other hand, he also notes that Israel is actually much more polyethnic than Switzerland yet the 'Swiss "nations" are more accommodated to each other than the Jewish "tribes".'[14]

In order to determine whether or not the Israeli party system provides a special, unique case beyond comparability, we need a research strategy that is both comparative and sensitive to historical detail and context without incurring the pitfalls and limitations of historical particularism.[15] We shall do this by (i) locating the *genesis* of the Israeli party system in the context of the emergence of democratic multi-party politics in early 20th-century Western Europe and (ii) examining how its subsequent development differed from those of the other West European party systems. It is indeed well known that Israel's electoral and party systems are rooted in the European legacy and heritage of the early makers of the two pre-state institutions, the Zionist movement and the Yishuv, which define the contours of the domestic political development of the State of Israel.[16] Therefore, the strategy allows us to see how 'Western' and 'European' the later developments of Israel's party politics have become. If we find substantial similarities in the development of the Israeli and West European party systems, we may be a step closer to refuting the *sui generis* thesis and understand Israel in its proper comparative context.

The development of the Israeli electoral and party system

Conventional wisdom in the comparative electoral and party systems literature holds that electoral rules shape the number of political parties. In a famous statement that subsequently became cited and known as Duverger's Law and Hypothesis, Maurice Duverger argued that first-past-the-post electoral systems reduced the number of parties to two while proportional representation (PR) electoral systems led to a fragmented multi-party system.[17] Although this statement spawned an extraordinary amount of scholarship as students of party politics looked for both supportive and disconfirming evidence, a reverse line of argument has also developed over time suggesting that electoral systems were the product rather than the cause of the party system in the first place.[18] The history of electoral systems in Western Europe provides substantial support for this view. Grumm notes that a number of West European countries (including Belgium, Denmark, Germany, Norway, Switzerland) had multi-party systems prior to and at the time of the adoption of a PR system.[19]

The logic of introducing PR in Western Europe was typically dictated by the strategic imperatives of large-scale electoral mobilization, thanks to the introduction of universal franchise, party system change, and the rise of socialist and labour parties in the early 20th century. The rising parties of the newly enfranchised masses demanded PR in order to increase the likelihood and scope of their parliamentary representation, while the parties of the established elite also preferred PR in order to keep their expected electoral losses under manageable control. In other words, PR emerged in Western Europe as a result of a compromise between the increasingly more powerful and organized parties of the working class, which sought to replace a majoritarian and plurality-based system with PR in order to benefit from lower thresholds of entry to parliament, and those established parties that felt most threatened by the workers' parties under the existing rules.[20] Table 4.1 shows the date when PR was adopted in selected states of Western Europe and in Israel, both before and after the creation of the State.

The adoption of the PR as the electoral system choice in the pre-state political institutions that would define the future contours of the State of Israel conforms to the West European historic logic. These two principal pre-state political bodies were the transnational Zionist Congress and the Elected Assembly (*Asefat Hanivharim*) of the Community of Israel (*Knesset Israel*) in Palestine, which not only provided 'direct experience for future Israeli parliamentarians [but] ... Israel's provisional organs of government, her major political parties, her system of elections and coalition government ... can also be traced to these bodies.[21] Representatives to both of these essentially voluntary institutions were always elected by PR to ensure the full cooperation and continued loyalty of the constituents. In the case of the Congress, elections at first took place along the lines of the territorial federations of the Zionist Organization, but by 1921 Congress delegates had been seated according to party groups. The three blocs of parties that came to define the party system of the Organization were the Labour,

Table 4.1 The introduction of PR in Israel and Western Europe

Country	Year PR was adopted
Belgium	1899
Sweden	1909
Denmark	1915
Germany	1918
Knesset Israel	1918
Netherlands	1918
Switzerland	1918
Italy	1919
Norway	1919
State of Israel	1948

Source: Colomer, 2004: 64.

the Religious, and the General Zionists.[22] It is interesting to note that a tri-polar party system structure has remained in place in Israel to this day.[23]

The adoption of PR in the Yishuv dates to the Election Regulations for the Palestine Jewry's First Elected Assembly at Jaffa in 1918, just one year after the Balfour Declaration.[24] Although the Mandate government did not cede legal recognition to the Assembly until 1926, prior elections took place in 1920 and 1925.[25] The PR system that was used in these elections featured (i) an open list of candidates, which allowed voters to cross out the name of an undesirable candidate; (ii) a single country-wide district for the purposes of allocating seats in the Assembly, except for the 1925 election that took place along district lines; and (iii) a significantly biased provision for universal franchise which was not corrected until the last pre-state election in 1944. These biases meant that in 1922, ultra-orthodox women did not vote; that in 1925 Yemenite voters cast their ballot after the elections and received special representation; and that in 1932, when elections took place in three distinct ethnic dialects (Ashkenazic, Sephardic, and Yemenite), nearly twice as many votes (793 versus 421) were needed to elect a Ashkenazi than either a Yemenite or a Sephardi representative. Although these biases were corrected for the purposes of the 1944 election, the Sephardic and the Revisionist parties of the Right boycotted the election after their demands for electoral reform failed.[26] As a result, voter turnout in the last pre-state election failed to reach its peak of 1920 even though the institutional biases in the franchise were remedied. Table 4.2 shows that only 67.5 per cent of the eligible voters exercised their right to vote in 1944. While this was almost 10 per cent higher than the turnout rate in the previous two polls, it was also 10 per cent less than the rate in 1920.

The electoral frameworks of the Zionist Organization and Yishuv provided important background for the adoption of PR after the State of Israel was declared. Although Section 10 of the UN Partitions Resolution of 1947 called for the creation of a 'legislative body elected by universal suffrage on the basis of proportional representation',[27] Medding notes that PR was eventually adopted because it was familiar to all parties in both the Zionist movement and the Yishuv.[28] Indeed, the Elections Committee of the Provisional State Council considered three main types of electoral systems (single-member majority rule; PR with multi-member districts; and PR with a single nation-wide district) but the status quo institution, i.e. nation-wide PR with closed lists of candidates, prevailed over the alternatives.

Table 4.2 Elections to elected Assembly of the Yishuv

Election year	Voter turnout (%)	Size of Knesset	Number of parties
1920	77.2%	314	20
1925	56.3%	221	26
1931	56.3%	71	12
1944	67.5%	171	18

Source: Sager, 1985: 14.

The PR system of the new State was novel, however, in terms of the number of seats that it allocated to the political parties in the Knesset. The Committee considered a Knesset of 71 seats (as in 1931), 131 seats (as in 1944), 101 seats and 120 seats. The latter was eventually settled upon as the compromise choice between the two extremes as well as its symbolic association with the size of the ancient Knesset Gedolah.[29]

Over the course of the past six decades, Israel's PR has shown remarkable resilience even though a number of proposals have been put forward to reform it.[30] In the early years, Prime Minister Ben Gurion suggested the introduction of the first-past-the-post electoral system; David Bar Rav-Hai, chair of the Elections Committee of the Provisional State Council, favoured PR with multi-member districts; while Yosef Serlin advocated a mixed-member system.[31] Yet the key features of the system, i.e. the closed-list character of the ballot; the single nation-wide district; and the number of seats in the Knesset, have remained intact. The main changes that took place pertained to three areas: presentation of candidate lists; the mathematical formula that converts votes into seats; and the election of the Prime Minister.

Prior to 1992, when the Parties Laws was passed and made the official registration of political parties a precondition to submit a candidate list, eligibility to submit a list was tied to the number of electors' signatures a party could collect.[32] As the size of the electorate grew, so did the number of required signatures, which increased from 250 in 1949 to 2500 in 1984.[33] The vote-to-seat conversion formula moved between the highest-average and the largest-remainder types, but the former has been in place since 1973.[34] Finally, for a brief period of time the Prime Minister was elected directly by the voters on a separate ballot in 1996, 1999 and 2001.[35]

In sum, this brief history of the electoral system in Israel shows close convergence with the West European historical pattern: when a multi-party system emerges, parties favour PR over other alternatives. Indeed, as we have seen, a multi-party system had already existed in the pre-state institutions, which paved the way for the unequivocal adoption of PR as the electoral system for the new state of Israel. In contrast to Western Europe, however, Israel was a new state with no prior electoral history to decide who controls the authoritative institutions of the state. As such, PR did not replace old and existing electoral rules, which was the case in Western Europe. Also, even though the elections in the Yishuv violated the 'one man one vote' principle, the electorate was fully mobilized via universal franchise by the time of the creation of the state and the adoption of PR.[36] In contrast, the struggles for PR and the extension of the franchised were joint processes in Western Europe.

Israel and Western Europe compared

Electoral systems have a number of important political consequences such as the fractionalization of the party system, the representation of ethnic and other minorities, electoral turnout, and the nature of government formation, and indirectly, government stability.[37] In this section, we assess the similarities and differences between the development of party competition in Israel and in West Europe in two of these areas: the number of parties and the nature of coalition governance. Unless otherwise noted, the empirical data on the Israeli cases are obtained from the website of Knesset, while for the comparable West European information we draw on data provided by Muller and Strom.[38]

There are a number of different measures that have been proposed in the literature to gauge the degree party system fragmentation. The simplest way is to count the number of parties that contest an election or that win parliamentary representation. While this measure is very easy to compute, its main drawback is that it does not provide any information about the distribution in the relative weights of political parties. For example, as we shall see, the actual number of party lists that have won seats in the Knesset has not changed much over time even though important changes have occurred in the relative weights of the parties represented. In order to compensate for this, comparative party systems researchers have relied more extensively on the 'effective number of parties' measure proposed by Laakso and Taagepera.[39] The calculation of this index is based on dividing into unity the sum of the squared vote or seat shares of every political party. For our purposes, we consider the seat share of political parties as those that have made it through the threshold of representation and won parliamentary seats.

Table 4.3 compares both the actual and the effective numbers of parties in thirteen West European states with those in Israel for the post-1945 period. The Table clearly shows that, on average, almost twice as many political parties have won legislative seats in Israel as in Western Europe. The highest number of parliamentary parties is found in Italy, the Netherlands and Belgium. Although they come close to the Israeli figure, the latter still remains much higher. The data in the 'effective number of parties' column tell the same story: even when taking parties' relative weights into account, the Israeli party system is more fragmented than those of Western Europe. The countries that come the closest to Israel are Finland, Belgium and the Netherlands. An interesting point concerning the effects of the electoral system is that in spite of its extreme proportionality, the Israeli electoral system results in a more pronounced reduction in the actual number of parties than the average case in Western Europe. In Israel, the effective number of parties is 2.4 times less than the actual number of parties, while the corresponding average figure in Western Europe is only 1.7. The only West European country where the effective number of parties is more deflated is Italy (with the actual number of parties exceeding the effective number of parties by 2.62) while the Netherlands comes close (with a ratio of 2.12).

Figure 4.1 shows that the effective number of parties moved within a predictable bend, between 3 and 6, for the most part in Israel's electoral history. In fact, it was not until after the introduction of the direct election of the Prime Minister that the number of effective parties started to rise meteorically. In the last Knesset elected before this institutional reform, in 1996, the effective number of parties was 5.61 whereas in the subsequent election, in 1999, the figure jumped to 8.69. Even though a clear upward trend had started as early as the 10th Knesset election (the effective number of parties was higher in every successive and newly elected

Table 4.3 The number of parties in Israel and Western Europe

Country	ENPP	Actual parties	Parties in cabinet
Austria	2.68	3.5	1.86
Belgium	4.96	8.5	3.24
Denmark	4.48	7.7	1.97
Finland	5.06	7.7	3.49
France	4.32	5	2.26
Germany	2.59	4	2.08
Ireland	2.9	4.8	1.64
Italy	4.01	10.5	2.88
Luxembourg	3.3	4.8	2.13
Netherlands	4.68	9.9	3.23
Norway	3.39	6.4	1.73
Portugal	3.21	5.4	1.91
Sweden	3.29	5.3	1.42
West Europe	3.76	6.4	2.3
Israel	5.16	12.4	3.96

Source: Muller and Strom, 2000: 565.

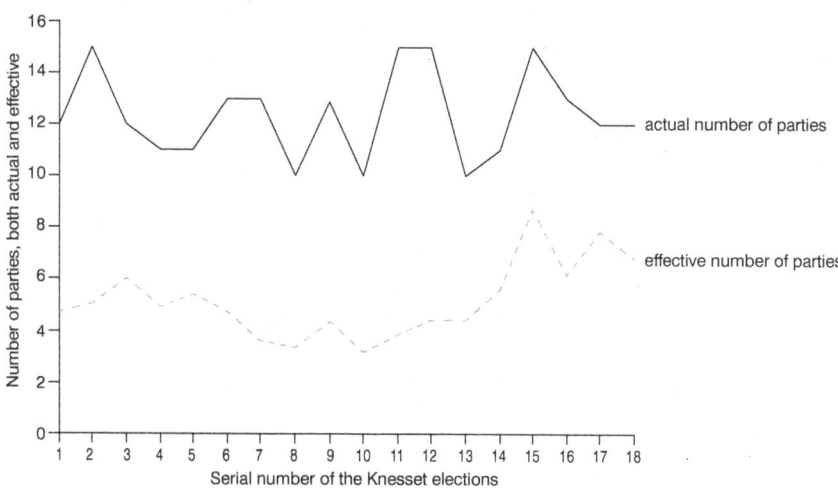

Figure 4.1 The number of parties in Israel

Table 4.4 Electoral turnout in Israel and Western Europe

Country	Turnout rate (%)
Austria	91.3
Belgium	92.5
Denmark	86.0
Finland	76.0
France	74.8
Germany	85.0
Ireland	73.2
Italy	89.8
Luxembourg	89.7
Netherlands	87.2
Norway	80.2
Portugal	75.7
Sweden	85.7
Western Europe	83.62
Israel	77.1

Source: IDEA 2004

Knesset between 1981 and 1999), the average change in the value of the index between every election pair in this period, i.e. 1981–84, 1984–88, 1988–92 and 1992–96, was only 0.62; a tiny fraction of the change from 1996 to 1999.

Prior to 1999, the Israeli party system was *not* more fragmented than the average of all West European cases combined. With an average effective number of parties of 4.53 between 1949 and 1996, the party system of Israel was actually less fragmented than that of Belgium and the Netherlands, and almost identical to that of Denmark.

PR electoral rules and multi-party systems generally lead to higher rates of electoral participation than plurality rules and less fragmented patterns of party competition.[40] Indeed, the average voter turnout rate in the thirteen Western European states, each of which has both PR and multi-party systems, is very high at 83.62 per cent for the 1945–2002 period.[41] As expected, Israel closely follows this pattern (see Table 4.4). The average voter turnout rate in all eighteen Knesset elections is 77.1 per cent, with a high of 86 per cent in the first election to the Constituent Assembly, and a low of 63.5 per cent in 2006. In fact, Figure 4.2 shows that prior to the election of 2003, voter turnout never dropped below 70 per cent. The recent decline in voter participation rate is unexpectedly deep. Whereas the average turnout rate over the fifteen elections held between 1949 and 1999 stood at 79.4 per cent, the corresponding figure for the past three elections is a mere 65.6 per cent, a difference of 13.8 per cent. Of the Western European cases considered, only France, Finland, Ireland and Portugal have registered lower average turnout rates than Israel in the post-war period.

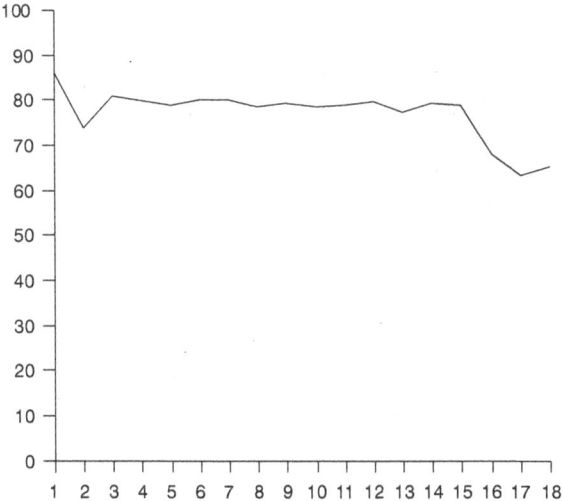

Figure 4.2 Electoral turnout in Israel since 1949

Source: http://www.knesset.gov.il/description/eng/eng_mimshal_res.htm

The historically high rates of electoral participation in Israel are especially impressive and ought to be considered in the context of a steadily expanding electorate. Whereas the number of eligible voters in the first election of 1949 was only around half a million, by 2009 the voter pool increased more than tenfold to over 5 million. Such an expansion in the voter base is unparalleled in Western Europe. That voter turnout in Israel has still remained high testifies not only to the continued political involvement of the population, but also to the successful political integration of the generations of new immigrants (*olim*). Luebbert notes that it was precisely the presence of an already well-institutionalized party system that prevented the explosion of the party system when the largest influx of immigrants arrived at the end of the Second World War.[42]

Government formation and stability

Since elections in fragmented multi-party systems do not normally produce a single-party majority outcome, parties tend to form coalition governments in order to ensure that the executive enjoys the support of a legislative majority. In Western Europe, 69.1 per cent of all post-war cabinets were indeed formed by such multi-party coalitions. The only countries that have never seen a single-party executive are Luxembourg and the Netherlands, while in Belgium, Finland and Germany single-party governments account for less than one-fifth of all cabinets. Of the thirteen countries examined by Muller and Strom, single-party governments have constituted a majority of the cases in only Ireland, Norway and Sweden. In general, West European coalition governments are small in terms of the number of parties forming them; on average, 2.3 parties were needed to form an executive.

The most numerous cabinets are found in the Netherlands (3.23), Belgium (3.24) and Finland (3.49), while Sweden (1.42), Ireland (1.64), and Norway (1.73) are at the opposite end of the distribution. It is worth noting that there is a significant positive correlation between the effective number of parliamentary parties and the number of parties forming the cabinet: the more fragmented the legislature, the more parties will be in the cabinet.

Most, but certainly not all, governments in Western Europe have controlled a parliamentary majority, i.e. the combined number of seats held by the coalition partners has exceeded the 50 per cent mark. Undersized minority governments accounted for only 37.3 per cent of all post-war cabinets with only one country never experiencing such an executive: Luxembourg. In the same three countries that have seen the most single-party governments, i.e. Sweden, Ireland and Norway, minority governments also account for the majority of the cases. However, the country with the highest frequency of minority executives (87.1 per cent) is Denmark.

Israel clearly follows these patterns. Similarly to Luxembourg and the Netherlands, each and every Israeli cabinet has been formed by multiple political parties, i.e. single-party cabinets simply do not exist. Furthermore, every Israeli government has had a parliamentary majority at the time of its formation. As mentioned earlier, the Knesset is more fragmented than the average West European parliament. Therefore, based on the above observation we would expect Israeli cabinets also to contain more parties than their West European counterparts. Indeed, the average number of parties in Israeli cabinets is 3.96, which is proportionately higher than in West European countries. However, this does not make Israel a unique or deviant case. While Israel is at the upper end of the distribution, i.e. it has a high number of parties both in the Knesset and in the cabinets, it does fit the broader West European trend.

The pattern of government formation in Israel also follows the West European model very closely in terms of electoral responsiveness. In Western Europe, the plurality party, i.e. the parties that have won the most seats in the election, normally forms the government. Indeed, among the thirteen countries we draw on for comparison, there is not a single one where the plurality party would not be in government in the majority of the instances. Within this, of course, there is variation. In the more fragmented party systems of Belgium, Denmark, Finland and the Netherlands, the largest party has been in government in only 79 per cent, 68 per cent, 78 per cent, and 59 per cent of the cases respectively. At the other end of the spectrum we find Austria and Portugal with 100 per cent each, followed by France (91 per cent), Italy (98 per cent) and Luxembourg (94 per cent).[43] Since 94 per cent of the Israeli governments included the plurality party, Israel seems to be more similar, in terms of the electoral responsiveness of government formation, to the less fragmented multi-party systems of Western Europe (e.g. Austria, Luxembourg, etc) than the more fragmented ones (e.g. Belgium, Finland).

Of the 32 Israeli cabinets, there were only two where the principle of electoral responsiveness was not followed. The first occurred after the May 1996 elections, the first time that the Prime Minister was elected on a separate ballot, in which the Israeli electorate delivered a split verdict: the Prime Ministerial contest was won

Table 4.5 Cabinet representation of the plurality party in Israel and Western Europe

Country	% of cabinets including the plurality party
Austria	100
Belgium	79
Denmark	68
Finland	78
France	91
Germany	85
Ireland	73
Italy	98
Luxembourg	94
Netherlands	59
Norway	65
Portugal	100
Sweden	81
West Europe	82.4
Israel	94

Source: Muller and Strom, 2000: 568.

by the Likud candidate (Benjamin Netanyahu) while the largest number of seats in the Knesset was grabbed by Labour. In the end, Netanyahu formed a six-party coalition government which did not include Labour. The second instance took place after the most recent election in 2009. In this election Kadima won the largest number of seats, although the margin of its victory over Likud was a mere single seat. Although President Peres gave Kadima leader Tzipi Livni the opportunity to explore the possibility of forming a Kadima-led coalition government, these efforts failed. As a result, the second largest party, Likud, was given a second opportunity, which led to the formation of a six-party cabinet.

The final dimension on which we assess the dynamics of multi-party politics in Israel and Western Europe pertains to the stability of the government formed. Table 4.6 shows that the average West European cabinet lasts for about two years in office (702 days). The variation across the countries, however, is considerable. The most stable cabinets are found in Luxembourg (1170 days), Ireland (891 days), Austria (854 days) and the Netherlands (808 days), while the least stable ones are in Italy (355 days), Finland (452 days) and Belgium (520 days). Interestingly, with 707 days, the average duration of Israeli cabinets is only a hair's breadth away from the overall West European average. This is surprising since the general pattern in Western Europe points to a negative association between the degree of parliamentary fragmentation and average cabinet duration: the more fragmented the parliament, the less stable cabinets tend to be. In Israel, however, a higher level of party system fragmentation generates coalition governments that are no less stable than what we find on the continent.

Table 4.6 Cabinet stability in Israel and Western Europe

Country	Average cabinet duration in days
Austria	854
Belgium	520
Denmark	626
Finland	452
France	625
Germany	699
Ireland	891
Italy	355
Luxembourg	1170
Netherlands	808
Norway	755
Portugal	597
Sweden	771
West Europe	702
Israel	707

Source: Muller and Strom, 2000: 585.

Conclusion

This chapter has demonstrated the inherent and essential Europeanism of the Israeli party system in three main points. First, the development of a multi-party system and a PR electoral rule in Israel was part of the same historical process that defined the political evolution and development of democracy of West Europe in the early 20th century. Second, although the Israeli electoral system is often blamed for inducing a high level of fragmentation in the party system, we showed that it was only when Israel departed from her established political tradition by introducing the direct election of the Prime Minister that the number of parties started to exceed the West European average. Third, we have also shown that Israel follows the same established patterns of coalition government formation and stability that we find in Western Europe. All in all, the findings suggest that Israel may be unique in many ways, but in terms of both the characteristics of her electoral institutions and the consequences that these generate, the country fits and follows the West European mode.

Notes

1 See the annual reports of Freedom House at www.freedomhgouse.org, which identifies Israel and Lebanon as the only two free and democratic states in the region prior to 1976. Thereafter, Israel remains the only free state in the region.
2 See, for example, J. Linz, 'The Perils of Presidentialism', *Journal of Democracy* 1, 1990, 51–69; M. S. Shugart and J. Carey, *Presidents and Assemblies: Constitutional*

Design and Electoral Dynamics, Cambridge: Cambridge University Press, 1992. For a recent dissenting view on the relationship between presidentialism and democratic instability, see J. A. Cheibub, *Presidentialism, Parliamentarism, and Democracy*, Cambridge: Cambridge University Press, 2007.

3   M. Barnett, Israel in *Comparative Perspective: Challenging the Conventional Wisdom*, Albany, NY: SUNY Press, 1996.
4   E. Gutmann, 'Israel', *Journal of Politics* 25, 1963, 706.
5   A. Arian and S. H. Barnes, 'The Dominant Party System: A Neglected Model of Democratic Stability', *Journal of Politics* 36, 1974, 592–614; M. Duverger, *Political Parties: Their Organization and Activity in the Modern State*, London: Wiley, 1954.
6   G. Luebbert, *Comparative Democracy: Policymaking and Governing Coalitions in Europe and Israel*, New York: Columbia University Press, 1986; D. Avnon, 'Parties Laws in Democratic Systems of Government', *Journal of Legislative Studies* 1, 1995, 283–300.
7   R. Hazan, *Reforming Parliamentary Committees: Israel in Comparative Perspective*, Columbus, OH: Ohio State University Press, 2001; R. Hazan and G. Rahat, *Democracy Within Parties: Candidate Selection Methods and Their Political Consequences*, Oxford: Oxford University Press, 2010; G. Rahat and R. Hazan, 'Israel: The Politics of an Extreme Electoral System', in M. Gallagher and P. Mitchell, eds., *The Politics of Electoral Systems*, Oxford: Oxford University Press, 2005, 333–52.
8   *Party Politics* 14, 2008.
9   M. Barnett, *Israel in Comparative Perspective*, p. 3.
10 Ibid., p. 4.
11 G. Sartori, *Parties and Party Systems: A Framework for Analysis*. Cambridge: Cambridge University Press, 1976.
12 Ibid., p. 146.
13 Ibid., p. 153.
14 Ibid.
15 M. Barnett, *Israel in Comparative Perspective*, p. 7.
16 G. Luebbert, *Comparative Democracy*; P.Y. Medding, *The Founding of Israeli Democracy 1948–67*, Oxford: Oxford University Press, 1990; S. Sager, *The Parliamentary System of Israel*. Syracuse, NY: Syracuse University Press, 1985.
17 M. Duverger, *Political Parties*.
18 For the former position, see G. Cox, *Making Votes Count: Strategic Coordination in the World's Electoral Systems*, Cambridge: Cambridge University Press, 1997. For the latter argument, see C. Boix, 'Setting the Rules of the Game: The Choice of Electoral Systems in Advanced Democracies', *American Political Science Review* 93, 1999, 609–24; A.M. Carstairs, *A Short History of Electoral Systems in Western Europe*, London: George Allan and Unwin, 1980; J. Grumm, 'Theories of Electoral Systems', *Midwest Journal of Political Science* 2, 1958, 357–76; S. Rokkan, *Citizens, Elections, Parties: Approaches to the Comparative Study of the Processes of Development*. Oslo: Universitetsforlaget, 1970.
19 J. Grumm, 'Theories of Electoral Systems', p. 374.
20 S. Rokkan, *Citizens, Elections, Parties*, 1970.
21 Sager, *The Parliamentary System of Israel*, pp. 5–6.
22 Ibid., pp. 3–7.
23 J. Mendilow, *Ideology, Party Change and Electoral Campaigns in Israel, 1965–2001*, Albany, NY: SUNY Press, 2003.
24 Sager, *The Parliamentary System of Israel*, p. 45.
25 D. Horowitz and M. Lissak, *Origins of the Israeli Polity: Palestine Under the Mandate*, Chicago, IL: University of Chicago Press, 1978, p. 42.
26 Ibid., pp. 42, 246, n.13.
27 United Nations Security Council. 1947. Resolution 181 on the Future Government of Palestine. http://www.un.org/documents/ga/res/2/ares2.htm.

28 Medding, *The Founding of Israeli Democracy*, pp. 15–6.
29 Ibid., p. 16.
30 A. Brichta, 'Forty Years of Struggle for Electoral Reform in Israel, 1948–88', *Middle East Review* 21, 1988, 18–26; G. Rahat, *The Politics of Regime Structure Reform in Democracies: Israel in Comparative Perspective*, Albany, NY: SUNY Press, 2008; Rahat and Hazan, *The Politics of an Extreme Electoral System*.
31 See http://www.knesset.gov.il/description/eng/eng_mimshal_shi.htm.
32 Avnon, 'Parties Laws in Democratic Systems of Government'.
33 Sager, *The Parliamentary System of Israel*, p. 46.
34 For a technical discussion of these and other formulae, see Gallagher and Mitchell, *The Politics of Electoral Systems*, pp. 579–97.
35 O. Kenig, G. Rahat, and R. Hazan, 'The Political Consequences of the Introduction and the Repeal of the Direct Elections for the Prime Minister', in A. Arian and M. Shamir, eds., *The Elections in Israel 2003,* New York: Transaction Books, 2005, pp. 33–61; G. Rahat, 'The Politics of Reform in Israel: How the Israeli Mixed System Came to Be?', in M.S. Shugart and M.P. Wattenberg, eds., *Mixed-Member Electoral Systems: The Best of Both Worlds?*, Oxford: Oxford University Press, 2001, pp. 123–51.
36 Luebbert, *Comparative Democracy*, pp. 93–4.
37 A. Blais and K. Carty. 'The Impact of Electoral Formulae on the Creation of Majority Governments', *Electoral Studies* 6, 1987, 209–18; A. Lijphart, *Electoral Systems and Party Systems: A Study of Twenty-Seven Democracies, 1945–1990*, Oxford: Oxford University Press, 1994; J. Blondel, 'Party Systems and Patterns of Government in Western Democracies', *Canadian Journal of Political Science* 1, 1968, 180–203; D. Rae, *The Political Consequences of Electoral Laws*, New Haven, CT: Yale University Press, 1971.
38 W. Muller and K. Strom, *Coalition Governments in Western Europe*. Oxford: Oxford University Press, 2000.
39 M. Laakso and R. Taagepera, 'Effective Number of Parties: A Measure with Application to West Europe', *Comparative Political Studies* 12, 1979, 3–27.
40 A. Blais and K. Carty, 'Does Proportional Representation Foster Voter Turnout?', *European Journal of Political Research* 18, 1990, 167–81.
41 See http://www.idea.int/publications/voter_turnout_weurope/upload/Full_Report.pdf.
42 Luebbert, *Comparative Democracy*, p. 94.
43 Muller and K. Strom, *Coalition Governments in Western Europe*, p. 568.

References

Arian, Alan and Samuel H. Barnes. 1974. 'The Dominant Party System: A Neglected Model of Democratic Stability'. *Journal of Politics* 36 (3): 592–614.

Avnon, Dan. 1995. 'Parties Laws in Democratic Systems of Government'. *Journal of Legislative Studies* 1(2): 283–300.

Barnett, Michael. 1996. *Israel in Comparative Perspective: Challenging the Conventional Wisdom*. Albany, NY: SUNY Press.

Blais, Andre and Ken Carty. 1990. 'Does Proportional Representation Foster Voter Turnout?' *European Journal of Political Research* 18 (2): 167–81.

Blais, Andre and Ken Carty. 1987. 'The Impact of Electoral Formulae on the Creation of Majority Governments'. *Electoral Studies* 6 (3): 209–18.

Blondel, Jean. 1968. 'Party Systems and Patterns of Government in Western Democracies'. *Canadian Journal of Political Science* 1(2): 180–203.

Boix, Carles. 1999. 'Setting the Rules of the Game: The Choice of Electoral Systems in Advanced Democracies'. *American Political Science Review* 93 (3): 609–24.

Bogdanor, Vernon and David Butler. 1983. *Democracy and Elections: Electoral Systems and their Political Consequences.* Cambridge: Cambridge University Press.

Brichta, Avracham. 1988. 'Forty Years of Struggle for Electoral Reform in Israel, 1948–88'. *Middle East Review* 21 (1): 18–26.

Carstairs, Andrew McLaren. 1980. *A Short History of Electoral Systems in Western Europe.* London: George Allan and Unwin.

Cheibub, Jose Antonio. 2007. *Presidentialism, Parliamentarism, and Democracy.* Cambridge: Cambridge University Press.

Colomer, Josep M. ed. 2004. *Handbook of Electoral System Choice.* Basingstoke, UK: Palgrave Macmillan.

Duverger, Maurice. 1954. *Political Parties: Their Organization and Activity in the Modern State.* London: Wiley.

Freedom House. Various reports. www.freedomhouse.org.

Gallagher, Michael and Paul Mitchell. eds. 2005. *The Politics of Electoral Systems.* Oxford: Oxford University Press.

Grumm, John. 1958. 'Theories of Electoral Systems'. *Midwest Journal of Political Science* 2 (4): 357–76.

Gutmann, Emanuel. 1963. 'Israel'. *Journal of Politics* 25 (4): 703–17.

Hazan, Reuven. 2001. *Reforming Parliamentary Committees: Israel in Comparative Perspective.* Columbus, OH: Ohio State University Press.

Hazan, Reuven and Gideon Rahat. 2010. *Democracy Within Parties: Candidate Selection Methods and Their Political Consequences.* Oxford: Oxford University Press.

Horowitz, Dan and Moshe Lissak. 1978. *Origins of the Israeli Polity: Palestine Under the Mandate.* Chicago, IL: University of Chicago Press.

IDEA 2004. *Voter Turnout in Western Europe.* Stockholm: IDEA. Available online at http://www.idea.int/publications/voter_turnout_weurope/upload/Full_Reprot.pdf.

Kenig, Ofer, Gideon Rahat, Reuven Hazan. 2005. 'The Political Consequences of the Introduction and the Repeal of the Direct Elections for the Prime Minister'. In Asher Arian and Michal Shamir. eds. *The Elections in Israel 2003.* New York: Transaction Books. pp. 33–61.

Knesset. http://www.knesset.gov.il.

Laakso, Marku and Rein Taagepera. 1979. 'Effective Number of Parties: A Measure with Application to West Europe'. *Comparative Political Studies* 12: 3–27.

Lijphart, Arend (1994). *Electoral Systems and Party Systems: A Study of Twenty-Seven Democracies, 1945–1990.* Oxford: Oxford University Press.

Linz, Juan. 1990. 'The Perils of Presidentialism'. *Journal of Democracy* 1: 51–69.

Luebbert, Gregory. 1986. *Comparative Democracy: Policymaking and Governing Coalitions in Europe and Israel.* New York: Columbia University Press.

Medding, P.Y. 1990. *The Founding of Israeli Democracy 1948–67.* Oxford: Oxford University Press.

Mendilow, Jonathan. 2003. *Ideology, Party Change and Electoral Campaigns in Israel, 1965–2001.* Albany, NY: SUNY Press.

Migdal, Joel. 2001. *Through the Lens of Israel: Exploration in State and Society.* Albany, NY: SUNY Press.

Muller, Wolfgang and Kaare Strom (2000). *Coalition Governments in Western Europe.* Oxford: Oxford University Press.

Rahat, Gideon. 2008. *The Politics of Regime Structure Reform in Democracies: Israel in Comparative Perspective.* Albany, NY: SUNY Press.

Rae, Douglas. 1971. *The Political Consequences of Electoral Laws.* New Haven, CT: Yale University Press.

Rahat, Gideon and Reuven Hazan. 2005.'Israel: The Politics of an Extreme Electoral System'. In Gallagher, Michael and Paul Mitchell. eds. *The Politics of Electoral Systems*. pp. 333–52. Oxford: Oxford University Press.

Rahat, Gideon. 2001. 'The Politics of Reform in Israel: How the Israeli Mixed System Came to Be?' in Matthew S. Shugart and Martin P. Wattenberg. eds. *Mixed-Member Electoral Systems: The Best of Both Worlds?* Oxford: Oxford University Press. pp. 123–51.

Rokkan, Stein. 1970. *Citizens, Elections, Parties: Approaches to the Comparative Study of the Processes of Development*. Oslo: Universitetsforlaget.

Sager, S. 1985. *The Parliamentary System of Israel*. Syracuse, NY: Syracuse University Press.

Sartori, Giovanni. 1976. *Parties and Party Systems: A Framework for Analysis*. Cambridge: Cambridge University Press.

Shugart, Matthew Soberg and John Carey. 1992. *Presidents and Assemblies: Constitutional Design and Electoral Dynamics*. Cambridge: Cambridge University Press.

United Nations Security Council. 1947. Resolution 181 on the Future Government of Palestine. http://www.un.org/documents/ga/res/2/ares2.htm.

Part II
Contested identities

5 Where East meets West

David Ohana

Zionism's ambivalence towards the East

The long history of interaction between the East and the West has been characterised by two opposite approaches: one that we may call 'the crusader approach', according to which the two must permanently be in opposition, and a violent confrontation between them is always imminent; the other, which we call 'the Mediterranean option', maintains that on the contrary, the two are in permanent dialogue, creative synthesis, and that it is in their reciprocal difference that each discovers itself.

Zionism was born in the West. It sprang up against the background of the rise of nationalism, the spread of secularism and the dominance of Eurocentricity. One of the chief cultural ambitions of the Zionist movement was to create a 'new man' – an idea that made its appearance in the period of the Enlightenment at the end of the 18th century, at the time of the historic encounter between the Jewish Diaspora and European culture. It was thought that the Jew could be transformed by the adoption of secularism and modernism, and so be made fit to join European society. However, the myth of the 'new Jew' came into being only when the idea of a separate Jewish nationality was accepted and realised in the East, in Israel. It was believed that there was an affinity between the people and the land: only in the land of the forefathers, in the East, would the desired change in the image of the Jew come about. Zeev Jabotinsky, in the Zionist Congress of 1905, spoke of the 'Palestinian personality', and Martin Buber believed in a mystical connection 'between the people and the land'. The realisation of Zionism in Israel linked ideology to geography, history to a spatial identity.

The 'new Hebrew' at the fin-de-siècle in East and Central Europe faced two directions: he looked to the East, the Levant, but he also had his back to it. Zionism was characterised from its earliest days by its ambivalent attitude to the East. The positive attitude to the East was first expressed by figures such as Moses Lieb Lilienblum, Mordechai Zeev Feierberg, Itamar Ben-Avi, Nahum Sokolov, Yitzhak Ben-Zvi and David Ben-Gurion Lillenblum saw the European Jews as aliens: 'We are alien to our own race. We are Semites among the Aryans, sons of Shem among the sons of Japhet, a Palestinian tribe from Asia in European lands.' Feierberg declared to the Jews in his famous essay *Whither?*, 'And you, my brethren, as you now go eastwards, you must always remember that you are orientals by birth.' Itamar Ben-Avi declared 'We are Asiatics', Sokolov wanted to create 'a great Palestinian culture',[1] and Ben-Gurion said in 1925 that 'the meaning of Zionism is that we are once again becoming an Oriental people.'[2]

Yigal Zalmona, the curator of The Israel Museum, wrote:

> The Israeli self-image has been oscillating between these two extreme attitudes towards the East ever since the beginnings of the Zionist settlement of this country. The issue of national and individual identity rises to the surface mainly in moments of crisis, at times of unrest or during periods of an impending encounter or confrontation with the East. The desire to form part of the East in the deepest existential and cultural sense, or, in contrast, to detach from it – these are the two major impulses that come to bear on the evolving Israeli sense of identity.[3]

The negative attitude was expressed in an *a priori* rejection of the Eastern option. Herzl declared in *The Jewish State*, 'For Europe we can be part of the defensive wall against Asia; we can be outposts of culture against barbarism.'[4] The historian Joseph Klausner saw his culture as a superior one, as he said in his article 'Fear' (1905): 'All our hope that we shall one day possess the land of our ancestors is not based on the sword, nor on the fist, but on the collective advantage we have over the Arabs and Turks.'[5]

Is this attitude of some of the thinkers of Zionism in its early stages an outstanding example of the orientalist thesis put forward by Edward Said? Were certain varieties of Zionist perception of the East an example of a paternalistic relationship of the West to the East, or, more precisely, to the area of the Eastern Mediterranean? Here we have something much more complex than the out-and-out European orientalism, because the East was seen not only as the site of the ancient history of the Jewish people but also as the supreme object of the people's return to itself according to its vision; but to the same degree that the East was seen as the cure for the national distress of the Jewish people and the insignia of its national identity, it represented the 'other', it was external to the Zionist Jew, and was perceived as 'there', whether as a strange or even alien entity or as an object of insatiable longings. The growing attraction of the East for the 19th-century European romantics may be ascribed to a longing for ancient and authentic roots and to a common feeling among the intelligentsia that the West was in decline. It was this attraction that impelled Jews of Zionist inclination to see the East not only as the cradle of their national identity or as a place of refuge but also as a source of values, strength and moral renewal for their people.

'Crusaders' and 'Mediterraneans' are two geopolitical metaphors frequently used by politicians, writers and scholars, both within Israel and outside it, to describe Israel's identity and its place in the region. The first indicates the alien character of a Western colonialism in the East. Israel's adversaries and certain elements within it both employ this metaphor, which signifies an imminent confrontation between East and West. For modern Arab nationalism the Zionist-crusader analogy was a political myth that enlisted the forefathers for the benefit of the heirs: the historical episode became an inspiring model for the descendants, who were thus incited to expel the 'Jewish infidels' from Palestine in the 20th century.

In contrast with other contentious images such as the Zionist-crusader analogy, 'Mediterraneanism' has the reputation of being a source of dialogue between the East and West. It is true that the annals of the Mediterranean Basin record an ongoing conflict for political hegemony, cultural control and economic imperialism. Yet, despite these historical confrontations, the Mediterranean includes both the Levant and the West, and out of this synthesis it created a space which did not give rise to a hegemonic and all-inclusive culture with a single, homogenous character. Instead it created a variety of historical models of cultural meetings and intellectual exchanges. The Mediterranean, without being a homogenous cultural unit, has historically been a region with an intense mixture of Eastern and Western cultures.

The ideology that characterised the first years of Israeli independence was that of the so-called 'melting-pot' – a policy that set out to create a unified Israeli identity and culture amongst all the Jews immigrating to Israel. It aimed to fashion the Zionist ethos, with its native secular outlook and modern Western orientation, into an Israeli identity with clearly defined borders. In contrast to this, the Mediterranean option offered a more wide-ranging Israeli identity, one with cultural mobility, a connection with tradition, multiple voices, and sustained intellectual and linguistic interchange.

The opponents of the Mediterranean option claim that its advocates are attempting to evade the issue of Israel's proximity to the Arab states and the Palestinians, and are taking refuge in the idea of a pleasant neighbourly relationship with the Europeans; an escape, say the critics, that has no basis in reality. For them it is an evasion of the basic problems of Israel and its neighbours/adversaries. Those who reject this criticism, for their part, claim that the Mediterranean option is a real cultural and political possibility and can therefore serve as a basis for a dialogue with Israel's neighbours, an option therefore offering a new and fresh perspective that is not dependent on the basic assumption of two contending sides. The validity of this option is contingent on the idea that there is a closeness and a rich fabric of geo-cultural affinities among the peoples living in the Mediterranean Basin – affinities with a vital political significance that can facilitate the creation of a broad dialogue and regional channels of communication, and to some degree moderate the Israeli-Arab dispute. This dispute is often said to be insoluble, and it is possible that this negative verdict may be due, amongst other things, to a disregard of the general Mediterranean context and of the things that are common to the heritage of all the peoples of the region, emphasizing instead only the different geographical interests these peoples have. Unlike the limiting old-new Middle Eastern option, a geopolitical term initiated in British and French colonial thought, this new option does not regard the Mediterranean as a 'theatre of confrontation', an area of conflict between Jews and Arabs. Furthermore, this option is by no means confined to the external relationships between the peoples.

Zionism not only sought to change the Jew's relationship to place but also to change his relationship to time.[6] It boasted of restoring the Jew to history, and claimed that this was necessary in order that he would cease to relate to time in a deterministic way, passively waiting for the end of days. The task of the modern Jew was to approach time in an active manner. The traditional Messianic approach to time, which was essentially cyclical and passive, was exchanged for an active, modern approach whose Messianism was Promethean and in which man, through his actions, achieved his own redemption in historical time. In contrast to this, the crusader and Canaanite narratives claimed the pre-eminence of time over man. The crusader narrative claimed that time would ultimately defeat the Israeli colonialist experiment, and the Canaanite narrative claimed that the mythological Canaanite time was more valid than the Jewish or Zionist time.

Underlying the Canaanite metaphor is the deterministic claim that the Hebrew national identity is native and owes nothing to human effort. It is not voluntary, modern or Western – that is to say Promethean – but primitive and fundamentalist. Thus, it undermines the Zionist pretension of effecting a transformation of the Jew: it held that it was impossible that an extra-territorial religious consciousness could become a native national identity. Conversely, the crusader metaphor also makes the deterministic claim that the Zionist project is a hopeless cause. However much the Zionist, Hebrew or Israeli seeks to strike roots in the place, he will inevitably be an alien implantation. Underlying both metaphors, which are in contradiction to one another, is the common basic assumption that the Zionist passion is doomed to failure from the start.

The paradox of Zionism laid in a new self-consciousness of many Jews in Europe at the time of the Enlightenment and the emancipation that as free individuals they were enslaved. From the time that the modern Jew began to think for himself and have his own values, he asked himself why he was enslaved to the national norms of his neighbours and colleagues. The inequality between him and his associates in Europe was made evident by the revolutionary universalistic assumptions of the Enlightenment and led to a positive and liberating thought. Universalism postulated the right of all peoples to self-determination, and thus the principle of equality encouraged a demand for national specificity. It was the reflexive consciousness that derived from the emancipation and not anti-Semitism that gave birth to modern Jewish nationalism. Zionism thus became the Promethean passion of many Jews in the modern era.

The uniqueness of the Zionist project lay in its combination of the creation of a new space with the moulding of a new historical individual. The Promethean will to the self-construction of the new Jew required first of all the annulment of the dichotomy inherent in the slogan of the Jewish Enlightenment: 'Be a Jew in your home and a man outside'. Two basic assumptions, which follow from one another, were implicit in this slogan: the Jew lived in a space that was not his, and as a result he was alienated from himself. In other words, the modern Jew was inauthentic because he lived in a hostile enclave and in a certain sense he was homeless: exile is not only a physical situation but a state of mind.[7] Zionism therefore sought to be a movement of self-liberation: liberation from the enslaving space would automatically free the alienated individual. Zionism was not only a transference of the Jews to a new space, the abandonment of a temporary place and a return to the territory of birth; it was also the aspiration to radically change the kind of man that grew up in the unnatural space that its thinkers and founders called exile. It was felt that it was necessary to create a new historical individual, and this would not only come about through education or through political developments such as the French or Russian revolutions or similar national ideologies, but through transference from one geographical and mental space to another. Place is space in the memory:[8] Zionism consequently sought to exchange a house that it considered empty for an old-new home full of modern Jewish meaning.

It was the place that would bring about the transformation of identity: from being a subject, the Jew in his homeland would become his own ruler, he would create his authentic personality; the Jew would become a Hebrew, the child of exile would become a native. Geography would change history, and in parallel with this conceptual transformation, a new philosophy of history would arise.[9] The Zionist philosophy of history that emerged presented a synthetic picture of past Jewish history in which it was deemed necessary to return and to reconnect with the initial, sovereign, Hebrew, heroic stage. Hence the emphasis placed on a whole series of symbols and myths rooted in Zion, the place of birth, and on the creation of a new human model: positive, heroic and tied to the land; and hence the obliteration of the concepts and memories that came into being between the end of Jewish independence in 132 CE and the Zionist national rebirth in 1948. Zionism was thus for many people a territorialization of Judaism, but in a deeper sense than merely restoring the Jews to their natural place.[10] It reflected a radical historical philosophy that sought to change the Jew into an old-new Hebrew. The meaning of the rebirth for the more radical thinkers was a return to Hebraism and not to Judaism, to the physical space and not to God. The paradox was this: only in the ancient historical space could the new man come into being; only a return to ancient roots would restore the Jew to modern history.

In the land of Canaan

The Israeli orthodox cultural critic Baruch Kurzweil's (1907–1972) first attack on the Canaanite ideology was not aimed at Ratosh and his group but took place in January 1948 against the Israeli journalist Uri Avnery's intellectual circle and their provocative journal. The Canaanites held that it is the nativistic and linguistic factors that govern the national consciousness. They were not ideologically marginal but had considerable sociological potential, and in April 1949 the philosopher Samuel Hugo Bergman declared that the Canaanites expressed 'clearly and unhesitatingly what others feel and experience timidly and halfheartedly'.[11]

What in fact was the Canaanite idea? Its main point was nativistic Israeli nationhood, the geographical conception that it was the plot of land that defined the national identity of a country's inhabitants. It was not the collective memory, the cultural heritage, ethnics or biology that created a nation, but the physical space, and the language obliterated differences and formed a national melting pot. It was the space that gave national significance: for example, Arabs and crusaders were assimilated into the Sidonian space, and that is how Lebanese nationhood came into being. This view was of course in contradiction to the classical Arab or Muslim viewpoint, as it explained the Sidonian civilisation as a geopolitical product of the crusader and Arab conquests. Among the Arabs, however, there were similar views, like the pharaonic conception in Egypt and the Syrian nationalism of Anton Sa'ada.[12] Here, the nativism in the Arab territorial nationalism ignored the invaders.

Unlike this nativistic variety, Zionism was a historical nationalism. Canaanism subverted it in seeing the present and not the past as the decisive time-factor, making 'nowness' the guiding principle of identity.[13] The significance of nativism as a metaphor is that it is not only a matter of being born in a place but an identity gained through a cultural concept that turns the immigrant into a native. The imagined Canaanite community is defined in the terms of Benedict Anderson's formulation: collective time – the present – a territory, and a common language. Many people call for economic migrants or non-Jews living in Israel to be not only citizens of the State of Israel but full partners in the Hebrew nation. Yaron London has praised Israel for 'granting citizenship to useful immigrants', explaining that 'love of a country is not conveyed through a heritage but through a creative culture, and Israel is a most effective producer of culture.'[14]

There have been many and varied expressions of the Canaanite idea (which is not necessarily identical with the poet Yonatan Ratosh's (1908–1981) 'Canaanite group') in the Israeli public sphere. The sociological and demographic changes that have taken place in Israel and the Jewish Diaspora have lowered the tone of the debate on the Canaanite option. The shrinking of the Jewish people in the Diaspora, the impressive demographic growth of the Israelis and especially of the 'Sabras', the immigration to Israel of over a million former citizens of the Soviet Union (a large part of whom are not of Jewish origin), the globalisation that has brought in its wake a large number of foreign workers, some of whom have children that were born in Israel: all this and more shows that the Canaanite idea is no longer the property of a closed sect, and is likely to be realised not as a deliberate plan and not as the fulfilment of a utopian vision, but through the force of events without any ideological intention.

Secular intellectuals in Israel have always been attracted by the Canaanite idea. They wished to eliminate the contradictions and tensions inherent in the process of the secularisation of the Jewish identity within the national framework. In the 'Canaanite hour', as the poet Haim Guri called the window of Hebrew opportunity in Eretz Israel (Palestine), many young people in the Yishuv (Jewish community) were enraptured by the possibility of acquiring a native identity free of remnants of the past, of the burden of history and of the imposition of the remains of exilic Judaism: a new identity that embodied self-construction and local autonomy. In describing the encounter with the Canaanite proposition as a 'change of religion' and a 'true religious experience', Guri recognised the nativistic idea as an existential or even religious awakening.[15] It was a kind of revelation, the possibility of acquiring a new identity along the lines of the Freudian 'Oedipus complex', a sort of rebellion against the parents who came from *there*, from the inauthentic place, from exile.

The radical innovation of Ratosh and his group was their total rebellion against Judaism as a religious, cultural and ethnic entity, and its replacement by a nativistic and linguistic experience. Ahad Ha-am understood its revolutionary potential when he saw the native-born 'Hebrews' as Canaanites on his visit to the country: 'Here you are bringing up ancient Jews. You want to obliterate two thousand years of exile and go back to the culture of ancient Canaan.' This was an observation about a subconscious Canaanism that sought to overcome a lack felt by the native-born by reverting to an ancient, primeval identity. The term 'Hebraism' was the war-cry of the Hebrew pioneers of the early 20th century, a flag by which they wished to demarcate the watershed between themselves, the native-born Hebrew-speakers with their Hebrew homeland, and the Jews in foreign countries who spoke a thousand languages. Hebraism was the nativistic consciousness that saw the motherland as the source of identity; and Canaanism was an ideological outlook that came out of it and transcended it by setting itself in opposition to the Jewish religion, history and Diaspora.[16]

The founders of Zionism did not accept the Canaanite claim, which of course was formulated much later, but its territorial logic was understood by all. They saw the Hebrew 'nation' as umbilically connected to the Jewish community. Zionism sought to link Jewish history in all its metamorphoses to the place where it all began: the Israelite place was the 'metaphorical womb' of Jewish history. Hence the belief that exile was the absence, the negation of Jewish autonomy, an autonomy that could only exist in Eretz Israel.[17] Exile was seen as a sickness and the native Hebrew identity as the cure. A.B. Yehoshua sees Zionism as 'the name of the cure for a certain kind of Jewish sickness called exile', with its various victims – religious, liberals, socialists, nationalists, bourgeois and anarchists.[18] In his opinion, exile was not imposed on the Jewish people but was a situation that was chosen by the Jews in order to escape from the basic conflict of Jewish identity: the one between Jewish nationhood and the Jewish religion.

Some, however, have seen the exile in a positive light. In their opinion, the shift from fidelity to the place itself to that of the memory of the place after the defeat of Bar Kochba was necessary in order to make the loss of the land surmountable.[19] Retaining the memory of the place helped the Pharisaic rabbis to overcome that loss. Not everyone has seen the exile as a punishment, and for some major Jewish thinkers the text was the most important factor. Hermann Cohen saw Jewish history as a progress from the national condition to the exilic condition.[20] Franz Rosenzweig, who saw the soil as a 'fetter' and the Jew as 'a travelling, wandering eminence', thought that 'a place where the nation loves its native soil more than it loves its life is always in danger [...].[21] Hannah Arendt pointed out the special value of the Jew as a 'pariah',[22] and Bernard Lazare called him a 'wanderer by choice'.[23] Edmond Jabès preferred the text as a homeland,[24] and, where George Steiner was concerned, the Jewish intellectual always lived on his suitcases and spread avant-garde, universalistic ideas.[25] Hebrew independence is the end of Judaism, an idea that the brothers Daniel and Jonathan Boyarin expressed as follows: 'The exile, not monotheism, is the major contribution of Judaism to the world.'[26]

Against these ideas, major Israeli intellectuals began to develop an anti-exilic ideology very close to the Canaanite outlook. The historian Yigael Elam distinguishes between Jewish nationhood, which only exists in Israel, and the Jewish religion, describing historical Judaism as a nation/religion that can only exist in exile. The nation-state of Israel is in the final analysis always the community of the Jewish religion.[27] The playwright Yehoshua Sobol continues this line of thought, and warns of 'the Jewish reaction that raises its head and threatens to engulf the Hebrew identity and the Hebrew spirit that made possible the creation of the Yishuv and its transformation from a state-in-the-making to a state like any other.'[28] The philosopher Yosef Agassi also thinks that 'if Israel is a nation-state, its theocratic clothing must be removed', and like Hillel Kook proposes separating the Jewish religion from the Israeli nation, making Israel into a liberal, democratic, Western nation-state.[29] Without Ratosh-like noises, Canaanite tom-toms and the mythological aesthetics of Baal and Ashteroth, the call for a Hebrew State is being heard once again, but this time not from the fringes of the cultural establishment but through the front door of an Israelism defined in terms of territory and language alone.

It is no wonder that even the Sabra Haim Guri recoiled from these Canaanite ideas. He too was unable to separate Ratosh the wonderful poet of *The Black Canopy* from Ratosh the ideologist. Canaanism worried him in denying the duality of the Israeli identity in the context of the return to Zion: 'This challenge had a great fascination, but I knew that the denial of any connection or affinity between the Jew and the Hebrew and placing them in opposition with such relentless hostility invalidated any possible explanation of our existence here and destroyed lofty cultural values which we saw as our property [...]. We have committed ourselves to the Hebrew, land-of-Israel alternative, not to cutting the Gordian knot. Making Zionism an enemy of the Hebrew renaissance makes Hebraism into a shallow spiritual salon, something meta-historical, a false romanticism in the name of the distant past.'[30]

In the short history of the crystallization of the Israeli identity, from the 'Hebrew', the 'pioneer' and the 'Sabra' to the itemization of the Hebrew image through an ever-increasing cleavage, who can guarantee us that the Canaanite option has completely disappeared? Perhaps its ultimate conclusion – separation between Israeli citizenship and the Jewish religion – is becoming so relevant that a complete split between the homeland (the Hebrew or Israeli) and the people (the assimilated Jew) will finally succeed. Perhaps this process will take place not as a deliberate act and not in the hope of realising a utopian vision, but simply through the force of reality, without any ideological factor.[31]

Is post-Zionism a secular, leftist neo-Canaanism? Post-Zionism as a guiding principle – going over from history to geography – is a nativistic conception that turns its back on the continuity of the history of the people, part of whom have returned to realise its nationhood in its land, and only recognises those who reside here and now.[32] Underlying the post-Zionist ideology is the assumption of the existence of a local society based on a civil rather than a national definition: the state belongs to its citizens, not to history.[33] Because Zionism completed its task in founding the state, one should remove its protective covering – i.e., cancel the Law of Return – effect a de-Zionization of Israel, and from that moment see the resulting secular democratic state as a 'state of all its citizens'. According to the nativistic conceptions of the new identity, which places at its heart the geographical factor and not the Jewish surplus value, the Israelis are formalistically defined as a collection of citizens living under a single roof. It is the *place* that defines the Israelis in this way. Some would say that the true significance of post-Zionism is thus the severing of the umbilical cord between the Israeli homeland and the Jewish people and culture, between the landscape of the country and its history, between the language and its sources, and in the words of one of those responsible for this phenomenon: 'Post-Zionism means the denial of all hidden threads binding together separate phenomena, of a special connection between the people of Israel today and yesterday whether in the country or in the Diaspora, between the Israeli culture and its sources or between the Hebrew language and its history.'[34]

Is Gush Emunim religious, right-wing neo-Canaanism? In the Messianic model proposed by the trinity Torah, land and people, the earthly locality is given first place. If post-Zionism makes connection with the place the sole identity card, Gush Emunim raises place to a sanctified level and settlement to the status of myth, enshrining return to the land as a supreme principle. In its settlement-political activities, Gush Emunim sought to restore the true model of the Greater Land of Israel. The frontiers of political compromise were replaced by the frontiers of the Promise. This movement, which blended political theology with the myth of settlement, was based on the precedence of the ancient Jews over the country's Arab inhabitants.[35]

The Six-Day War once again brought about a fusion of the transcendental Messianism and the Promethean Messianism: theology was once again joined to politics. The outstanding example was the story of the return to Kfar Etzion. In the more than sixty years that the State of Israel has existed, the politics of memory have not known any achievement more impressive than that of a small group of skullcap-wearers, the sons of Kfar Etzion. The orphans and widows of the 240 fighters who fell at Kfar Etzion in the 1948 war had an extraordinarily developed consciousness of memory and sense of national mission. They consistently practised a politics of memory for nineteen years, in the period from 1948 to 1967, and in this way linked the Zionist-Israeli memory of 1948 with the Jewish-Messianic memory of 1967. For the majority of Israelis, the commemorative activities of the sons of Gush Etzion created a common Israeli past that became a central element enjoying a wide consensus in the general national consciousness.[36]

The crusader myth

If the Canaanite paradox was a protest against the continuity of 'Jewish time', the Zionist-crusader analogy was a protest against the 'Jewish space'. Is there any truth in the claim of the poet and translator Aharon Amir, one of the founders of the 'Canaanite group', in a forecast made one year after the founding of the State that the final outcome of Jewish theocracy would be the establishment of a 'crusader kingdom of Israel'?[37] Everyone knows how the crusaders in Palestine ended. The crusader narrative describes invaders coming from Europe in the belief that the land was promised to them, but who eventually yielded to the logic of the place and returned, defeated, to their countries of origin. The rooted, authentic presence of the Arabs and the bellicose counter-culture of Islam, the desert and the Orient, defeated the foreign intruders, resulting in the re-conquest of the land. All that remained were lifeless relics: empty castles with Latin names, the transplantation of a cultural and mental place that was not in its place. From the Zionist point of view, the crusader narrative is the most negative myth that can be imagined: it raises the possibility of annihilation. Whereas the Zionist founding myths like Massada and Tel Hai were placed in time and space like monuments, ceremonies or pilgrimages, the crusader myth has no physical or ritualistic quality.[38] The crusader narrative was a founding myth that represented, in the words of sociologist Michael Feige, a 'Meta-trauma': the existential fear of the possibility of an end of the Zionist national enterprise.[39] It is present-absent, and it is this quality precisely that intensifies the mythical dimension of anxiety and dread described by the scholars of myths Claude Lévi-Strauss and Leszek Kolakovski in their study of existential threats and confrontation with contradictions that have no solution.[40] The crusader myth is deductive in that it can be understood through a decoding of the Zionist genome that contains in itself the fear of its own end.

There are three conclusions to be drawn from the definition of Zionism as a return to the place: the place is ours, the place is *only* ours, the place is not theirs. These are based on historical claims, native experience, religious faith or a national outlook (and to these can be added the classic Zionist claim that the other places, where the Jews live in the Diaspora, are not ours). The crusader myth counters these assertions by aiming three arrows at the heart of Zionism: namely, do the Israelis *really* belong to the place? Do the Israelis not belong somewhere else: for example, Europe? Perhaps the others (the Palestinian natives) belong to the place more than the Israelis? The crusader myth subverts the Promethean passion of Zionism. It asserts that the claim that a change in the Jewish historical individual would take place in the new space was unfounded, that the three-sided transformation that Zionism sought to effect with regard to the land, the people and the individual had no real chance of succeeding, and that the Jewish people were never meant to create a country or a nation, to settle in a national territory or to play an active role in history. Their foreignness to the place, their religious heritage, their racial composition, their cosmopolitan propensity to dispersion and their dependence on external foreign powers are not compatible with the Promethean desire of the modern Jews to re-establish their national entity in their ancient homeland. In questioning the modern Western linearity, the crusader myth undermines the basis of the Zionist identity and brings to the surface all that is repressed. What is repressed is both the 'old' Jew who lived in a cyclical world in expectation of a Messiah, and the East: the space in which Zionism operated and from which many of its citizens came. Critical thought in our time conceptualises these two forms of alienation, exile and the Arab East as representing one and the same alienation.[41]

The crusader anxiety is an extreme expression of the orientalist ideas of Edward Said, and it also reflects the present sense of a cultural war between East and West, as conceived by Samuel Huntington.[42] From the end of the 19th century, with the description of Western Zionism as a colonialist project, to the beginning of the 21st, with the Iranian nuclear threat and Bin Laden's attack on the 'crusader-Jewish alliance', the myth opposed an invading West to an imaginary East. The colonialist-crusader image depicts the primitive, threatening, dangerous and exotic Levant once again taking the Holy Land out of the linear history represented by Europe. This binary approach does not permit the hybridity allowed by post-colonialist ideas or the Mediterranean option that proposes a dialogue between East and West. The ideological violence and the uncompromising power struggle inherent in the Zionist-crusader analogy inhibits the possibility of cultural dialogue, intermingling in the space or political rapprochement in the future.

What are the reasons for the crusader anxiety of the Israelis? The anxiety exists on several levels, the highest being that of security: the fear of the actual physical destruction of the State of Israel, a fear that was present in Israel's wars with its Arab neighbours and is aroused by the present nuclear threat from Iran. The declared Arab threat of politicide (the destruction of the State), and on occasion of genocide, inevitably arouses an existential fear and an anxiety for the future. One should of course not minimise the importance of the memory of the Holocaust in nurturing and strengthening this existential fear, although this fear also exists independently. It is planted deep within the national consciousness already in the Bible in an immanent uncertainty about belonging to the place, and in the two historical precedents in which the fear was concretised in an actual historical destruction.

In order to explain the nature of the connection between the Jewish people and its land, one must realise that Eretz Israel was seen as a land of choice and an objective, but not as a land of birth. God makes clear to Abraham the arbitrariness of the connection between the people and the land that by chance it meets on its way. In the Jewish tradition, the land belongs to God and is given to the people only on a provisional basis, and for that reason it can also be taken away. Existence there is essentially fragile and arbitrary. There is always some fly in the ointment that prevents a union of the 'small place' of reality with the 'large place' of imagination and hope.[43] This tension between the concrete and the utopian explains why the Jewish soul throughout history harboured in its depths the crusader anxiety. The anxiety existed long before the crusaders entered history, and it exists long after they disappeared. Parallel with this, one must remember that for most of history the Jewish people did not have direct knowledge of a physical homeland. The history of Jewish nationalism was abnormal, and the years of exile distorted the self-confident relationship between the people and its homeland, between the citizens and their state, between the subjects and their historical origins.

Place and exile

The consciousness of exile among many believing Jews in the physical exile (the 'non-place') took the form of a testimony to the destruction of the Temple and the land, and this fuelled the disparity between the longing to return to the Holy Land and the fear of realising that utopia. A metaphysical fear of the holy place and a religious awe of the sacred existed side by side with the attraction to the land of Israel. Avi Ravitsky, historian of Jewish thought, pointed out that Eretz Israel fascinated and attracted its children, and especially those exiled from it, but it also aroused in them an awe and dread of its metaphysical demands, to such a degree that the exiles recoiled before the extreme holiness of the land, and it sometimes became a taboo, something forbidden to touch. Redemption in place was not possible without redemption in time: Eretz Israel, the ultimate place, was out of reach until the ultimate time, the days of the Messiah. To this alternation between enchantment and fear, attraction and repulsion, was added the demonic factor of the destruction of the Temple 'which laid upon the destroyed Temple Mount and the deserted land of Israel a threatening shadow of desolation.'[44] Zionism's return to the designated place required the tension to be broken, the fear to be dispelled, and the new Jew to be anchored once again in his Hebrew homeland.

According to Mircea Eliade, the holiness ascribed to a place bestows meaning on man and his world.[45] The sanctity of the space transforms the chaos of life into something with order and organisation, into an anchoring in a point that holds back the chaos, so that the concrete place becomes transcendental, a place beyond place. One moves from a static place devoid of meaning and a time without purpose to an existence with deep significance in time and place. The national movements of the modern age, including Zionism, secularised the language conceptualising metaphysical sanctity into modern terms, endowing the secular place with mythical significance.[46] This metaphysicalisation of the secular place was one of the chief instruments in the construction of national communities.[47] Places in Israel were sanctified both by secular Zionism and by religious tradition. The sanctification of the secular place by the Jewish community in Eretz Israel was the basis for the later claim by the settlers of Gush Emunim that they were not content only with the biblical level of sanctity but were the continuation of the secular Zionist utopia. It is not surprising that the members of Kfar Etzion were fond of the analogy of Tel Hai, a secular place sanctified by both the Zionist left and right.[48]

The form of the Zionist claim to legitimacy, which gives Zionism the right to the country, simultaneously arouses the crusader anxiety. Zionism had an extensive time-frame, being linked to the far-off days of the Bible, while the Palestinians, who related to the more recent past, had a shorter time-frame (although there have been Palestinian attempts, as yet unsuccessful, to link up to a Canaanite-mythological past).[49] The semiotics of the place, when the Jews arrived, were Palestinian, Arab, oriental. Evidence of their lack of ownership was everywhere apparent; the national symbols of the return to the land were taken straight from the enemy dwelling in the land, and that same enemy readopted these symbols in its own national struggle.⁵⁰ Is it surprising if the fear of banishment and of the cyclical nature of history has been a continuous and disturbing, if hidden, presence in Israeli history? The elimination of the crusader – that is, the revival of the 'true' nature of the country – is a two-sided concept. Firstly, it is military and external: the Arabs will expel the Israelis if they do not become Canaanites, if they are not sufficiently connected to the place. But an Israeli insistence on the connection to the place immediately gives rise to the charge of a crusader-like invasion. The Canaanism of the Israelis prevents them from becoming crusaders inasmuch as their rooting in the place provides a guarantee of territorial security, strength and endless patience. This is perhaps also the reason for the obsessive activism of the Israelis, making perceptible to themselves what Slavoj Zizek described as a concretisation of the concrete.⁵¹

The threat is also an inner one. The anxiety can appear as a fear of spiritual annihilation, of a dissolution within the space in the form of Levantinisation. The Israelis are liable to become 'Arabs', to be conquered from within. This is the same anxiety as that aroused by the Muslim influx into Europe, as though the former natives of the colonies now turned to their colonialist enslavers of yesterday, and said, 'Then you were in our place, now we are in your place!' There is consequently a fear of an orientalisation of the Jews, a fear of a symbolic destruction that in certain respects is worse than physical expulsion. As they see it, their recoiling from a dissolution into the East and an amalgamation in the space is more valid than the Zionist logic of overcoming the place. For example, the tomb of the Jewish Sepharadic saint Baba Sali, located in the south of Israel, is now given the function, which he had in life, of serving as an intermediary between the mass of believers and God, and there are many other such cases in peripheral Israel.⁵² The fear of the conquest of the centre by the periphery is comparable to the greater fear of the conquest of Israel by its enemies in the Arab space. The discourse concerning the fear of the East is not a new one. Its roots go back to the beginnings of Zionism, where there was the ambivalence of an attraction to the East and a repulsion towards it, the dual face of the 'new Hebrew' who looked towards an imagined East and whose gaze was always turned towards the West as a source of cultural identity. The discourse concerning the East continues today among the post-colonialist scholars who condemn the hegemonic culture in Israel as modern Western nationalism and as a colonial ethnic project repressing both the East and the Orientals, as well as what remains of Palestine.⁵³

Whereas the Israelis translate the crusader anxiety into literary metaphors like the arson of a forest of the Jewish National fund in A.B. Yehoshua, the return of the swamps in Meir Shalev or the wailing of jackals in Amos Oz, the Palestinians do not feel themselves to be potential victims but actual victims of the Israeli 'crusaders', who pay the price for the progress of Zionism by the burial of what went before. They ask themselves if the strata covered over by the process of destruction and creation still exist and can facilitate their redemption. Are there orchards still blossoming beneath the car parks? Many post-Zionists see the Israeli place in terms of the redemption envisaged by Walter Benjamin, and they allot themselves the task of telling the tale of the defeated and the losers, brushing history against the grain and sticking pins in the Zionist-crusader narrative, which they describe in a reversed form: The historical crusaders were defeated and disappeared; the metaphorical crusaders – the Zionists – were victorious, and the Palestinians of today are swept under the carpet of history. The names of their villages are removed, the olive trees are uprooted, and the bulldozer builds on the ruins of their homes in the first Hebrew city the edifices of the children of those who came from the sea.[54]

An examination of some of the main features of the crusader discourse among the Israelis reveals a fascinating episode in the intellectual history of the State of Israel and constitutes a scrutiny of the Israeli narrative in its deepest sense. In the 'crusader prism' we have opted to study, major cross-currents of Israeli thought are reflected. Although the crusader-Zionist analogy has not been central to the Israeli discourse, the many treatments the subject has been given show that the historical parallel which Arab circles have made between the medieval Christians in the Holy Land and the modern Jews in Israel has not been lost on Israeli intellectuals.[55] Even when not dealing directly with the local conflict, the Israelis amongst themselves have discussed the crusader equation with an acute sense of their own 'foreignness' in the area: in this perspective, the 'other' becomes 'us'. The Israeli participants in the crusader's discourse engaged in a veiled dialogue in which the analogy was not the subject of a historical debate or of a factual investigation of the truth. What was involved here were the origins, no less than the future, of the Jewish state at the heart of the Arab-Muslim East. Did the analogy itself become a kind of mobilising symbol? How did each side select principles, images and perceptions corresponding to its political viewpoint and general outlook?

A historical episode in the history of Palestine unconnected with the Jewish history of the land of Israel became a fascinating episode in the elucidation of the Israelis' identity and self-image. It is as if a picture of some historical subject had been painted and those who looked at it asked themselves if they saw themselves within it. The Arabs answered positively; the Israelis for the most part answered negatively. The analogy served as a pretext for posing the question 'Who are we?', this time in its contrary form, 'Who aren't we?'. The question 'Are we crusaders?' preceded the question 'Are we colonialists?', and this was without specifically identifying Zionism with settler movements with a colonialist element. In other words, the Zionist-crusader analogy reflected a veiled debate, sometimes turning to alarm, in which the colonialist question was broached without being called by its name. Thus, an interpretation of the Zionist enterprise as a colonialist project was hinted at in this way until the advent of the post-Zionists who renewed the open discussion of the question.

In view of the fascinating, lively 'crusader discourse' in historiography, literature and art, in political life and in essays, the crusader parallel runs like a thread through the Israeli discourse at all levels. This preoccupation has come to the fore especially in three periods: around the time of the 1948 war, before the 1967 war and around the time of the El Aqsa intifada. The apprehensions of the Israelis embodied in this parallel are a consequence both of external factors like the Arab threat internalised as a future which resembles the past, and of internal factors like the political controversy between right and left or the post-Zionist questioning which has renewed the colonialist-crusader discourse about the beginnings of Zionism. More than the crusaders have been the object of a historical comparison, the subject now serves as a litmus test to clarify attitudes towards Zionism. Those who sympathise with the Zionist point of view totally reject the Zionist-crusader analogy, while the post-Zionists make the analogy. They have a 'Christian' theory of original sin with regard to the Zionist movement and the State of Israel, reaching the conclusion that the sole solution to the problem is the negation of the State of Israel in its present form as a Jewish democratic state and its replacement by a 'state of all its citizens'.

Looking out to sea: The Mediterranean option

Israelis can promote a geopolitical and cultural dialogue that will involve the Eastern and the Southern shores of the Mediterranean. The conflict between the Palestinians and Israelis today is part of a situation in which the Mediterranean region is engulfed in national, political, ethnic, and religious conflicts that have contributed to a destabilisation not only in the area but even in Europe and beyond. Against this backdrop, the Mediterranean option can play a key cultural and political role in re-stabilising this tense environment and creating a new geo-strategic alignment.[56]

The idea of the Mediterranean as a cultural-political entity that holds together a multiplicity of ethnic, religious-cultural and economic units predates late 20th-century proposals and programs of the type issuing from Brussels, Barcelona, Malta or Paris. Earlier ideas of the Mediterranean were informed by realities of trade, conquest, migration and subtler geographical affinities that were conducive to a regional unity though never to uniformity or to political unification. Whether or not this collective regional identity was disturbed (as is argued in Henri Pirenne's famous thesis) by the Moslem conquest is an important historiographical issue for investigation. But, whether as the result of this conquest, of early modern imperialism, or of other social forces – both prior to and following the Enlightenment in Europe, it is clear that the older idea of the Mediterranean gave way to a more parochial, nationalist *mare nostrum* conception.

The early appearance of Jacqueline Kahanoff's (1917–1979) polyphonic voice was in contradiction to the 'Nimrodian' Israeli culture – Eurocentric, secular, socialist and masculine – in the country's first two decades. Her novels, essays and short stories were liminal in that they disregarded borders, blurred polarities such as East/West or hegemonic/'other', and possessed a hybrid quality of reciprocity, stratification, variety, lack of dogmatism, and played down the 'oppositional' undercurrents. By those who view her as representative of Mediterranean culture, Kahanoff is regarded as one of the primary intellectual sources of the Mediterranean idea in Israel.[57]

What Kahanoff proposed with her modern perspective was the simultaneous adoption of the various points of time and space of the Levant made up of different viewpoints, relationships and cultural dimensions. Thus, the Levant is revealed as a rich mosaic, a mirror in which many angles are reflected, a fertile and creative kaleidoscope which is not restricted to a one-dimensional ideology of East or West. Her constant stress on the Eastern part of the Mediterranean as the Levant shows that she saw this area as the cultural space that made possible a living dialogue of East and West.

At the end of her introduction to her projected collection of essays in English, Kahanoff confessed that her articles reflected a certain ambivalence about a past that was not entirely free from the outlook of the period between the two World Wars, or the dilemmas of an immigrant from an oriental country who was none too enthusiastic about her process of absorption. Her gaze, she wrote, was focused on the past rather than the future. The 1967 war, however, had brought Israel back to the Levant as a force that could change the old order. She hoped it would be a positive force, a modern and progressive one. The 1967 war changed Kahanoff's perspective on Israel and the Levant. After the founding generation, which came from Eastern and Central Europe, a new generation had been born in the country. It looked at the Levant differently from its parents. The territories conquered in the war also produced an unmediated contact between Israelis and Palestinians. This was Kahanoff's view when she wrote her articles, which had an optimistic conciliatory flavour together with a modern outlook. Human beings had made history, and they could therefore make a different history. It was the generation before the *intifadas* and the massive enterprise of colonialist settlement. As a result, Kahanoff could hope that Israel had changed its approach to the Levant; that it was integrating into its surroundings and would not be as preoccupied with the Jewish aspect as it had been in the past. Perhaps she should have known already then that the narcissistic Jewish attitude of the first settlers that found its fulfilment in the conquest of the territories would not give birth to a modern Levantinism, but would cause the conflict to increasingly degenerate into a fundamentalist national and cultural confrontation. Kahanoff did not delude herself that the pluralistic alternative she proposed would prevent future wars, but at the same time her gaze was directed towards the Braudelian *longue durée* (long term): 'In the long run, it might help Israel integrate in the Levant.'

The Levantine option is not only a cultural possibility but a concrete political proposal. In place of pan-Arabism on the one hand and Zionism on the European-Ashkenazi model on the other, Kahanoff proposed a political culture of the Levant, the essence of which was 'live and let live'. The reconstruction of the Levant, the product of the old encounter between Byzantium, Islam and Judaism, could help to redefine the relationship of the Israelis to the political and cultural space in which they reside.

The Mediterranean dialogue has three facets: creating a new agenda that will confront the most threatening dangers currently at hand; revealing and examining the common heritage of the peoples of the region; and creating new channels of communication based on their reciprocal influences and interactions.

The time has come to examine and evaluate the Mediterranean option for Israel, an Israeli geopolitical and cultural policy for peace in the Middle East. The

Mediterranean cultural discourse seeks to detach the region from conflict and to fashion a broader cultural framework in which Israelis and their Arab neighbours are not alone with each other, but work together in a broader context and partnership. In other words, it is an attempt to create a dialogue that has a different perspective and focus. Such a broad perspective, with its strategic orientation, has been missing from the scholarly literature on the Mediterranean Basin. The contribution of this article is to take the emerging Mediterranean identity of the Israelis – a multi-cultural, heterogenic, mixed society, situated between East and West – as a point of departure. What lessons can be learned from examining its characteristics? Can this Mediterranean model be projected onto the entire region in order to develop strategies for evolving a unified but polycentric Mediterranean civil society?

The idea that Israel is a Mediterranean society in the making has been encouraged by three historical processes. The first process was the frequent fluctuations in the peace process between Israel and its neighbours in the last decade, and the state of confrontation culminating in the current conflict with the Palestinians that erupted in October 2000. The conflict raised questions concerning the dynamics of Israeli collective identity and what may be called the 'Israeli spatial identity'. Many Israelis have thus started to think in terms of 'Mediterraneanism' rather than in terms of 'Middle Eastern' culture. Such thinking was assisted by Israeli accessibility to the Southern and Eastern shores of the Mediterranean Sea – i.e., Turkey and the Maghreb in the 1990s.

The second process was the transition of Israeli society from a mobilised and ideological society to a civil, sectorial society, one that is in constant search of its own identity while it tries to maintain an internal dialogue among its various sociological components, and, in addition, an external dialogue with other people and cultures in the Mediterranean geopolitical region. The ideology of the 'new man' gave way to the old-new idea of a non-ideological Mediterranean melting pot blending together immigrants from East and West, from the Christian countries and the Muslim countries. Zionism sprang up against the background of the rise of nationalism, the spread of secularism and the dominance of Eurocentricity. One of the chief cultural ambitions of the Zionist movement was to create a 'new man'. But this ideological myth, when finally fulfilled, was applied to a nation that was made up of people of flesh and blood: people who, for sixty years now, have constituted a society on the Eastern shore of the Mediterranean Sea. Their new identity is not ideologically based; it is constructed out of geography and culture.

The Mediterranean option offers a dialogue, not a cultural war. It proposes a voyage, a slow and reflective voyage, a journey between shores and not a cultural war in which, as in all wars, there are only losers. It is a journey within the space of our own consciousness, to our cultural and intellectual origins, to the landscape of our own sea. It is a journey rather than a flight from our immediate neighbourhood, the Arabs and the Palestinians. We are travelling to the space where everything was born: Western and Eastern civilisation, monotheism and Hellenism, the polis and the Renaissance, the Old and the New Testament. The Mediterranean option for Israeli society represents a philosophical challenge, a socio-cultural identity and a political programme.

Notes

1. David Ohana, *Origins of the Israeli Mythology: Neither Canaanites Nor Crusaders*, Cambridge 2011; Amnon Rubinstein, *From Herzl to Rabin, 100 Years of Zionism*, Tel Aviv 1997, p. 74.
2. Cited in Shlomo Ben-Ami, *A Place for All*, Tel Aviv 1998, p. 321.
3. Yigal Zalmona, 'Estward! Eastward? On the East in Israeli Art', eds. Y. Zalmona and T. Manor-Friedman, *Kadima – The East in Israel's Art*, Jerusalem 1988, 47–93.
4. Theodor Herzel, *The Jewish State*, Hank Overberg (tran.), New Jersey 1997, p. 34.
5. Joseph Klauzner, 'Fear', *Hashiluach*, 17, 574–576 [Hebrew].
6. Eyal Hovers, 'Time in Zionism: The Life and Afterlife of a Temporal Revolution', *Political Theory*, vol. 26, no. 5, (Oct. 1998), pp. 652–685; Robert Pine, 'Jewish Ontologies of Time and Political Legitimation in Israel', Henry J. Rutz, ed., *The Politics of Time*, Washington D.C. 1992, pp. 150–170.
7. Anita Shapira, 'What Happened to the "Denial of the Exile"?', *Alpayim*, vol. 25, 2003 [Hebrew], pp. 9–54.
8. Michel Halbwachs, *The Collective Memory*, New York 1980.
9. Eric Hobsbawm and Terence Ranger, eds., *The Invention of Tradition*, Cambridge 1983.
10. Boas Evron, *A National Reckoning*, Tel Aviv 1988 [Hebrew].
11. Samuel Hugo Bergman, 'On the Formation of the Nation's Character in Our State', *Ha-Poel Ha-Tzair*, vols. 26–27, 10.4.1949 [Hebrew].
12. Albert Hourani, *Arabic Thought in the Liberal Age 1798–1939*, Oxford 1962, pp. 319–323; Elias Khoury and Ahmad Baydoun, 'La Mediterranee libanaise', in: T. Febre et R. Ilbert, *Les representation de la Mediterraneei* (Paris, 2000); Edward Al-Kharrat and Mohamad Afifi, 'La Mediterranee egyptienne', in T. Faber and R. Ibert, *Les representation de la Mediterraneei* (Paris, 2000).
13. Hannan Hever, 'An Imagined Native Community: "Canaanite Literature" in Israeli Culture', *Israeli Sociology*, 2, 1, (1999), p. 148 [Hebrew].
14. Yaron London, 'Toto Tamuz and the Law of Return', *Yediot Aharonot*, 9.7.2007.
15. Haim Gouri, 'The Canaanite Hour', *Maariv*, 26.12.1975 [Hebrew].
16. Yonatan Ratosh, 'Birth of the Nation', *Reshit Yamim, Ptihot Ivriot*, Tel Aviv 1982, p. 38 [Hebrew].
17. Avi Sagi, *The Jewish–Israeli Voyage, Culture and Identity*, Jerusalem 2006, p. 235 [Hebrew].
18. Ruvik Rosenthal, ed., *The Heart of the Matter, Redefining Social and National Issues*, Jerusalem 2005, p. 59 [Hebrew].
19. Harry Berger, 'The Lie of the Land: The Text Beyond Canaan', *Representations* 25 (1989); William David Davies, *The Gospel and the Land: Early Christianity and Jewish Territorial Doctrine,* Berkeley, CA 1974; Regina M. Schwartz, 'Nations and Nationalism: Adultery in the House of David', *Critical Inquiry*, 19, 1 (autumn 1992).
20. Eva Jospe, ed., *Reason and Hope: Selections from the Jewish Writings of Hermann Cohen*, Cincinnati, OH 1971.
21. Franz Rosenzweig, *The Star of Redemption*, Jerusalem 1970, p. 324 [Hebrew].
22. Hanna Arendt, *The Jew as Pariah: Jewish Identity and Politics in the Modern Age*, New York 1978.
23. Bernard Lazare, *Job's Dungheap*, New York 1949.
24. David Ohana, *Israel and its Mediterranean Identity*, New York 2011.
25. George Steiner, 'The Wandering Jew', *Ptahim*, 1 (1969), pp. 17–23; Idem, 'The Exile Jew', *Haaretz, Galeria*, 7.11.1999 [Hebrew].
26. Daniel and Yonatan Boyarin, 'No Homeland to Israel: on the Place of the Jews', *Theory and Criticism*, 5 (1994), p. 100 [Hebrew].
27. Igal Elam, *End of Judaism: Religion–Nation*, Tel Aviv 2000, p. 253 [Hebrew].
28. Yehoshua Sobol, 'Not a People of Masters', *Haaretz*, 11.5.2005 [Hebrew].

29 Yosef Agasi, *Between Religion and Nation – Towards Israeli National Identity*, Tel Aviv 1984, p. 165; Yosef Agasi, Yehudit Buber Agasi and Moshe Berant, *Who is Israeli*, Tel Aviv 1991 [Hebrew].
30 Haim Gouri, 'A Call to the Hebrews', *Davar*, 12.8.1983 [Hebrew].
31 David Ohana, 'The Meaning of Jewish-Israeli Identity', in: Eliezer Ben–Rafael, Yosef Gorny and Ya'acov Ro'i, eds., *Contemporary Jewries, Convergence and Divergence*, Boston, MA 2003, pp. 65–78.
32 Adriana Kemp, David Newman, Uri Ram and Oren Yiftachel, eds., *Israelis in Conflict: Hegemonies, Identities and Challenges*, Sussex 2004; Ephraim Nimni, ed., *The Challenge of Post-Zionism: Alternatives to Fundamentalist Politics in Israel*, London 2003; Tom Segev, *Elvis in Jerusalem: Post-Zionism and the Americanization of Israel*, New York 2003; Hagit Boger, 'Post-Zionism Discourse and the Israeli National Consensus: What has Changed?', *Response* 66 (1996), pp. 28–44; Herbert Kelman, 'Israel in Transition from Zionism to Post-Zionism', *Annals of the American Academy* 555 (1998), pp. 46–61; Deborah Wheeler, 'Does Post-Zionism have a Future?', in: Laura Zitttrain Eisenberg, *Traditions and Transitions in Israel Studies – Books on Israel* 4, New York 2003, pp. 159–180.
33 Silberstein, *The Postzionism Debates: Knowledge and Power in Israeli culture*, Routledge, New York 1999.
34 Yosef Dan, 'On Post-Zionism, Oral Hebrew, and Futile Messianism', *Haaretz*, 25.3.1995 [Hebrew].
35 Michael Feige, *Settling in the Hearts: Jewish Fundamentalism in the Occupied Territories*, Detroit, MI 2008; Janet Aviad, 'The Messianism of Gush Emunim', *Studies in Contemporary Jewry* 7, pp. 197–213; David Newman and Tamar Hermann, 'A Comparative Study of Gush Emunim and Peace Now', *Middle–Eastern Studies* 28 (1992), pp. 509–530; Ian Lustick, *For the Land and the Lord: Jewish Fundamentalism in Israel*, New York 1991; Ehud Sprinzak 'Gush Emunim: The Iceberg Model of Political Extremism', *Jerusalem Quarterly* 21 (1981), pp. 28–47; David Weisburd and Vered Vinitzky, 'Vigilantism as Rational Social Control: The Case of the Gush Emunim Settlers', in: Myron Aronoff, ed., *Cross Current in Israeli Culture and Politics*, New Brunswick 1984; L. Weisburd and E. Waring, 'Settlement Motivations in Gush Emunim Movement: Comparing Bonds of Altruism and Self-Interest', in: *The Impact of Gush Emunim*, London 1985, pp. 183–199.
36 Ohana, 'The Community of Memory and the Myth of Return', *Israel Studies* 7, no. 2 (summer 2002), pp. 145–174. 22.
37 Yehoshua Bentov (Aharon Amir), 'The Crusader Kingdom of Israel?', in: *The Canaanite Group – Literature and Ideology*, Collection ed. by Nurit Graetz and Rahel Weisbrod, The Open University, Tel Aviv, 1986, p. 28 [Hebrew].
38 Ohana, 'The Crusade–Zionist Analogy in the Israeli Discourse', *Iyunim Bitkumat Israel*, 11(2001), pp. 486–526 [Hebrew].
39 Michael Feige, 'The Meta-Trauma of The Israeli-Crusader Myth', *A Lecture in the Annual Conference of the Israeli Association for Sociology and Anthropology*, 2006 [Hebrew].
40 Claude Levi-Strauss, 'The Structural Study of Myth', *Structural Anthropology*, trans. Claire Jacobson and Brook Grundfest Schoeff, New York 1963; Leszek Kolakowski, *The Presence of Myth*, trans. by Adam Czerniawski, Chicago, IL 1989.
41 Yehuda Shenhav, *The Arab Jews, A Postcolonial Reading of Nationalism, Religion, and Ethnicity*, Stanford, CA 2006.
42 Edward Said, *Orientalism*, New York 1978; Samuel Huntington, *The Clash of Civilizations and the Remaking of World Order*, New York 1997.
43 Zali Jurevitch and Gideon Aran, 'The Land of Israel: Myths and Phenomenon', *Studies in Contemporary Jewry*, X (1994), pp. 195, 210.
44 Aviezer Ravitzky, ed., Preface, *The Land of Israel in Modern Era Jewish Thought*, Jerusalem 2004, p. 3 [Hebrew].

45 Mircea Eliade, *Images and Symbols*, Paris 1952, pp. 33–72; Benjamin Zeev Kedar and Raphael Jehuda Zwi Werblowski, eds., *Sacred Space: Shrine, City, Land*, London 1998.
46 Nachman Ben-Yehuda, *The Masada Myth: Collective Memory and Mythmaking in Israel*, Madison, WI 1995; Yael Zerubavel, *Recovered Roots: Memory and the Making of National Tradition*, Chicago, IL 1995.
47 Benedict Anderson, *Imagined Communities: Reflections on the Origin and Spread of Nationalism*, London 1991.
48 'In Those Days and at That Time – Conversations With the Old-Timers of the Gush on the Events of 1948', *Gushpanka* 88 (February 1988) [Hebrew].
49 Yehoshua Porath, 'Hebrew Canaanism and Arabic Canaanism'; Ifrach Zilberman, 'Palestinian Canaanim', in: Danny Jacoby, ed., *One Land, Two Peoples. Selected Issues in the History of The Yishuv and The State of Israel*, Jerusalem 1999, pp. 83–93; 96–103 [Hebrew].
50 Ahmad H. Sa'di, 'Catastrophe, Memory and Identity: Al-Nakbah as a Component of Palestinian Identity', *Israel Studies*, 7, No. 2 (summer 2002), pp. 175–198 [Hebrew].
51 Slavoj Zizek, *Welcome to the Desert of the Real*, London 2003.
52 Yoram Bilu and Eyal Ben-Ari, 'Modernity and Charisma in Contemporary Israel: The Case of Baba Sali and Baba Baruch', in: Ohana and Robert Wistrich, eds., *The Shaping of Israeli Identity: Myth, Memory and Trauma*, London 1995, pp. 224–237.
53 Colin Shindler, *A History of Modern Israel*, Cambridge 2008, pp. 91–97; Hannan Hever, Yehouda Shenhav, Pnina Motzafi-Haller, eds., *Mizrahim in Israel: A Critical Observation into Israel's Ethnicity*, Jerusalem 2002.
54 Meron Benvenisty, *Sacred Landscape: The Buried History of the Holy Land Since 1948*, trans. Maxine Kaufman-Lacusta, California 2000. See also Homi K, Bhaba, 'The Other Question: Difference, Discrimination and the Discourse of Colonialism' in: Russel Ferguson et al, eds., *Out There: Marginalization and Contemporary Cultures*, Cambridge, MA 1990.
55 David Ohana, 'Are Israelis the New Crusaders? The Radical Religious Symbolism of the Zionist-Crusader Takes on New Significance', *Palestine-Israel Journal of Politics, Economics and Culture*, 13, 3 (2006) pp. 36–43.
56 David Ohana, 'Israel Towards a Mediterranean Identity', *Munich Contributions to European Unification, Special Issue: Integration and Identity: Challenges to Europe and Israel*, 4 (1999), pp. 81–101.
57 Jacqueline Kahanoff, *From East the Sun*, ed. Aharon Amir, Tel Aviv 1978; Idem, *Between Two Worlds*, ed. David Ohana, Jerusalem 2005 [Hebrew].

6 The irresolvable geographies of Mediterranean-Israeli music

Amy Horowitz

Following the mass migration of Jews from European, Middle Eastern, and North African homelands after World War II, Israel became a site for new genres of music combining styles, instruments, and traditions from quite different cultures. Jews from Islamic lands found an already present European-dominated national music (and here I refer to *Ha Shir Ha Eretz Yisraeli* – The Song of the Land of Israel) that specifically excluded their music as too Arabic, too Turkish, or not European enough.[1] Although European-Israeli artists borrowed elements of Middle Eastern and North African musical styles, the music and musicians who originated the music were relegated to display occasions at official folkloric events or specific ghettos of radio broadcast time. Against a backdrop of cultural and political exclusion, Jews from Islamic lands formed a pan-ethnic community of communities called Mizraḥim (or Easterners) and developed their own musical genres and styles. One of the new genres, Mediterranean-Israeli music, emerged in working class Mizrahi neighborhoods as the first Israeli-born generation of Middle Eastern and North African Jewish children came of age in the late 1960s and early 1970s.

Mediterranean-Israeli music developed in the disjuncture between a European vision of a Jewish national homeland and an actual Israeli nation in the Middle East. The music, a creation of the first generation of Israeli Jews from Islamic countries in the 1970s to 1990s, issued a visceral aesthetic challenge to the European sense of what a Jewish home/land should sound like. Its texts, melodies, and aesthetic intention combine Eastern vocals with Arab and Hebrew lyrics, Western pop and Eastern classics, and secular and liturgical themes. Spilling from marketplace booths, the music resisted and re-formed the sonic if not political borders of Israel and her neighbors.

All this can be traced musically. In Mediterranean-Israeli music, as in all emergent cultural styles, traditional elements are being rearranged and foreign elements are being introduced to create a new musical formation. Sounds that used to be outside a musical tradition begin to trouble its edges and wedge themselves in, because communities once separated become neighbors, because those who used to be outside marry into families. When for reasons of politics, propinquity, or sentiment musical styles get forced together, new possibilities become available, not all of which get exploited. When they are exploited, the musical result is not a copy of the social landscape but a new aesthetic space undergoing its own formation, which may in turn play back into politics or be recognized there, but which neither foreordains nor reflects it.

If the actual musical elements were to be mapped out, they would bear traces of the reconfigured family, neighborhood, and global territories. The vocal line is a characteristically melismatic signature[2] that centers the music and signals the Eastern roots of the singers. Orbiting this are various shifting musical elements that may be called into service on an East-West continuum, for example: bass guitar is a Western sound mode; a Greek melody is Eastern enough without going too far, the bent guitar notes

are blues enough to simultaneously evoke the quarter-tonality of an *'ud* and an African-American subversion of Western guitar technique, and the drum machine can be programmed for either Arabic *darabukka* or rock 'n' roll drums.[3]

Mediterranean-Israeli music developed a loosely confederated but recognizable generic brand by the late 1970s, stirred a national debate in the 1980s to 90s, and is still forming and fomenting debate in the new millennium.[4] This essay focuses on one Mediterranean-Israeli music performer, Zehava Ben, a Moroccan-Israeli woman from the impoverished Shukhnat Dalit neighborhood of Be'er Sheva, who arrived on the scene in the early 1990s when Mediterranean-Israeli music was beginning to seep through the ghetto walls and trouble mainstream channels and Euro-Israeli resistance. Her ascendency between 1992 and 2000 coincided with a pivotal moment between hope and disappointment that began with the initiation of a renewed peace process in 1992 and encompassed the aftermath of the assassination of Prime Minister Rabin in October 1995. It was during this historically liminal period that Ben catapulted out of neighborhoods, radio ghettos and cassette booths, and assumed the role of a homespun soundtrack to the elusive peace process of the mid-1990s.

In the early 1990s, Turkish melodies had been circulating freely in the public domain when Moroccan composer Dani Shoshan found *Dil Yarasi*, composed by Orhan Gencebey, the father of the Arabesque style, reupholstered it with Hebrew lyrics, and offered it to Zehava as *Tipat Mazal* (A Drop of Luck).[5] Before radio editors knew her name, Zehava's amplified voice blared in all directions from dozens of cassette booths that occupied retail space between vegetable, appliance, and clothing booths in Tel Aviv's outdoor marketplace. This outdoor commercial cassette market had been developed by Mizrahi entrepreneurs in the late 1970s as a creative remedy to their exclusion by the Euro-sonic Israeli music industry. Within three months there were unsubstantiated estimates that Zehava Ben had sold an astounding eighty-thousand copies of her new *Tipat Mazal* cassette. When listeners flooded the radio with requests for the song, radio editors and record storeowners took notice.

According to Shoshan, Mizrahi composers had previously relied on Greek music because it was safely European; Turkish music's unequivocal Middle Easternness, what Rino Tsror called 'Turkish, Turkish',[6] resonated with Mizraḥi reclamations of their cultural roots. Shoshan also noted that Greek tunes required royalty payments, whereas Turkish tunes did not, because in the early 1990s there was no intellectual property agreement between Turkey and Israel. As a result, he was able to borrow '*Dil Yarasi* from the 'public domain'.

As Ben's voice penetrated mainstream public spaces in the early 1990s, European Israelis began to comment on the eastward and specifically Turkish shift in the soundscape of Mizrahi popular music. Mizrahi soldiers affixed the cassette cover of *Tipat Mazal* on their weapons. Ashkenazi Israeli writer Yonatan Gefen lamented a Turkified Tel Aviv when he indirectly referred to Ben in a May 1992 *Ma'ariv* newspaper column:

> As much as I tried I couldn't avoid hearing the 'Turkish' singer whose name I intentionally deleted and who blessed the State of Israel with a medley of Turkish melodies as the audience screamed. After 44 years of solitude we have returned to the roots of Istanbul. The Turks have conquered the city.[7]

Gefen's hostile response to Zehava Ben's music (so strong that he consciously deleted her name and any notoriety that might result from his use of it), and his use of the metaphor of political conquest of a historical occupier of the land, indicate the potentially turbulent power of such boundary-crossing music in a context of ethnic polarization among European and Mizrahi Israeli groups. Yonatan Gefen was not alone in lamenting the shifting Mizrahi preference away from the safety of Greek Mediterranean party music and toward the Turkified, Arabized songs rendered by Zehava Ben and other Mizrahi performers. Sarcastic terms such as *Shire bekhi* (crying songs) and 'Turkification' acknowledged the dissolution of certain boundaries at the same time that they resisted it. Nonetheless, Ben seemed to enjoy at least token notice by the Israeli mainstream.

Ben's success in bridging East and West harkened back to a 'discovery' piece that had appeared in one of Israel's major daily papers, Ha-Aretz in 1981, where Michal Ohad had ironically reworked Rudyard Kipling's classic observation about the incompatibility of East and West, foreshadowing the trajectory of the still (in 1981) nascent style:

> Kipling said the east and the west will never meet. Kipling is wrong. After the singers from the east proved their box office potential, the Western establishment accepted them with open arms and signed contracts and gave their songs successful recordings and nice covers.
>
> (Ohad, 1981)[8]

Despite Ohad's claims of the ability of Mediterranean-Israeli music to heal the East-West divide, it was not possible simply to locate the music somewhere on an East-West continuum. The music behaved like a lightning rod that attracted the conflicting social currents rumbling in the political air. Economic and social terms that described Mizrahi inequality, such as *kipuah* (deprivation), *ha-geto* (the ghetto), and *Shehorim* (blacks), were also applied to the performance culture. Like lightning, the emerging music not only attracted but also conducted the social currents and provided a site that forced a confrontation between aural polarities and revealed them as interconnected sound clusters.

In 1992 a popular rock band called Etnix (Ethnics) invited Zehava Ben to perform one song with them for their new recording, *Masala*. In her guest appearance on this mainstream recording, Zehava Ben shares the vocal lead with Zev Nehama, the band's lead singer, whose parents are Sephardi Jews from Bulgaria. While the Etnix incorporated some Middle Eastern motifs within their rock sound, their music was basically European pop/disco. The band's duet with Zehava Ben on the song '*Ketourna Masala*'[9] shifted more to the East than most of their repertoire in this period. The main meeting of Eastern and Western styles occurs in the refrain, which takes the form of a call and response between Zev Nehama and Zehava Ben. Nehama sings the verses in a standard rock vocal style, though he inserts some slow and simple trills reminiscent of his Bulgarian heritage, while Zehava Ben sings the refrain in an Arabic vocal style, demonstrating her mastery of quartertones and Eastern aesthetics. The synthesizer provides an Eastern feeling by emulating the sounds of the *santur*[10] and other 'indigenous' instruments. The song was extremely popular and won first place in the 1992 Israeli *Mits'ad ha-pizmonim* (Israeli Hit Parade).

Two seemingly oppositional directions met in collaborations such as this, where Mizraḥi musicians performed duets with mainstream Ashkenazi performers.[11] The Mizraḥi vocalists maintained and even embellished their Middle Eastern vocal elaboration as a counterpart to the Western styles of their vocal partners. These collaborations did not represent a true reciprocity but rather reinforced existing asymmetries and separate constituencies. At the same time, they permitted a degree of appreciation of Mizraḥi music on the part of European Israelis, who were willing to incorporate selected elements of this music into their own compositions. The fact that Etnix kept the two styles distinct may have contributed to the composition's positive reception. By keeping the Arab vocal style (contained in the refrain) separate from the European rock style (in the verses), Etnix avoided anxieties about blurred categories. Zehava Ben's Eastern vocal refrain reverberates only faintly within the rock frame of '*Ketourna Masala*', but in bringing together the two styles without blending them, her collaboration with Etnix breaks into new territory.

Ben's collaboration with Etnix helped set in motion a musical transformation that spanned the Israeli-Palestinian moves towards peace over the same period. It was in the course of this bold, yet fragile, period that Ben's interethnic soundtrack began shifting its position in the national landscape. By early 1995, Ben issued a CD of abridged versions of Umm Kulthum's repertoire, entitled *Zehava Ben sharah Aravit* (Zehava Ben Sings Arabic).[12] Umm Kulthum, a Muslim-Egyptian singer who died in 1975, was so widely beloved that Cairo shut down on the day of her funeral and 4 million people tried to attend. Umm Kulthum is considered the most renowned Arab singer of the 20th century. Zehava Ben's tentative but heartfelt gesture toward Umm Kulthum's repertoire helped bring Arab music into the mainstream for Mizraḥim, who had kept their unwavering appreciation of this iconic Egyptian singer quietly confined to neighborhood events.[13]

While the peace negotiations between Israel and the Palestinians seemed to be moving forward, European-Israeli audiences, who had rejected both Mizraḥi attempts to emulate Euro-sonic Israeli songs as too Arab-sounding and the emerging Mizraḥi pan-ethnic genre as too confusing, embraced Zehava Ben's performances of an unquestionably 'authentic' Arab music, a music that they could now claim – through her – as their own. Was the Egyptian repertoire of Umm Kulthum considered more generically 'pure' than hybrid Mizraḥi popular music by world music and highbrow European-Israeli listeners? World music, a marketing concept and emergent genre that took hold in the late 1980s, had resituated Arab music as legitimate for Euro-Israeli music consumers who might own a copy of an Umm Kulthum recording without personally appreciating the music itself. In a way, the world music boom prepared the European-Israeli 'ear' for Zehava Ben's reclamation of Umm Kulthum.

While Zehava Ben's manager, the savvy Eli Banai, no doubt saw the commercial potential of producing an Israeli cover of a renowned Egyptian singer, Ben's performance was more than a successful marketing ploy. She presented her performance of Umm Kulthum and other Arab singers as a homage to revered masters. The album cover for *Zehava Ben sharah Aravit* (Zehava Ben Sings Arabic), which features Umm Kulthum as well as several other Arab music selections, merges a drawing of her own face with Umm Kulthum's, and includes photographs of her pilgrimage to Umm Kulthum's grave in Egypt. She defined herself as a daughter of Arab music rather than an outsider, evidenced by her choice of a CD title that emphasizes her reclamation of the Arabic language that was part of her inheritance. Although this move was contested by some Israelis as either too Arabic or too transparently exploitative of the peace process,[14] and by some Arabs as thievery and fakery, many Arabs and Israelis appreciated both her boldness and the quality of her decidedly Arab music.

Among the Israeli Jews who supported Ben's gestures across Arab-Israeli and intra-ethnic Israeli divides was a young Moroccan-Israeli filmmaker, Erez Laufer. Laufer's documentary, *Zehava Ben, Solitary Star*,[15] filmed in 1996, captures a narrow but crucial swath in Ben's career as she moved between spatial, political and musical contrarieties under pressure at once to intensify a partisan position among Mizrahim and to abandon the differences among and between them and European Jews in the interests of the blending of the exiles. As the incongruous juxtapositions in Laufer's documentary demonstrate, Zehava Ben resisted partisanship and dissolution, opting to sing across irresolvable geographies.[16] Geographer Marie Cieri suggests that complexly situated, multi-dimensional cultural contexts cannot be reduced to positions of longitude and latitude. She argues that artists at once embody and transcend contested and indeterminate spaces like East-West, Israel-Palestine.

Sonically, in the brief period recorded in Laufer's documentary, Zehava Ben traversed the bifurcated fissures of Israeli ethnicity, class, and polity as she was called into service to cross into Arab and official Euro-Israeli territory. I suggest that performers like Zehava Ben do more than embody and transcend irresolvable geographies; they trespass unapologetically across these impassable and contradictory intra- and interethnic boundaries. In doing so, they attract unlikely audiences in multiple marketplaces and create counter-constituencies that resonate beyond the music itself.

Laufer's documentary captures Ben's spatial, cultural and musical transgressions during 1996. Examples of her performances across political, ethnic, and religious divides include: 1) *Sidi h'bibi*, a Moroccan love song for a predominantly right-wing Likud party Mimouna festival,[17] 2) *Shir le-shalom*,[18] Yakov Rotblitt's Euro-sonic peace song for a left-wing Meretz party event, 3) Mohamed Al-Ashkar's *Dalaly Dalaly*[19] for an audience of Palestinian men at a Jericho beachfront, 4) Haifa Wehebe's *Haramt Ahebak*[20] for Palestinian families at a wedding hall in Jericho, 5) Aviv Gefen's Euro-sonic pop song, *Lanetzah Achi*,[21] for Israeli government officials at a UNESCO dedication of a memorial to Prime Minister Rabin, and 6) Umm Kulthum's *Enta Omri*[22] for a mixed Arab and Jewish audience in southern France. On each occasion, Ben travels through irresolvable geographies and challenges binary configurations. At the heart of Ben's spatial and cultural trespasses are musical choices that underscore Mediterranean-Israeli music as an open genre in which old sources conjoin with contemporary styles in unstable (and thereby robust) juxtaposition that invite harmony, while at the same time figuring one sound starkly against the other; insisting on, announcing, difference.

Irresolvable geographies and counter-constituencies one: Singing right and left

The campaign leading up to the May 31, 1996 election unfolded in the shadow of Prime Minister Yitzhak Rabin's assassination by a religious Yemenite Jewish man the previous fall. Yigal Amir's bullets were aimed as much at the peace negotiations that Rabin had initiated and the concessions of land that were likely to follow as at the body of the Prime Minister. The election to replace him was largely a contest between right-leaning Likud candidate, Bibi Netanyahu, and centrist Labor candidate, Shimon Peres. Bumper stickers and campaign signs supporting one or the other decorated cars, balconies, and community events as voters expressed their support or opposition to Palestinian national aspirations. In this context, the Mimouna festival, a pan-ethnic Israeli celebration that originated as a Jewish celebration in Morocco on the final days of Passover, became even more politically charged than in past years.[23] Most of the participants displayed pro-Netanyahu signs, with a sprinkling of signs for Peres.

Zehava Ben performed at the Mimouna in the southern coastal town of Ashkelon, just eight miles from the Gaza border in April 1996. Dressed modestly in a white t-shirt and black jacket and pants, Ben stood on a makeshift stage covered with a patchwork of tarps and surrounded by festive families tending to barbeque grills that had been set up next to white plastic outdoor chairs and tables and coolers throughout the site. As Zehava's back-up band began the instrumental introduction to a well-known Moroccan song, *Sidi H'bibi* (*Where Are You, My Love*), Zehava grabbed her mic and offered a dedication to the residents of the northern border town with Lebanon, Kiryat Shemoneh, who, like the community in Ashkelon, had experienced missile attacks from across the border: 'To the residents of Kiryat Shemoneh, I wish them a happy holiday and my heart is with them.' As she spoke, Erez Laufer filmed audience members already clapping and moving to the rhythm of the song, fanning their grills with homemade election posters reading 'Netanyahu, I am confident' and the like. One young man fanned his grilling meat with a small poster reading 'Blow Peres away from the government' as the smoke from his almost palpable lamb wafted up in rhythm with the song itself. As the audience sings the refrain of the song, 'bibi, bibi' (*friend* in Arabic), the camera zooms in on an audience member holding a poster showing Bibi Netanyahu's image against the backdrop of an Israeli flag and above the caption, 'a fighter, a politician, a leader', as if to create a homonymous pun between the audience predilection for a Euro-American right-wing politician and their competence and affinity with Arabic language, culture and music. The scene cuts immediately to undulating young women demonstrating proficiency in Middle Eastern dance while several older women ululate at a high vocal pitch, their tongues creating the staccato contact with the roof of their mouths, in approval of the reference to song, their candidate of choice, and Zehava's performance. When I asked Laufer why he had translated the Hebrew slogans on the poster instead of the Arabic lyrics of the song, he seemed not to have noticed the visual-aural pun the juxtaposition would have produced. In the next scene, Ben is talking with a stage manager backstage at a Meretz political event, where she and Euro-Israeli pop singer, Dana Berger, will film a campaign ad for the left-wing party. The song they perform, Yakov Rotblitt's *Shir le-shalom* (song of peace), is the song that Yitzhak Rabin had just finished singing when he was murdered. The song lyrics were still in his pocket.[24]

Zehava Ben's singing across irresolvable geographies and counter-constituencies makes audible the incongruity of what Michael Herzfeld calls cultural intimacies. Ben herself denies that performance for any group displays partisanship. She fervently believes in a two-State solution but she takes her performances on political occasions as work she does for her living. Ben sees no contradiction in expressing her affinity with the Likud-leaning Moroccan community in Ashkelon and immediately after performing *Shir l'shalom*, so her singing holds together personal as well as political contraries in the same performance. Despite her disdain for journalists who presumed that her Meretz or Likud- Mimouna appearances indicated her voting preference, her connection to these performances is intimate and honest – she resonates with Moroccan-Israeli culture and heritage.

Ben expressed her experience of overlapping counter-intimacies during this profound period of grieving over Prime Minister Rabin's death and the unsettled peace prospects by making appearances in Jericho as well as at the dedication ceremony in Paris for UNESCO's Square of Tolerance in memory of the fallen leader, where her somber vocal melisma moved Aviv Gefen's *Lanetzach Achi* a tad more eastward than he may have intended.[25]

Counter-constituencies two: Singing Israel and Palestine

'I am not a politician, I am an artist, I perform for Jews and Arabs all over the world. I am a singer. I make art. I think we shouldn't act that way to them. Just like we wouldn't want them to treat us that way.' Laufer pans to a close-up of Zehava Ben lighting a cigarette as she emphatically talks to the security guards who had mistreated several Palestinian fans as she made her way to the dressing room before her concert in Jericho. The scene cuts to Ben, dressed modestly in a long white shirt and black pants singing Mohamed Al-Ashkar's *Dalaly Dalaly* before an audience of Palestinian men clad in bathing suits at a Jericho beachfront. The men, animated and on their feet, clap along as they answer Ben's line in a call and response fashion:

> In your beautiful eyes,
> Knives appeared in my heart...

That evening, Palestinian families seated around tables at a formal banquet clap as Zehava Ben sings her rendition of *Haramt Ahebak* (I forbid myself to love you), made famous by Warda. Women in *hijabs* fed their babies and sang along and young Palestinians came up on stage to have their photographs taken with the Israeli singer. The crowd's modest attire was in sharp contrast to the bare-chested male audience earlier in the day. What is shared is the warm reception Zehava receives and the warmth she returns at a moment when the elusive window to the peace negotiations is already closing.

Two weeks later, Ben performed Aviv Gefen's *Lanetzach Achi* (Forever my brother) at the inauguration of the Square of Tolerance (dedicated in memory of Yitzhak Rabin) at the UNESCO headquarters in Paris.[26] Somber and somewhat subdued, her eyes cast downward as if to ward off tears, Ben renders Gefen's[27] lyrical song, written in memory of a lost friend, as Rabin's widow, Leah Rabin, Shimon Peres, and other Israeli government officials look on.

Counter-constituencies three: Singing in Arabic for Arabs and Jews together

At this very moment of extreme cultural and political fragility in the fall of 1996, Ben's ongoing project of mastering Umm Kulthum's repertoire gathered momentum. Learning classical Arabic – quite different from the Judeo-Moroccan language spoken at home during her childhood in Be'er Sheva – was an almost insurmountable challenge. By the fall of 1996, Ben had studied classical Arab music, language, and performance, and developed a higher level of competence in Umm Kulthum's repertoire. For the performance of her fifty-seven minute version of Umm Kulthum's classic *Enta Omri* (You Are My Life) in Southern France, Ben replaced her earlier synthesized accompaniment with the Arab Orchestra of Haifa, comprising Palestinian and Israeli instrumentalists. The Arab and Jewish audience hummed along with Ben as she presented her emotional rendition and rose as one to its feet in a thunderous ovation at the end of the piece.

Ben's encounter with Umm Kulthum's life story and artistry was personal and emotional. Umm Kulthum's flexible religious identity and poor rural background resonated with Ben's own non-dogmatic religious upbringing, impoverished childhood, and cultural marginality. And Umm Kulthum's service to the pan-Arab, anti-Israel program of Abdul Nasser did not diminish Ben's devotion to the singer, whom she understood as a disadvantaged woman, like herself, committed to building bridges through her music.

Ben's vision of a hybrid musical formation that could bridge enemy cultures was realized in a specific performance seven years later, when, on November 12, 2003, al-Jazeera, the Arab TV network, invited Zehava Ben to perform at the celebration of the one hundredth anniversary of the birth of Umm Kulthum. The inclusion of Ben was remarkable in that not only had Israeli Jews come to appreciate an Israeli singer singing Arab music but that, despite the increasingly dim prospects for peace, Arabs did, too.

Music may rise above borders through the airwaves but it can never transcend culture on the ground. Whether musicians and scholars like it or not, music has a culturally situated politics. Even if music stays the same as it travels globally, it takes on different significance in different locations. The politics in question do not disappear into a blend in the music but are figured there, within a song, a repertoire, or a performance context in the form of contrasts whose aesthetic effect is dialogical rather than harmonious. Eventually, as with the development of any new genre, future audiences will no longer hear the allusions to contrasting musical traditions in Mediterranean-Israeli music. Many contemporary listeners do not discern Jewish, Arab, and European strains that were forced together, but rather a particular genre. It is this absorption of that which was once other that leads to new aesthetic formations. At historical periods on elusive cusps between enmity and unity, amid tentative alliances such as those in Israeli society in the 1990s, music makes the political aesthetic. The political is not only perceptible in the aesthetic, but it is transformed there. The dissonant, the conflicting held together, play with and off each other harmoniously. Harmony is not seamless blending; difference is still heard, but together. Musicians like Zehava Ben make audible this politics of the aesthetic. They suspend together in the same composition, in the same historical moment, difference – not to create wholly new forms but to hold together old forms in a harmonic matrix, literally and figuratively, in a way that does not dissolve difference but announces it. It is this announcement that makes the aesthetic of Mediterranean-Israeli music political.

Singers negotiate between cultural memories of Arab or Islamic countries and Jewish national loyalties to create what Mediterranean-Israeli singer, Haim Moshe, called in the early 1980s 'the new, authentic, Israeli expression'. This renewal subverted a previous 'new Israeli authenticity' formulated by Eastern and Central European musicians whose own search for national identity and authenticity had privileged European styles and embellished these with Middle Eastern, and particularly Yemenite, elements. This attitude manifested itself in the exoticization of locality, and the adoption of 'native' elements such as Bedouin dress, Yemenite dance, and Arab tunes.[28]

On the other hand, many Mediterranean-Israeli musicians resolved a different need for 'authenticity' by including in their repertoire Middle Eastern or North African songs, like Ben's *Sidi Ha-bibi*, echoing her roots in Morocco, or Umm Kulthum's canonic song, *Inta Omri*, signaling competence in a pan-Arab music tradition from which she descends. Next to these familial and traditional elements Ben incorporates Western elements such as harmony that, according to Peter Manuel, signify power and modernity to the non-Western listener.[29] Songs in Ben's repertoire such as Rotblitt's *Shir le-shalom* an Gefen's *Lanetzach Achi*, although Western compositions, are written in minor keys – a bridge between the East and West. Musical instruments such as the *darbuka* and *'ud* may reside next to the electric bass and synthesizer at Ben's beachfront performance of *Dalaly Dalaly*. According to Richard Middleton, popular culture is neither pure resistance nor superimposition, but rather an arena of negotiation.[30] This arena of negotiation is illustrated by Haim Moshe's comments in 1984, a decade before Zehava Ben arrived on the scene: 'The truth is, we are in the Middle East, surrounded by Lebanon, Syria, Iraq and strongly influenced by Arabic music. We are also strongly inspired by England, America, and France. So maybe in another twenty years we'll have a music style and people will not say, "This is Eastern; this is Western." In another twenty years it will be known as original, authentic, Israeli music.'[31] As Zehava Ben illustrated little more than a decade later, Moshe's prediction appears prophetic. In 2011, Israelis no longer categorized popular music as Eastern or Western as much as they did in 1984 or even 1996, but they still invented claims of indigeneity and authenticity to privilege some music and disparage others. So although Mediterranean-Israeli musicians who were silenced in the 1970s and 1980s found voice and new Mizrahi styles emerged, a politics of the aesthetics is still at work.[32]

Amnon Shiloah noted that the Israeli national anthem, Naftali Herz Imber's 'ha-Tikvah', written in 1878, instantiated the peculiarly pre-1948 diasporic Jewish dialectic between the East as both the future and the past. For European Jews, who would relocate to become Israeli citizens in the modern Israeli state, the present – the diasporic spread from which they emigrated to Israel – was outward and westward; the future, like the past, was inward and eastward, so that going East (though of course some Middle Eastern Jewish communities traveled West to Israel) was both going forward and going back, the myth of the eternal return.[33] The refrain of Imber's ballad captures this equation: *U-lefa'ate* (turn) *mizrah* (East) *kadimah* (forward!), 'Turn forward, toward the East'. This concept of turning eastward, characterized by movement forward, toward a cultural future, was also a turning back to a historical memory, a religious past. Shiloah further notes: '*Kadimah* on its own is a call for action: "Forward"'. Yet in the synonymous pair *Kedmah-Mizrahah*, it is an intensification of *mizrah* with the emphasis not on action, but on place. The relationship between the future and the East, and the past and the West, was already controversial when Imber wrote his ballad in the late 19th century, during the period in which European Jews began to settle lands they regarded as the once and future Israel. It is still controversial.

What Imber could not anticipate from his romantic European vista in the late 1800s was how East-West longing would undergo a Bakhtinian inversion[34] over the next fifty years as the West became both the past and the preferred future destination for many Israeli Jews who now emigrate in increasing numbers to New York, Los Angeles, and Paris.

Aesthetics and politics refuse separation; they insist on getting entangled, plunging themselves, with all their complexities, over each other's borders. Aesthetics and politics are never purged of each other, but they are not replications of one another either. What is antithetical in politics might hold together in music; what presents itself or wants to present itself as politically seamless reveals its musical seams; what arouses ire or argument in politics lifts music toward the transcendent. As Zehava Ben sings across irresolvable geographies and counter-constituencies, she embodies this possibility of music as a reflection through a glass darkly, of a politics that music neither mirrors nor breaks but whose alternative formations it figures and whose entangled histories it echoes.

Notes

1 The predominant music transmitted in Israel at that time in schools, at official occasions, on the radio, as well as throughout the ma'abarot was the ha-Shir ha-Erets Yisre'eli (the Song of the Land of Israel), a repertoire created by European Jews consisting largely of Eastern European melodies and Hebrew lyrics unfamiliar to Jews from Yemen, Morocco, Syria, and elsewhere. Both this European-dominated national music and the marginalized music genres created by Mizrahim involved appropriation and reappropriation. Both soundscapes can be described as pan-ethnic formations that borrowed melodies and visual aesthetics from local contexts in Russia, Poland, Czechoslovakia, Greece, Turkey, and Palestine, and reconfigured them in new communal contexts in Israel. See Natan Shahar, 'The Eretz-Yisraeli Song 1920–1950: Sociomusical and MusicalAspects', Ph.D. diss., Hebrew University, 1989; Motti Regev and Edwin Seroussi, Popular Music and National Culture in Israel (Berkeley, CA: University of California Press, 2004), 49–89.

2 A melisma is 'a group of more than five or six notes sung to a single syllable'. Richard L. Crocker, 'Melisma', *Grove Music Online,* ed. L. Macy, http://www.grovemusic.com.

3 The *'ud* is a 'short-necked plucked lute of the Arab world, the direct ancestor of the European lute, whose name derives from al-'ūd ('the lute').' Christian PocheÅL, "Ūd', in Macy, *Grove Music Online.* The *darabukka* is 'a single-headed goblet drum. It is made from pottery, wood or metal; the bottom is open and the skin head is directly attached by nails, glue or binding.' William J. Conner, Milfie Howell/Tony Langlois, 'Darabukka', in Macy, *Grove Music Online.*

4 The genre received minimal attention during the 1980s to 90s. See: Erik Cohen and Amnon Shiloah, 'Major Trends of Change in Jewish Oriental Ethnic Music in Israel', *Popular Music* 5 (1985): 199–223, Jeffrey Halper, Edwin Seroussi, and Pamela Kidron, 'Musica mizrakhit: Ethnicity and Class Culture in Israel', *Popular Music* 8, no. 2 (1989): 131–41, Mordechai [Motti] Regev, 'The Coming of Rock: Meaning, Contest and Structure in the Field of Popular Music in Israel' (Ph.D. diss., Tel Aviv University, 1990), 175, Amy Horowitz, '*Musika Yam Tikhonit Yisraelit* (Israeli Mediterranean Music): Cultural Boundaries and Disputed Territories', Ph.D. diss., University of Pennsylvania. For more recent attention see: Motti Regev and Edwin Seroussi, *Popular Music and National Culture in Israel* (Berkeley, CA: University

of California Press, 2004); for the first book-length study see: Amy Horowitz, *Mediterranean Israeli Music and the Politics of the Aesthetic* (Detroit, MI: Wayne State University Press, 2010).
5   Zehava Ben, *Tipat mazal* (A Drop of Luck) (1992), Eli Banai Productions, Ultratone Studios.
6   Rino Tsror, 'The Neighborhood Abandoned Hebrew', *Ma'ariv* (Tel Aviv), June 1991.
7   Yonatan Gefen, 'ha-Etsev hu Ashkenazi' (Sadness Is Ashkenazi), *Ma'ariv* (Tel Aviv), 15 May 1992, 3.
8   Michael Ohad, 'Libi ba-Mizrah' (My Heart Is in the East), *Haaretz* (Tel Aviv), 25 September 1981, 16.
9   Ben, Zehava, 'Etnix' (Ethnics). *Keturna masala* (When Luck Returns) (1991). Composed by Ze'ev Nehama and Amir <liski. Masala. Helicon.
10 The santur is the 'Dulcimer of the Middle East, south-eastern Europe and South and East Asia. It is used in Iran, Iraq, India, Kashmir, Turkey, Greece, Armenia, China and Tibet. The prototype instrument may be seen in a harp carried horizontally and struck with two sticks'. (Jean During, Scheherazade Qassim Hassan, and Alastair Dick, 'Santur [sadouri, santūr,sant'ur, santuri, sintir, tsintsila]', *Grove Music Online*, ed. L. Macy [Accessed (22 March 2007)], <http://www.grovemusic.com>).
11 Their collaboration was a new phenomenon of the 1990s. In this interview, Mediterranea-Israeli singer, Jackie Makayton, asks Israeli superstar Shemer if she would perform a duet with him. Her answer is honest and clear, that this would smell like a gimmick since they did not really know each other. Shemer, Nomi and Jackie Makayton, 'She'elot mi Jackie Makayton le-Nomi Shemer'. In *Aprion*, 45–6, 1985, 18.
12 *Zehava Ben sharah 'Aravit* (Zehava Ben Sings Arabic) (1995). Eli Banai Productions.
13 Virginia Danielson, *The Voice of Egypt: Umm Kulthum, Arabic Song, and Egyptian Society in the Twentieth Century*. Chicago, IL (University of Chicago Press), 1997.
14 Recently at the conference out of which this anthology emerges, one of the participants, an Iraqi-Israeli Jew who is fluent in Arabic and teaching Arabic literature at Haifa University, complained that Ben's Arabic renditions of Umm Kulthum reflected an impoverished command of that language – and that her Arabic is not convincing to native Arabic speakers, pointing to the cultural, linguistic and economic deprivation she experienced.
15 *Zehava Ben: Solitary Star*, written and directed by Erez Laufer, produced by Dalia Migdal (Tel Aviv: Idan Productions, 1997). This 84-minute documentary is in Hebrew and Arabic, with English subtitles.
16 Marie Cieri, 'Irresolvable Geographies', Ph.D. diss., Rutgers University, 2004.
17 Algerian Jewish singer Salim Halali sings Sidi Ha-bibi: http://www.youtube.com/watch?v=U9YWBW7DGu0.
18 http://www.hebrewsongs.com/song-shirlashalom.htm.
19 Mohamed Al-Ashkar Dalaly Dalaly http://www.youtube.com/watch?v=h6YFKKlxdc4.
20 Haifa Wehbe singing Warda's "Harramt Ahebak" http://www.youtube.com/watch?v=CBOp81N0Prg.
21 http://www.hebrewsongs.com/song-lanetzachachi.htm.
22 http://www.youtube.com/watch?v=tB0neJ3BLPU&playnext=1&list=PL6E0F16E4A396181F.
23 *Mimouna* is a North African Jewish celebration of the first baking of leavened bread immediately following the last day of Passover. It has become a pan-ethnic Mizrahi festival in Israel. For a discussion of the politicization of Mimouna see: Guy Haskell, 'The Development of Israeli Anthropological Approaches to Immigration and Ethnicity: 1948–1980', *Jewish Folklore and Ethnology Review* 11, nos. 1–2 (1989): 23–24.
24 This amateur video contains footage of Rabin singing at the rally and a shot of the bloodstained lyrics that were found in his pocket. http://www.youtube.com/watch?v=tmhoau5eYAE&feature=fvwrel.

25 Ironically, Aviv Gefen is the son of Yonatan Gefen who had bemoaned Zehava's Turkish song as conquering Tel Aviv and moving it eastward.
26 The monument is an environmental sculpture beside the Headquarters building. It includes a mature olive tree standing before a stone wall engraved with words from the Preamble to UNESCO's Constitution in ten languages, including Hebrew. It was designed by Israeli artist Dani Karavan.
27 Ironically, Aviv Gefen is the son of Yonatan Gefen, mentioned earlier in the chapter as authoring a satirical essay (note 7) in which he credits Ben's Turkish songs as the equivalent of the Ottoman reclamation of Tel Aviv. Here in a counter-subversion, Ben relinquishes her Turkish occupation of Tel Aviv, returning it to its right Ashkenazi soundscape through Aviv's lament.
28 Itamar Even-Zohar, 'The Emergence of a Native Hebrew Culture in Palestine: 1882–1948', *Studies in Zionism* 4 (1981): 171–73.
29 Peter Manuel, *Popular Musics of the Non-Western World: An Introductory Survey* (Oxford: Oxford University Press, 1988), 21–22.
30 Richard Middleton, quoted in ibid., 21–22.
31 Haim Moshe and Meir and Asher Reuveni, interview by author, Tel Aviv, 5 August 1984.
32 Disdain for Mediterranean-Israeli Music is still palpable among scholars, critics, and musicians. See the recent media debate over mainstream Sephardi singer Yehoram Gaon's disparaging remarks about the music covered in Ha'aretz: http://www.haaretz.com/print-edition/news/veteran-singer-yehoram-gaon-sparks-storm-by-terming-mediterranean-music-rubbish-1.348222. Gaon is quoted as referring to Mediterranean-Israeli music as 'rubbish' and disgusting. In *Playing Across the Divide: Israeli Palestinian Musical Encounters*, Benjamin Brinner notes that the most salient factor linking his three ethnic music case studies (Aley Zayit, Yair Dalal, and Bustan Abraham) is their desire not to be mistaken for Mizrahi music, a style that they 'detest'. pp. 77.
33 Amnon Shiloah, 'Eastern Sources in Israeli Music', *Ariel* 88 (1992): 4. Imber's source for the melody of 'ha-Tikv.ah' is a controversial topic in itself. Claims include a Moldovian or Romanian folksong and a theme from a tone poem by Czech composer Bedrich Smetana, likely derived from folk melodies familiar to the artist. Other possibilities include a Sephardi liturgical tune. It is most likely that the melody of 'ha-Tikv.ah' was a European import like much of the *ha-Shir ha-Erets Yisre'eli* repertoire composed around the same time. See the YIVO Institute for Jewish Research website for a discussion of this debate: http://epyc.yivo.org/content/13_6.php.
34 Mikhail Bakhtin, *The Dialogic Imagination: Four Essays by M. M. Bakhtin*, ed. Michael E. Holquist, trans. Caryl Emerson and Michael E. Holquist (Austin, TX: University of Texas Press, 1981), 270.

7 The architect and critic Leo Adler and the definition of Tel Aviv as a modern Mediterranean city

Yossi (Joseph) Klein

Introduction

From its start, the definition of modern Zionist culture was generally subject to controversy, as was the geo-historical and geo-cultural definition of Eretz Israel, as well as the ultimate characteristics of the Zionist 'place', architecture and city. On the one hand, Zionists, under the leadership of Theodor Herzl and Max Nordau, wished to 'expand the borders of Europe to Asia' and accordingly to adopt the cultural repertoire of Western Europe in its entirety; and on the other hand, circles, led by 'Ahad Ha'am', saw in the 'cultural issue' the essence of the redemptive Zionist project and demanded that it be focused on developing 'authentic' cultural concepts which would be integrated into regional history.[1] In this context, 'East' and 'West' were metaphors and models used in defining Zionist architecture which, at this time, was notable for its jumble of 'European', 'Oriental' and 'Moorish' styles. Thus it was in Tel Aviv, in particular, where until a relatively late period (the late 1920s), eclectic, historicist architectural 'Hebrew styles' were created by the leading Zionist architects, among them Alexander Baerwald, Joseph Berlin and the artist and the founder of Bezalel Academy of Art Boris Schatz.[2] Later, British colonial architects who were active in Palestine during the British Mandate period also emphasized historic-regional and local ties, especially in Jerusalem,[3] though also in Tel Aviv under the direction of the Scottish architect Patrick Geddes, who made a unique contribution to the planning of the city and to the Zionist integration into the 'Oriental' cultural and geographical *Regio*.[4]

From the mid-1920s, imported modernist architectural norms began to be adopted in Palestine and especially in Tel Aviv, the city that led the modernization processes through 'Europization' and 'Americanization'[5] of local Zionist architectural culture. During this period, in which the national conflicts between Arabs and Jewish communities were aggravated, Tel Aviv's modern architecture was interpreted mainly as 'National', 'European' and 'International' expression,[6] but as is proved primarily by some recent cultural research, perceptions of the essence of the modern Zionist space were particularly broad, including trends geared towards developing a modern 'local', 'regional'[7] and 'Mediterranean' Zionist architecture.[8] Thus it was, especially in Tel Aviv, where modern architecture because of its

Figure 7.1 Architect Leo Adler (1891–1962); picture courtesy of Nurit Arnon

'white' puristic qualities 'more closely resembled the local architectural style, even more than the exotic, "pseudo-Arabic" and "Hebrew" architectonic style'.[9] In this context, it appears that the abstract ambivalent character of modern architecture facilitated its adoption as an 'agreed practice' within the fading of the controversies among Zionist planners whose ideological, political and cultural approaches contradicted each other.

This article focuses on commentary regarding the Eretz Israel work of the Jewish architect, theoretician and critic Leo Adler (1891–1962) who emigrated from Germany to Tel Aviv in 1933. Adler, whose name has almost disappeared from the contemporary historiographical Israeli discourse,[10] was an extraordinary figure among the local Zionist architects during the 1930s and 40s, one of the few who were also engaged in theory and criticism. Although Adler was not the only one who was involved in these fields, he was definitely one of the best-known and most authoritative architectural theoreticians and historians active in Palestine, at least until 1948.[11]

As will be seen in the following discussion, Adler's unique contribution – which was rejected by the 'center' – was his authoritative, scholarly criticism of the Zionists' sweeping use of 'functional', 'international', and 'a-historic' architectural norms, emphasizing the need for renewed theoretical and formal links between the 'modern', the 'classical' and the 'regional'. Hence, it appears that Adler may be considered one of the first Jewish modernist architects active in pre-state Palestine, and perhaps even the first, who strived towards the development of an authentic Zionist modern architecture which would be integrated into the regional culture, of the *Regio* of the Mediterranean.

Though the point of departure for this article was limited biographical research, in retrospect it seems to have helped reveal the depth of the controversies over the ideological and formal origins of modern Zionist architecture, highlighting the existence of modern-regional architectural options. In this context, Adler's unique and scholarly counter-efforts joined those of other modernist architects, among them Erich Mendelsohn[12] and Ya'akov Pinkerfeld,[13] who also strived to formulate a modern Zionist architecture with reference to regional and local precedents.

As for the historiographic perspective, this paper follows early and later attempts of historians in the European, American and Mediterranean arenas who dispute the 'monolithic' historical descriptions claiming that modern architecture is 'architecture without precedents' that reflects only utopian, universal and functional visions, emphasizing in addition links between the modern and the historical, the classical, and the regional.[14]

Leo Adler's German and Eretz Israeli biography (1891–1962)

Leo Adler was born in 1891 in the city of Kersch in Southern Russia. In 1910, he moved to Germany, where he began studying Architecture in Berlin, and later he completed his studies at the Technische Hochschule in Munich. In 1914 Adler was drafted into the German army; he fought in World War I and was wounded. After recovering, he completed his doctoral thesis at the Technische Hochschule in Dresden, focusing on the analysis of 'Historical Expressions of Architectonic Development'.[15]

Adler was known in Germany as an historian and one of the important architecture critics. Among his major published texts are: *Wasmuths Lexikon der Baukunst* (1926–1931), a wide-ranging, five-volume encyclopedia of architecture that he edited; his book *Vom Wesen der Baukunst* (1926), a discussion of theoretical issues; and *Neuzeitliche Miethäuser und Siedlungen* (1931), a book dedicated to architectonic innovations in popular residential architecture. Adler also edited, from the early 1920s, the magazines *Wasmuths Monatshefte für Baukunst* and *Architectura*, which served as major platforms for modernist architectonic debate. During this period Adler also published a few articles in the Jewish journal *Menorah*.

Adler's German career as a theoretician and critic reflects his attempts to link architectural theory, history, methodology, and practice in a wide phenomenological and universal 'view', an attitude which can defined as a continuation of architect Gottfried Semper's early efforts to formulate 'a practical aesthetic' (*Praktischer Aesthetik*).[16] The American historian Paul Zücker describes Adler's singularity in the theoretical definition of the essence of architecture as translation of an *'a priori'* purposeless aesthetic space concept into the visual purposeful reality of three-dimensional space.[17] 'Functionality', according to Adler's concept, was currently influencing only structural elements, while the essence of the architectonic act,

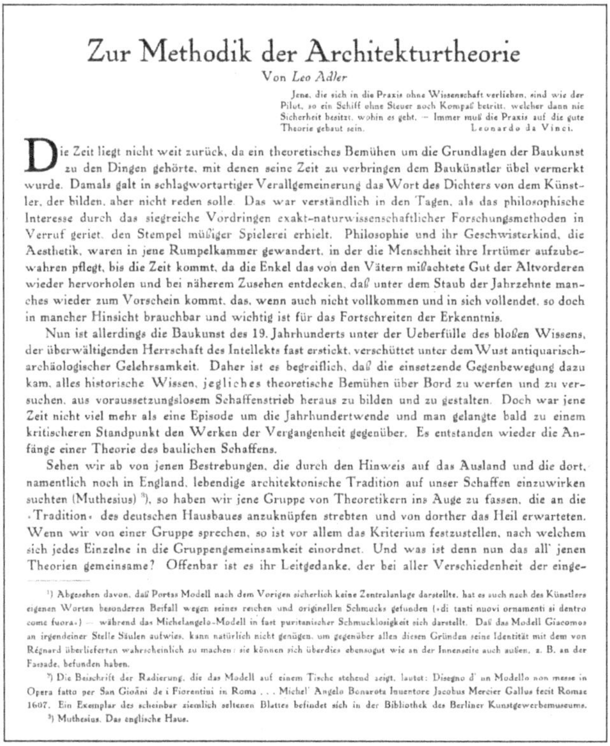

Zur Methodik der Architekturtheorie

Von *Leo Adler*

Jene, die sich in die Praxis ohne Wissenschaft verlieben, sind wie der Pilot, so ein Schiff ohne Steuer noch Kompaß betritt, welcher dann nie Sicherheit besitzt, wohin es geht. – Immer muß die Praxis auf die gute Theorie gebaut sein. Leonardo da Vinci.

Die Zeit liegt nicht weit zurück, da ein theoretisches Bemühen um die Grundlagen der Baukunst zu den Dingen gehörte, mit denen seine Zeit zu verbringen dem Baukünstler übel vermerkt wurde. Damals galt in schlagwortartiger Verallgemeinerung das Wort des Dichters von dem Künstler, der bilden, aber nicht reden solle. Das war verständlich in den Tagen, als das philosophische Interesse durch das siegreiche Vordringen exakt-naturwissenschaftlicher Forschungsmethoden in Verruf geriet, den Stempel müßiger Spielerei erhielt. Philosophie und ihr Geschwisterkind, die Aesthetik, waren in jene Rumpelkammer gewandert, in der die Menschheit ihre Irrtümer aufzubewahren pflegt, bis die Zeit kommt, da die Enkel das von den Vätern mißachtete Gut der Altvorderen wieder hervorholen und bei näherem Zusehen entdecken, daß unter dem Staub der Jahrzehnte manches wieder zum Vorschein kommt, das, wenn auch nicht vollkommen und in sich vollendet, so doch in mancher Hinsicht brauchbar und wichtig ist für das Fortschreiten der Erkenntnis.

Nun ist allerdings die Baukunst des 19. Jahrhunderts unter der Ueberfülle des bloßen Wissens, der überwältigenden Herrschaft des Intellekts fast erstickt, verschüttet unter dem Wust antiquarisch-archäologischer Gelehrsamkeit. Daher ist es begreiflich, daß die einsetzende Gegenbewegung dazu kam, alles historische Wissen, jegliches theoretische Bemühen über Bord zu werfen und zu versuchen, aus voraussetzungslosem Schaffenstrieb heraus zu bilden und zu gestalten. Doch war jene Zeit nicht viel mehr als eine Episode um die Jahrhundertwende und man gelangte bald zu einem kritischeren Standpunkt den Werken der Vergangenheit gegenüber. Es entstanden wieder die Anfänge einer Theorie des baulichen Schaffens.

Sehen wir ab von jenen Bestrebungen, die durch den Hinweis auf das Ausland und die dort, namentlich noch in England, lebendige architektonische Tradition auf unser Schaffen einzuwirken suchten (Muthesius) [3], so haben wir jene Gruppe von Theoretikern ins Auge zu fassen, die an die »Tradition« des deutschen Hausbaues anzuknüpfen strebten und von dorther das Heil erwarteten. Wenn wir von einer Gruppe sprechen, so ist vor allem das Kriterium festzustellen, nach welchem sich jedes Einzelne in die Gruppengemeinsamkeit einordnet. Und was ist denn nun das all' jenen Theorien gemeinsame? Offenbar ist es ihr Leitgedanke, der bei aller Verschiedenheit der einge-

[1]) Abgesehen davon, daß Portas Modell nach dem Vorigen sicherlich keine Zentralanlage darstellte, hat es auch nach des Künstlers eigenen Worten besonderen Beifall wegen seines reichen und originellen Schmucks gefunden (»di tanti nuovi ornamenti si dentro come fuora«) – während das Michelangelo-Modell in fast puritanischer Schmucklosigkeit sich darstellt. Daß das Modell Giacomos an irgendeiner Stelle Säulen aufwies, kann natürlich nicht genügen, um gegenüber allen diesen Gründen seine Identität mit dem von Régnard überlieferten wahrscheinlich zu machen; sie können sich überdies ebensogut wie an der Innenseite auch außen, z. B. an der Fassade, befunden haben.

[2]) Die Beischrift der Radierung, die das Modell auf einem Tische stehend zeigt, lautet: Disegno d' un Modello non messe in Opera fatto per San Gioãni de i Fiorentini in Roma . . . Michel' Angelo Bonarota Inuentore Jacobus Mercier Gallus fecit Romae 1607. Ein Exemplar des scheinbar ziemlich seltenen Blattes befindet sich in der Bibliothek des Berliner Kunstgewerbemuseums.

[3]) Muthesius, Das englische Haus.

Figure 7.2 Leo Adler, 'Zur Methodik der Architekturtheorie'; published in: *Wathmus Monatshefte fur Baukunst,* 1–2(1921)

he claimed, reflects 'total' and given truths. According to Zücker, Adler's ideas were part of the broadening of historic-architectonic theory into an approach that reflected not only logical developments but also aesthetic ones.[18] It seems that Adler was well aware of the difficulties in conceptualizing a comprehensive architectonic theory against the background of the European Enlightenment, which he described as characterized by an over-emphasis on the theoretic and the historic, which he claimed did not contribute to improving the quality of the architectural product. But in his critiques, Adler did not intend to return to historicist interpretation of a 'golden age', maintaining rather that aesthetics is not a speculative-normative theory but a scientific-empiric discipline based on the study of architectonic examples that disregard the 'hierarchy' determined by historic and political processes. According to Adler, only methodological and empirical study (based in part on modern archaeological discoveries) would lead to the future definition of a modern '*Baukunst*' with similar characteristics.[19]

Adler's outstanding career in Germany was abruptly ended when the Nazis assumed power in 1933; violence against Jews was spreading, and he was arrested. According to the testimony of his granddaughter Nurit, Adler felt that he was in danger and decided 'that very same night'[20] to flee with his family to

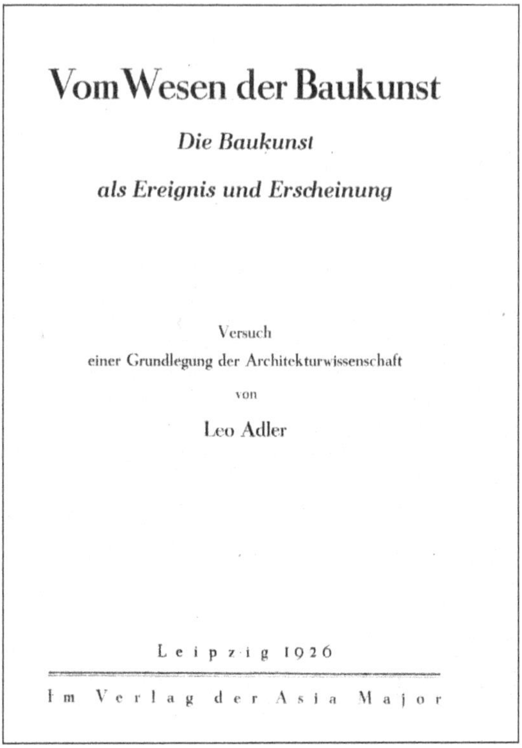

> **Vom Wesen der Baukunst**
>
> *Die Baukunst*
>
> *als Ereignis und Erscheinung*
>
> Versuch
> einer Grundlegung der Architekturwissenschaft
> von
> Leo Adler
>
> Leipzig 1926
>
> Im Verlag der Asia Major

Figure 7.3 Leo Adler, 'Vom Wesen der Baukunst', Verlag der Asia Major, Leipzig, 1926

Palestine, where, like other immigrant architects, he found it difficult to replicate his success in Europe.

In Palestine, Adler tried to combine architectonic practice and theory. It appears that only five buildings planned by Adler were constructed in Eretz Israel, all of them in Tel Aviv and its periphery (see details, following). As a theoretician and critic, Adler published a number of non-consecutive articles in Eretz Israel journals, among them the *Journal of the Engineers and Architects in Eretz Israel*, and in the art magazine *Gazith*, but in this context his most important activity was his participation in the unique (though sporadic) effort of a group of modernist architects, members of the Architects' Circle (the *'Hugg'*), to edit and publish a 'modernist' architectural journal, *Habinyan*.[21]

Until 1948, Adler also participated in various professional competitions, and in 1937 he won second prize in the important competition to plan the main avenue of Haifa, Kingsway; the architect Adolf Radding won first prize.[22] Adler's proposal included the construction of a continuous, modernist urban avenue appropriate to local climatic conditions, at the end of which was planned a 'colonnaded hall', a cool and shaded multipurpose space.[23] As will be described later, this kind of rhetoric testifies to Adler's orientation, according to which modern urban planning in Eretz Israel was based on typologies borrowed from the local-classical lexicon.

In the years 1949–51, Adler participated in the team that prepared the National Master Plan, known as the 'Sharon Plan'. His role, apparently, was to define sites of historic significance,[24] but even in this period he had difficulty establishing a significant, ongoing career in Palestine/Israel.

In the early 1950s Adler moved to Kibbutz Ein Harod. During this period he served as the planner for the Gilboa Regional Council and took part in planning the Ta'anach belt, which was led by the engineer Emmanuel Yalan.[25] The concept of the 'triple-neighbourhood village' was realized for the first time in the Ta'anachim.[26] Leo Adler died in 1962 at Kibbutz Ein Harod.

Leo Adler as a practising architect in Tel Aviv (1923–1948)

The first building by Adler that was built in Palestine was the Isser Romanov house, located at 25 Nahmani Street in Tel Aviv. This building was planned by Adler between 1923–25 in Berlin while the Tel Aviv architect Moshe Cherner was in charge of supervising the statutory procedures and the physical construction.[27] The Romanov house was planned according to a Berlin dwelling typology, where the residential spaces (32 rooms on three floors) were organized along a central corridor.[28] The Romanov house was dubbed the 'the Falling Building' because of its diagonal-vertical *'brise-soleils'* elements, which created the optical illusion of falling. The combination of large, high, shaded apertures aimed to provide maximal ventilation. There are those who believe that the building's facade is anachronistic, forced upon Adler by Tel Aviv's romanticist municipal engineer, Dov Hershkowitz,[29] but in fact there appear to be signs of modernist Art Deco in this building, as well as shade-providing diagonal-vertical modernist elements that Adler also used in the architecture of the Blum factory in Nahalat Yitzhak, which was built in the mid-30s as modernism was reaching its peak in Tel Aviv.[30]

Adler also planned the Schlagman office building for a chemical company located at 22 Lilienblum Street in Tel Aviv. The planning of this building probably began in 1933, and its construction was completed close to 1935. The Schlagman office building was erected on the demolished Izmuzik house,[31] one of the first buildings in the Ahuzat Beit, the first neighbourhood of Tel Aviv founded in 1909. This 'founding fathers' building was not the only one to be destroyed[32] and replaced with a modernist building as part of the demographic and functional changes that were occurring in this neighbourhood from the mid-20s onward.

It seems that Adler – who was aware of the commercial value of visual conspicuousness facing Herzl Street, the neighbourhood's main street – originally intended to include a round element in the Schlagman office building.[33] Apparently this proposal was rejected by the municipal engineer, and Adler inserted a conspicuous vertical element in its stead. The Schlagman office building was designed around a half-open courtyard with the offices concentrated in the northern wing, whose facade included large 'ribbon' windows that allowed occupants to depend on natural lighting.

During the same period Adler also planned the factory for the 'American Company for Ceramic Teeth' in Tel Aviv's Nahalat Yitzhak neighbourhood,

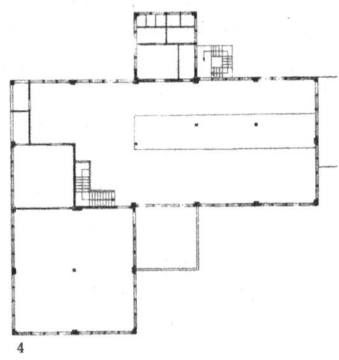

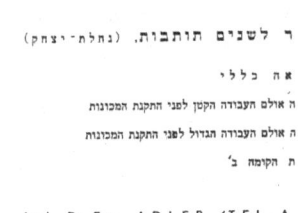

Figure 7.4 Leo Adler, the Blum factory built in Nahalt Yizhak, Tel Aviv, during the 30s; picture courtesy of Nurit Arnon

established in 1935 by Shmuel Shimson Blum.[34] For this factory Adler planned an industrial structure of large proportions whose plan reflects simplicity and functional efficiency. Its outstanding architectonic elements are constructional combined with diagonal '*brise-soleils*' (previously used by Adler in the Romanov House).

Two other buildings that he planned, discovered in the course of this research, were previously unknown. These are small one-storey residential buildings constructed before 1936 in the Bayit Vagan[35] neighbourhood (today the city of

Figure 7.5 Leo Adler, Schlagman House built in Tel Aviv during the 30s; picture courtesy of Irmel Kamp Bandau

Bat Yam). The modest architecture of these buildings also included elements to shade the interior and exterior spaces.

In a comprehensive analysis, it appears that the Schlagman office building and the Blum factory, both built in Tel Aviv, were the most eloquent modernistic architectonic examples planned by Adler in pre-state Palestine. These buildings exemplify Adler's attempt to 'localize' European architectural norms, an attempt that was combined with the gradual abandonment of 'functional' modernistic 'rhetoric'. It should be noted though that while Adler's architectural ideas were well founded on deep theoretical and historical observations, his practice through the whole period under discussion remained limited – a gap that indicates the difficulty to apply 'regionalist' patterns within the controversial national dispute with the Arabs.

Leo Adler as critic – Towards a modern Mediterranean architecture in Tel Aviv

Adler consistently decried the 'illogical' way in which European architectural modern norms were being adopted by the Zionist architects in the essentially different local climatic conditions. A criticism of this kind was expressed mainly in the article 'The Architecture in Our Land',[36] in which Adler broadened his criticism against 'importing' European norms, emphasizing the importance of multicultural and multigenerational processes comparing the historical development of national architecture in America – the land of immigration *par excellence* – with the contemporary Eretz Israel's cultural and political context. 'From this perspective,' Adler notes, 'what stands out is the similarity in the development of a national architectural style in America and in Eretz Israel', but he adds that 'native' heritage is not relevant, and 'just as the Indians' art of construction did not serve as a source for American architecture, so Arab architecture can never be the (only) source of Jewish national architecture in Eretz Israel'.[37] Another article by Adler, entitled 'Hygienic consideration in Ancient Construction', was published in 1943 in the art magazine *Gazith*.[38] Although this article addresses a specific technical subject, he broadens the scope of the topics included in 'Architecture in Our Land' and reveals his attitude towards the development of local and regional urban and dwelling typologies. Actually, in both 'Architecture in Our Land' and 'Hygienic consideration in Ancient Construction', Adler claims that a multitude of regional 'Eastern' typologies that were developed in a broad range of historic and geographic context, beginning in the ancient East, Egypt, Greece, etc., carry significant weight in the development of the 'Western' European architectural culture. These 'Eastern' typologies, Adler claims, were borrowed and refined by the Greek and Roman architects and later by Europeans according to classical rules, stressing in addition the importance of the Italian Renaissance to the formation of the modern European architectonic culture. It seems that these positions as expressed in Adler's critical writing can be seen as a 'scholarly' detailed call to establish the modern Tel Aviv space upon regional-classic precedents, and specifically, as will be discussed below, on the three 'aureate' typologies: the atrium house, the colonnaded street and the colonnaded hall.[39]

'European modernism passing away' and Adler's call for a 'return to order'

The emphasis by Adler on establishing renewed links between the 'classical' and 'modern' architecture was formulated in the context of trends that were developing in Europe toward the end of the 1920s, based on the principle of a 'return to order' – *Rappel á Retour á Order.*[40] The post-Futurist manifesto '*Apres le Cubism*' served as the foundation of this new trend, stressing not the 'ephemeral', the 'extraordinary', nor the 'exceptional of a protesting nature', but the opposite: expressions that reflect the ever-lasting and 'eternal' order.[41]

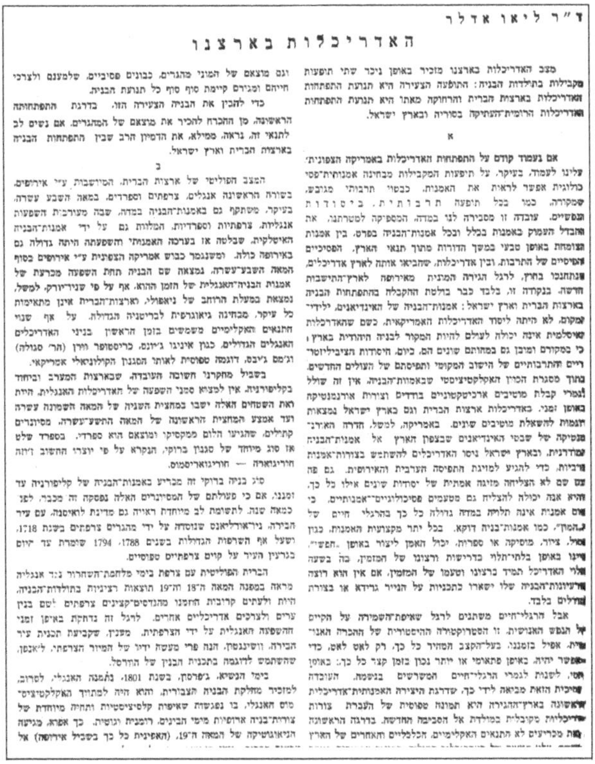

Figure 7.6 Leo Adler, 'The Architecture in our country'; published in *Gazith* (8–9)1936

The call for a 'return to order' was developing primarily in the ultra-nationalist and fascist realms, where architectural norms were being subordinated to racist doctrine.[42] In another trend, led most notably by Le Corbusier, the links between the 'modern' and the 'classical' were also emphasized, but with a focus on ancient Greek and Roman precedents, emphasizing the 'abstract' and 'universal' nature of classical architecture. This reflected the autonomy of the artistic creation and, in many ways, the 'nature' of architecture (especially modern architecture) as a 'Mediterranean discipline'. In this context, Adler apparently claims that 'the modernism of Central Europe is passing away in the world of construction'[43] and calls for a reformulation of modern paradigms newly linked to the classical tradition: 'a renaissance of the great and classical ideas about construction'.[44] It should be noted that in his first Eretz Israel article, 'Why? Impressions of a New Immigrant',[45] Adler was seeking only minor technical adaptations of European architectonic paradigms to fit local climatic conditions, but later he declared that 'folding shutters are but a sad accessory, and alone they cannot fill the local need for shade and ventilation',[46] calling for a more essential change in the orientation of local architecture, whose condition he defines as so absurd that it seems that 'German architects from the 1920s and 30s are its fathers'.[47] In fact, Adler's criticism of 'functionalist' rhetoric is also reflected in his early German articles, which praised other modern models, particularly the modern Mediterranean 'rational' architecture that developed in Italy within a 'true' classical historical context.[48] In this context Adler demanded explicitly that the 'Northern' Eretz Israel norms be abandoned to make way for the modern development of local classic typologies. 'There is no longer a good, appropriate role other than to continue the truly great building concepts of ancient times and to develop them according to the advanced, modern, technical construction methods of our time, concrete, iron and glass, the internal courtyard, the colonnaded hall and street – these are the three foundations of construction ... and of necessity, we must build them in a way that suits our times: in my opinion, this is the role of the coming generation of architects in Eretz Israel'.[49]

Between ideal types and real spaces – Atrium houses, colonnaded streets, and colonnaded halls in modern Tel Aviv

Adler regarded Roman architecture and city planning as the ideal models for the new modern Zionist architecture. His arguments for this orientation were both cultural and functional. He praised the universal character of 'the Roman art of building', which he maintained integrated Mediterranean and European architectonic cultures until it became the 'mother and father of all those cultures that were influenced, directly or indirectly, by Mediterranean culture ... Western Christian cultures', but also 'the Moslem art of building'.[50] Adler described Roman architecture and the Roman city – *civitas* – as reflecting universal values: 'It makes no difference whether those who produced this architecture were pagan Germans, Christian Armenians or Moslem Arabs';[51] therefore, with its emphasis on objective and functional proportions, it reflects the achievement of all human (European) 'civilization'. But more than that, Adler claimed that it was the clear advantages of Roman architecture over ancient vernacular examples that, 'thanks to skills of the Roman builders', achieved their 'perfect', classical qualities, such as the atrium and the peristyle, 'that gradually became true 'aureate' spaces.[52] In fact, these typologies: 'the atrium house, the colonnaded street, and the colonnaded hall' were, according to Adler, fundamental elements of a universal architecture prevalent in the first and ancient global context 'from Britannia to Baal Beck and Palmyra'.[53]

'The Roman atrium house', the first primary component of ancient Roman universal space, is in Adler's view a 'Southern house' comparable to a parasol.[54] The historical origins of the atrium, he claimed, were to be found in every corner of 'our region', starting with 'Tel el-Amarna in the Egyptian kingdom ... in Greece in Homer's day ... on the island of Knossos, etc.'[55] Thus, this 'Southern' dwelling type reflects both universal, national and shared regional heritage, while its origin can also be found in 'Abraham's ancient homeland'. Archaeologists like Yizhar Hirshfeld confirmed the mere existence a shared rich culture of dwellings in ancient Eretz Israel: imported 'high' elitist atrium houses which primarily served the urban aristocracy, as opposed to simpler vernacular types that were being developed in the villages. The simple vernacular type later became the source of the traditional Arab residential typologies, which were also documented by the architect Ya'akov Pinkerfeld at the start of the 1940s.[56]

As mentioned, Adler considered the 'atrium house' not just an ideal historical architectural example, but also a relevant 'counter example' to the apologetic semi-rural European 'garden city' dwelling typologies that were carried out by Zionist planners also in the new 'Hebrew Metropolis' Tel Aviv. Adler maintained that it was a mistake to implement the 'Northern' dwelling type in Tel Aviv described as 'a cube … with tiny courtyards of 2–4 meters from all sides, leaving the fate of a family's life to the eyes and ears of their neighbours', and suggested replacing it with 'the Southern dwelling type',[57] the atrium house. It seems that this suggestion refers mainly to the construction of a real urban fabric around 'shared internal courtyards for whole blocks of buildings'. He proposes that, 'instead of these inadequate courtyards, shared internal courtyards should be arranged for whole blocks of buildings'.[58]

The direct advantages of adopting the atrium type in modern Tel Aviv were, in Adler's opinion, 'ventilation, shade and privacy', but more than that, he believed that the urban planning of the first Hebrew city based on the 'atrium house' typology would comprise a revolution of urban public spaces, in which 'the colonnaded street' would become a significant, renewed modern element. Implementing this typology, Adler further claimed, would facilitate the creation in Tel Aviv of 'street lines with a consistent monumental character … from the perspective of urban construction', which would make it possible to create multi-storied terraces and shaded 'colonnaded streets' that would follow the 'examples in the ancient Eastern cities of Italy and Spain'.[59]

The colonnaded street was the second primary element of the Roman city in Eretz Israel and also within the Eastern areas of the Empire. It developed as a functional solution for shading and protecting commercial streets and for ornamenting the sacred streets that led to various temples (*via sacra*).[60] Assumptions regarding the origin of this urban element are controversial, but most researchers seem to agree that the colonnaded street was developed in the Eastern part of the Mediterranean, where 'the Hellenistic tradition was strong, and from there it spread to all parts of the Empire'; perceived mainly as a 'creation of the East', it should be considered a 'local element'.[61] The colonnaded street became the universal urban element that was widely adopted in Europe and other far-flung regions until it was abandoned by modernist urban planners after World War I. It was only as part of the post-modern critique that the importance of the historic city generally and of traditional urban patterns in particular were once again emphasized, as was the significance of the traditional street and the colonnaded street as permanent urban elements. So it was, for example, with the 'Mediterraneanist' architect Bernard Rudofsky,[62] and most notably with post-modern architects like Aldo Rossi, the Krier brothers and others.

It seems that Adler's call to use the colonnaded street and other traditional Mediterranean urban typologies in Tel Aviv was part of his criticism of the dominant Zionist trends, especially in Tel Aviv, which he claimed reflected, at best, old Eastern European concepts imported by Jewish immigrant architects, and modernist-socialist attitudes that aimed to dismantle the city as a physical and cultural phenomenon by replacing the traditional street with 'neighbourhood units' and other semi-rural elements. This anti-urban Zionist trend changed gradually and only partially when, in the early 1940s, a number of arcades were built in Tel Aviv,[63] and in the 1950s when the city's longest colonnaded street was inaugurated – Ibn Gvirol Street. Ya'akov Ben Sira, the municipal engineer, supported these late climatic, architectonic adaptations of the Tel Aviv street typology.

The third foundation of Adler's new Tel Aviv space was the 'colonnaded Roman hall', a typology combining the basilica, the peristyle, and the stoa, multi-columned urban public structures that were meant to provide protection from the climate. The impact of Hellenistic and Roman architecture and of the secular basilica on the architecture of the synagogue[64] was also stressed in the finds of 'Hebrew' archaeological excavations[65] conducted by Jewish and non-Jewish researchers in Eretz Israel at the start of the 20th century (in Beit Alpha and Korazin, for instance). One can assume that Adler was aware of the discoveries of 'Hebrew archaeology' since, in the *Wasmuths Lexikon der Baukunst* he edited, the architecture of Galilean synagogues was described as having been influenced by classical-Hellenist culture. In fact, the ancient basilica became the transitional model adopted, for a range of reasons, by Jews.[66] For Adler, the rhetorical use of classical Hellenist-Roman concepts was also meant to emphasize traditional Jewish openness to secular values and universal forms, a viewpoint characteristic of the 'Western' German Jewry;[67] for others it connoted the return to the 'golden age' of religious life in Eretz Israel. An example of the claims regarding the renewed use of the basilica typology is provided in an article by Shmuel Krois, 'The Basilica in the Talmud', published at the start of the 1930s,[68] in which he writes, 'now that the question arises of what style and typology to build … in the style to which we are accustomed in the lands of the Diaspora, or in the style that was acclaimed in Eretz Israel during the Golden Age of our religious life?'. The answer, Krois continues, 'was discovered in the ruins of the Galilean synagogues; the classical type of the basilica'.[69]

History, archaeology, and architecture

The development of modern Zionist architecture was connected to the development of geo-historical and architectural-historical research. Until a relatively late period (the start of the 20th century), these disciplines were based on philological research of Biblical texts, particularly their descriptions of the temples.[70] It seems that Adler, who was well aware of the methodological disadvantages of these initial attempts, tried to establish an 'alternative' historical outline based on 'real' archaeological findings. He explains that his preference for the archaeological is based on the 'fact' that 'historical documents are given to biased interpretation, whereas the archaeological remain is unambiguous'.[71.]

This position is essentially rooted in the methodologies of art history research developed in the German and Austrian cultural arenas starting in the 18th century, according to which the 'archaeological is the historical' since it can provide a 'real' experiential, historical picture. This connection to archaeology, especially to Roman remains, actually denotes the beginning of the new modern, scientific, empirical discipline of the history of (European) art and architecture as formulated for the first time by Winckelmann.[72] He regarded the classical model as an 'absolute model' that constituted the basis of German architecture and German historiography of architecture at least until the end of the 19th century. Goethe, Schinkel and Heine were instrumental in including the classical as a 'German' element equivalent to the Gothic and defining it as a perfect model that integrated beauty with efficiency. Such paradigms developed as a result of the 'Grand Tours' to the South, mainly Italy, where Roman and Greek remains were studied.[73]

Adler complains that 'the connection between the archaeological discoveries to the work of the architect is too loose'.[74] On one hand, this is another piece of his criticism of the severance from the classical. However, the very attempt to subordinate the architectural to the archaeological reflects an intention to draft an historical outline that would delineate for the first time the development of architecture in Palestine using 'scientific' and 'objective' tools. According to Adler, only such an outline might serve as a worthy basis for establishing a modern construction art – *Baukunst* – based on those same principles. Accordingly, Adler chose to use as a source of inspiration the Roman architectural heritage, described as 'of engineering quality' and therefore closer to the *Neue Sachlichkeit*. It should be noted that in the 1920s and 30s the findings of many archaeological studies in Palestine and the Mediterranean basin stressed the link to the Greek-Roman heritage – a link that was emphasized in the findings of many archaeological investigations in the 1920s and 30s in Palestine and in the Mediterranean basin, and particularly the remains of the cities Baalbeck and Palmyra (Tadmor), which Adler mentions.[75] As related in the *Wasmuths Lexikon der Baukunst*, these excavations also 'proved' the Helleno-Roman influences on the architecture of the local synagogues.

'Southern Europe' and the definition of modern European architecture as Mediterranean

According to Adler, the examples upon which the modern Tel Aviv space will be based are from 'Southern Europe'.[76] This European geo-cultural concept developed in the 18th century parallel to the discovery of the South by scholars and artists on their Grand Tours. The cultural importance of these journeys cannot be overestimated: they led to a real revolution in the definition of many branches of European culture including art and architecture, which were redefined as emanating from a double heritage: 'classical', but also based on 'the diversity ... and on the sensuality' that typified the Southern regions. [77]

The influence of the Grand Tour in the South can also be seen in the development of new geographic, historical perceptions, to which German researchers made a significant contribution (Ben Artzi, 2004; Goren, 1999).[78] Ritter advanced beyond the scientific-physical perceptions of Humboldt, and

Ratzel developed anthropogeography – human geography that 'wished to balance the deterministic influences and emphasized the influence of man's activity as landscape-designing'. Ratzel defined the Mediterranean region as 'European', the reason being his perception that 'in the cultural sense, history is more important than the physical or ethnographic structure', a definition also reflected in Adler's writings explaining the development of Jewish architecture in ancient times as integrated into the regional culture. These definitions paved the way for the 'modern' definitions of Mediterranean geography by Braudel.[79]

Modernistic architectural rhetoric also related to the 'Mediterranean characteristics' discovered in 'the South of Europe'. For example, in *Towards a New Architecture*, Le Corbusier argues for the development of modern architectural aesthetics 'of engineers' from the study of universal aesthetics laws reflected in classical architecture. Indeed, Le Corbusier describes Roman architecture as 'bad taste' although it does reflect modern values: efficiency, order and rationalism. It is hinted also that 'Southern Europe' is the 'cradle of the architectural discipline' where the 'Mediterranean sun' is a kind of a mechanism that enabled the discovery of 'eternal' harmonious artistic and architectonic proportions. Adler's formulations are almost identical; he declares that 'determining good proportions between the entire wall and the openings', in the light of 'the strong rays of the Palestinian sun', is 'fundamental of good architecture'.[80] These definitions are probably based on a later interpretation of the ancient Greek 'theory of climate' that connected geographic and human characteristics. It is argued that due to the geographic characteristics of the Greek islands, philosophy and artistic architectural creation developed in these 'Southern' areas where 'Homer's sun' shined on Attica and its pure light 'assisted in designing refined philosophical concepts and fostered sculptural perception that sees things in three-dimensional molds and relief and not like painting, as two-dimensional figures'.[81]

Conclusion – The universal is the local

Modern Zionist architecture developed from the end of the 19th century in a unique, paradoxical context: on the one hand, Zionism as a national movement stressed the importance of historical and geographical dimensions, but on the other hand, the physical situation in the 'ruined' and 'abandoned' land did not provide sufficient and real material evidence of the Jewish architectural heritage. In this situation, the range of invented historical interpretations regarding the ancient national architectural heritage was extremely wide. At first, philological research filled the historical gaps, when Biblical descriptions (especially of Solomonic Temple) and 'oriental' typologies served as a basis for 'constructing' a historicist national 'Hebrew' architectural style.[82] At the beginning of the British Mandate in Eretz Israel, new modernist architectonic norms imported from Europe were adopted enthusiastically. It should be noted that those who led the use of these paradigms in Tel Aviv were mainly members of the 'Architects' Circle' who belonged to the socialist wing and, at least on the rhetorical level, related with hostility to the 'city' in general and to Tel Aviv in particular. During the same period, those architects who did not belong to the dominant socialist 'center' were marginalized; so too, it would appear, was Adler.

Modern Tel Aviv was the pride of Zionists who described the city, even when it was a small town, as a European metropolis. In contrast, Adler (like other modernist architects) described the 'First Hebrew city' only as 'a city that is not a city', where the 'Eastern European *shtetl* left its impression in the form of the individual building and on the idea of city planning ... where the main axis is a *boulvar* [a word, typically taken from the French, which penetrated the Russian architectural vocabulary and became naturalized there] ... there is almost no mid-sized Russian city that doesn't have a *boulvar*.'[83] ('Russian' was denoted by Western Zionist as 'underdeveloped'). It appears that in this context Adler tried out his alternative pro-urban concepts, according to which the architectonic space of Tel Aviv should be based on three essential assumptions:

1. Eretz Israel, with Tel Aviv at its center, belongs to the Mediterranean South European geo-cultural zone;
2. New Zionist architecture should reflect new trends, according to which 'modernism is passing away from the world of construction';
3. Tel Aviv new urban and architectural spaces will be based on ancient historical classical precedents as discovered, documented and analyzed in archaeological excavations in Palestine.

These criteria constituted a counter-model to the dominant Socialist-Zionist modernist paradigms, while the South of Europe as a geo-cultural definition marked the call to replace the Eastern European pastoral anti-urban orientations with a Western liberal one. The mention of Roman architectural remains discovered in the 'daring excavations' in the Mediterranean basin,[84] which allegedly proved that the ancient Jewish heritage integrated within it universal Hellenist-Roman culture, reflects a call to universalize Zionist paradigms with a link to local climatic conditions. Mentioning the ruins of ancient cities in Eretz Israel was also meant to highlight the permanent importance of the city in Jewish history, and, accordingly, to the contemporary Zionist reality. This view reflects Adler's opposition to the Zionist establishments, which adopted physiocratic, socialist, anti-urban approaches,[85] and the apologetic, semi-rural model of the garden city, which dominated in Israel at least until the end of the 1950s.[86] In this connection it should be noted that for Lewis Mumford and Patrick Geddes, the Scottish planners of Tel Aviv's urban space, the Roman metropolis represented a real dystopia presaging the end of civilization.[87]

Regarding Adler's attitude towards Muslim architectural culture: his proposal to rely on Roman 'universal' precedents would seem to reflect a rejection of oriental-Levantine culture. But Adler similarly rejected the main Zionist trends and was far from such views. He described the outstanding universal quality of Muslim art and architecture and even compared it to Jewish art.[88] Furthermore, he totally and consistently rejected nationalist and racist biological 'theories' and, consequently, any connection between 'nation', 'race' and architectural style.[89]

These theories, Adler stressed, citing Kant, 'are not scientific'. Instead, Adler argued that the socio-cultural dimension is the dominant one, therefore in Europe there are no races in the usual sense. The *volk*, for Adler, is but an expression of the 'cultural merging' of people of different origins in one territory, while cultural patterns, including architectural ones, are 'community' social conventions and not of a geographical organic nature.[90]

In conclusion, Adler insists on abandoning modernistic functional planning models in Tel Aviv and calls to develop spaces based on classical Mediterranean precedents interpreted by him as a common denominator of European and Jewish culture. This stance also reflects an intention to integrate into the regional culture. However, Adler's emphasis on the importance of the classical is a typical formalistic 'expert view' reflecting an essentially Eurocentric tendency. According to Pavlides,[91] European modernists' focus on regional typologies, particularly the classical Mediterranean one, served only as a means to underscore rational and objective viewpoints aimed at ending the exclusive focus on architectonic styles. Regarding the Zionist context until 1948, it seems that Adler's similar approach was antithetical to both the dominant Zionist functional socialists' trends and also to the social-anarchist who aimed at the development of new local and vernacular space 'from below' – attitudes described by Pavlides as 'anthropological-vernacular'.[92]

Indeed, if Adler's proposals had been implemented, Tel Aviv – whose architecture was based merely on bureaucratic and functional planning norms – would have gained monumental architectural qualities and 'high momentum shaded public spaces'.[93] But beyond that, Adler's proposals to lean on classical values, developed in the Mediterranean basin, were an outspoken criticism of any attempt to reduce 'eternal' universal human values to any limited national, ethnic, racist, regional, local, Jewish, Arab, or German cultural expression. In this context, the classical-modern option scholarly formulated and advocated almost exclusively by Adler was meant to be a wide-range counter-option to the Zionist narrow functional and ethnocentric trends; for him, *the universal is the local.*

Notes

1 For discussion of the impact of the 'culture dispute' (*kulturfrage*) over the developmental of 'Western' and 'oriental' artistic expressions in the Zionist arena, see: A. Holtzman, *Aesthtics and National Revival: Hebrew Literature Against The Visual Arts* (Hebrew), Tel Aviv: Zmora Bitan, 1999, pp. 25–30, 78–82; M. Berkowitz, 'Art in Zionist Popular Culture and Jewish National Self-Consciousness, 1897–1914' in: *Studies in Contemporary Jewry* 5, 1990, pp. 9–42; Y. Shavit, ,Hundred Years of Israeli History as Reflected in Art', in: *A People Builds its Land* (Hebrew), Herzeliya: Herzeliya Museum, 1988. pp. 9–48. On 'Oriental' Zionist artistic expressions, see: Ariel Hirschfeld, 'Kadima – The Orient in Israeli Culture' in: Yigal Zalmona and Tamar Manor-Friedman (eds.), *To The East – Orientalism in Israeli Culture* (Hebrew), Jerusalem: The Israel Museum, 1998, pp. 11–31; Yigal Zalmona, 'To The East -Orientalism in The Arts in Israel', in: Zalmona and Manor-Friedman (eds.), ibid. pp. 47–93.
2 Architect Alexander Baerwald, considered the father founder of early Zionist architecture, depended on regional architectural examples from 'southern Syria';

Joseph Berlin used 'southern European' neo-classical precedents, while Boris Schatz, Josef Barsky and Y.Z. Tabachnik tried to establish an 'authentic' Hebrew architectonic style based on Biblical descriptions; see: Y. Klein, 'Zionist Disputes Reflected in The Urban Patterns and Architectural Styles in Ahuzat-Bayit' (Hebrew), in: *Zmanim*, 106, 2009, pp. 22–35; see M. Levine, 'Five Attitudes to The Oriernt in Israeli Architecture' (Hebrew), in: *Zmanim*, 96, 2006, pp. 38–47. See also: N. Harpaz, 'The First Hebrew City and its Architecture – A Local Original Style in "Little Tel Aviv"'(Hebrew), in: *Haaretz Museum Yearbook*, 20–21, Vol. 2–3, 1986, pp. 227–291.
3 R.A. Fuchs. *Austen St. Barbe Harrison: A British Architect in the Holy Land.* (PhD Dissertation), Haifa: Technion, 1992; Benjamin Hyman, *British planners in Palestine 1918–1936.* Boston Spa: British Library Document Supply Centre: 1994; N. Hysler-Rubin, 'Planning the Artistic City: Charles Robert Ashbee in Jerusalem', (Hebrew), *Cathedra*, 117, 2005, pp. 81–101.
4 W. Volker. *Biopolis: Patrick Geddes and the city of life*, Cambridge, MA: MIT Press, 2002. pp. 71–72.
5 Y. Klein, *The Americanization of Tel Aviv*, Jerusalem: Carmel, 2010.
6 Nitzah Szmuk presents the panoply of influences on Tel Aviv architecture, and especially emphasizes the connection to the Bauhaus ignoring the contradiction between the leftist-radical political orientation of the Bauhaus and the conservative and liberal/revisionist majority in mandatory Tel Aviv, see: N. Szmuk, *Building from the Sand.* (Hebrew). Tel Aviv: Misrad Habitahon, 1994. pp. 19–36.
7 On Mendelsohn's 'regional' contribution see: A. Shiftan, ‹Contested Zionism – Alternative Modernism: Erich Mendelsohn and the Tel Aviv Chug in Mandate Palestine', *Architectural History*, 39, 1999. pp. 147–180.
8 D. Ohana, *Neither Canaanites Nor Crusaders* (Hebrew), Ramat-Gan: Shalom Hartman Institute, Bar Illan University, Ketter Publishing House, 2008; A. Nocke, *The place of the Mediterranean in modern Israeli identity*, Boston, MA: Brill, 2009.
9 A. Helman, *Urban Culture in 1920s and 1930s Tel Aviv* (Hebrew), Haifa: Haifa University Press, 2005. p. 25.
10 For articles devoted to a discussion of Adler's activity, see: M. Warhaftig, *They Laid the Foundation: Lives and Works of German Speaking Jewish Architects in Palestine 1918–1948*, Berlin: Wasmuth. 2007, pp. 256–263; M. Warhaftig, 'Leo Adler 1891-1962', *Bauwelt*, 39, 1991 p. 208; a documentary file prepared by the architect Nitza Mezger-Szmuk in the context of the conservation of the Romanov house includes additional information on Adler's activity. See: N. Mezger-Szmuk, *The Romanov House-Documentation Survey.* Tel- Aviv, 2006. These are informative articles which focus primarily on Adler's activities in Germany. In the course of our research, two unknown buildings planned by Adler were discovered in the Bayit Vagan neighbourhood (today in the city of Bat Yam), as well as five critical articles which have not yet been the subject of research or commentary.
11 It must be noted that additional architects played a part in the attempt to base relevant historic and theoretical outlines, among them Erich Mendelsohn, Julius Posener, Eugene Ratner, Paul Engelmann, and Yaakov Pinkerfeld. The best-known and most authoritative were Mendelsohn, who was considered an architect of international repute, and Adler, who upon his arrival in Eretz Israel was known as a reputed architecture critic on the German scene. Ratner and Posener emphasized consensual commentary, while Mendelsohn, Pinkerfeld, Adler and Englemann, who did not belong to the 'center', expressed opposing positions, the main point of which was a call for modern interpretation based on local-regional precedents.
12 See, for example, E. Mendelsohn, *Palestine and the world of tomorrow*, Jerusalem, 1940.
13 Y. Klein, 'The Red Side of Tel Aviv – Pinkerfeld's Architecture in the Kibbutz Sphere', *Docomomo Journal*, 40, 2009. pp. 46–51.
14 See: A. Colquhoun, 'The Concept of Regionalism', in: Gulsum Baydar Nalbantogulu, Wong Chong Thai (eds.) *Postcolonial Spaces*, New York: Princeton Architectural

Press, 1977; *Modernity and the Classical Tradition*, Massachusetts: MIT Press. 1991; H.J. Henket, H. Hilde, *Back From Utopia – The Challenge of The Modern Movement*, Rotterdam: 010 publishers, 2002; Rowe, Collin. 1972. *'Introduction to Five Architects'*. [in] HAYS, Michael (ed). *Architecture Theory since 1968*. Cambridge: MIT Press, 2002, pp. 73–84; M. Umbach, B. Huppauf, (eds.), *Vernacular Modernism*, Stanford, CA: Stanford University Press. 2005.
15 Warhaftig, *They Laid the Foundation*, op. cit. p. 256.
16 Kieren Martin, 'Der Stoff der idée Machen', in: L. Adler, *Von Wesen der Baukunst*, (reprint), Berlin: Gebr. Mann Verlag, 2000, pp. 1–18.
17 P. Zücker, 'The paradox of architectural theories at the beginning of the Modern Movement', *Journal of The Society of Architectural Historians*, 3(1951), p. 11.
18 Ibid.
19 L. Adler. 'Zur Methodik der Architekturtheorie', *Wasmuths Monatshefte für Baukunst*, 1–2, 1921, pp. 45–49.
20 Interview with Nurit Arnon, Ein Harod, May 2009.
21 It was published irregularly from 1934–38. Beginning in 1937, Adler co-served as the editor with S. Steinbuch. The journal's name, *Habinyan*, was borrowed from the German term *Baukunst*, a modernist 'alternative' name for the 'new-architecture'. The name of the 'Hugg' was also borrowed from the name of a group of avant-garde German architects, 'the Ring'. Symptomatically, when Adler began to serve as editor of *Habinyan* he changed its name to '*Habinyah Bmisrah Hakarov- a Palestine Periodical for Architecture in The Near East*'. In his memoirs, the architect Arieh Sharon reports on the founding of the '*Habiyan*', but he does not mention Adler at all, either here or in connection with his part in preparing the National Master Plan in 1949. See: A. Sharon, *Kibbutz+Bauhaus*, Tel Aviv: Massada Publishing Ltd; A. Sharon, 'Tel Aviv – Past and Present', Gazith, 393–408, 1984, pp. 249–252.
22 H. Gilbert, and S. Sosnovsky, *Bauhaus on the Carmel and the crossroads of empire: Architecture and Planning in Haifa during the British Mandate*. Jerusalem: Yad Izhak Ben-Zvi, 1993. pp. 133–140. Pfankuch, *Adolf Radding*, Berlin: Gebr. Mann Verlag, 1970. pp. 104–105.
23 This was a joint proposal by Adler, Patki, and Lesovsky. In the article summarizing the results of the competition, Adler praises the common denominator of the winning proposals, the planning of urban towers, which he describes as 'vital elements', in: Adler, 1937.
24 Interview with the architect Shmuel Yavin, a member of the planning team, Tel Aviv, May 2009.
25 A. Israeli, *The Taanach Settlement: Planning versus Practice*, Haifa University, 1970.
26 E. Yalan, *Land Planning of Agricultural Settlement Physical Planning*, R.B.R.C, 1964.
27 N. Mezger-Szmuk, *The Romanov House-Documentation Survey*, op. cit.
28 M. Warhatig, *They Laid the Foundation*, op. cit., p. 257.
29 A letter by Tel Aviv city engineer, Dov Hershkowitz, to Adler (29.7.1924) includes a demand to change the building facades, claiming that 'The license to build ... will be received only after authorization [of] the changes to the facade, which must be presented to the Technical Department' in: N. Mezger-Szmuk, *The Romanov House-Documentation Survey*, op. cit.
30 Yaakov Shifman (Ben Sira), the municipal engineer of Tel Aviv between1929–1951, became known for his tendency to coerce planners into using modernist architecture alone.
31 David Izmuzik (1873–1953), one of Tel Aviv's merchants, traded in wood and building materials. He was a member of the City Council and for some time presided as the Vice-Mayor and as a board member of the Municipal Department of Commerce; see: M. Naor, A. Levinsohn, 'Who were the 66 founders of Tel Aviv?', *Idan* 3 (1984), pp. 5–31.

32 'Today the entire historic fabric of Ahuzat Bayit is already demolished', A. Brawer, 'Geography and Geography of Tel Aviv', in: A. Druyanov, *The Tel Aviv Book*, (Hebrew), Tel Aviv: Vaad Hasefer, 1936, p. 313.
33 Letter from Leo Adler to the municipal engineer Yaakov Shifman dated May 26, 1935, building file, Tel Aviv Engineering Department archives.
34 Y. Zimen, *The History of Nahalt Yitzhak*, Tel Aviv: David Tidhar, 1946, p. 73.
35 These two buildings, originally located at Rothschild Street number 1 or 3, were demolished during the 60s. I am grateful to Architect Shmuel Groag and Mr. Ya'akov Ziv, of the 'Bat Yam Founders' Association', for their assistance in trying to locate these buildings.
36 L. Adler, 'The Architecture in our country', (Hebrew) in: *Gazith*, 8–9 (1936), pp. 61–64.
37 Ibid.
38 L. Adler, 'Hygienic considerations in Ancient Construction', in: *The Journal of Architects and Engineers in Eretz Israel*, 1(1943) p. 3–5.
39 L. Adler, 'The Architecture in our country', op. cit.
40 *'Retour á Order'* – call for a return to order, characteristic of the French scene after the end of the First World War, in which even the futurist Gino Severini published in 1917 the manifesto *'Du Cubism au Classicisme'* ; see: K. Frampton, 'Rappel a l'Order: the case for the Tectonic'. In: Nesbitt, Kate (ed). *Theorizing a new agenda for Architecture: an anthology of architectural theory*. New York: Princeton Architectural Press, 1990. p. 516–526.
41 R. Banham, *Theory and Design in The First Machine Age* (Hebrew version), Tel Aviv: Dvir, 1978. pp. 210–258.
42 F. Borsi, 1987. *The Monumental Era*, New York: Rizzoli, 1987, pp. 9–13; B. Miller-Lane, *Architecture and Politics in Germany 1918–1945*, Cambridge, MA: Harvard University Press, 1968, pp. 189–196; R. Etlin, *Modernism in Italian Architecture 1890–1940*. Massachusetts: MIT Press, 1991, pp. 391–438.
43 L. Adler, 'The Architecture in our country', op. cit.
44 Ibid.
45 L. Adler, 'Why? Impressions of a New Immigrant', *Habiyan*, 1 (1943), p. 11.
46 Ibid.
47 'The Architecture in our country', op. cit.
48 L. Adler, 'Modernistisces in Italien' Sttutgart und so wiiter', *Wathmus Monatshefte für Baukunst*, 2(1927), pp. 402–406.
49 L. Adler, 'The Architecture in our country', op. cit.
50 Ibid.
51 Ibid.
52 Ibid.
53 Ibid.
54 L. Adler, 'Hygienic considerations in Ancient Construction', op. cit.
55 Ibid.
56 Y. Hirschfeld, *Dwelling Houses in Roman and Byzantine Palestine*. Jerusalem: Yad Ben-Zvi, 1986, pp 7–54.
57 L. Adler, 'The Architecture in our country', op. cit.
58 Ibid.
59 Ibid.
60 It is claimed that the colonnaded street first developed in Alexandria, in Egypt, and in Delos in Greece, but there are those who also mention Josephus Flavius (Joseph ben Mattitiyahu), who describes in his writings a colonnaded street in Antioch as the first colonnaded street. Others consider the colonnaded avenues built in the second and first centuries BCE in Ostia and Pompeii as the source of this urban element. It actually seems that the *stoa* inspired the colonnaded avenue, or more precisely the changes that this architectonic element underwent at the end of the Hellenistic period; see: A. Segal, *From Function to Monument: Urban Landscape of Roman Palestine, Syria,*

and Provincial Arabia, Oxford: Oxford Books, 1997; Y, Tsafrir, *Eretz Israel from the Destruction of the Second Temple to the Muslim Conquest* (Hebrew), Jerusalem: Yad Ben-Zvi, 1984. pp. 59–99; J. Ward-Perkins, 'From Republic to Empire: Reflections on Early Provincial Architecture in The Roman East', in: *Journal of Roman Studies*, 55(1979), pp. 1–19.61 Y. Tsafrir, ibid.

62 B. Rudofsky, 1982. *Streets for People*, New York: Reinhold, 1982.
63 For example, Zeev Rechter's plan for the new Tel Aviv synagogue compound (1938), in: M. Zak, *Zeev*, (Hebrew, exhibition catalogue) Tel-Aviv: Halalait, 2009, p. 6.
64 Early research by Kohl and Watzinger emphasized that regional Hellenist-Roman influence on ancient Eretz Israel architecture served as the basis of the modern research on synagogue Architecture; see: H. Kohl, C. Watzinger, *Antike Synagogen in Galilaea*, Leipzig: 1916.
65 On national meaning of Hebrew archeology see: M. Fiege, 'Introduction', in: M. Fiege, Z, Shiloni. Archeology and Nationalism in Eretz Israel, Sede Boker: Ben Gurion Research Institute, 2008; Y. Ben-Arie, 'Jewish of General Archeology: Study of the Land of Israel before 1948', (Hebrew),ibid, pp. 19–42.
66 S. Fine (editor), *Art and Judaism in the Greco-Roman World*, Cambridge, MA. 2005.
67 The modern synagogues of Europe built during the 19th century were designed in neo-classical, neo-Gothic and neo-Muslim styles. German Jewry was characterized by its use of the neo-classical style, and afterwards by similar receptiveness to 'new building' (*Neues Bauen*), see: Brenner, M. *Renaissance of Jewish Culture in Weimar Germany*, (Hebrew), Jerusalem; Merkaz Shazar, 2003, pp. 154–184.
68 S. Krois. 'Habsilica ba- Talmud' (Hebrew), *Ha-Shiloach* , 221 (1931), pp. 1–16.
69 Ibid.
70 Y. Ben-Arie, 'Eretz-Israel Historical–Geography Literature in the 19th Century'. (Hebrew), in: Y. Ben-Arie, (2001). *A Land reflected in its past*, Jerusalem: The Hebrew University Magnes Press. pp. 239–253.
71 L. Adler. 'Hygienic considerations in Ancient Construction'. op. cit.
72 On Winckelmann, see: M. Barasch, Approaches To Art 1750–1950 (Hebrew), Jerusalem: Mosad Biyalik,1977, pp. 29–34.
73 D. Watkin, *The Rise of Architectural History*, London: Architectural Press, 1983; D. Watkin, M. Tilman, *German Architecture and the Classical Ideal,* Cambridge, MA: MIT Press, 1986, pp. 8–15.
74 L. Adler. 'Hygienic considerations in Ancient Construction'. op. cit.
75 Ibid.
76 Ibid.
77 Y. Shavit, D. Mendesohn, 'The Discovery of Italy and The "South" in European Literature' (Hebrew), in Y. Shavit (editor) '*A Mediterranean Anthology*, Tel Aviv: Yediot Ahronot, Tel Aviv University, 2004. pp. 51–67.
78 Ibid.
79 Y. Ben-Artzi, 'The Mediterranean Regio in the German Geography during the 19th and the 20th Century' (Hebrew), in Y. Shavit, (editor) *A Mediterranean Anthology*, op. cit. pp. 175–195.
80 L. Adler, 'Why? Impressions of a New Immigrant', op. cit.
81 Y. Shavit, *Judaism in the Greek Mirror and the Emergence of Modern Hellenized Jew.* Tel Aviv: Am Oved. pp. 360–378.
82 Y. Klein, 'Zionist Disputes Reflected in Urban Patterns and Architectural Styles in Ahuzat Bayit', op. cit., pp. 22–35.
83 L. Adler, 'The Architecture in our country', op. cit.
84 L. Adler. 'Hygienic considerations in Ancient Construction'. op. cit.
85 Thus, for example, Yoseph Neufeld, editor of the *Habinyan*, defines Eretz Israel architecture as 'organic', and dependent on nature. Tel Aviv city engineer Ya'akov Shifman describes his preference for open, semi-rural urban planning; this trend changed partly after 1948.

86 M. Zaidman, R. Kark, 'The Beginnings of Tel Aviv: The Ahuzat bayit Nieghbourhood as a 'Garden city'?, *Zmanin*, 106 (2009). pp. 8–21.
87 R. Laurence, 'Writing the Roman Metropolis', Parkins, H. (ed.), *Roman Urbanism*, London: Routledge, 1997, pp. 1–21.
88 L. Adler, 1928. 'Jüdische Kunstfeindlichkeit', *Menorah*, 1, pp. 52–57.
89 Nazi propaganda dubbed modern architecture as 'Semitic' and 'Jewish'; such racist and xenophobic views are expressed in a photo montage in which the *Weissenhof* exhibition in Stuttgart (1927) was described as a Semitic 'Arab village'. The innovations presented at this modernist exhibition were one of the sources for planning the modern architecture of the 'White City' of Tel Aviv. See: K. Kirsch, Karin, *The Weissenhofsiedlung*, New York: Rizzoli, 1989. p. 200.
90 L. Adler, 1926. *Vom Wesen der Baukunst*, Leipzig: Verlag der Asia Major, pp. 109–112.
91 E. Pavlides, 'Four Approaches to Regionalism in Architecture', in: Aanizaro, Vincent (editor), *Architectural Regionalism-collected writings on Place, Identity, Modernity and Tradition*, New York: Princeton Architectural Press, 2007. pp. 157–167.
92 Ibid.
93 Ibid.

8 Double exclusion and the search for inessential solidarities

The experience of Iraqi Jews as heralding a new concept of identity and belonging

Reuven Snir

> Woe to those who, to the very end, insist on regulating the movement that exceeds them with the narrow mind of the mechanic who changes a tire.
>
> (Georges Bataille)[1]

Introduction

The chapter deals with the changes in the concept of identity and belonging among Iraqi Jews, especially the Baghdadi among them, during the 20th century. My main argument is that due to some processes that the Iraqi Jews had experienced and because of some global developments, they gradually developed a negative sensitivity toward the notion of stable identity, whatever identity; asserting instead their particular singularities and searching for alternative forms of identification, mostly various kinds of inessential solidarity and belonging. From a sample of partial investigations, however, I have a solid basis for the hypothesis that the same developments have occurred, if in different rhythms and intensity, among other communities of Arabized Jews[2] as well.

In the last section of his essay 'Ideology and Ideological State Apparatuses (Notes towards an Investigation)' (1971),[3] the French Marxist philosopher Louis Pierre Althusser (1918–1990) coined the term 'interpellation', theorizing the constitutive process by which individuals acknowledge and respond to ideologies, thereby recognizing themselves as subjects. Stating that (a) 'there is no practice except by and in an ideology'; and (b) 'there is no ideology except by the subject and for subjects', Althusser comes to his central thesis that 'Ideology Interpellates Individuals as Subjects' (p. 160). Althusser defines ideological recognition as the act of 'interpellation', of identification of a subject and that subject's recognition of himself as the one addressed ('hailing') – this recognition 'guarantee[s] for us that we are indeed concrete, individual, distinguishable and (natural) irreplaceable subjects.' To be interpellated is to identify with a particular idea or identity; it is the process by which you recognize yourself to belong to a particular identity. To illustrate how interpellation functions in the context of ideology, Althusser used the example of the policeman who shouts 'Hey, you there!'. At least one

Double exclusion and the search for inessential solidarities 141

individual will turn around (most likely the right one) to 'answer' that call. At this moment, when one realizes that the call is for oneself, one becomes a subject relative to an ideology, and in that case, the ideology of law and crime. This is the way in which ideology generally functions, as we are all always caught up in the process in which we voluntarily acknowledge the validity or relevance of some ideology in which we live for ourselves and thus subject ourselves to it. Ideology functions as a mediator between systems of power and individuals; it allows for hegemonic power to reproduce itself by obscuring traditional forms of repression and incorporating individuals into the power structure.

The process of identification creates identity and we recognize ourselves when we are hailed – you identify me and I become that me that you have identified. I know that it is me who is being called as I unconsciously accept the subject position and my subjectivity is thus created or modified – it is as if I had always already been there. By subjectivity I mean the inner life processes and affective states as they have been expressed in words, images, institutions, and behaviors, through which people actually represent themselves to themselves and to one another. This understanding is accompanied by the awareness that subjects are themselves unfinished and unfinishable as well as by the recognition that, because individuals are members of cross-cutting and often conflicting associations, subjectivity and characterization shift widely between multiple perspectives and no single analytic framework can fully account for the inner lives of people and their intersubjective relations.[4] The apparent freedom with which we recognize and accept that position only serves to cement us further into it. Interpellation can be considered as 'recruitment' as it invites a person into a subject position, but it is rarely as specific as being addressed by name, as it is rather being addressed as a member of an audience or any collective. One can immediately see the connection between interpellation and rhetoric, as I will elaborate on below. When we recognize that we are being spoken to, we not only engage more deeply with the hailing, we also accept the social role being offered to us: young, white, female, gay, athletic, liberal, etc, and in the context of our present study: Arab, Jew, Muslim, Israeli, Zionist, as well as Mizrahi, Levantine, Oriental, Sephardi, Black, etc. Speaking about terminology, it should be noted that while the term 'Mizrahi' had been invented by the systems of power, it has also been used as a subversive catchword by militant Middle Eastern and North African Jewish intellectuals and activists to express resistance to the conception of Israel as a Zionist and Western country.[5]

For the purpose of my investigation into the identities of Arabized Jews throughout the documented history of the last sixteen centuries (the first known Arabic text by a Jew was attributed to Sārra al-Qurayẓiyya, whose elegy for 350 noblemen of her tribe killed in a battle in 492 AD has been frequently cited in Arabic sources[6]), I have broadened the scope of interpellation to encompass all human interactions. This process, in Althusser's analysis, occurs chiefly through Ideological State Apparatuses (ISAs) – public/private education, media, religion, the family, etc –and, when necessary, Repressive State Apparatuses (RSAs) – the police, the army. But since we are always already in ideology, we generate systems of ideologies ourselves, always already implicated as subjects of and subjects (re)producing interpellation. 'Man is an ideological animal by nature,' says Althusser (p. 160), and therefore as 'good' subjects we are always already interpellating others as 'subjects' in the 'work' of achieving our own recognition.

When Althusser published his essay, the concept of 'identity' had actually started to become a prism through which many dimensions of contemporary life were spotted, grasped and examined. In the late 1960s and early 1970s, Robert Jay Lifton had already published his preliminary versions about what he called 'the protean self', after Proteus, the Greek sea god of many forms. Referring to the many-sided self that is in constant motion, Lifton suggested that in the modern world we were becoming 'fluid and many sided. Without quite realizing it, we have been evolving a sense of self appropriate to the restlessness and flux of our time.' The protean self emerges from confusion, from the widespread feeling that we are losing our psychological moorings. We change ideas and partners frequently, and do the same with jobs and places of residence. Whether dealing with world problems or child rearing, our behavior tends to be ad hoc, more or less decided upon as we go along. We are beset by a contradiction: schooled in the virtues of constancy and stability – whether as individuals, groups, or nations – our world and our lives seem inconstant and utterly unpredictable. We readily come to view ourselves as unsteady, neurotic, or worse.[7]

Throughout the last three or four decades, scholars have pointed out the veritable discursive explosion around the concept of identity: the critique of the self-sustaining subject at the centre of post-Cartesian Western metaphysics has been comprehensively advanced in philosophy; the question of subjectivity and its unconscious processes of formation has been developed within the discourse of a psychoanalytically influenced feminism and cultural criticism; the endlessly performative self has been advanced in celebratory variants of postmodernism. Within the antiessentialist critique of ethnic, racial and national conceptions of cultural identity and the 'politics of location', some adventurous theoretical conceptions have been sketched in their most grounded forms. What, then, 'is the need', asks Stuart Hall in 1996, 'for a further debate about "identity"? Who needs it?'.[8] In 2009, however, Zygmunt Bauman still refers to the same 'discursive explosion' around the concept of identity which has even 'triggered an avalanche'.[9]

In the labyrinths of these theoretical and sometimes bewildering discussions about identity, one can notice that most deliberations have been conducted around two models: the first assumes that there is an essential content to any identity which is defined by common origin or common structure of experience. The second one, which stands in the centre of the present study, emphasizes the impossibility of fully separate distinct identities. Any identity depends upon its difference from some other identity – 'identity is a structured representation which only achieves its positive through the narrow eye of the negative', writes Hall, 'it has to go through the eye of the needle of the other before it can construct itself.'[10] Identity is thus always a temporary and unstable effect of relations that define identities by marking differences, which means that the multiplicity of identities and differences and the emphasis on connections or articulations between the fragments or differences are inevitable. While identity of someone cannot be explored or challenged without a simultaneous investigation of another, this is rarely the case in practice and most investigations in cultural studies deal with the construction of subaltern, marginalized or dominated identities. Rarely are the two ever studied together, as mutually constitutive, as the theory would seem to dictate.

Also, identities arise from the narrativization of the self, but the necessarily fictional nature of this narrativization in no way undermines its discursive, material or political effectivity, even if the belongingness, the 'suturing into the story' through which identities arise, is partly in the imaginary (as well as the symbolic) and therefore always partly constructed in fantasy, or at least within the fantasmatic field. Identities refer to the meeting point, that very point of *suture*, between on the one hand the discourses and practices that attempt to interpellate, speak to us or hail us into place as the social subjects of particular discourses, and on the other hand, the processes that produce subjectivities, which construct us as subjects who can be 'spoken'. All identities are thus only 'points of temporary attachment to the subject position which discursive practices construct for us.'[11] Because we are always in the process of being exposed to new interpellating machines and processes, reacting always consciously *and* unconsciously to them with our own complicated and unique singular subjectivities, there is no escape from elusiveness and fluidity. Bauman describes contemporary society as a place in which everything is elusive, and where the disorientation and insecurity caused by living in society cannot be solved by parading past certainties and established systems.[12] In other words, identities deal with the past only on the exterior level, simply because they cannot be but present- and future-oriented projects: they are about questions of using the resources of history, language and culture in the process of becoming rather than being: not 'who we are' or 'where we came from' so much as 'what we might become', 'how we have been represented' and 'how that bears on how we might represent ourselves'.[13]

Postmodernity and globalization have undoubtedly problematized and invigorated even more the notion of identity. In traditional pre-modern[14] societies, one's identity was generally fixed, solid, and stable. One was born and died a member of one's clan, of a fixed kinship system, and of one's tribe or group with one's life trajectory fixed in advance. Identity was not problematical and, at most, not subject to any reflection or discussion. Individuals did not undergo identity crises, or radically modify their identity, at least not in the contemporary sense. In modernity, however, identity becomes more mobile, multiple, personal, self-reflexive, and subject to change and innovation. It becomes also social and Other-related – the Other is a constituent of identity in modernity – but its form is also relatively limited, fixed and substantial, though the boundaries of possible identities are continually expanding. There is still a structure of interaction with socially defined and available roles, norms, customs, and expectations, among which one must choose, appropriate, and reproduce in order to gain identity in a complex process of mutual recognition, but in modernity identity becomes increasingly problematical, and, more than that, the issue of identity itself becomes a problem – how we constitute, perceive, interpret, and present our self to ourselves and others.[15] Postmodern thought has by and large rejected the essentialist and rationalist notion of identity building on the constructivist notion, which it in turn problematizes. Postmodern identity tends more to be constructed from *images of leisure and consumption* and is liable to be more unstable and subject to change. Both modern and postmodern identities contain a level of reflexivity, an awareness that identity is chosen and constructed. In contemporary society, however, it may be more 'natural' to change identities, to switch with the *changing winds of fashion*. While this produces an erosion of individuality and increased social conformity, there are some positive potentials of this portrayal of identity as an *artificial construct*. For such a notion of identity suggests that one can always change one's life, that identity can always be reconstructed, that one is free to change and produce oneself as one chooses.[16] In other words, identity becomes a freely chosen game, a *theatrical presentation of the self*, in which one is able to present oneself unconcerned about shifts, transformations and dramatic changes.[17]

If the modern problem of identity was how to construct an identity and keep it solid and stable, the postmodern challenge is how to avoid fixation and keep all options open: the catchword of modernity was *creation* while the catchword of postmodernity is *recycling*.[18] We are 'migrant animals in the labyrinths of the metropolis', says Alberto Melucci, 'in reality or in the imagination, we participate in an infinity of worlds. And each of these worlds has a culture, a language, and a set of roles and rules that we must adapt to whenever we migrate from one to another.'[19] Thus, added Melucci, we are subjected to mounting pressures to change, to transfer, to translate what we were just a moment ago into new codes and new forms of relation. We transform ourselves into sensitive terminals, transmitting and receiving a quantity of information that far exceeds that of any previous culture. Related to our migration in the labyrinths of the global village is the impact of the internet, which has been enthusiastically embraced so far by more than a quarter of the world population. Communication through the internet, more than through other means, enables us not to stick to one identity but to play with our identities. I am not speaking about creating fake identities but about the way the internet provides us with the ability not to commit ourselves to a single identity.

More than that, in an article published in 2006[20] Ulrich Beck and Natan Sznaider called for a re-conceptualization of the humanities and social sciences by asking for a cosmopolitan turn. There is no uniform interpretation of cosmopolitanism, and the boundaries separating it from competitive terms such as globalization, transnationalism, universalism, and glocalization are not distinct; internally it is traversed by all kinds of fault lines.[21] Yet all other concepts presuppose basic dualisms, such as *domestic/foreign, national/international, local/global, us/them*, all of which in reality have become ambiguous. In fact, all these dualities have dissolved and merged together in new forms that require new conceptual analysis. The basic idea is that the light of the great cultural problems has moved on from a nation state definition of society and politics – the modern construct of the nation state is under constant pressure from the forces of globalization – to a cosmopolitan outlook, which means that in doing research or theorizing we cannot anymore take it for granted that society is equated with national society, and the unit of analysis should not be the national society or the national state or the combination of both.

The recent changes and developments in the attitude to the notions of identity and belonging are thus a natural outcome of the intense globalization, the wide migration, the growing social and political uncertainty and insecurity, the development of communication, and the cosmopolitan turn; all this in addition to the heritage of postmodernism, post-structuralism, psychoanalysis and post-feminism. They could not have happened, however, without what has been described as the market triumphalism in our era, which has witnessed 'the expansion of markets and market-oriented reasoning into spheres of life traditionally governed by non-market norms.'[22] All of us are '*in* and *on* the market', says Bauman, 'simultaneously customers and commodities. No wonder that the use/consumption of human relations and so, by proxy, also our identities … catches up, and fast, with the pattern of car use/consumption, imitating the cycle that starts from purchase and ends with waste disposal.'[23] More than 70 years after Robert Musil's *The Man Without Qualities* (1930), Bauman suggested the 'Man without Bonds' as the hero of our liquid modern society: 'if you wish "to relate", keep your distance; if you want fulfillment from your togetherness, do not make or demand commitments. Keep all doors open at any time.'[24]

These changes could not have happened either without the classlessness of the bourgeoisie: 'If we had once again to conceive of the fortunes of humanity in terms of class', says Giorgio Agamben, 'then today we would have to say that there are no longer social classes, but just a single planetary petty bourgeoisie, in which all the old social classes are dissolved: The petty bourgeoisie has inherited the world and is the form in which humanity has survived nihilism.'[25] Global capitalism, explains René ten Bos, 'is indifferent to whether products are being sold to Moslems, Christians, Buddhists, Hindu, or atheists. It is also indifferent to national or political identities. It only takes an interest in anonymous and acquisitive citizens.'[26]

Processes of collective interpellation and exclusion

In the modern history of the Iraqi Jews, we may notice some processes that already around the middle of the twentieth century led to the creation of embryonic forms of such singular subjectivities, which some decades later would be celebrated globally, as we have just shown, among intellectual and academic circles in the West. The following analysis is based on an investigation of the subjectivities and singularities of more than a hundred Iraqi-Jewish intellectuals, writers, and artists (see the list at the end of the chapter).[27] As previously mentioned, I have a solid basis for the hypothesis that the same developments have occurred among other communities of Arabized Jews as well. Because the Iraqi Jews have been the topic of my studies during the last two decades, I will concentrate here on them. Also, I will try to trace the exclusionary operations that the Iraqi Jews experienced during the last century. 'Once it is understood that subjects are formed through exclusionary operations', says feminist theorist Joan Scott, 'it becomes necessary to trace the operations of that construction and erasure.'[28] The Iraqi Jews as a whole experienced during the twentieth century at least four major processes of collective interpellation, two of them at the same time intense exclusionary operations and erasure:

1. Hailing the Iraqi Jews as Arabs.
2. Hailing the Iraqi Jews as 'Zionist' (*first exclusion*).
3. Hailing the Iraqi Jews as 'Arabs' (*second exclusion*).
4. Hailing the Iraqi Jews as one side in a binary monolithic category.

The quotation marks around 'Zionist' and 'Arabs' in the second and third processes (the first and the second operations of exclusion) mean that, in each case, the hailing ascribed to them a specific identity, while at the same time ignoring whether the subjectivities of the interpellated people were at all ready to positively respond to such a hailing. I have focused my investigations on the ways by which Iraqi Jews articulated their cultural preferences, defined their identities, and expressed their identification and belonging before and after their immigration. In other words, I am interested more in their subjectivities and less in the identities ascribed to them.

Before elaborating on the four processes, it is essential, as I previously pointed out, to emphasize the necessary connection between interpellation, rhetoric, and identity – after all, Parmenides's question of 'the one and the many', of the self's relation to others, is a problem not only for philosophy but also for rhetoric, which interests itself in the speaker or writer's capacity to engage and to move an audience, to have an effect on others.[29] Offering a rhetoric of relationality that hypothesizes no unity of self, no positive identity as such, Kenneth Burke turns our attention toward the question of the *many in the one*, suggesting that what goes for one's individual 'substance' amounts to the incalculable totality of one's complex and contradictory identifications, which are never reducible to one identity. Starting with a 'weak' or inessential subject that cannot rest upon itself, Burke argues that there is no identity, no one at all, that has not already been identified and hailed into existence as a subject via the very others to which it would address itself. This rhetoric necessarily presumes an exposed and so radically non-self-sufficient and non-figurable 'subject' – we might in fact say that it presumes *love's* subject.[30] We are clearly in the region of rhetoric, says Burke, when considering the identifications whereby a specialized activity makes one a participant in some social or economic class. 'Belonging' in this sense is rhetorical.[31] Burke's rhetor is charged with hailing his audience into existence, pulling together a community of readers or citizens by figuring them as such and prompting them to identify with some representable condition of belonging that they are presumed to hold in common. The rhetor's task, adds Carolyn Miller, is *'to construct one out of many, over and over again.'*[32] Barbara Biesecker refers to 'the power of persuasive discourse to constitute audiences out of individuals, to transform singularities into collectives, *to fashion a "we" out of a plurality of "I's"*, and to move them to collective action.'[33]

First process: The Jews are Arabs

From the late nineteenth century and even after the 1917 Balfour Declaration, the Jews living in Arab societies had been hailed, in one way or another, as Arabs; they were considered part of the Arab collective from the linguistic aspect – they spoke Arabic. In the conclusion to his four-volume *Ta'rīkh al-Ṣiḥāfa al-'Arabiyya* (History of the Arab Press), the pioneer scholar of Arabic journalism, Philip de Ṭarrāzī, wrote in 1933 about Islam, Christianity and Judaism as 'the leading religions to which the Arabic writers of the world belong'.[34] The Balfour Declaration was considered by many Arabized Jews as encapsulating the vision and hopes of only European Ashkenazi Jews. For most of the Iraqi Jews, the idea of establishing a Jewish nation state in Palestine was at the time a far-off cloud, totally undesired. Sir Arnold Talbot Wilson (1884–1940), the Acting Civil Commissioner in Mesopotamia (1918–1920), wrote in 1936 that he discussed the declaration with several members of the Jewish community and they remarked that Palestine was a poor country, and Jerusalem a bad town to live in. Compared with Palestine, Mesopotamia was a Paradise. 'This is the Garden of Eden', said one of the Jews, 'it is from this country that Adam was driven forth – give us a good government and we will make this country flourish – for us Mesopotamia is a home, a national home to which the Jews of Bombay and Persian and Turkey will be glad to come. Here shall be liberty and with it opportunity! In Palestine there may be liberty, but there will be no opportunity.'[35]

The real national vision of most of the Iraqi Jews at the time, certainly of the intellectual secular élite, was Iraqi and Arab. It was a vision that had its roots in the nineteenth century with the start of the process of secularization, when cultural barriers between the Jews and the wider local society had begun to crumble. The connection between interpellation, rhetoric and identity was expressed, for example, by Emir Fayṣal (1883–1933); on 18 July 1921, one month before his coronation as King of Iraq, he addressed the Jewish community leaders:

> In the vocabulary of patriotism, there is no such thing as Jew, a Muslim, or a Christian. There is simply one thing called Iraq. ... I ask all the Iraqi children of my homeland to be just Iraqis, because we all belong to one origin and one tree, the tree of our ancestor Shem, and all of us are related to the Semitic root, which makes no distinction between Muslim, Christian or Jew. ... Today we have but one means [to our end]: influential patriotism.[36]

The aim of Fayṣal was to create 'an independent strong Arab state, which will be a cornerstone for Arab unity' – the Jewish citizens were an integral part of that vision. Sāṭi' al-Ḥuṣrī (1880–1968), Director General of Education in Iraq (1923–

1927) and Arab nationalism's first true ideologue, argued that 'every person who is related to the Arab lands and speaks Arabic is an Arab'.[37] The Iraqi constitution of 21 March 1925 (al-Qānūn al-Asāsī al-'Irāqī) stated that 'there is no difference between the Iraqi people in rights before the law, even if they belong to different nationalities, religions and languages'.[38]

The evident inclusive rhetorical expressions toward the Jews and the hailing of them as Arabs should not be surprising since Arab nationalists at their earliest phases had already considered the Jews living among Arabs as part of the Arab 'race'. A manifesto of Arab nationalists disseminated from Cairo by the Arab Revolutionary Committee at the beginning of the First World War, some sections of which were published from Istanbul in a French translation in 1916, served as a strong interpellating machine: 'Arabes chrétiens et israélites unissez-vous à vos frères musulmans. N'écoutez pas ceux qui disent qu'ils préfèrent les Turcs sans religion aux Arabes de croyances différentes; ce sont des ignorants qui méconnaissent les intérêts vitaux de la race.'[39] Another manifesto printed in December 1918 in Damascus hailed the children of all three monotheistic religions as Arabs: 'You are Arabs before you are Muslims, before you are Christians, and before you are Jews. The Land is your land and the fatherland is your fatherland, and you must join together to defend its independence.'[40]

It is thus not surprising to find the intellectual secular élite of the Jews in Iraq rallying behind the efforts to make it a state for all its citizens – Muslims, Christians and Jews. Even in the late 1930s, Iraqi-Jewish educator 'Ezra Ḥaddād (1900–1972) declared that 'we are Arabs before we are Jews' (naḥnu 'Arab qabla an nakūna yahūda).[41] On 20 July 1938, his compatriot the poet Anwar Shā'ul (1904–1984) emphasized the Arabism of the Iraqi Jews and their rejection of Zionism.[42] Another Iraqi-Jewish writer, Ya'qūb Balbūl (1920–2003), indicated that 'a Jewish youth in the Arab countries expects nothing from Zionism other than colonialism and domination.'[43] The English historian of Lebanese origin A.H. Hourani (1915–1993) wrote in 1947 that 'the Iraqi Jews, like the Oriental Jews, are for the most part not Zionists by conviction; some of them indeed profess to Arab nationalism and are hostile to Zionism.'[44] In his survey of Jewish Communities in the Muslim Countries of the Middle East, published in 1950, the German scholar Siegfried Landshut (1897–1968) wrote that except for a natural interest in developments in Palestine, there has never in Iraq been any feeling of solidarity with the political aspirations of Zionism.[45] Considering themselves an integral part of Arab-Muslim culture and the Iraqi nation, Iraqi Jews were full of confidence that Iraq was their only homeland and that the Jewish community in Iraq would endure; as Iraqi-Jewish writer Shālom Darwīsh (1913–1997) was to put it, 'to the days of the Messiah'.[46]

Second process: The Jews are 'Zionist' (first exclusion)

Siegfried Kracauer (1995) makes a distinction between two kinds of communities: On the one hand, there are 'communities of life and fate', whose members 'live together in an indissoluble attachment rather than being welded together solely by ideas or various principles'. Instances of this kind are the family and the nation: they envelop any person born into them just the way he is, from his birth through to his death and even beyond his death. These communities, whose origins and purposes are irrational, devote themselves to an 'endless multiplicity of objectives, though they never find their definitive significance in any of them'. On the other hand, there are those communities whose accord is based on an idea with which they arise and perish. Their unity 'is not an immanent part of organic, growing life, but is fully encompassed by a specific concept that will come to life through them'.[47]

For the Jews, Iraqi society was certainly of the first kind: it was a community of life and fate whose members had been living together in an indissoluble attachment. Suddenly, however, that community was denied to them and they were excluded as the 'Others' – they were not considered *true* Iraqis and *real* Arabs anymore. It was the Balfour Declaration that started a process which interpellated the Iraqi Jews into Zionism, while at the same time interpellated the Arab Muslims and Christians as a unified Arab community calling upon themselves to operate exclusionary operations against Jews, whatever Jews. Because of the escalation of the Arab-Jewish conflict over Palestine during the late 1940s and the beginning of the 1950s, the Iraqi-Arab identity of the Jews, which had been firmly consolidated during the 1920s and 1930s, underwent a speedy fragmentation in a way that left them no alternative but to immigrate. Among the immigrants we can hardly find even one, no matter what his political point of view, who did not lament that exclusion. Here it should be noted that the controversy of whether the Arabized Jews lived in perfect harmony with Muslims and Christians or whether this is only a myth current in left-wing intellectuals is irrelevant. At any event, unlike popular conceptions, the well-known myth of 'golden age' and harmonious Muslim-Jewish relations prior to the rise of Zionism, as well as the 'neo-lachrymose' countermyth, which views Jewish history under Arab Islam as a story of intolerance, persecution and unending nightmare of oppression and humiliation, are both highly exaggerated and no serious professional scholar of Jewish history under Islam holds to either of them.[48]

After the immigration of the Iraqi Jews to Israel, their subjectivities, certainly those of their offspring, were gradually 'enriched' by new components of identity, the most outstanding of which were the Zionist, the Israeli, and the Hebrew layers of identity. No Arabized Jew who immigrated to Israel could resist the strong interpellating processes administered by the State, not even those in whose subjectivities the Arab component was dominant. The new Zionist-Israeli rhetoric of identity overwhelmingly swept all of them.

The Zionist and Israeli processes of interpellation lead us to both the third and fourth processes of interpellation which the Iraqi Jews have experienced. These processes were somehow temporally overlapping, though we refer to them here as two different processes. I mean the hailing of them as a population in need of 'education' due to their *Arabness* (primitiveness), and at the same time, the hailing of them, together with all other communities of Arabized Jews in Israel, as a monolithic population.

Third process: The Jews are 'Arabs' (second exclusion)

The third process of interpellation is thus the second exclusion of the Iraqi Jews, this time in Israel. After their exclusion in Iraq, they realized that they were excluded again, and now precisely because of their Arabness, by none but their fellow coreligionists. Before their immigration, they had found themselves excluded because of their *Jewish* identity, and now, in Israel, they found themselves excluded because of their *Arab* identity. Both exclusions were based on a kind of unspoken agreement and a substantial identity of interests between both national movements, Zionism and Arab nationalism, seeing *Jewishness* as equated with *Zionism* and later even with *Israeliness*, to the point that the three identities have been considered by both movements as virtually synonymous. In order to be part of the new Israeli-Jewish-Zionist collective, the immigrants were encouraged to change their Arab names, to stop using Arabic in public spaces, to train themselves to adopt Israeli-Hebrew culture, to remodel their family patters, to 'refine' their life style, etc. In retrospect, many of the Arabized Jews would consider this process as a 'cultural ethnic cleansing'.[49] They were Jews and they immigrated to the state of the Jews, but they discovered that Israeli society was not for them a community in which they could live together with the others, in Kracauer's terms, in 'an indissoluble attachment'. For most of them, certainly after their very immigration, the bond with the other Jewish majority members was only a bond of religion.

But there was another process, simultaneous and overlapping, to that process: the second exclusion was accompanied by labeling the immigrants as one side in an evaluative binary.

Fourth process: The immigrants are Sephardim, 'Edot Mizrah, Mizrahim, etc.

For the purpose of my argument, there is no difference if the monolithic category is Sephardim, *'Edot Mizrah*, Mizrahim, Easterners, Orientals, Levantines or any derogatory name like blacks, Franks or Aryeh Gelblum's description of one community of Arabized Jews as 'people whose primitivism is at a peak, whose level of knowledge is one of virtually absolute ignorance, and worse, who have little talent for understanding anything intellectual.'[50] Now, it is widely recognized that any such monolithic category is inadequate, but this insight of the inadequateness of the monolithic hailing had always been a matter of fact among all communities of Arabized Jews, certainly among the Iraqis. In their reflections on the study of Middle Eastern Jewries within the context of Israeli society, Harvey E. Goldberg and Chen Bram showed how 'analysis based on explicit and implicit binary models skews the understanding of some historical developments'. Furthermore, 'critical approaches have provided useful insights into how hegemonic structures have excluded Jews defined as "Eastern", but have been less successful in documentation and grasping developments reflecting the distinctiveness and creative categories and assumptions of those groups themselves.'[51] From my investigations into the identities of the Arabized Jews from Iraq – and I do not have any reason to believe that something fundamentally different happened with Arabized Jews immigrating from other places – it is clear that Goldberg and Bram were too cautious in their critical comments of the binary-oriented analytical methods and critical approaches.

Such monolithic categories were never adopted by Arabized Jews in the way they were meant to interpellate and hail them by the systems of power. From the point of view of the Iraqi Jews, this process of interpellation has been the weakest among all four processes. But it has served the aims of the state and of the dominant and hegemonic systems and structures, precisely as any exclusionary operations serve the aims of any state or any system of power. The influence of such a process was very significant but by no means in the direction the interpellating systems desired, particularly because it coincided with the previously mentioned global processes that created the tendency to escape into inessential subjectivities and to prefer singularities, and also because it did not take into account the double exclusion of the previous two processes. Unfortunately, for political and ideological reasons, scholars have preferred mostly so far to emphasize only one side of that double exclusion – either that exercised in the Arab countries before the Jews' immigration, or that exercised in Israel after their immigration. Measured in their combined effect, the significance of both exclusionary operations cannot be underestimated. Most of the Iraqi Jews realized that what was very convenient for the State might be convenient for them as well as long as they could behave as singularities. What is the difference if I am personally hailed as Mizrahi, Sephardic, Easterner, *'Edot Mizrah*, Iraqi, Frank, Black or any other identity ascribed to me (and in person I have faced *all* those very labels), if I insist in my personal life to behave according to my own singularity without affirming, in my own subjectivity, any stable identity?

The search for Inessential solidarities

The global developments were not fully effective during the middle of the twentieth century, but the contemporary political, social and cultural circumstances had prepared the Iraqi Jews to gradually develop a negative sensitivity toward the notion of stable identity, whatever identity. If it were only the first exclusion, it would have sufficed for them to be aware that belonging and identity were not cut in a rock, and that they were not secured by a lifelong guarantee. What were they to expect after they would be excluded again in their very promised homeland, 'promised' by both those who pulled them – the Zionists – as well as by those who pushed them – the Iraqi authorities and the Arab national activists? Was there any chance for them to think that belonging and identity were cut in a rock? Following that very double exclusion, and after adapting and adjusting to the new Israeli society, they found themselves, separately and not collectively, preferring to assert their own singularities and at the same time to reject any essential identity. To paraphrase a declaration by writer Sami Michael (born 1926), each chose to build his own unique 'State' which consists of only one citizen – himself.[52] During less than half a century, they had witnessed a rapid process by which their Iraqi-Arab-Jewish identity was firmly consolidated (1920s to 1940s), to be followed by another process that resulted in its speedy fragmentation (1950–51). Many hoped that their uprooting from Iraq might be a blessing in disguise, dreaming that their immigration to the new Jewish land would guarantee for them a full integration into a unified new Israeli-Jewish identity without renouncing their Arabness. Instead of that, they were left excluded from both old and new identities.

It was thus the absurdity of both exclusionary operations that paved the way to the rejection of the notion of whatever fixed identity, simply because each of these operations was aiming at the heart of a *major* component of their identity: in Iraq, precisely when the Jews felt themselves *more Arab and Iraqi than Jewish*, they were excluded as the 'Other' Jews in a way that left them no alternative but to immigrate to the state of the Jews. In Israel, precisely when they should have felt themselves *more Jewish than Arab and Iraqi*, they were excluded as the 'Other' Iraqis and Arabs. But now, unlike the first exclusion, there was no other abode that would serve as a new promised haven. The political circumstances in the Middle East, which were the direct cause to that double exclusion, accelerated among many of the immigrants a tendency, which at the time was globally and universally still in its infancy, to reject in principle the notion of stable and fixed identities, to assert their particular singularities, and to search for alternative forms of identification, mostly various kinds of inessential solidarity and belonging. The local, regional, and global developments, sometimes simultaneous and overlapping, served as fertile ground for the formation among many of them of such a form of subjectivity which responded to the natural human need for identification and belonging and, at the same time, was flexible enough to provide them with some shield against additional frustrations and disappointments. Singularity has been the preferred option, but not by default. It has been a conscious choice which has fit the local, global, and, in most cases, the personal circumstances.

I believe that the aforementioned analysis of the subjectivities of the Iraqi Jews is also applicable, in one way or another, to other immigrants from Arab countries. There are of course significant differences between the Iraqi Jews and other Arabized immigrants, with respect to the attitude to Arabic language and culture. But I found that the tendency towards inessential solidarities had *nothing* to do with the Iraqi Jews' well-known Arab cultural preference; it was rather because of the two processes of exclusion, which most if not all the Arabized Jews had undergone. Already in the 1950s, three decades before the global/local dialectics could be clearly noticed in Israel as well, most of the intellectuals among the Arabized immigrants felt the same dialectics but tripled: global/regional/local – and this dialectics involved their very existence: as members of the Israeli-Hebrew society, they spoke *Hebrew* but they were also part of the *Arabic* speaking Middle East, and, at the same time, they could not escape the *global* developments. Whoever lived this double exclusion could not have adhered to any notion of stable identity and, if he wished to survive, he must have thought about the need to be flexible and adapt himself to the changing circumstances, emphasizing his own singularity in which each of the major layers of collective identities, such as Arabness, Jewishness, Hebrewness, Israeliness, Zionism and Communism, played a different role, in addition of course to various more specific components like gender, profession, hobby, local environment, etc.

As for the new generation of Neo-Arab-Jewish intellectuals, those radical Mizrahi leftist scholars such as Yehuda Shenhav (born 1952), Ella Shohat (born 1959), Sami Shalom Chetrit (born 1960) and their followers, it seems that all of them adopted Arab-Jewish or Mizrahi identity as part of identity politics in Israel, which is not isolated from what appears to be switching with the changing winds of fashion during the last decades. Following Edward Hallet Carr's constructive suggestion 'to study the historian before you begin to study the facts',[53] I have studied the 'identities' of the three of them in the same way I have studied the subjectivities of the Iraqi-Jewish writers and intellectuals during the last century. It is paradoxical that my investigations have led me to one solid conclusion: all of them have been recycling their identities according to changing circumstances, preferring, in one way or another, to adhere each in his own way to various inessential solidarities as well. All of them are moving towards what G. Agamben has described as the 'Coming Community', which is a community of human beings devoid of any stable or fixed identity. In other words, they are not viewed, and do not see themselves, as belonging to a particular group by virtue of some essential feature of theirs. They do not have any identity in the usual sense: Shenhav, Shohat, and Chetrit are not determined as having an essence which is necessary and without which they would not be themselves. More than that, even if they speak in favor of Arabism and Arabic, they are excellent examples of Arabic which has been gradually disappearing as a language mastered by Jews. Proficiency in Arabic can mainly be traced now to two cases: Jews who immigrated from Arab lands having already mastered the language (and their number, of course, is rapidly decreasing), or those who make a living from their knowledge of Arabic whether in the Israeli governmental, educational or security services (and their number, of course, is always increasing). The Jewish or Israeli canonical élite, among them these very Mizrahi intellectuals, do not see Arabic language and culture as an intellectual asset as proven by their attitude to it in their daily life and professional practice. What is more interesting is their reluctance to master Arabic or to touch upon Arabic *belles lettres*, especially that written by Jews. Even those who speak for the importance of reviving the hybridic Arab-Jewish option have a cultural identity that is more a political or imported academic tool than an ethnic or cultural one. Paradoxically, the way those radical intellectuals refer to the historical Arab-Jewish identity implies conceiving the notion of identity as essential, and at the same time playing down the fluidity of the subjectivities of immigrants, whatever immigrants.

Conclusion

Identity is a double-edged sword. Sometimes, the edge of identity is turned against 'collective pressure' by individuals who resent conformity; at another time, it is the group that turns the edge against a larger group that is accused of a wish to destroy it. In both cases, 'identity' appears to be a war-cry used in a defensive war: an individual against the assault of a group, or a weaker group against a stronger totality.

But is Arab-Jewish identity currently a war-cry at all?

First, there were Jews that identified themselves as Arab, but no Jewish community has ever declared itself as Arab-Jewish. We can only find retrospective allusions to Jewish communities who lived in Arab societies as such. It goes without saying that no Arab-Jewish community currently exists.

Second, all current references to any historical Arab-Jewish identity do not aim to celebrate the past but only to express present and future ideological and political desires and aspirations.

Third, Arab-Jewish identity has been paradoxically reinvented precisely when those who could have been mostly interpellated as Arab Jews were in the process of escaping such a recruitment. More than that, the interpellating machine is now being administrated by people who pretend to be such, but never had the potentiality of such an identity.

Fourth, most of the individuals who, during the last decades, have been identifying themselves as Arab Jews, have only been using such an identity as a war-cry against Zionism.

Fifth, the radical Mizrahi intellectuals have succeeded in provoking 'real' Arabized Jews, mostly Iraqis (e.g., Nissim Rejwan [born 1924], Sami Michael [born 1926], Shimon Ballas [born 1930], Sasson Somekh [born 1933]), to 'reclaim' their Arab-Jewish identity and to use it as a war-cry against those very radical intellectuals themselves. Now that Arab-Jewish identity has become something to be proud of in certain circles, those Arab-Jewish 'veterans' rightly feel that if there is any credit to be given for having such an identity, *they* deserve it more than anyone else.

Sixth, Muslim and Christian Arab intellectuals in general do not pay any attention to the emergence of the new 'fashion' of Arab-Jewish identity in Israel. If they do, it is mostly for political reasons only and as a tool against Israel and Zionism.

Last but not least: in the preface to his *The Black Atlantic*,[54] Paul Gilory mentioned two aspirations that he would like to share with his readers before they embark on the sea voyage that he would like his book to represent. I have three aspirations; two of them are essentially Gilory's ones adapted to my needs: the first is my hope that the present study articulates transparently the notion of the inescapable intermixture of ideas of all communities and persons, and at the same time the dangerous obsessions with essential purity which have been circulating for more than a century inside and outside Zionist-Jewish or Arab-Muslim national politics and cultures. The second is my desire that the study's heartfelt plea against the closure of the categories with which we conduct our cultural and political lives will not go unheard. The history of the Arabized Jews during the last century yields a course of lessons as to the instability and mutability of identities which are always unfinished, always being remade. My third aspiration is that scholars of Jewish, Muslim and Arab cultures and identities, who have produced dozens of excellent scholarly studies, will benefit more from the theoretical insights of thinkers and philosophers who have been working on notions of identity and belonging. In this context, fresh identity debates based on genetic studies, such as 'Who Are the Jews'[55] or new controversies around the invention of peoples,[56] are irrelevant. There is instead an urgent need, to quote Dian Davis, to 'shoot for a thinking of fluidity and a fluidity of thinking'.[57] Thinking, as Hélène Cixous writes, 'is trying to think the unthinkable: thinking the thinkable is not worth the effort.'[58] After all, to borrow Georges Bataille's saying which appears as a motto to the present study, we, as scholars dealing with such delicate issues, must find ways to stop 'regulating the movement that exceeds [us] with the narrow mind of the mechanic who changes a tire.'

Appendix: Iraqi-Jewish intellectuals, writers, and artists

'Anbar, Sulaymān (1875–1941)
Nissīm, Ibrāhīm Mu'allim (1876–1952)
Isḥāq, Salīm (1877–1948)
Moshe, Salmān (1880–1955)
al-Kabīr, Heskel (?–)
al-Kabīr, Ibrāhīm (1885–1973)
Khaḍḍūrī, Sasson (1886–1971)
Baṭṭāṭ, Rūbīn (1888–1962)
Ḥūraysh, Yūsuf (1889–1975)
Shahrabānī, Khaddūrī (1894–1982)
al-Kabīr, Salmān Ṣāliḥ (1895–1976)
al-Kabīr, Yusūf Ṣāliḥ (1898–1990)
Shīna, Salmān (1899–1978)
Ḥaddād, 'Ezra (1900–1972)
Sūsa, Aḥmad Nissīm (1900–1982)
Za'rūr, Mnashshī (1901–1972)
Aharon, 'Ezra (1903–1995)
Shā'ul, Anwar (1904–1984)
al-Kuwaytī, Ṣāliḥ (1904–1986)
Mu'allim, 'Izzat Sāsūn (1904–2004)
al-Kuwaytī, Dāwūd (1905–1976)
Murād, Salīma (1905–1974)
Mīkhā'īl, Murād (1906–1986)
Khaddūrī, Shā'ul Nājī (1907–2005)
al–Shibbath, Salīm (1908–)
Aghāsī (Agasi), Iliyāhū (1909–1991)
Ḥaddād, Shā'ul (1910–2010)
Shā'ul, Ya'qūb (Jack) (1909–1967)
Baṣrī, Na'īm (1910–1971)
Darwīsh, Salmān (1910–1982)
Baṣrī, Mīr (1911–2006)
Ilyās, Albert Shā'ul (1912–1961)

Darwīsh, Shālūm (1913–1997)
Qaṭṭān, Masrūr Ṣāliḥ (1913–1978)
Sūdā'ī, 'Azīz Ibrāhīm (1913–)
Ben–Yaacob, Abraham (1914–2005)
Ḥaddād, Meir (1914–1983)
Makmal, Yūsuf (1914–1986)
Sāllā–Salmān, Dā'ud (1914–1992)
Ṣiddīq, Yehūda (1914–1949)
Ṭuwayq, Na'īm Ṣāliḥ (1916–1989)
Dankūr, Na'īm (1916–)
Nissīm, Nissīm 'Ezra (1917–)
Isḥayyiq, Shā'ul (1917–)
Barshān, Yahūda (Gurjī) (1918–)
Shā'ul, Idwār (1918–)
Balbūl (Lev), Ya'qūb (1920–2003)
Nāwī, Eliyahū (1920–2012)
Ibrāhīm, Ibrāhīm Mūsā (1921–)
Ilyās, Arieh (1921–)
al-'Imārī, Sīmūn (1921–1989)
Kojaman, Yeheskel (1921–)
Tuwayna, Na'īm (?–1999)
Mu'allim, Meir (1921–1978)
al-Shārūnī, Abraham (1922–)
al-'Imārī, Murād 'Abd Allāh (1923–2012)
Hillel, Shlomo (1923–)
Khazzūm, Iliyāhū (1923–)
Obadyā, Ibrāhīm (1924–2006)
Rijwān, Nissīm (1924–)
Zilkha, Nūrī'īl Nūrī (1924–)
Shemtov, Yūsuf (1924–2007)
Kedourie, Elie (1926–1992)

Mīkhā'īl, Sāmī (1926–)
Najāt (1926–1989)
Shammāsh, Richard (192?–)
Shahrabānī, Naʻim (1926–)
Shaʻshūʻ, Salīm (1926–2013)
Zakariyyā, Meir (?–1993)
Bār-Moshe, Isḥāq (1927–2003)
al-Baṣṣūn, Salīm (1927–1995)
Ḥabba, Heskel (1927–)
Hārūn, Zakkay Binyāmīn (1927–)
Ilyās, Alber (1927–)
Ḥaddād, Heskel M. (1928–)
Qaṭṭān, Naʻīm (1928–)
Sagiv, David (1928–)
Shoḥet, Nīr (1928–2011)
Gilʻadī, Naeim (1929–)
ʻIvrī, David (1929–)
Khayrī, Suʻād (1929–)
Zamīr, Shlomo (1929–)
Ballas, Shimon (1930–)
Kohen, Isparūns (1930–)
Fattāl, Salīm (1930–)
Kazzaz, Nissim (1930–)
al-Kātib, Sālim (1931–)
Kāḥīla, Najīb (1931–)
Murād, Imīl (Emil) (1931–)
Moreh, Shmuel (1933–)

Murād, ʻEzra (1933–)
Semah, David (1933–1997)
Somekh, Sasson (1933–)
al-Sūdāʼī, Max (1933–)
Qaṣṣāb, Nuzhat (1934–)
al-ʻAlālī, Yaʻqūb (1934–)
Ḥāyik (Hayek), Yoav (1935–)
Mercado, Esther (1935–)
Dāwūd, ʻAbd (1936–)
ʻAmīr, Elī (1937–)
al-Mullā, Maryam (?–)
Moreh, Mordechai (1937–)
Zubayda Sāmī (1937–)
Levi, Shoshana (1938–)
Naqqāsh, Samīr (1938–2004)
Rabeeya, David (1938–)
Smooha, Sammy (1941–)
Dabbī-Joury, Lilian (1942–)
Ishayyiq, Idmūn (1944–)
Alfī, Yossi (1945–)
Darwīsh (Lecker), Tikva (1945–2002)
Jalāl, ʻAzīz (1947–)
Someck, Ronny (1951–)
Shenhav, Yehuda (1952–)
Yaḥyā, Munā (1954–)
Shoḥat, Ella Habiba (1959–)

Notes

1 Georges Bataille, The Accursed Share: An Essay on General Economy (trans. Robert Hurley), New York: Zone Books, 1988, I, pp. 26–27.
2 In the chapter, I will use the term 'Arabized Jews' following Ross Brann, 'The Arabized Jews', in: M.R. Menocal, R.P. Scheindlin, and M. Sells (eds.), *The Cambridge History of Arabic Literature: The Literature of al-Andalus*-ambridge: Cambridge University Press, 2000, pp. 435–454. On the question of terminology, see Moshe Behar, 'What's in a Name? Socio-Terminological Formations and the Case for "Arabized-Jews"', *Social Identities* 15:6 (2009), pp. 747–771.
3 Louis Althusser, 'Ideology and Ideological State Apparatuses (Notes towards an Investigation)', in: *Lenin and Philosophy and Other Essays* (trans. Ben Brewster), London: NLB, 1971, pp. 121–173.
4 Based on João Biehl, Byron Good, and Arthur Kleinman (eds.), *Subjectivity: Ethnographic Investigations*, Berkeley, CA: University of California Press, 2007, pp. 1–23 (introduction). For tracing the history of some of the philosophical insights that have shaped current understandings of subjectivity, see Amélie Oksenberg Rorty, 'The Vanishing Subject: The Many Faces of Subjectivity', in: Biehl, Good, and Kleinman, *Subjectivity: Ethnographic Investigations*, pp. 34–51.

5 According to Ella Shohat, one of the first of these radical thinkers, the aim is 'to relink [our]selves with the history and culture of the Arab and Muslim world, after the brutal rupture experienced since the foundation of Israel' (Ella Shohat, 'Antinomies of Exile: Said and the Frontiers of National Narrations', in: Michael Sprinker [ed.], *Edward Said: A Critical Reader*, Oxford, UK and Cambridge, MA: Blackwell, pp. 121–143 [the quotation is from p. 141, n. 4]). See also Lital Levy's remark on the term 'Mizrahi' in her essay 'Reorienting Hebrew Literary History: The View from the East', *Prooftexts* 29, 2009, pp. 127–172.
6 Abū Faraj al-Iṣbahānī, *Kitāb al-Aghānī*, Cairo: n.pub., 1964, XXII, pp. 102–105; Michèle Bitton, *Poétesses et lettrées juives: une mémoire éclipsée*, Paris: Les Editions Publisud, 1999, pp. 43–46.
7 Robert Jay Lifton, *The Protean Self: Human Resilience in an Age of Fragmentation*, New York: Basic Books, 1993, p. 1.
8 Stuart Hall, 'Introduction: Who Needs "Identity"?' in: Stuart Hall and Paul Du Gay (eds.), *Questions of Cultural Identity*, London: SAGE Publications, 1996, p. 1.
9 Zygmunt Bauman, 'Identity in the Globalizing World', in: Anthony Elliott and Paul du Gay (eds.), *Identity in Question*, Los Angeles, CA: Sage, 2009, p. 1.
10 Stuart Hall, 'The Local and the Global: Globalization and Ethnicity', in: Anthony D. King (ed.), *Culture, Globalization and the World-System: Contemporary Conditions for the Representation of Identity*, Binghamton, NY: Dept. of Art and Art History, State University of New York at Binghamton, 1991, p. 21.
11 The quotations in the last sentences are from Hall, 'Introduction: Who Needs "Identity"?' pp. 5–6.
12 Zygmunt Bauman, *Liquid Modernity*, Cambridge, UK: Polity Press, 2004. See also his *Liquid Times: Living in an Age of Uncertainty*, Cambridge: Polity Press, 2007.
13 Hall, 'Introduction: Who Needs "Identity"?' p. 4.
14 I use 'modern' here not in the temporal sense but as consisting of three dimensions: a preference for secular rationality, the adoption of religious tolerance with tendencies toward relativism, and individualism.
15 Douglas Kellner, 'Popular Culture and the Construction of Postmodern Identities', in: Scott Lash and Jonathan Friedman (eds.), *Modernity and Identity*, Oxford, UK and Cambridge, MA: Blackwell, 1991, pp. 141–143.
16 Kellner, 'Popular Culture and the Construction of Postmodern Identities', pp. 153–154. (My emphasis – R.S.)
17 Kellner, 'Popular Culture and the Construction of Postmodern Identities', p. 158. (My emphasis – R.S.)
18 Zygmunt Bauman, 'From Pilgrim to Tourist', in: Hall and du Gay, *Questions of Cultural Identity*, p. 18 (my emphasis – R.S.). Cf. Zygmunt Bauman, *Globalization: The Human Consequences*, New York: Columbia University Press, 1998, pp. 77–102.
19 Alberto Melucci, 'Identity and Difference in a Globalized World', in: Pnina Werbner and Tariq Modood (eds.), *Debating Cultural Hybridity: Multi-Cultural Identities and the Politics of Anti-Racism*, London & New Jersey: Zed Books, 1997, p. 61.
20 Ulrich Beck and Natan Sznaider, 'Unpacking Cosmopolitanism for the Social Sciences: A Research Agenda', *The British Journal of Sociology* 57.1, 2006, pp. 1–23 (also published in a special issue of *The British Journal of Sociology*: 'Shaping Sociology over 60 Years', Volume 61, 2010, pp. 381–403).
21 When Tony Judt uses the term 'globalization', referring to 'the last great era of internationalization' in the 'imperial decades preceding World War I', he probably means the era of cosmopolitanism as we mean in the present article. In any event, Judt argues that 'the story of globalization combines an evaluative mantra ("growth is good"), with the presumption of inevitability: globalization is with us to stay, a natural process rather than human choice.' In his view, however, 'we should by now have learned that politics remains national' (Tony Judt, *Ill Fares the Land*, New York: The Penguin Press, 2010, pp. 190–197).

22 Michael J. Sandel, *Justice: What's the Right Thing to Do?* Penguin Books, 2009, p. 265. Sandel's hero is Robert F. Kennedy (1925–1968) who tried to confront what he called 'the poverty of satisfaction', as in the following quotation: 'But even if we act to erase material poverty, there is another great task. It is to confront the poverty of satisfaction – a lack of purpose and dignity – that inflicts us all. Too much and too long, we seem to have surrendered community excellence and community values in the mere accumulation of material things' (18 March 1968).
23 Bauman, *Liquid Modernity*, p. 91.
24 Zygmunt Bauman, *Liquid Love: On the Frailty of Human Bonds*, Cambridge, UK: Polity Press, 2003, pp. vii, x.
25 Giorgio Agamben, *The Coming Community* (trans. Michael Hardt), Minneapolis, MN: University of Minnesota Press, 2003 [1993], p. 63.
26 See René ten Bos, 'Giorgio Agamben and the Community Without Identity', *The Sociological Review* 53.1, 2005, p. 22.
27 On these intellectuals, writers, and artists, see my work on Iraqi Jews published during the last two decades, especially '*Arviyut, yahadut, tsiyonut: Ma'avak zehuyot ba-yetsira shel yehude 'iraq* (Arabness, Jewishness, Zionism: A Struggle of Identities in the Literature of Iraqi Jews), Jerusalem: Ben Zvi, 2005.
28 Linda Nicholson, 'Introduction' in: Seyla Benhabib et al. (eds.), *Feminist Contentions: A Philosophical Exchange*, New York & London: Routledge, 1995, p. 12.
29 The following section is based on Kenneth Burke's *A Rhetoric of Motives*, Berkeley, CA: University of California Press, 1969, and Diane Davis's reflections on identity and belonging and their connections with rhetoric, especially Diane Davis, *Inessential Solidarity*, Ph.D. Thesis, The European Graduate School, 2003, pp. 3–6.
30 Cf. Agamben, *The Coming Community*, pp. 1–3.
31 Burke, *A Rhetoric of Motives*, p. 28.
32 Carolyn Miller, 'Rhetoric and Community: The Problem of the One and the Many', in: Theresa Enos and Stuart C. Brown (eds.), *Defining the New Rhetorics*, Newbury Park, CA: Sage Publications, 1993, p. 91 (my emphasis – R.S.).
33 Barbara A. Biesecker, *Addressing Postmodernity: Kenneth Burke, Rhetoric, and a Theory of Social Change*, Tuscaloosa, AL: University of Alabama Press, 1997, p. 1 (my emphasis – R.S.).
34 Philip de Ṭarrāzī, *Ta'rīkh al-Ṣiḥāfa al-'Arabiyya* (History of the Arab Press), Beirut: al-Maṭb'a al-Adabiyya, 1933, IV, pp. 486–487.
35 Arnold T. Wilson, *Loyalties Mesopotamia: 1914–1917; A Personal and Historical Record*, London: Oxford University Press, 1936, I, pp. 305–306. Wilson writes afterwards: 'Vain words, no doubt, but they concealed perhaps the seeds of economic truth.' This comment, however, was presumably added in retrospect, in the light of the escalation in the national conflict in the Middle East and the increasing tension between the Jews and the Iraqi authorities. Elie Kedourie, however, argued that even in the 1940s 'the Zionist cause did not seem to me as a matter of any political wisdom. The expectancies which Zionism was creating were too high and unrealistic' (*Dvar ha-shavu'*, 7 April 1988, p. 9).
36 The original text was first published in *al-'Irāq*, 19 July 1921. For the text of the speech, see *Fayṣal ibn al-Ḥusayn fī Khuṭabihi wa-Aqwālihi* (Fayṣal ibn al-Ḥusayn in his Speeches and Sayings), Baghdād: Maṭba'at al-Ḥukūma, 1945, pp. 246–249. In an address Fayṣal had delivered before the Arab Club in Aleppo, on 9 June 1919, he had already emphasized that 'there are no religions or sects, for we were Arab before Moses, Mohammed, Jesus, and Abraham. We Arabs are bound together in life, separated only by death. There is no division among us except when we are buried' (Abū Khaldūn Sāṭi' al-Ḥuṣrī, *Yawm Maysalūn: Ṣafḥa min Ta'rīkh al-'Arab al-Ḥadīth* (The Day of Maysalūn: A Page from the Modern History of the Arabs), Beirut: Manshūrāt Dār al-Ittiḥād, 1965, p. 231. Translation according to Abū Khaldūn Sāṭi' al-Ḥuṣrī, *The Day of Maysalūn: A Page from the Modern History of the Arabs*

– *Memoirs* (trans. Sidney Glazer), Washington D.C.: The Middle East Institute, 1966, p. 113. In January 1919, Fayṣal signed with Chaim Weizmann (1874–1952), who acted on behalf of the Zionist Organization, the Fayṣal-Weizmann Agreement (for the text of the agreement, see George Antonius, *The Arab Awakening: The Story of the Arab National Movement*, London: Hamish Hamilton, 1938, pp. 437–439). Although attempts have been made to marginalize Fayṣal's readiness at the time to accept the Zionist programs, even considering the agreement as a failed attempt 'to secure by fair or unfair means an Arab endorsement of the Balfour Declaration' (for example, Abd al-Latif Tibawi, *Arabic and Islamic Themes: Historical, Educational and Literary Studies*, London: Luzac & Company, 1974, pp. 315–323), no one, to my knowledge, has gone so far as to doubt Fayṣal's goodwill and sincere intentions.

37 Abū Khaldūn Sāṭi' al-Ḥuṣrī, *al-'Urūba Awwalan!* (Arabism First!), Beirut: Dār al-'Ilm li-l-Malāyīn, 1965 [1955], p. 12.

38 For the text of the constitution, see 'Abd al-Razzāq al-Ḥusnī, *Ta'rīkh al-Ḥukūmāt al-'Irāqiyya* (The History of Iraqi Governments), Beirut: Maṭba'at Dār al-Kutub, 1974, I, pp. 319–334; the quotation is from p. 319.

39 *La Vérité sur la question syrienne*, Stamboul: Imprimerie tanine, 1916, p. 35. For the full original Arabic text of the manifesto, see Aḥmad 'Izzat al-A'ẓamī, *al-Qaḍiyya al-'Arabiyya* (The Arab Case), Baghdad: Maṭba'at al-Sha'b, 1932, IV, pp. 108–117. For an English translation, see Sylvia G. Haim, *Arab Nationalism – An Anthology*, Berkeley, CA: University of California Press, 1962, pp. 83–88.

40 Eliezer Tauber, *The Formation of Modern Syria and Iraq*, Ilford: Frank Cass, 1995, p. 49.

41 Nissim Rejwan, *The Jews of Iraq, 3000 Years of History and Culture*, London: Weidenfeld and Nicholson, 1985, p. 219.

42 Muḥammad 'Izzat Darwaza, *Mudhakkirāt Muḥammad 'Izzat Darwaza: Sijjil Ḥāfil bi-Masīrat al-Ḥaraka al-'Arabiyya wa-l-Qaḍiyya al-Filasṭīniyya Khilāla Qarn min al-Zaman; 1305–1404H/1887–1984* (The Memories of Muḥammad 'Izzat Darwaza: An Abundant Register of the History of Arab Movement and Palestinian Case during a Time of a Century; 1305–1404H/1887–1984), Beirut: Dār al-Gharab al-Islāmī, 1993, III, p. 545.

43 *Al-Akhbār*, 21 July 1938; cited in Khaldūn Nājī Ma'rūf, *al-Aqalliyya al-Yahūdiyya fī al-'Irāq bayna Sanat 1921 wa-1952* (The Jewish Minority in Iraq between 1921 and 1952), Baghdad: al-Dār al-'Arabiyya li-l-Ṭibā'a wa-l-Nashr, 1976, II, p. 70. It was argued that notices published by well-known Jews in the Iraqi press during the 1930s declaring that they were loyal to their motherland and that they had no connections with Zionist activities were initiated by the authorities against the background of the anti-Jewish atmosphere created following the disturbances in Palestine (Elie Kedourie, 'The Break between Muslims and Jews in Iraq', in: Mark R. Cohen and Abraham L. Udovitch (eds.), *Jews among Arabs: Contacts and Boundaries*, Princeton, NJ: The Darwin Press, 1989, pp. 28–29). The same, of course, might be said about the testimonies included in *Iraqi Jews Speak for Themselves*, Baghdad: Dar al-Jumhuriyah Press, 1969.

44 A.H. Hourani, *Minorities in the Arab World*, London: Oxford University Press, 1947, p. 104.

45 Siegfried Landshut, *Jewish Communities in the Muslim Countries of the Middle East*, London: The Jewish Chronicle, 1950, p. 45.

46 Shālom Darwīsh, 'The Relations between Communal Institutions and the He-Ḥaluts Underground Movement in Baghdad' (Hebrew), in: Zvi Yehuda, *Mi-bavel li-yrushalayim* (From Babylon to Jerusalem), Tel-Aviv: Iraqi Jews' Traditional Cultural Center, 1980, p. 83.

47 Siegfried Kracauer, *The Mass Ornament: Weimar Essays* (trans. Thomas Y. Levin), Cambridge, MA: Harvard University Press 1995, p. 144.

48 See the debate in *Tikkun*: Mark R. Cohen, 'The Neo-Lachrymose Conception of Jewish-Arab History', *Tikkun* 6, 1991, pp. 55–60; Norman A. Stillman, 'Myth,

Countermyth, and Distortion', *Tikkun* 6, 1991, pp. 60–64. In *The Dispersion of Egyptian Jewry: Culture, Politics, and Formation of a Modern Diaspora* (Berkeley, CA: University of California Press, 1998), J. Beinin rejects both approaches and opts instead for a Marxist interpretation of the political events and the question of identity (see especially pp. 1–28).
49 See, for example, David Rabeeya, *The Journey of an Arab-Jew in European Israel*, Philadelphia, PA: Xlibris Corp., 2000, p. 27.
50 *Ha'aretz*, 22 April 1949.
51 Harvey E. Goldberg and Chen Bram, 'Sephardic/Mizrahi/Arab-Jews: Reflections on Critical Sociology and the Study of Middle Eastern Jewries within the Context of Israeli Society', in: Peter Y. Medding (ed.), *Sephardic Jewry and Mizrahi Jews*, Oxford & New York: Oxford University Press, 2007, pp. 227–256 (quotations from pp. 242, 247 respectively).
52 In the documentary film *Forget Baghdad* (2002), made by the Iraqi-Swiss director Samir Jamal al-Din, Michael says: 'When I first arrived here in Israel, I decided to found a state called "Sami Michael". [There has been] an ongoing fight between [the State of] Israel and [the state of] myself. Of course, both the State and myself wanted to be [victorious]. But today I can say that I have won' (this is the written translation of his Arabic original text which appears in the subtitles of the film with necessary modifications. The exact wording of the original Arabic spoken text was slightly different).
53 E.H. Carr, *What is History?*, Harmondsworth: Penguin Books, 1965, p. 32.
54 Paul Gilroy, *The Black Atlantic: Modernity and Double Consciousness*, Cambridge, MA: Harvard University Press, 1993.
55 See Michael Balter, 'Who Are the Jews? Genetic Studies Spark Identity Debate', *Science* 328, 11 June 2010, p. 1342.
56 Such as that evoked following the publication of Shlomo Sand, *The Invention of the Jewish People* (trans. Yael Lotan), London ; New York: Verso, 2009; and see Anita Shapira's review essay: 'The Jewish-people deniers', *The Journal of Israeli History* 28.1, 2009, pp. 63–72. See also Sharon Begley, 'The DNA of Abraham's Children: Analysis of Jewish Genomes Refutes the Khazar Claim', *Newsweek*, 3 June 2010.
57 D. Diane Davis, *Breaking Up [at] Totality: A Rhetoric of Laughter*, Carbondale, IL: Southern Illinois University Press, 2000, p. 15.
58 Hélène Cixous, *Three Steps on the Ladder of Writing*, New York: Columbia University Press, 1993, p. 38.

9 Remote participants

Lessons about Israeli identity from the experience of Israeli parents in America

Udi Sommer and Michal Ben Zvi Sommer

The research presented here examines the implications of the immigration of Israelis to America in terms of their identity, and what we can learn from their parenting experience about Israeli identity more broadly. Immigrant families are becoming an increasingly common element of American society with important political implications for the United States as well as for their homelands. According to the Center for Immigration Studies, the number of immigrants living in the United States reached a record high of 37.9 million in 2007, a figure comparable in its proportions to those from the turn of the twentieth century. What is more, approximately one in every ten people identifying themselves as Israeli resides in the United States on a permanent basis. Yet despite the growing significance of this group, scholars have not thoroughly explored the challenges immigrant families face and the political implications related. Based on a series of in-depth interviews and workshops with Israelis, who live in the big metropolitan areas in North America, we examine how political and national identities are influenced by immigration. To examine this question, we focus on the parenting experience. We investigate the processes of identity evolution and formation as those are reflected in the experience of emigrants as parents, and then draw conclusions about Israeli identity more broadly.

'Think about your experience as a parent. How is it shaped by the place where you grew up, Israel, and the way you were brought up there?'. This was the opening question in all the interviews conducted for the purposes of this study. 'It has had a major effect on me as a parent' was the initial response of Yael, a single mother living in Manhattan with her four-year-old daughter. She then carried on with her parenting narrative, starting with her decision to leave Israel nine years earlier and continuing on to her recent plans to go back to the place she still calls home.

The move to the land of endless possibilities – the United States – allowed Yael to pursue her dream of many years; she wanted to become a mother. 'The minute I set foot in this city,' she tells us about New York later in the interview, 'I had a feeling that everything was possible. All sorts of things may happen; there were no limits. For the very first time in my life, I had the feeling I could do anything I set my mind to – that I could go the distance.'

Immigration caused a fundamental change in Yael's life. She celebrated the freedom she felt away from all those who knew her too well and used to judge every move she made. At last she could connect with her desire to have a baby.

However, while the constraints imposed by people around her were gone, just as in Israel she was still unable to form a steady relationship in New York. Yet in this new city, which she felt offered her everything and anything, she was ready to make this move – with or without a partner by her side.

Six years later, on a humid New York summer evening, we met in her apartment. The walls were covered with pictures and souvenirs from trips to different parts of the country and different corners of the world. At this point in her life, however, Yael wanted to go back to Israel. She wanted to raise her daughter, who was sleeping in the next room, in the 'tribal' experience, as she dubbed it, provided by her family back in Israel. In addition, Yael had plans to have another baby. Returning to Israel, she felt, was necessary to successfully support a larger family. In her eyes, the support network in Israel was invaluable. For both practical and emotional reasons, this was the right place for her and her family to be. 'It is important to me that my daughter sees how family members support each other,' she explained, 'and when people live close to each other, relationships of a different nature are formed. The connection is there, even if you do not intend for it to happen. And when it is there, when it is present, it is priceless.'

Our seven-year-old daughter, Talia, our son, Ori, who is four a half, and our six-month-old baby, Inbal, were born in the United States. Much of what we heard from individuals interviewed for this project and who took part in workshops we conducted all over North America was similar to our own parenting experience as Israelis in America.

Just like Yael and the authors of this paper, all of the interviewees either grew up in Israel or spent a formative period of their lives there. They all think of themselves as Israelis. However, another thing they all have in common is the fact that either in the present, or at some point in the past, they raised children in America. As such, their relations with Israel are an issue they often deal with, and in some cases ceaselessly so – emotionally and ideologically.

This research project deals with the parenting experiences of Israelis who are 'remote participants' in America. They identify themselves as Israelis but have an American identity as well. As reflected in the parenting experience of most of them, over time the latter identity becomes increasingly central to who they are. Because parenthood is a crossroads – between the personal and private on the one hand and the public and political on the other — this article seeks to clarify the concept of Israeliness itself using what we can glean about it from the parenting experience of Israelis abroad. As far as the public and political are concerned, in many cases it is the parent who is the key agent of socialization. A mother teaches her children their identity as members of the society in which they live and grow up. They learn about their religious affiliation, citizenship, their family's political persuasion, as well as about partisanship, ideology and other components of their social identity.[1] Parents teach their children who they are as social creatures. On the other hand, the relationship between parents and their children is personal and private. What happens in the family forms children's inner worlds. Their emotional stability, their attachment style, their ability to form interpersonal connections successfully are to a large extent a function of the parenting they received.[2]

Both the public and political as well as the personal and private came up in the interviews and workshops we conducted. There are certain emotional relations and attachment styles that are more frequent among Israeli parents. Likewise, there are certain political and ideological messages that appear more regularly in the relations those parents form with their children. Key to our argument is the notion that since parenting plays such a central role in the lives of many, and in particular in the lives of almost all those who participated in our project, how parents aim to form the identity of their children, the kind of messages they have for them and the relationship that is created as a result are highly instructive as far as the identity of those parents themselves is concerned. When dealing with the identity they would like to instill in the next generation, parents come in close contact with their own identity. Therefore, when they shared their parenting experience with us, what they essentially did was discuss not only their relationship with their children or the identity of their children, but their own identity as well. When a person discusses her parenting experience, when she talks about what she would like to pass on to the next generation, what she engages in is fundamentally discussing her perceptions of who she is.

In the Israeli experience, personal and psychological issues are often part and parcel of what happens on the national level and on the level of ideology. Being Israeli, therefore, is a complex experience that stays with many of those who grew up in Israel for the rest of their lives.[3] Consequently, those who start a family are influenced in their role as parents by this profound experience. On the other hand, the reality of life across the Atlantic Ocean, thousands of miles away from the Middle East, is different. Anything from moral values and language to culture and mentality is dissimilar to what they had known in Israel. One way or another, immigrant parents live on a daily basis within this gap between their home country and their new reality.

For people all over the world, immigration has become a part of modern life.[4] Indeed, hundreds of thousands of Israelis leave their homeland to live overseas.[5] For some, this is a temporary arrangement, while others leave for good. By far the most popular immigration destination for Israelis is the United States. After Israel, the United States is the nation most populated by Israelis and former Israelis. The largest concentrations of Israelis are in several of the major metropolitan areas in America. Those include New York, Los Angeles, Boston, Chicago and the San Francisco Bay area.

Like all immigrants, Israelis become part of their new home. They learn the language, find a job, go to school, and weave for themselves a new life. In addition, many of them start a family or expand the one they have. Interestingly, the immigration of Israelis to America has been studied in the scholarly literature[6] and discussed extensively in the Israeli media. Yet, apart from the occasional mention, the parenting experience of those same Israeli immigrants in America is largely a neglected topic.

In fact, even the literature about immigration more generally focuses mainly on the second generation,[7] comparing the children of immigrants to their counterparts in their country of origin or, alternatively, in America.[8] The challenges, difficulties and joy involved in raising those children are largely understudied.[9] Furthermore, the challenge of immigration, and of immigrant parents in particular, can teach us much about Israeli identity in America, as well as in Israel. These are the purposes of this article.

Parenting and immigration – Two life-changing experiences

The story we are telling here involves two life-changing experiences. Parenting and immigration, even when experienced separately, fundamentally alter one's life. Combining them raises two major questions. First, is the experience of immigrant parents different in any meaningful way from the experience of non-immigrant parents? Judging by the interviews and workshops conducted for this project, there is much in common. When their children are born, parents go through several of the most dramatic changes in their lives. They deal with the education of their children, pass on values and traditions they cherish, experience love of a sort never before experienced, and face the huge challenges involved in raising the next generation. At the same time, as the personal stories revealed to us during the individual interviews and workshops indicate, important aspects of childrearing are fundamentally dissimilar when parents live away from their homeland.

The second question is the extent to which immigration is different for parents compared to individuals who go through the same process with no children of their own. Here, too, one finds many points of similarity. Immigrants live through an identity crisis, experiencing a torn identity as Americans who in certain ways are still connected to their country of origin. While they long for the place where they grew up, they are both excited and anxious about living up to the challenges of a new language, a new culture, a new society and a new life. But again, as the narratives of the immigrant parents we met indicate, parenting gives immigration a whole new dimension. This paper is largely about the additional dimensions of parenting and immigration experienced by immigrant parents and reflected in the identity they form over time.

Our key contention is that parenting provides immigrants with a milieu in which to mend their torn identity. How parents work through their identity crisis affects their own lives and those of their children. The parent strives, in some way or form, to relate the life he used to have with the new reality in which he lives. In fact, raising children requires parents to do so. Yet as parents they have a unique setting, both in the outside world and in their mind, in which they can deal with their identity crisis.

This article is about the different ways in which emigrants in general, and emigrants from Israel in particular, shape their new identity, benefiting from their role as parents and their relationship with their children. As such, this project offers insights into the world of immigrant parents more generally. In addition, since the group studied is parents who emigrated from Israel, the project is also about what it means to be Israeli, how Israeli identity develops and what happens to national identity (Israeli and otherwise) when living away from the homeland.

The different identities of parents

A parent passes her identity on to her children. She explains where the family came from and who they are. Parents associate themselves with certain identities – national, professional, religious, personal, and ethnic. Typically, parents would like to see their offspring associate themselves with similar identities; they would like to see their children live in the same identity circles. For this to happen, however, parents should first explore their own identity. Who are they? What circles of identity do they place themselves in?

Every person identifies herself in certain ways. Yet, not infrequently, there is tension between the different identities one carries. In the case of immigrants, the tension between her new identity as an immigrant and her identity from the country of origin is critical to who the immigrant becomes. In fact, because of the abrupt changes inherent in the immigration experience, there is often a disconnect between who the immigrant used to be and who this person is now. This disconnect is experienced as an identity crisis. By its nature, the transition from Israel to America is not smooth. Immigration involves a drastic change, a change that fundamentally alters the life narrative of the immigrant. This change leads to a sense of a torn identity, which is key to understanding the parenting experience of immigrants.

Every parent, indeed every person, experiences conflicts, questions and crises. Yet for our interviewees and for participants in the workshops, the crisis associated with immigration was the most dramatic and influential. The interviews indicate that the attempt to find the middle ground between Israeli and American identities occurs largely as a part of the parenting experience. How immigrants shape their parenting, the way they deal with the challenges involved, and the role parenting takes in their lives influence how parents attempt to regain a balanced sense of who they are.

The balance each of them finds between Israel and America may be different. There are those who raise their children principally as Israelis. Others think of their children simply as Americans. However, most parents mentioned that, as parents, they try to pass on to their children an identity that is somewhere in between. An identity that has in it Israeli elements as well as American ones.

Parenthood, therefore, has an intermediary role. Both Israeli and American identities live within Israelis in America. Within their parenting experience, parents mediate between two realities – the American and the Israeli. In order to pass on a coherent identity to the next generation, immigrants, within their parenting experience, attempt to bridge (in many cases successfully) the reality they left behind in Israel, and the one they currently live in America.

To provide their children with a coherent identity, parents have to face the split in their own identity caused by the decision to move to the United States. At the same time, the very same experience offers a setting in which parents can work through their identity crises and find ways to mend their torn identity. Parenting is born with the first child, and it changes and grows over the years. An immigrant's identity as a parent, therefore, grows, develops and forms alongside the children.

As such, parenting is a place in which immigrants can deal with their torn identity, process it and often even come to peace with it.

Methodology – The interviewees, the interviews and the interviewers

For the purposes of this study, a diverse sample of participants was interviewed. Some of them have traditional families,[10] while others are single parents. Some are in their 80s, while others are young parents in their late 20s. Some became parents not long before they met us, whereas others had adolescent grandchildren. While some are living in the US on a temporary basis, most view themselves as temporary visitors but are immigrants in reality. One couple arrived in America in 1947, before Israel's establishment; others immigrated in the 1970s and 1980s; and still others only in recent years. Interviewees' lines of business included everything from music, business consulting and medicine to contracting, academic research, and occupational therapy. Some of them were descendants of Jews who immigrated to Israel from Arab countries, while others were sons and daughters of European Jews. Their reasons for leaving Israel vary, with some moving to the US for medical reasons, others for business or to pursue higher education, and still others for a trip that turned into a long-term stay. For some of the interviewees, raising their children was a major concern in life, while others mostly trusted their spouses with the task.

One thing all interviewees had in common was their choice of a place to live. All live in the major metropolitan areas popular among their compatriots. Our sample included interviewees living in major cities in California and on the East Coast (New York, Los Angeles, Boston, San Francisco and San Diego), as well as in the Chicago area.[11]

Recruiting participants for this study proved challenging in some cases. Interviewees were not always forthcoming or happy to discuss a topic they found particularly personal. In some cases, ads posted in community centers or via electronic mailing lists were the best way to reach potential interviewees. In other cases, snowball sampling allowed us to get to new interviewees via word of mouth from those who had already participated. Almost without exception, however, our in-depth psychological interviews, which focused on a topic many of them felt conflicted about, made parents hesitant about taking part in the project. In fact, despite efforts to obscure participants' identity, some of those who eventually decided to participate still expressed anxiety about the possibility that their identities might be revealed.

To protect their privacy, interviewees were asked to choose their own pseudonyms. Furthermore, their places of residence were changed, as were some details about their background. All interviewees received verbatim transcripts of their interviews with the details of their identities changed to ensure they were sufficiently comfortable with the text. It was not uncommon, when we contacted participants months after the interview, to find that their lives had changed considerably. In some cases, their families had moved back to Israel. In others, they had expanded, moved elsewhere in the United States or experienced other life-changing developments.

The conversations themselves were in-depth psychological interviews.[12] During the interviews, we were attentive to both conscious and subconscious messages. We paid particular attention to places where the flow of speech slowed or stopped or where the tone changed, and often made an attempt to go back to those points, where complex and painful issues often arose. Together with the interviewee, we made attempts to examine and analyze such issues.

In structure, the interviews resembled a classic psychological interview.[13] However, in addition to what subjects told us concerning their psyches, we were also mindful of additional aspects of their stories. As mentioned above, parenting brings up personal and psychological issues side by side with sociological and political topics. In order to fully investigate the complexities of the lives of Israelis in America and their multifaceted identities, we also paid close attention to the cultural, sociological, and political aspects of their stories.

Apart from the opening question, the interview itself was not structured – 'Think about your experience as a parent. How is it shaped by the place where you grew up, Israel, and the way you were brought up there?'. With no exceptions, the opening question provoked emotional reactions from all the interviewees, and from this point on they shared their parenting narratives with us with little prodding on our part. The parents and their stories dominated the interviews. When we did ask questions later on, it was done for clarification purposes or to echo and thus mirror sentiments of the interviewees. When there was something we wanted to underscore or examine further, we would echo the sentiments they expressed, asking them to elaborate. Different interviews therefore proceeded in different directions, with the interviewees leading them where they desired.

Once an interview was over, the interviewers would typically be engrossed for days with everything they had heard. Right after the interview, we would attempt to give the interviewee a short summary of the insights about the narrative she had just shared. But the ability to link the psychological, political, sociological and historical aspects of the stories required the perspective of time. And so, with the benefit of time, we have deeper analytical insights to present here.

This project is based on 30 interviews conducted over a period of 18 months and over 15 workshops with approximately 20 participants in each. Many of the interviews were very long, with some of them lasting more than three hours. Only a subset of the interviews is shared. Yet all interviews were crucially important for the writing.

A large variety of narratives are apparent. In some cases, the interviewees are raising babies. Others have toddlers. In some of the interviews, parents talk about their adolescent children, and in some cases the people we spoke with were octogenarian grandparents. We made every effort to minimize the editing of the interviews, attempting to provide the reader with an authentic impression of the subjects and of their stories. Some of the variation between the stories is doubtless lost in translation. For instance, the interviewees largely spoke in Hebrew as it was spoken when they left Israel for America. A rapidly evolving language, Hebrew was one thing when Rachel and her husband left Israel more than six decades ago, and was fundamentally different when Yael left the country 10 years ago, or when Michelle left for the US three years before we met her. While there was an attempt to reflect the differences in vocabulary, grammar and speaking style during the translation process, some of those differences were lost.

The different ways in which individuals relate their stories are fascinating. Each person we spoke with had her own way of presenting her life, emotions and the challenges she faced as a parent. Their inner worlds affected their choice of words and the vocabulary they tended to use. Michelle's husband, Uri, a businessman, works for a major high-tech company on the West Coast. During the interview, he often fell back on a vocabulary reflecting his vocation. This vocabulary was infused with masculine metaphors reflecting a goal-oriented state of mind. Conversely, Michelle, a midwife, makes use of feminine language to describe her experiences, emotions and state of mind. For example, Uri expresses his thoughts about Israel in the manner of an investment banker. 'In the early days,' he relays, 'when the state was a young startup…' Later, when describing why he considers it dangerous to raise children in Israel, he described risk in the following way: 'There is a calculated risk that you have to take if you decide [to raise your children in Israel], just like when I board an airplane for one of my business trips. Obviously, it is a relatively safe way to travel from place to place, but there is some risk involved. If I were a salesman who travels by air on a daily basis, I would clearly increase the risk I take. When this increased risk concerns me only, it is one thing, but when children are involved, it is a different story altogether. The risk is greater by orders of magnitude.'

Another interesting aspect of the interviews is the insights that many of the interviewees reached during the interviews. Many of the interviewees preferred to begin the interview with more general comments about parenting. Only after they warmed up did they reveal the more personal aspects of their stories, in some cases coming to certain realizations for the first time during the interview itself. For example, during our interview, Michelle realized that she was able to articulate emotions she had never previously experienced on a conscious level. Likewise, Yael came to recognize that her move to the United States was largely motivated by her desire to have a baby; it was the move to a new country that allowed her to live away from those who would not let her take this step. It was during the interview with Dawn that she became aware of a major theme in her life as a parent – making amends. As the interview with her moved forward, Michelle came to realize that parenthood has become a central axis around which many of the recent transformations in her life had taken place. Furthermore, she came to realize that these transformations, which stemmed partly from becoming a mother, would not have taken place had she not left Israel.

Our own status as Israeli parents in America added to the complexity of the situation. Much of the content in the interviews echoed our experience as parents. We would not be exaggerating if we said that the understandings we have of our children and ourselves were often influenced. Yet during the interviews, we made every effort not to let our own story influence the situation. After all, the interviews were about the interviewees, not us. Sharing stories during the interview might have limited their ability to express themselves freely.

With that in mind, there were also certain advantages. The familiarity with the life circumstances of the interviewees often allowed us to better understand the challenges, difficulties and joys they shared. To create a sense of closure at the end of the interviews, we would share our feelings. Often, this sense of a common experience made interviewees feel that they had been understood. We were touched by much that we heard, and for days after the interviews would be busy thinking about what had happened. As much as possible, there was an attempt to include those feelings and thoughts in this project.

Israeli parents in America

A growing number of immigrants from Israel (and elsewhere) are raising their children in the United States. Their parenting experience is influenced both by their personal narratives and by the political and social environments in which they grew up. The parenting they received as children influences who they are as parents. The social and political contexts in which they were raised have an impact on the parents they are today. Indeed, on one level or another, the vast majority of parents we spoke with still associate themselves with Israel, which is particularly evident in the way they raise their children. The vast majority make every effort to speak Hebrew at home, give their children Israeli names (although some of these names, such as Daniel or Maya, work just as well in English), and engage in passing on what it means to be Israeli in their eyes to the next generation.

One example of how deeply ingrained being an Israeli is comes from the interview with Edith. She lives with her husband and two young children (a one-and-a-half-year-old and a 4-year-old) in a big metropolitan area on the East Coast. At a certain point in the interview, she says, 'We mostly speak Hebrew at home. But recently, I have come to realize that my son, who goes to a public school, speaks increasingly more English, much more than he used to when he was home with me. His Hebrew, which has always been better than his English, still is. But his proficiency in English is almost as good. He watches television and plays computer games in English. His playmates and friends from school are American. So English has become very dominant in his world in the last year. It really troubles me, because the issue of speaking Hebrew is near and dear to me. It is not only that I want him to know Hebrew, but I want his language to be at a certain level. I would like him to have a rich vocabulary. It's important to me, because I want him to have what I have, to be what I am. And what I am is still, to a large extent, Israeli.'

Regardless of their particular country of origin, immigrant parents' homeland and mother tongue remain important to them. Yet what characterized many of the Israeli parents we interviewed was the sense that they are in America on a temporary basis.[14] Notwithstanding how long they had been in this country, many of them considered themselves visitors or transient rather than immigrants. This temporary aspect of their life, whether real or mostly in their minds, affects how they raise their children.

How they perceive their position in their new country affects how immigrants behave and feel as parents. When the 'temporary' nature of their life becomes permanent, their parenting experience is affected as well. Israel, which would have been central to their lives had they stayed there, remains relevant because of the possibility of moving back. Naturally, it also affects how their children are raised. The option of returning to Israel one day makes it hard for parents to ignore their homeland when raising their children. 'If there is a chance my children ever live in Israel,' many of the parents think to themselves, 'then it is important that I incorporate certain elements of Israel into our family's lifestyle.'

The parenting experience of Israeli expatriates is interesting also because of their reasons for moving to America. The overwhelming majority, including almost all the interviewees, immigrated by choice. Political persecution, discrimination, and other forms of distress are rarely the reasons that Israelis immigrate to the United States. Rather, their immigration is part of a global trend; the ability to move from place to place is a desirable part of life in a globalized world. Immigrants typically move to a new country in pursuit of greater freedom professionally, financially or in terms of educational opportunities.[15]

In light of all this, it is interesting to examine the complex relationship Israeli immigrant parents have with their country of origin. Even if their ability to immigrate is part of a success story, or at least represents a degree of freedom and the ability to control their own lives, Israel continues to play a central role. The centrality of Israel arises in the interview with Edith when she says, 'In my view, children need a broader frame of reference. They need a context in which they can place themselves, their lives and their story. The larger context we as parents can pass on to them are the things we know. Essentially, it is who we are. As Israelis, what we are most familiar with is the place where we were born and raised, Israel. This is our cradle, this is where we come from, and this is what we know best.'

One situation in which parents' origins come to the fore is when they get angry with their children. When our daughter, Talia, was younger, she used to walk in Central Park with her friends Elijah (whose parents were African American) and Leonardo (whose parents had emigrated from Italy). If the kids happened to climb a tree or a rock that the mothers deemed particularly dangerous, the warnings were simultaneously and instantly transmitted in three languages. Each mother fell back on her mother tongue, so that Talia's warnings came in Hebrew, Elijah's in English, and Leo's in his mother's mother tongue, Italian.

That said, even when calm, Israeli parents largely associate themselves, emotionally and ideologically, with Israel. When it comes to parenthood, many become nostalgic. Amir, a musician and his spouse, Lilly, who was engaged in research in chemistry, told me:

Amir: When you are away from Israel, you get a different perspective on things. We were watching some YouTube clips of a music festival from the 1980s with Shimi Tavori [a well-known Israeli singer] with Saul [their 3-year-old son]. Watching the kind of music productions they used to have in Israel made me nostalgic. In fact, it really gave

	me the blues. All of a sudden, I longed for the country, for the music, for the people. I felt sad.
Interviewer	Why did you feel sad? Was something lost?
Amir:	You cannot turn back time. Watching Saul sitting there with me, watching clips from days that will never return, and from a place that seemed so far away, made me feel sad. At the same time, though, there was a sense of comfort. It was something I felt connected to fundamentally, and it was nice to have Saul there with us.
Interviewer:	Does it have to do with the fact that you now live in America?
Amir:	Definitely. Things look different from across the Atlantic.
Lilly:	I think the only reason we even watched Shimi Tavori on YouTube was because we were here. It was snowing outside, and we could not leave the house. But in addition, when you are here, these kinds of things become particularly meaningful. It is something you cherish.
Amir:	I agree. We did those things for Saul. We wanted to entertain him. We wanted to show him the songs we used to love so much.
Lilly:	The nice thing was that Saul found it really amusing, too. He really loved it.
Amir:	It's about what you experienced when you were young, and now you're trying to give your kids something similar.

Although less than a year had passed since they arrived in the United States, Amir and Lilly had already developed nostalgic feelings toward Israel. Those feelings came up most strongly in connection with their son. As fall passed and they were bracing themselves for the cold New England weather, the temperatures outside felt particularly unwelcoming. Watching YouTube clips of their favorite 80s hits turned out to be a perfect activity for the entire family. Nostalgia for Israel appeared in many of the stories we heard from Israeli immigrants, particularly in the context of raising their children.

Ironically, the way those immigrants are viewed in Israel is largely negative. In the media, in academia, and in political speeches, they are perceived as having abandoned the country, parting with the idea of Zionism and choosing to live away from their families. As such, all references to Israeli expatriates in America, even when not openly ideological (for instance, when personal stories of those immigrants are discussed), revolve around the question of whether they plan to return, and if so, when.

This project, which focuses on their parenting experiences, takes a different perspective. Interviews about parenting, with its obvious social and political components, shed new light on their lives. That said, the possibility of a return to Israel also remains a pertinent question in their role as parents. In sum, not least because so many of them live while pondering that option, Israel is a major element in how they raise their kids, and therefore remains a major element in the parents' identity. This, however, is not easily transferable to the next generation.

The desire to pass on a coherent identity is almost universal. At the same time, the understanding that parents' identity is multidimensional is commonplace, particularly among immigrants, for whom identity crises are a part of life. As such, parents in general, and immigrant parents in particular, have to work through their own identity issues and crises before feeling ready and able to pass a clear sense of who they are on to their children. Simultaneously, parenthood provides immigrants with a framework within which they can process their identity issues. For many of them, our interviews indicate, it is within parenthood that their identity can take on its new form after the rupture of immigration.

Conclusions

'It's possible to take the Jews out of exile, but not to take the exile out of Jews.' There are those who cite this as one reason that there are Jews, some of them Israeli, who prefer to live in places other than Israel, their national home. We do not know if there's genetic truth to this statement, or any truth at all. Based on the interviews, we would amend this to say, 'It's possible to take Israelis out of Israel, but not to take Israel out of Israelis.' Israelis can leave Israel and live elsewhere, but it is very hard for them to stop their constant internal dialogue over Israeliness. This dialogue with their identity as Israelis is conspicuous in their experience as parents.

A majority of our interviewees were a part of the business, artistic, academic or professional communities in the US. They were familiar with the American way of life, and had succeeded in going about their business within it. And yet, in their own homes, the Israeli experience remains central in a way that is clear when it comes to raising children. The identity crisis brought on by immigration plays a central role for Israeli parents in the US. Yet their identity as Israeli is very much alive in the parenting experience of the vast majority of our interviewees.

Each of the interviewees experiences her role as a parent in the most profound and meaningful way. Among a portion of them, parenthood takes center-stage immediately after the birth of their first child. The standout example was Michelle, whose life changed completely after her daughter was born and she changed her career, switching over from business consulting to being a midwife. By contrast, there were others for whom parenthood, and particularly the Israeli component of parenthood, became meaningful only after a while. Only after he became a grandfather did Benjamin come to recognize the cultural divide that had opened between him and his son, and only after his son's family moved to Australia did he allow himself to decry the emotional and ideological distance between them.

Subjects such as continuity, identity, assimilation and isolation are central concerns among Israeli parents in America, as are issues of values, the Hebrew language, Jewish identity and connections with family in Israel. Struggles over these issues are shared among many of those we spoke with. They sense that these are the things that form the basis of their identities, both individually and as parents.

And yet each interviewee has her own predilections. Not all the parents are trying to raise Israeli children. There are those trying to do the complete opposite. Reuma, for example, wants her daughter to know a language other than English –

but it does not matter to her whether this second language is Spanish or Hebrew. There are those who feel liberated from family ties after leaving Israel. For others, the pain of separation burns in their bones even years later. There are those who are happy to see their children grow up with American manners and discipline, and those who would prefer to see them 'waste' more time on games, rather than learn to read and write before they hit four.

And yet everyone, without exception, is almost always negotiating with his Israeliness, questioning how much they can, or want to, pass on to the next generation.

In its different variations, Israeliness remains dominant in the lives of Israeli parents in America, with their identity crises a central axis around which raising children revolves. Yet among those whose children have grown and left home, it's not clear that Israeliness can truly be passed on. After they leave their parents' homes, whether for college or work, most children move farther from the Israeli world of their parents. They may identify as Israeli-Americans, but few of the qualities valued by their parents remain. The features that do survive will, for the most part, be Jewish and thus religious in nature, and not those of secular Israelis.

What does all this mean, broadly, about Israeliness? What does it say about the Israeliness of the Israelis still living in the Middle East, in Israel? It is difficult to make a clear-cut determination. It is obvious that national identity remains important for immigrants, and that the identity of Israelis is particularly strong. This identity stays with them upon leaving Israel, and manifests itself most strongly at key moments in life and in experiences as important as parenthood.

And yet Israeliness as a national identity is very much connected to the place where it sprouts: is Israel. Israeliness is a dynamic idea, and the meaning of being Israeli is different today than a year ago (when Chavezelet and Amir moved to America), five years ago (when Reuma left Israel), or 25 years ago (when Naomi immigrated).

Consequently, it is hard to develop Israeliness, or even to preserve it, overseas. By this we mean that while the parents may have a clear component of Israeli identity, the same may not apply to their children. Parents identify as Israelis to themselves as well as to their friends and family years after their children have stopped sharing the same identity, if they ever did. Parents have talked about their attempts at passing Israeliness on to the next generation, but at the same time admitted, in most cases, the futility of such efforts. For better or worse, the American way of life carries the next generation to distant places, far from what the parents left behind. Even if some traces of Israel remain, such as language, names or religious components, it seems that something elemental, at the root level, is lost.

Parents' identity crises as immigrants remain central during the process of raising children. It's an issue accompanying many of their most important struggles as parents. Yet when Israeliness is cut off from its roots back in Israel, it struggles to bloom. Even if parents draw on these roots as they deal with their experience as Israeli parents in America, with the passage of time it becomes relatively peripheral in their lives, and in particular in the world of their children.

Notes

1 B. R. Berelson, P. F. Lazarsfeld and W. N. McPhee, *Voting*, Chicago, IL: University of Chicago Press, 1954.
2 J. Bowlby and M. Ainsworth, *The Effects of Mother-Child Separation: A Follow-Up Study*, Cambridge University Press, 1956; C. Chazan and P. Shaver, 'Romantic Love Conceptualized as an Attachment Process.' *Journal of Personality and Social Psychology*, 52(3), 1987, 511–24; A. K. Driscoll, S. T. Russell and L. J. Crocket, 'Parenting Styles and Youth Well-Being Across Immigrant Generations', *Journal of Family Issues*, 29, 2008, 185–209; M. Rutter, 'Implications of Attachment Theory and Research for Child Care Policies'. In J. Cassidy, P. R. Shaver, *Handbook of Attachment: Theory, Research and Clinical Applications*. New York and London: Guildford Press, 2008, pp. 958–74.
3 Z. Eisenbach, 'Jewish Emigrants from Israel in the United States'. In Elazar Leshem and Judith J. Shuval, *Immigration to Israel: Sociological Perspectives*, Transaction Publishers, New Brunswick and London, 1988; A. Friedberg and A. Kfir, 'Jewish Emigration from Israel', *Jewish Journal of Sociology*, June, 1988, 5–15; S. Gold, 'The Emigration of Jewish Israelis', In U. Rebhum and C. I. Waxman, *Jews in Israel: Contemporary, Social and Cultural Patterns*, Brandeis University Press, Hanover and London, 2004; G. Lahav and A. Arian, 'Israelis in a Jewish Diaspora: The Dilemmas of a Globalized Group'. In R. Koslowski, *International Migration and the Globalization of Domestic Politics*, Routledge: London and New York, 2005; D. Mittenberg and Z. Sobel, 'Commitment, Ethnicity and Class as Factors in Emigration of Kibbutz and Non-Kibbutz Members from Israel', In E. Leshem and J. J. Shuval, *Immigration to Israel: Sociological Perspectives*, Transaction Publishers, New Brunswick and London, 1998.
4 R. D. Alba and V. Nee, *Remaking the American Mainstream: Assimilation and Contemporary Immigration*, Cambridge, MA: Harvard University Press, 2003; A.-M. Ambert, 'An International Perspective on Parenting: Social Change and Social Constructs', *Journal of Marriage and the Family* 56, 1994, 529–43; A.-M. Ambert, *Immigrant and Minority Parents: The Effects of Children on Parents*, New York: The Hawthorn Press, 2001; S. A. Camarota, 'Immigrants in the United States, 2007: A Profile of America's Foreign-Born Population', Center for Immigration Studies, 2007 (accessed on 19 December 2008: http://www.cis.org/immigrants_profile_2007); Y. Choi, M. He, and T. W. Harachi, 'Intergenerational Cultural Dissonance, Parent-Child Conflict and Bonding, and Youth Problem Behaviors Among Vietnamese and Cambodian Immigrant Families', *Journal of Youth Adolescence*, 37, 2008, 85–96; K. T. Dinh, B. R. Sarahson and I. G. Sarahson, 'Parent-Child Relationships in Vietnamese Immigrant Families', *Journal of Family Psychology*, 8, 1994, 471–88; N. Foner, *In a New Land: A Comparative View of Immigration*, New York University Press, New York, 2005; J. Georgas, J. W. Berry, F. J. R. Van de Vijver, C. Kagitcibasi and Y. H. Poortinga, *Families Across Cultures: A 30-Nation Psychological Study*, Cambridge, MA: Cambridge University Press, 2008; N. Glick Schiller, L. Basch and C. Blanc-Szanton, 'Transnationalism: A New Analytic Framework for Understanding Migration'. In *Toward a Transmittional Perspective on Migration: Race, Class, Ethnicity and Nationalism Reconsidered*. New York: New York Academy of Sciences, 1992, 1–24; P. Kasinitz, J. H. Mollenkopf, M. C. Waters and J. Holdaway, *Inheriting the City: The Children of Immigrants Come of Age*, Harvard University Press, Cambridge, MA and London, England, 2008; A. Ong, *Flexible Citizenship: The Cultural Logics of Transnationality*, Duke University Press, Durham and London, 1999.
5 S. Gold, *The Israeli Diaspora*, Seattle, WA: University of Washington Press, 2002.
6 S. Cohen, 'Israeli Émigrés and the New York Federation: A Case Study in Ambivalent Policymaking for 'Jewish Communal Deviant', *Contemperary Jewry*, 7, 1986, 155–6; G. Sheffer, 'The Israelis and the Jewish Diaspora', in U. Rebhum and C. I. Waxman,

Jews in Israel: Contemporary, Social and Cultural Patterns, Hanover and London: Brandeis University Press, 2004; M. Shokeid, 'One-Night Stand Ethnicity: The Malaise of Israeli Americans' in E. Leshem and J. J. Shuval, *Immigration to Israel: Sociological Perspectives*, Transaction Publishers, 1998; Z. Sobel, Migrants from the Promised Land, Transaction Books, New Brunswick and Oxford, 1986; N. Uriely, 'Patterns of Identification and Integration with Jewish Americans Among Israeli Immigrants in Chicago: Variation Across Status and Generation', *Contemporary Jewry*, 16, 1995, 27–49; N. Uriely, 'Rhetorical Ethnicity of Permanent Sojourners: The Case of Israeli Immigrants in the Chicago Area', in E. Leshem and J. J. Shuval, *Immigration to Israel: Sociological Perspectives*, New Brunswick and London: Transaction Publishers, 1998.

7 Y. Quinones-Mayo and P. Dempsey, 'Finding the Bicultural Balance: Immigrant Latino Mothers Raising "American" Adolescents', *Child Welfare*, 84, 2005, 649–67; M. K. Shields and R. E. Behrman, 'Children of Immigrant Families: Analysis and Recommendations', *The Future of Children*, 14, 2004; Z. B. Xiong, P. A. Eliason, D. F. Detzner and M. J. Cleveland, 'Southeast Asian Immigrants' Perceptions of Good Adolescents and Good Parents', *The Journal of Psychology*, 139, 2005, 159–75; Y.-W. Ying, P. A. Lee, J. L. Tsai, Y. J. Lee and M. Tsang, 'Relationship of Young Adult Chinese Americans With Their Parents: Variation by Migratory Status and Cultural Orientation', *American Journal of Orthopsychiatry*, 71, 2001, 342–9.

8 G. P. Carreón, C. Drake, A. C. Barton, 'The Importance of Presence: Immigrant Parents' School Engagement Experiences', *American Educational Research Journal*, 42, 2005, 465–98; J. A. M. Farver, X. Yiyuan, R. Bakhtawar, S. Narang and E. Lieber, 2007, 'Ethnic Identity, Acculturation, Parenting Beliefs, and Adolescent Adjustment', *Merrill-Palmer Quarterly*, 53, 2007, 184–215; C. Goldenberg, R. Gallimore, L. Reese and H. Garnier, 2001, 'Cause or Effect? A Longitudinal Study of Immigrant Latino Parents' Aspirations and Expectations, and Their Children's School Performance', *American Educational Research Journal*, 38, 2001, 547–82; J. C. Gorman, 'Parenting Attitudes and Practices of Immigrant Chinese Mothers of Adolescents', *Family Relations*, 47, 1998, 73–80; A. G. Inman, E. E. Howard, R. L. Beaumont and J. A. Walker, 'Cultural Transmission: Influence of Contextual Factors in Asian Indian Immigrant Parents' Experiences', *Journal of Counseling Psychology*, 54, 2007, 93–100; A. S. Neetu and K. M. Sheldon, 'Parental Autonomy Support and Ethnic Culture Identification Among Second-Generation Immigrants', *Journal of Family Psychology*, 22, 2008, 652–7; L. M. Pachter and T. Dumont-Mathieu, 'Parenting in Culturally Divergent Settings: Handbook of Parenting: Theory and Research for Practice'. M. Hoghughi and N. Long, Eds. London: Sage Publications, 2004; K. M. Perreira, M. V. Chapman and G. L. Stein, 'Becoming an American Parent: Overcoming Challenges and Finding Strength in a New Immigrant Latino Community', *Journal of Family Issues*, 27, 2006, 1383–414.

9 E. J. Calzada and S. M. Eyberg, 'Self-Reported Parenting Practices in Dominican and Puerto Rican Mothers of Young Children', *Journal of Clinical Child and Adolescent Psychology*, 31, 2002, 352–63; A. J. Fuligni, 'Authority, Autonomy, and Parent-Adolescent Conflict and Cohesion: A Study of Adolescents From Mexican, Chinese, Filipino, and European Backgrounds', *Developmental Psychology*, 34, 1998, 782–92; C. Izzo, L. Weiss, T. Shanahan and F. Rodriguez-Brown, 'Parental Self-Efficacy and Social Support as Predictors of Parenting Practices and Children's Socioemotional Adjustment in Mexican Immigrant Families', *Journal of Prevention and Intervention in the Community*, 20, 2000, 197–213; S. Jambunathan, D. C. Burts and S. Pierce, 'Comparisons of Parenting Attitudes Among Five Ethnic Groups in the United States', *Journal of Comparative Family Studies*, 31, 2000, 395–406.

10 Interviewees included parents living in traditional families, as well as single mothers. While we were able to locate gay Israeli parents, we found it very difficult to get them to take part as interviewees. The same applies to religious Zionist Israelis.

11 Uriely studied the Israeli community in the Chicago metropolitan area: Natan Uriely, 'Rhetorical Ethnicity of Permanent Sojourners: The Case of Israeli Immigrants in the Chicago Area'. In Elazar Leshem and Judith J. Shuval. *Immigration to Israel: Sociological Perspectives*, Transaction Publishers, New Brunswick and London.
12 H. S. Sullivan, *The Psychiatric Interview*, New York: Norton, 1954.
13 The classic is: H. S. Sullivan, *The Psychiatric Interview*, New York: Norton, 1954.
14 Ong, *Flexible Citizenship*.
15 Z. Bauman, *Globalization: The Human Consequences*. New York: Columbia University Press, 1998.

10 The Israeli triangle

(De)constructing the borders between Israeliness, Jewishness and migrant workers

Robin A. Harper and Hani Zubida

Introduction/general context

The physical borders of the state of Israel have been in heated contention since the establishment of the state less than a century ago. There has also been another border dispute, much less visible to the outside world, but just as critical to the definition of the Israeli nation-state: what is it to be Israeli? Despite Arabs comprising 20 percent of the Israeli population, since the founding of the Jewish state, being Israeli has been understood to be at its core Jewish. As the state matures, and absorbs various populations, it wrestles with liberal and republican citizenship discourses as well as how to define itself, its Jewish and its long-standing and newer non-Jewish members. In part, this unclear identity is nothing more than a continuation of centuries-old questions of the nature of Jewish peoplehood, so inimical to both internal and external Jewish questions in Europe. In part, the question reflects the hybrid nature of the Israeli state,[1] composed of both European and Middle Eastern Jews, geographically situated in the Middle East while politically, culturally and economically at the crossroads of Africa, Asia and Europe. Finally, it engages the core question of the nature of a Jewish and democratic state in Israel. As an ethnocracy,[2] Israel has traditionally given preference to members of the nation of Jews over the non-Jewish citizens of Israel. But, as the number of non-Jewish citizens and residents has grown, the state, as well as state and non-state institutions, are now forced to ascertain 'what is the definition of Israeli?'

The residency of now about 400,000 migrant workers[3] poses a new challenge for the integrity of the Jewish state itself: Is there a way for the state to remain a Jewish state and include these non-Jewish newcomers into the national story? What possible directions are available for Israel: Can it (or should it) follow the lead of many Western countries that try to boost declining birthrates, aging populations and political legitimacy by, at least formally, accommodating guest workers into the polity? Or should it follow the Middle Eastern state practice of keeping foreign workers on the periphery, and sustain the dominant Jewish character of the state? Is it even possible to maintain the unique cohesiveness of being the world's only Jewish state if it extends accommodation to these foreign workers and their children? But can it maintain the mantle of being a democratic state if it does not? Which understanding should Israel claim as its own: Eastern or Western, liberal or republican, and all the while remaining Jewish; clearly, not an easy balance to imagine, implement or sustain.

Inclusion is complicated as the foreign workers and their children are unlike any of the other marginalized groups in Israel, such as the Israeli Arabs, the Ethiopians and the non-Jewish immigrants from the former Soviet Union. The Israeli Arabs hold formal citizenship and the Ethiopians are Jews. The new immigrants from the former Soviet Union (FSU),[4] known as 'the Russians' (regardless of their actual ethnicity), are settled under the amended Israeli Law of Return,[5] which recognizes them as eligible for *aliya* under the Law of Return regardless of the fact that some of them are not Jewish according to *Halacha* (Jewish law). As a result they can bridge the difference between Israeliness and Jewishness in a way that simply is unavailable to the migrant workers.[6] In contrast, the foreign workers remain what their name states: foreign and workers. Exclusion is equally complicated as their numbers have swollen beyond a manageable level to enforce deportation and as the Israeli economy is increasingly becoming dependent on this source of cheap labor.

In this chapter, we explore conceivable boundaries for 'Israeli' by listening to arguably the most marginal residents of Israel, the foreign workers. We observe that foreign workers' presence is putting pressure on the boundaries of 'Israeli' and as a result, increasing the tension between Israeliness and Jewishness. Through examination of multiple methods (survey and interview data) with 126 foreign workers in Israel, many of whom are parents of children in Israel, we explore how these migrants perceive their experiences in Israeli society, their own and their children's identities, prospects for incorporation and permanence, perceptions of social borders and entry points and intersection between Israeliness and Jewishness. Through our analysis, we argue that the foreign workers' presence has a profound impact on what it is to be Israeli from demographic, symbolic, practical, ideological and policy perspectives. We conclude that the decision to include or exclude has substantially higher stakes for the state of Israel, thrusting it to either a Western or an Eastern paradigm. And in so doing, regardless of the orientation, causing cleavage throughout society, including in the power structure of the state itself.

Eastern and Western paradigms: Where does Israel fit?

There are many research studies examining what it is to be Israeli from the perspective of the dominant population groups, whether Israeli Jews[7] or Israeli Arabs.[8] As the number of foreign workers rises, we thought we should shift our examination away from the dominant voices to examining how those on the margins perceive themselves in Israel and how their presence is affecting contemporary understandings of 'authentic' Israeliness. Although rarely cited as an integral part of Israeli society, the foreign worker population is not insignificant in Israel, but now comprises about 5 percent of Israel's population – more than twice as many as the Ethiopians, the Druze or the Bedouin, groups that are common populations of study when examining peripheral groups in Israel.

Israel is caught between two paradigms: an Eastern one and a Western one. The Eastern paradigm for migrant worker management is most closely associated with the oil-rich Gulf states (and abandoned in Western Europe in the 1970s). This approach, where the local population is dependent on migrant labor, which is pushed to the periphery of the society and citizenship and its concomitant rights are accorded exclusively to coethnic members of the state and nation, is well documented.[9] Migrant policy here is probably best described as '*accommodation*',[10] as a way of managing the large numbers (who often outnumber nationals) of contract workers settling in the region, especially to provide labor for oil production but also for construction, light industry, services and household administration. Workers indenture themselves either individually or through their home government-sponsored programs to work in the receiving state for a delimited time. Depending on the state and the sending countries' arrangements, they reside either in closed work camps or in private facilities. Workers remain at the pleasure of the receiving country and thus can be deported at will, or repeatedly renew work contracts. Again, in cases where the labor was organized by their home country, e.g., South Korea, China and Sri Lanka, workers' movements are constrained and their departure, as a group, is enforced by the sending country.[11] Foreign labor sources have been used not just to buoy insignificant local labor supplies but also to eliminate the development of a politically astute working class which could threaten the local political hegemony.[12] The workers are not perceived as potential nationals; they are simply providing labor: contract workers. As Choucri[13] explains about Asian workers in the Gulf, who are considered completely peripheral to Gulf society and political life:

> Asians had a distinct political advantage: Asian workers were unlikely to make claims for citizenship. Asians were alien and could continue to remain disenfranchised. They were regarded as more likely to be passive observers of political processes rather than as potential activists or claimants on social services and other benefits of citizenship. (p. 252)

Workers benefit by receiving wages and the ability to provide development aid to their home states, and the Gulf states benefit through development. Some scholars and nongovernmental organizations are less sanguine and have even defined this type of labor as a form of modern-day slavery.

Overall, the policy is characterized by a recognition that national development is tied to the importation of foreign labor and that workers maintain, and are conferred, no residency rights beyond those tied to their labor, no citizenship rights and no expectations for integration for the workers or their children. In some cases, the labor is perceived as a mechanism for homeland development (mainly through state-managed and informal remittance mechanisms) and is managed by local representatives of their home governments. Any government-provided benefits, i.e., health care, are universally available and not tied to rights maintained by the individual migrant worker. Residency is tied to employment under the *kafeel* (sponsorship) system,[14] with the employer responsible for and retaining the rights to the labor of the migrant. Contract conclusions, cancellations or rescission provokes removal.

In Israel, this Eastern approach appears in the worker recruitment policy and in the care for workers. The Israeli government issues permits to specific firms for a given number of migrants per year who indenture workers in agriculture, construction, hospitality, ethnic cookery/catering, nursing/caregiving, welding and industrial professions. In all but caregiving, there are fixed annual quotas. Population control is managed primarily through deportation and forced rotations. Israel uses deportation as the main mechanism to compel repatriation. As the foreign worker population has grown, Israel has tried other inducements, including offering repatriation payments and making life in Israel more distasteful by limiting mobility[15] or renting apartments.[16] Still, the population grows. In 2008, Israel initiated a special immigration police called '*Oz*' ('courage' in Hebrew) to escalate deportations.

Like the Gulf states, Israel leaves the protection and management of the foreign workers to the manpower companies that issue permits. This can be problematic, as these companies profit not by finding new positions for current workers or for those who have fallen out of legal status but by bringing in new workers who pay new contract fees.[17]

The expectation for foreign workers is that they will pay contract fees, come to Israel and work, provide service to the Israeli state, receive remuneration for their services and then leave. There is no expectation for permanent residency or eventual naturalization. There is no legal means for adjudication of legal status for foreign workers to become Israeli citizens (except in exceptional cases).[18] Children of foreign workers also lack a means for permanence in Israel. Perhaps more generously than in the Gulf states, Israeli law grants pregnant foreign workers 14 weeks' maternity leave. However, until April 2011 it required mothers to leave Israel thereafter. Many remain with their children who are neither temporary workers nor citizens, and thus have no legal status in Israel.[19]

In contrast, the contemporary Western paradigm is one in which democracy, legitimacy and human rights norms and economics are expected to trump coethnic claims. One-time invited temporary contract workers (guestworkers) were eventually accepted as permanent members of the receiving state based on democratic, legitimacy, human rights norms and the realization that declining birthrates coupled with shrinking social security coffers for the elderly were not sustainable without infusions of younger workers.[20] In the case of democracy, legitimacy and human rights norms, these Western states accepted that it was contrary to their accepted political and social values to maintain large, growing unincorporated populations in the state, including children born, raised and socialized within the state, some knowing no other country but the receiving state, without any direct political voice or ability to politically incorporate. This Western pattern of incorporation is also well documented.[21] Although Germany is perhaps the poster child for this transformation – from cries in the street of '*Kinder statt Inder*' (children not Indians) to launching a birthright citizenship initiative to extend citizenship to children of some long-term guestworkers, changing an almost 100-year-old citizenship law that conferred German birthright citizenship only to ethnic Germans – many other states have transformed their citizenship laws to make room for long-term noncoethnic residents.[22]

Israel has included some human rights and labor protections. Israel recognizes that it has a responsibility to treat these workers fairly *de jure* (whether it does or not *de facto* is really another question); then again, Israel has made some good faith efforts in that direction. Israeli law tries to protect the workers by mandating rest time, religious practice time, setting wage and labor standards and establishing grievance procedures. Israel even published a multilingual guide of foreign workers' rights.[23] However, as explained previously, labor standards are complicated for the workers, as the government has relegated much of the worker protections to the very firms indenturing the workers, meaning that employers provide work and are responsible for tending to workers' complaints about that work. The civil rights of the foreign workers are always undercut by the fact that their legal status is tied to their employment (and therefore can be rescinded easily) or, when illegally present, may maintain fundamental civil rights of speech, assembly, etc. but no right to presence and residency. That said, the foreign workers, both legal and illegally present, have engaged (often through religious institutions) Israeli rights to religious practice, assembly, press and speech, and are permitted to access public services.[24] Noncitizens (in even most Western states) accessing these rights can put their residency rights in peril.

In the Western paradigm, population management has proven difficult and ineffective, as getting undocumented immigrants to leave requires state capacity and the commitment to deport, thus coming into conflict with normative human rights standards. Deportation does transpire, but it is not commensurate with the scope of the problem as the number of the undocumented vastly surpasses the state's ability to control the population growth. In Israel, cyclically, the implementation of a mass deportation policy is met with public backlash and curtailed, only to begin again. Some argue that the growth of undocumented workers is a desired public policy and thus the state's inability to deport is really an expected outcome and reflection of the state's desire to maintain surplus populations to depress wages and perform dirty, dangerous and dull work.

Since there are so many illegal aliens in the country with no opportunity for legalization of status and other problems like statelessness and lack of political voice, Israel could choose to follow the Western, European path, by instituting some form of adjudication of status. Yet, if Israel were to follow the Western model, it would compromise the ability of the state to maintain a Jewish majority in Israel, a core principle of the state. If this were to transpire and the Jewish majority were imperiled, this would pose a major problem for democratic, demographic and symbolic reasons. Thus, incorporating the foreign workers means being true to the Western path, but generating cleavage between Jewishness and Israeliness. So, where does this leave Israel? Western? Eastern? Jewish? In the next section, we examine this new Israeli reality.

The problem

The mutually exclusive nature of 'Israeliness' was, and remains, the contextual setting for many academic research efforts. For decades, the social and national understanding of Israeli as Jewish-held, mainly because it serves the Jewish-Arab divide. Although the question of 'who's a Jew?' is highly contested, up to the late 1980s, 'Israeli' meant 'Jewish'. Some non-Jewish groups, like the Druze or the Bedouins, were formally included in the state but have remained largely outside of national mythology. Perhaps the most recent major challenge to the perception of 'Israeli as Jewish' occurred with the arrival of the new FSU migrants. It is supposed that at least one third or more than 300,000 of them are not according to Jewish law (Halacha) actually Jewish[25] and yet, because of their familial relationships to Jews and modifications to the Law of Return, they were able to secure residency and Israeli citizenship.

The arrival of the foreign workers resulting from the closure of Israeli borders to Palestinian day laborers during the 1980s and 1990s because of the first and second Intifada poses a new socio-demographic reality: they are not Jews and most of them are not Arabs or Muslims either, so they do not fit into extant discourses about the Israeli public. Israeli law accommodates them only for short-term contract work and there is no legal provision for permanence. Although some have found in Israel a home, they largely live at the margins of Israeli society. Nonetheless, some migrant children – the official estimate is 1,200 – self-identify as Israelis, and through the school system are being socialized as Israelis. Political debate over whether these children – some of whom remain stateless, as their parents' countries of origin cannot or will not recognize them – should be deported or can be accommodated into Israel formally has occupied much political debate in 2009. In the summer of 2010, an official committee that was instituted by the Israeli government to examine the status of these children finally reached a decision on the matter. According to the decision, 800 of the children will be allowed to stay and be naturalized in the future, while the remaining 400 will be deported at a later date.

The migrant workers

Despite being an ethnonational state, Israel has used foreign workers to supplement labor supplies since the pre-state – the *Yishuv* – period. Then, most of the workers were Palestinians, commuting daily to Israel proper to perform dirty, dangerous and dull work. There were thousands of Palestinian migrant workers employed in Israel; they did not threat the hegemonic identity of the Israeli society nor did they intensify the tension between the two core identities of Israeli and Jewish. This was mainly due to the fact that although they were in Israel every day, they served as 'the other', and their presence provided contrast to Israeliness as Jewishness. Further, they had a home to return to on a daily basis and it was not Israel. This 'home' was not recognized as Palestine – this area referred to until recently as the occupied territories, and only in recent years as the Palestinian Authority. The Palestinians, according to this argument, were not trying to make Israel their home or acquire an Israeli identity; they were 'the other', 'the enemy', and as such were no threat to the core identity of the Israeli nation. Hence, they were not treated as 'regular' migrant workers.[26] On December 1987, the first Palestinian Intifada broke out and Israel sealed its borders to Palestinian workers. Israeli employers clamored for workers to replace Palestinians, as crops needed harvesting and housing had to be provided for the more than 1 million immigrants from the FSU who were entitled to resettlement provisions under the Law of Return. Rather than modernize conditions or make jobs more appealing to Israelis,[27] the firms pressured for expansion to even more low-paid, low-prestige jobs, including for eldercare and household assistance.[28] Table 10.1 reflects figures of legal foreign workers in Israel. According to various estimations there are now between 300,000 and 400,000 foreign workers – about two thirds of whom have fallen out of legal status. They account for 10 percent of the labor force, coming from throughout Africa, Asia, Europe and South America.[29]

Migrant workers' children

Israel estimates that there are 1,200 children of foreign workers resident in Israel, although estimates are as high as 2,000 such children. Some have citizenship from their parents' countries of origin, but many have never visited these countries and have no attachment to them beyond their legal claim to citizenship, often not even speaking the national language. Some are even stateless as their nations of origin do not, or will not, recognize them.

In June 2005, the government recognized the growing number of foreign workers' children resident in Israel who fell into this precarious non-legal status but were socialized into Israeli society.[30] It developed an amnesty for children whose parents entered Israel legally but overstayed their visas or fell out of status, and were at least 10 years old, lived continuously in Israel, studied at Israeli schools, spoke Hebrew and deemed 'removing (these children) from Israel would be akin to 'cultural exile' to a country with which (they have) no cultural ties'.[31] Parents could apply for status for minor children. If granted, the parents and any minor siblings would gain renewable temporary residency status through their children. Once the children served in the Israeli army, they and their siblings would become Israeli citizens and their parents would gain permanent residency. The Population Authority stipulated that 460 families, accounting for 1,400 people, have applied for status; 35 families have been approved.[32] Then PM Ehud Olmert noted that the Israeli state had a special responsibility to these children:

> The State of Israel will lose its moral standing if it evades its responsibility towards the weaker ... including the children of foreign workers who grow up among us and love our country, and wish to be part of it. It is not only our duty towards them. It is first and foremost our duty towards our moral standards.

Table 10.1 Distribution of 'legal' migrant workers in Israel (2008)

Country of Origin	Total Number (in thousands)
Total	114.7
Asia[a] Total	89.2
India	4.6
Turkey	2.6
Nepal	6.9
China	12.2
Sri Lanka	2.2
Philippines	29.3
Thailand	29.7
Other	1.7
Africa Total	0.4
Europe Total	23.7
Bulgaria	1.7
FSU[b]	9.8
Germany	0.1
United Kingdom	0.1
Romania	10.9
Other	1.1
America Oceania Total	1.0
USA	0.4
Others	0.6
Unknown	0.2

Source: Central Bureau of Statistics

a Includes Asian Republics of FSU
b Includes only European Republics of FSU

The state uses an odd, and potentially troubling expression, to describe the transformation of foreign worker children into Israeli citizens, by saying that it 'will enable the "laundering" of foreign workers in Israel'.[33] Whether the government means that the children's (and their parents') status will be cleansed of any legal wrongdoing through adjudication of migration status or whether this will symbolically purify them to join mainstream Israeli society, and what this means for the larger acceptance of these children, remains unclear.[34]

As noted, Israel is at a crossroads and has successively ordered and stayed deportation for certain Israeli-socialized foreign workers' children. A few NGOs led by 'Israeli Children' launched a public relations campaign against the deportation order, which is debated as we write. Thus, the real dilemma: do these children pose a real threat to what was once considered synonymous: Jewishness and Israeliness? And if they are, which treatment will the state of Israel undertake: Western or Eastern?

Methodology

In order to go beyond the visually obvious (changes in demographics, race and symbolism) and unpack the evolving concept of 'Israeli', in the winter and spring of 2010, we conducted a multiple methods research design. We interviewed 26 temporary workers from 11 countries about their thoughts, experiences, and opinions about life in Israel for foreign workers and opportunities for inclusion in and exclusion from the Israeli polity.

To provide a biographical sketch of our interview partners we note that our participants were predominantly female, with 3:1 ratio and a mean age of 32. Their range of tenure was between 4 and 23 years, with a mean of 8.5 years. They came from across the globe with most from Asia (60 percent), then Africa (30 percent) and finally Latin America (10 percent). Half were caregivers; about a quarter were cleaners and the rest were a mix of construction workers and gardeners, with one office worker.

Initial contact was made through postings and outreach at NGOs and through snowballing. Interview partners were informed of their rights and gave consent before the interviews, all of which took place in public places. All but three interviews were conducted in English; the remainder were in Spanish. Interviews were digitally recorded, transcribed, and coded according to standard grounded theory practices.[35] We engaged interview data to see Israeli life through foreign workers' eyes, since there are few studies that explore foreign workers' experiences. They are hard to reach and the Israeli social and political scene is dynamic. This type of small N study is common where there is limited available data and can serve as a basis for future quantitative theory testing.

To supplement the interview data, we also conducted a short survey. We relied on the available subjects technique as the lack of sampling prevented us from using a probability sample. We sampled people at worship places (after receiving consent from the pastors) and at the new central bus station in Tel Aviv Yaffo, a place that is known to be a major attraction to the migrant workers. We sampled 100 foreign workers. The average age was 35 and the age range was between 18 and 61; other characteristics are displayed in Table 10.2.

Findings and discussion

The new Israeliness and Jewishness

As argued, the arrival of migrant workers to Israel has impacted Israeli society by further deepening the cleavage between Israeliness and Jewishness, and in so doing, redefined the social borders of the Israeli collective. In this section, we will discuss some of the more prominent facets of this phenomenon using the data at our disposal.

Table 10.2 Survey sample characteristics

	Gender		Race			Country of Origin	
	Frequency	Percent		Frequency	Percent	Frequency	Percent
Male	14	14	Asian	60	60	Philippines	64	64
Female	61	61	Black/African	11	11	Nepal	2	2
Missing	25	25	Indian Subcontinent	1	1	Ghana	10	10
						Ethiopia	1	1
						Nigeria	1	1
			Missing	28	28	Missing	22	22
Total	100	100	Total	100	100	Total	100	100

Changing Israeli demography

Auguste Comte's oft-repeated line that '*demography is destiny*' could be the leitmotiv for Israeli citizenship politics. The argument is that a *Jewish state* must retain a Jewish majority or, even in a democracy, risk subjection to persecution, as experienced in Diaspora. Lustick[36] unveiled the issue in the Israeli context and argued that the Jewish majority is at risk as a result of the mass immigration from FSU, and that the large numbers of the migrant workers made this 'threat' imminent. Therefore, a major state focus is preserving the Jewish majority and it does so by three means – increasing Jewish births; *aliya*; and preventing non-Jewish immigration and/or naturalization. The state engages aggressive measures to increase births to Jewish women, including generous state subsidies and public policy to encourage in vitro fertilization.[37] It encourages *aliya* through resettlement programs and even birthright trips for all Jews,[38] and it provides no legal means for permanent non-Jewish immigration to Israel. Should they enter Israel, there is no legal way for them to naturalize (except for those related to Jews who are eligible for *aliya* and citizenship under the Law of Return).

A core principle for Israel is that it is a 'Jewish and democratic'[39] state whose primary goal is to be a place for 'in-gathering of the (Jewish) exiles', thus creating a synonymity between Israeliness and Jewishness. For those who are residents, but neither members of the state nor of the nation, the migrant workers are by their very presence a threat to this dominant understanding of the body politic. Raijman and Semyonov[40] argue that the migrant workers are perceived to pose a dual threat as seen from the Israeli public opinion '…threat to social and economic well-being of individuals as well as threat to national identity and Jewish character of the state.' The visible presence of foreign workers and asylum seekers becomes more prevalent as the number of foreign workers tips 5 percent of the population and since 2006 more than 17,000 migrants have claimed asylum in Israel.[41] This fuels the perception that migrant workers pose a demographic threat.[42]

Changing the complexion

Phenotypic characteristics of foreign workers mark them as outsiders. Most foreign workers are non-white and many come from places not normally associated with Jewish communities, especially Southeast Asia and Africa. This disadvantages them in the Israeli context, as in Jewish-Israeli society most people are white, with the exception of Ethiopian immigrants who compose only about 2 percent of the entire population and whose blackness was perceived as a barrier to inclusion into the Israeli society, despite their Jewish roots.[43] As a result, tolerance for racial difference has not been exercised, and thus acceptance levels are low and foreign workers appear hypervisible, especially in communities where there are large concentrations and few tourists.

Changing symbols of Israeliness

The inclusion of migrant workers also alters the long-honed image of 'sabra' in Israel. A major aspiration with the founding of the state of Israel was that the Jew would no longer be the wandering inner city nebbish but a strong, self-assured individual intrinsically connected to land, who through physical labor and communal action could build a Jewish state. As foreign workers increasingly undertake menial tasks in Israel, they challenge this image of the 'sabra' who makes the desert bloom through ingenuity and hard work; the meaning of a unified community, as embodied in the almost mythic image of kibbutz (communal farm); and the bedrock ideology of state for the Jews, the *Judenstaat*, as Herzl envisioned it – as a state comprising Jewish people, not just Jewish principles.

Identity

Foreign workers understand themselves not as Israelis in the ethnic sense, but in the sense that Israel is a practice of everyday life. Our survey data reveals that the Israeli identity is not an available identity for the foreign workers. They did not see themselves as becoming ethnically Israelis through being in Israel. In the survey, we asked respondents to rank their three top identities (see Table 10.3). None mentioned Israeli identity.[44] As can be seen in Table 10.3, the most important identity is their sending country's national identity, pointing to the idea that adult migrant workers feel strong commitment to their homeland, and are not a 'threat' to the integrity of the Jewish-Israeli collective. This was perplexing in that the respondents noted that they had positive feelings about Israel, which only increased after being in Israel. Our interview data helped to shed light on the fact that none felt 'Israeli' and yet they felt affinity with Israel. Rather than feeling Israeli, they felt 'of Israeli society', having taken on (their own variations of) Israeli customs, Israeli foods, celebrating Israeli holidays, etc., pointing to the fluidity of borders and the malleability and elasticity of identity. A black South African cleaner explained that she is not ethnically Israeli but she *is* Israeli, as she has been accepted as a trusted member of the community:

Table 10.3 Identity ranking

	Most Important Identity	Second Most Important Identity	Third Most Important Identity
National	30	13	2
Ethnic	1	6	13
Religious	19	13	3
Professional		2	8
Other	1	2	2
Racial		1	2
Missing	49	63	70
Total	100	100	100

* responses are percentages of 100 respondents

I am not an Israeli, but now I am Israeli. I feel like I am Israeli. Big time! You know I have keys from different families. My bag is full of keys. Do you think now if I go to America and Florida now, can somebody one day say that this is not my house key? I am sleeping in *my* house with *your* keys. ... You see, so when somebody, when you have somebody's key, that means that person is trusted.

Between identities and belonging

Migrants perceive themselves on the periphery, almost voyeuristic of Israeli life, even when there is no barrier, largely because of language, work schedules, and limited time off. Some mentioned invitations to Israelis' homes and led active civic lives in nongovernmental organizations and churches. Women, especially, were frequently present at family functions both as guests and as caregivers for elderly relatives. Visiting Israelis' homes was less true for males who were not caregivers, and they had fewer interactions with Israelis outside work, resulting in additional social exclusion. All of those interviewed recounted episodes of generosity from individual Israelis (watching their children, carrying water bottles, sharing meals or holidays, treatment from doctors, nurses and teachers, etc.) but noted that on a policy level, no matter how they felt about themselves, they were still the 'other'. A Filipina caregiver explains:

The situation and the treatment, it's different than what I expected. They don't want us to join. Israel is for Israelis.

Foreign workers' children's identity

In contrast, those with children reported that their children's experiences were completely different from their own. The foreign worker parents noted that their children's identities were remarkably shaped through socialization in Israeli schools and among Israeli peers. They described preparations for Israeli holidays, playing with Israeli children, sleepovers and doing homework together. Since Israeli society has no real (legal or social) term for these children, the children themselves were able to shape their own identities; their parents described them as being Israeli. Parents reported children speaking Hebrew, even when the parents either did not or had limited knowledge of Hebrew. Ironically, many spoke to their children in English and refrained from teaching the native tongue as they believed that Hebrew and English would serve them better in Israel. This reflects a parental confirmation that Israel is a *permanent home* for the children (regardless of Israeli governmental choices). Parents lamented their children's lack of native tongue skills but were proud of the children's achievement in Hebrew and asserted that a life in Israel meant developing a knowledge of Hebrew. Parents noted that when their children stated their (formal) nationality, the children expressed a distance from those places, as if they were foreign countries and not their own countries. A Filipina female caregiver remains in Israel, against her own desires, because her son wants to remain in Israel, noting 'He considers himself Israeli. He knows his blood is Filipino, but he considers himself Israeli.'

The plasticity of children's identity extends beyond nationality to religious identity. Even though Judaism is perceived (in Jewish law) as passed through blood, 'Jewish', through socialization, is nonetheless an available identity for these children. A Colombian housecleaner sent her children to a religious school because 'it's better', stating that despite her Catholicism, her children engage in Jewish practice at home, following what they were socialized to do in school:

> When the kids are asked where they are from, they say they are from Colombia. They always identify as Colombian. Always. In terms of religion? They need to study in a Jewish school. Whatever. They live in the school. I understand they want to be Jewish rather than Catholic or Christian. Because when they get in home, and kiss the mezuzah, they say 'Mom, let's pray before eating.' My son puts on a yarmulke. So they are closer to the Jewish religion than mine.

However, the dominant identity for these children is Israeli. Through the practice of Israeli civic religion (the flag, the military, the symbols of Israeli life, etc.), the children have managed to adopt Israeliness independent of any Jewish affect.

Religiosity

Like temporary workers the world over, our sample members had financial difficulties in their home country and came to Israel to make money. (Even those with political problems explained that it made it impossible for them to make a living.) However, expectations were far less concerned with pecuniary matters. Our interview data reveals that foreign workers can choose from a number of countries for work. In line with other work on Christian religiosity in Israel,[45] many choose Israel because of their deep-seated religious beliefs (or ironically intensified Christianity during their time in Israel.) Table 10.3 reveals that religious identity is consistently mentioned as most important identity or second most important identity. They imagined life as described in the Bible: of holiness, surrounded by holy people, acting holy. They were intrigued by the idea of 'coming to the sacred place where Jesus was born ... and living with the characters from the Bible'. Echoing many of the interviews, a Filipino caregiver described her expectations:

> I was thinking really, because I am a Christian. I am a Christian and Israel is a holy place. So what I did expect is that I will find people who will be as good as what I have read from the Bible because of our religion. To be kind, to be always, to be God fearing and to be working like or doing good things, every good thing they can do.

Experiencing isolation and vulnerability, local ethnic churches provided community, belonging and were often the only places where foreign workers could meet regularly with other foreign workers in a non-work environment. Our informants were not merely looking for the holy in Israel but also to spark it in themselves, to strengthen their Christian identity. They came to the holy land to work, but also to experience something holy. A Filipina caregiver explained:

> The most beautiful experience is to be born as a Christian. When I realized how blessed I am to be in the holy land, the promised land, where Jesus stepped on. When I realized I am very, very blessed, because I came to this land for the purpose of God.

Permanence

Jewish migration to Israel is expected to be unidirectional and permanent. Y*erida*, emigration, in Hebrew means 'descending ' (from Israel) and has a derogatory meaning. Yet research shows that there is a high degree of emigration, as high as 90 percent in the pre-state period and around 30 percent in the early years,[46] and it is generally around 10 to 15 percent.[47] The stated purpose of temporary foreign workers is that they fill a niche and leave. In our survey, foreign workers perceive their tenure as flexible, with about half expecting to stay 5 years or less but 71 percent remained longer than intended. They are not looking to remain in Israel at least at the *declarative* level: they are coming with the intention of making money and returning. Clearly, some suffer from the 'myth of return', or wanting to stay just long enough to attain x amount of money, only to find that a new need arises, forcing them to stay longer to achieve the new goal.[48] This is typical of temporary migrants the world over, following what Philip Martin[49] once called the 'iron law of labor migration', (p. 86) meaning that 'there is nothing more permanent than temporary workers'. Our survey data reveals that 72 percent stayed longer than anticipated because of financial reasons. However, none suggested any permanent resolution of status (except for those with children). Our respondents were firmly lodged in the day-to-day present. As a Filipino caregiver explained:

> We are not going to live here, we just need a job. We are not going to live here for the rest of our lives, we just need a job.

One could argue that this alternative short-term view reflects the policy goals for these migrants and does nothing to change what it is to be Israeli. And yet, in practice, as some migrants remain even longer than some Jewish *olim*, they are reflecting not just globalization but the transitory experience of migrants (Jewish and non-Jewish) to Israel, and underscoring the possibility that even for Israelis, perhaps it is possible to think of emigration in a different way.

Conclusions

As can be seen, there are multiple dimensions to the migrant workers in Israel. We presented some of the key facets: demography, identity, Israeliness and/or

Jewishness, religiosity and the question of migrant workers' children and their permanence. While these are introduced as separate issues, they are all intertwined and eventually lead to the current situation.

Foreign workers are in an odd position because of their religiosity and are unlikely to find political allies because of the Israeli-Jewish divide. The option they face is joining secular Israelis in the search for liberal citizenship and the Western approach to migrant workers' societal inclusion, since they cannot join religious Israelis with a circumscribed sense of republican, ethno-Jewish citizenship. Through their religiosity, they are introducing a whole new category of Israeli religious identity as neither Jew nor Arab, Muslim nor Christian. Their religious fervor brings them outside of the Israeli 'normal' politics as they are neither religious nor secular Jews, but religious and non-Jewish, injecting a whole new category of religious residents (communities and hierarchies) in Israel. However, regardless of their religiosity they are shifting the demographic composition and balance of Israel, as Lustick[50] argues, from a state with Jewish majority to one that is increasingly growing in the non-Jewish majority, and as such they are an indirect threat to the Jewishness of the Israeli state. Thus, the Zionist majority and the core political institutions, including the religious institutions, view them as a threat to the current state definition. However, their presence could be perceived as a bulwark to the Israeli majority, as the foreign workers' major advantage is that they are not Arabs, and as their numbers grow, so shrinks the importance of Arabs as a percentage of the total population.

As our data reveals, although the foreign workers do not envision a permanent stay in Israel for themselves, for their children it is a different story. These children have one consolidated identity, they view themselves as Israelis; and unlike their parents, they view Israel as their homeland. Demanding that their children be allowed to stay in Israel is probably the only political demand made by these people, and it could have serious implications for defining what and who is Israeli and how those determinations are made. By asking that children born in Israeli territory and/or educated in Israel be considered Israelis (i.e. broadening the definition to more than just Jewish parentage), the foreign workers' demand has the propensity to change the fundamental citizenship structure in Israel, moving from a nation-based, blood-based citizenship (*ius sanguinis*) to a territorially based understanding of citizenship *(ius soil)*, introducing the first effort to institutionalize soil-based citizenship. This understanding would move Israel toward a modern Western orientation where an individual is born into the state and away from a blood-based system.

This path of action is probably the ultimate threat to wedge between Jewishness and Israeliness, and the nature of the Israeli state as a Jewish state. In Israel, citizenship had been exclusively conferred based on Jewish lineage (a form of *ius sanguinis*). Arab-Israeli citizenship, an aberration to the dominant blood-based citizenship model, was conferred by *ius domicili*, the law of residency, based on presence at the foundation of the state of Israel. Israel confers Arab citizenship (including ascriptive citizenship) to the descendants of those present at the time of the foundation and excludes all other claims for non-Jewish citizenship. By introducing *ius soli* as a policy for transmitting citizenship, the policy would displace the hegemony of the religious as the keepers of the Jewish people (who's a Jew?) and the gate keepers for Israeli citizenship (what is Israeli?). Through this power shift from the religious to the state, the Israeli state would be strengthened. By moving to an *ius soli* system, in any form, the state would assume primacy over the 'borders' of the Israeli people and make the 'who's a Jew' discussion an exclusively religious – and not civic – matter for religious authorities exclusively, as it would no longer would impact state membership. Certainly, this introduction of non-Jews, regardless of the number (the number of foreign worker children is between 1,200 and 2,000, a negligible demographic figure), is a symbolic chink in the demographic integrity of the Israeli-Jewish state, but the stakes are far higher than these children. By even considering an *ius soli* system, the foreign workers' presence can shift the state apparatus and generate a real departure in what is Israeli and who is in charge of determining what and who is Israeli. This would more firmly shift the Israeli discourse to the Western paradigm and away from the Eastern one. However, it would generate great stress on the Jewish nature of the state, and how Israel would be able to manage this divide remains a yet unanswerable question.

Notes

1 H. K. Bhabha, The Location of Culture, London: Routledge, 1994. R. Young, Colonial Desire: Hybridity in Theory, Culture and Race, London: Routledge, 1995.
2 D. Alan, 'Is Israel Democratic? Substance and Semantics in the "Ethnic Democracy", Debate' Israel Studies, 4(2), 1999, 1. S. Smooha, 'The model of ethnic democracy: Israel as a Jewish and democratic state', Nations and Nationalism 8(4), 2002, 475–503. O. Yiftachel, 'Israeli society and Jewish-Palestinian reconciliation: "Ethnocracy" and its Territorial Contradictions', The Middle East Journal, 51(4), 1997, 505.
3 The official numbers are as follows: 125,000 legal and 125,000 illegal migrant workers; however, the estimations of most scholars are that the numbers are much higher and the migrant workers in Israel, legal and illegal, are estimated much closer to 400,000. See: R. Harper and H. Zubida, 'Making Room at the Table: Incorporation of Foreign Workers in Israel', Policy and Society, 29(4), 2010, 371–383.
4 These are the immigrants that came to Israel during the late 1980s and throughout the 1990s.
5 The law of return and amendments: http://www.mfa.gov.il/MFA/MFA Archive/1950_1959/Law%20of%20Return%205710-1950.
6 N. Elias and A. Kemp, 'The New Second Generation: Non-Jewish *Olim*, Black Jews and Children of Migrant Workers in Israel', Israel Studies, 15(1), 2010, 73–94. I. S. Lustick, 'Israel as a non-Arab State: The Political Implications of Mass Immigration of no-Jews' The Middle East Journal, 53(3), 1999, 417–433.
7 B. Kimmerling, 'Religion, Nationalism, and Democracy in Israel', Constellations, 6(3), 1999, 339–363. Y. Peled, 'Inter-Jewish Challenges to Israeli Identity', Palestine-Israel Journal, 8(4) 2001 and 9(1), 2002, 12–23. D. Rabinowitz, 'Borderline Collective Consciousness', Palestine-Israel Journal, 8(4) 2001 and 9(1) 2002, 2002, 38–49. E. Schweid, 'Jewishness and Israeliness', Palestine-Israel Journal, 8(4) 2001 and 9(1) 2002, 2002, 2002, 84–93. A. Shachar, 'Citizenship and Membership in the Israeli Polity', in T. Aleinikoff & D. Klusmeyer (Eds.), From Migrants to Citizens: Membership in a Changing World, Washington D.C.: Brookings Institution Press, 2000, 383–429.
8 A. Ghanem, The Palestinian-Arab Minority in Israel, 1948–2000, Albany, NY: State University of New York Press, 2001. J. S. Migdal and B. Kimmerling, 'The Odd

Man Out: Arabs in Israel', in Through the Lens of Israel: Explorations in State and Society, J. S. Migdal (Ed.), Albany, NY: State University of New York Press, 2001, 173–194. R. L. Basem, 'The Cana'anite Factor: (Un) Defining Religious Identities in Palestine and Israel', Palestine-Israel Journal, 8(4) 2001 and 9(1) 2002, 2002, 108. N. M. Rouhana, 'Outsiders' Identities: Are the Realities of "Inside Palestinians" Reconcilable?', Palestine-Israel Journal, 8(4) 2001 and 9(1) 2002, 2002, 61–70.
9   M. Z. Ispahani, 'Alone Together: Regional Security Arrangements in Southern Africa and the Arabian Gulf', International Security, 8(4), 1984, 152–175. M. Humphrey, 'Migrants, Workers and Refugees: The Political Economy of Population Movements in the Middle East', Middle East Report, No. 181, Radical Movements: Migrants, Workers and Refugees (Mar. – Apr.), 1993, 2–7. S. Khalaf, and S. Alkobaisi, 'Migrants' Strategies of Coping and Patterns of Accommodation in the Oil-Rich Gulf Societies: Evidence from the UAE', British Journal of Middle Eastern Studies, 26(2), 1999 (Nov), 271–298. L. Huan-Ming Ling, 'East Asian Migration to the Middle East Causes, Consequences and Considerations', International Migration Review, 18(1), 1984 (Spring), 19–36. S. Miers, 'Contemporary Forms of Slavery', Canadian Journal of African Studies, 34(3), 2000, 714–747. J. Chalcraft, 'Monarchy, Migration and Hegemony in the Arabian Peninsula', Kuwait Program on Development, Governance and Globalization in the Gulf States, London School of Economics, 2010.
10 S. Khalaf, and S. Alkobaisi, 'Migrants' Strategies of Coping and Patterns of Accommodation in the Oil-Rich Gulf Societies: Evidence from the UAE', p. 271–298.
11 R. Owen, 'Migrant workers in the Gulf', Minority Rights Group Report, 68, 1985.
12 N. Disney, 'South Korean Workers in the Middle East', Middle East Report, 61, 1977, 22–26. J. Chalcraft, 'Monarchy, Migration and Hegemony in the Arabian Peninsula', 2010.
13 N. Choucri, 'Asians in the Arab World: Labor Migration and Public Policy', Middle Eastern Studies, 22 (2), 1986, 252–73.
14 Bahrain ended the system in 2009.
15 In 2008, the government restricted migrants from living between Gedera and Hadera (two cities located 20 miles north and south of Tel Aviv) to reduce the numbers of migrant workers in the Tel Aviv area. The policy was rescinded after protests both from refugee organizations – because of community isolation and restrictions on freedom of movement – and from municipalities outside the region – for increasing the number of foreign workers under their jurisdiction.
16 Although not a state action, in 2010, 24 rabbis in Tel Aviv banded together and declared renting apartments to foreign workers was against Jewish law. See: D. Weiler-Polak, July 8, 2010: http://www.haaretz.com/news/national/tel-aviv-rabbis-renting-apartments-to-foreign-workers-violates-jewish-law-1.300815.
17 Employers may terminate workers at will, thus work complaints may engender contract rescission and loss of legal status, as status is tied to employment visas. As a result, there is a chilling effect on workers' complaints and some employers take advantage, knowing there is little recourse. This also means that many workers choose to become illegal workers if dissatisfied with working conditions or facing expiring contracts. Ironically, illegal workers have more freedom than their legal counterparts as they may live where they can find housing, charge the price they wish for their labor, and take or leave jobs at will. However, clearly they trade employment freedom for more precarious residency status.
18 See the section on foreign worker children for such exceptions.
19 In April 2011, the Israeli Supreme Court decided that pregnant women could not be forced to choose to send their children out of the country or lose their visas. Other issues remain contested before the Supreme Court.
20 We are not suggesting that this transition has been easy or is in any way completed. It is a complicated transition process that has been met with much political and social backlash. Further, the position of these former guestworkers and their children is not

The Israeli triangle 195

uniformly good or without discrimination and other serious social, economic and political problems.

21 R. Brubaker, (Ed.), Immigration and the Politics of Citizenship in Europe and North America, New York: University Press of America, 1989. R. Bauböck, (Ed.), From Aliens to Citizens: Redefining the Status of Immigrants in Europe, Brookfield, VT: Ashgate Publishing Company, 1994. A. Aleinikoff, and D. Klusmeyer, From Migrants to Citizens: Membership in a Changing World, Washington, D.C.: Carnegie Endowment for International Peace, 2000. R. Chin, The Guest Worker Question in Postwar Germany, New York: Cambridge University Press, 2007.

22 For a discussion of the ways of inclusion in the actual process of citizen making, see: R. Schmidt Sr., D. Yanow, M. Van Der Haar, R. Lozano, and K. Völke, 'Citizen-making in four countries: An interpretive analysis of citizenship policies for international migrants in the USA, Canada, the Netherlands, and Israel', Presented at the Western Political Science Association Annual Meeting, San Francisco, 2–5 April 2010.

23 Foreign workers' rights handbook can be found on the web at: http://www.piba.gov.il/ PublicationAndTender/Publications/Pages/Zchuyot2.aspx.

24 Ministry of Foreign Affairs, World Conference against Racism: Durban – Foreign Workers, 20 August 2001: http://www.mfa.gov.il/MFA/MFAArchive/2000_2009/2001/8/ Foreign%20Workers Z. Rosenhek, 'Migration Regimes and Social Rights: Migrant Workers in the Israeli Welfare State', in D. Levy and Y. Weiss (Eds.), Challenging Ethnic Citizenship: German and Israeli Perspectives on Immigration. New York: Berghahn, 2002, 137–153. A. Kemp, and R. Raijman, 'Christian Zionists in the Holy Land: Evangelical churches, labor migrants, and the Jewish State', Identities: Global Studies in Culture and Power, 10, 2003, 295–318. Kav L'Oved, Restaurant workers demonstrate for their wages, April 7 2006: http://www.kavlaoved.org.il/media-view_eng.asp?id=2379. R. Raijman, and A. Kemp. 'Consuming the Holy Spirit in the Holy Land: Evangelical Churches, Labor Migrants, and the Jewish State', in: Y. S. Carmeli and K. Applbaum (Eds.), Consumption and Market Society in Israel, Oxford: Berg, 2004, 163–184.

25 I. S. Lustick, 'Israel as a non-Arab State: The Political Implications of Mass Immigration of non-Jews', 417–433.

26 Other issues concerning the Palestinian workers are not included here but are discussed in: Y. Peled, 'Ethnic Democracy and The Legal Construction of Citizenship: Arab Citizens of The Jewish State', American Political Science Review, 86(2), 1992, 432–43. G. Shafir, and Y. Peled, 'The Dynamics of Citizenship in Israel and the Israeli-Palestinian Peace Process', in G. Shafir, (Ed.), The Citizenship Debates, Minneapolis, MN and London: University of Minnesota Press, 1998, 251–62. G. Shafir, and Y. Peled, Being Israeli: The Dynamics of Multiple Citizenship, Cambridge: Cambridge University Press, 2002.

27 D. Bartram, 'Foreign Workers in Israel: History and Theory', *International Migration Review*, 32(2), 1998, 303–325.

28 Israel usually refers to eldercare, childcare and household assistance as 'caregiving'. We use this moniker as well.

29 Israeli Central Bureau of Statistics, 2009.

30 Adriana Kemp provides an interesting analysis of internal politics, see: A. Kemp, 'Managing Migration, Reprioritizing National Citizenship: Undocumented Migrant Workers' Children and Policy Reforms in Israel', Theoretical Inquiries in Law, July 2007, 663–700.

31 Ministry of Foreign Affairs Communiqué, 2005: http://www.mfa.gov.il/MFA/ Government/Communiques/2005/Cabinet+Communique+26-Jun-2005.htm.

32 R. Sa'ar, 'Prime Minister Vowed to Help Foreign Workers' Kids, but the State Wants to Deport Them', Ha'aretz Newspaper, May 7, 2006.

33 Ministry of Foreign Affairs Communiqué, 2006: http://www.mfa.gov.il/MFA/ Government/Speeches+by+Israeli+leaders/2006/Address+to+Knesset+by+PM+Olm ert+on+presentation+of+31st+government+4-May-2006.htm.

34 The Israeli government frequently invokes terms like 'washing', 'laundering' and 'cleansing' with respect to the removal of foreign workers. We discuss the issues of rhetoric on purity and policy implementation in: R. Harper and H. Zubida, 'Making Room at the Table: Incorporation of Foreign Workers in Israel', 371–383.
35 A. Strauss, and J. Corbin, Basics of Qualitative Research: Techniques and Procedures for Developing Grounded Theory, Thousand Oaks, CA: Sage Publications, 1998.
36 I. S. Lustick, 'Israel as a non-Arab State: The Political Implications of Mass Immigration of non-Jews', 417–433.
37 C. Shalev, and S. Gooldin, 'The Uses and Misuses of In Vitro Fertilization in Israel: Some Sociological and Ethical Considerations', A Journal of Jewish Women's Studies & Gender, 12, 2006, 151–176.
38 S. Kelner, Tours That Bind: Diaspora, Pilgrimage, and Israeli Birthright Tourism, New York: NYU Press, 2010. L. Saxe, and B. Chazan, Ten Days of Birthright Israel. Lebanon, NH: Brandeis University Press, 2008.
39 See declaration of establishment of state of Israel at: http://www.mfa.gov.il/MFA/Peace%20Process/Guide%20to%20the%20Peace%20Process/Declaration%20of%20Establishment%20of%20State%20of%20Israel.
40 R. Raijman and M. Semyonov, 'Perceived threat and exclusionary attitudes towards Foreign workers in Israel', Ethnic and Racial Studies, 27(5), 2004, 780–799.
41 K. F. Afeef, 'New Issues in Refugee Research: A promised land for refugees? Asylum and migration in Israel', Research Paper No. 183, UNHCR, December, 2009.
42 R. Raijman and M. Semyonov, 'Perceived threat and exclusionary attitudes towards Foreign workers in Israel', 780–799.
43 N. Elias and A. Kemp, 'The New Second Generation: Non-Jewish *Olim*, Black Jews and Children of Migrant Workers in Israel', 73–94. U. Ben-Eliezar, 'Becoming a Black Jew: Cultural Racism and Anti-Racism in Contemporary Israel', Social Identities, 10(2), 2004, 245–266. S. Kaplan, 'Can the Ethiopian Change His Skin? The Beta Israel (Ethiopian Jews) and Racial Discourse', African Affairs, 98, 1999, 535–550. S. Weil, 'Religion, Blood and the equality of rights: the Case of Ethiopian Jews in Israel', International Journal on Minority and Group Rights, 4, 1997, 397–412.
44 As we explain later, our findings hold only for the adults in our sample. We found that among children, Israeli was indeed an important self-descriptor.
45 R. Raijman and A. Kemp, 'Consuming the Holy Spirit in the Holy Land: Evangelical Churches, Labor Migrants, and the Jewish State', in Consumption and Market Society in Israel, 2004, 163–184. S. Willen, Transnational Migration to Israel in Global Comparative Context. Plymouth, MA: Lexington Books, 2007. G. Sabar, 'The Rise and Fall of African Migrant Churches: Transformations in African Religious Discourse and Practice in Tel Aviv', in S. Willen, (Ed.) Transnational Migration to Israel in Global Comparative Context, Plymouth: Lexington Books, 2007, 185–202.
46 A. Arian, Politics in Israel: The Second Republic, (2nd Ed.), CQ Press, 2004.
47 Israeli Central Bureau of Statistics, 2009.
48 M. Jones-Correa, 'The Politics of Discontent: Comments on "Immigration and Public Opinion"', in Marcelo Suarez-Orozco (Ed.), Crossings: Mexican Immigration in Interdisciplinary Perspective, Cambridge: DRCLAS and Harvard University Press, 1998, 404–412.
49 P. Martin, 'US immigration: Benign Neglect Toward Immigration', in W. Cornelius, P. Martin and J. Hollifield (Eds.), Controlling Immigration: A Global Perspective, Stanford, CA: Stanford University Press, 1994, 83–100.
50 I. S. Lustick, 'Israel as a non-Arab State: The Political Implications of Mass Immigration of no-Jews', 417–433.

Part III
Cinema and identity

11 Israeli cinema's 'I'm in the East and my heart is in the West'

Igal Bursztyn

The aesthetic and the sociological – introductory remarks

Dozens of books and probably hundreds of publications have been produced in the last two decades on the subject of East/West relations in Israeli cinema. Almost all of them discuss the films from sociological, gender, political and ideological perspectives, completely disregarding film aesthetics.[1] This omission is not surprising if one considers the virtual absence of cinema from the Israeli cultural discourse till the late 1980s. Very little had been published on it besides press reviews, nor was it considered a worthy partner for any serious intellectual discussion. 'Plato didn't go to movies and yet he was one of the greatest men in history. And so was Moses, a great man, though he never watched TV' argued David Ben-Gurion in the mid-1960s.[2] The 150-year history of Zionism favored the struggle for language, for Hebrew, which provided the ingathering of fugitives with a national identity. So did, to a lesser degree, music, painting, dance, and from 1917, Hebrew theater (since the establishment of the Moscow Habima Theater which moved into the Land of Israel in 1928. It was preceded by the amateur 'Lovers of the Hebrew Stage' who operated in the Land of Israel in the years 1904–1914, mainly in schools and community centers to promote the use of Hebrew language). Film, first conceived as an instrument of propaganda and fund raising, later as a commercial enterprise, was of secondary cultural importance.

While plots, characterizations and language of early Hebrew literary works by Moshe Smilansky, Haim Brenner, Asher Barash, Haim Hazaz, Shai Agnon and later Izhar Smilansky confronted the complexities of the national conflict between Jews and Arabs and Oriental/Occidental ethnic divisions within the Jewish society, the cinema of their time avoided these confrontations or simplified them for propaganda purposes. Its heart yearned so much for the East that it developed a very imaginary picture of it.

The refusal to face reality, which persisted in films till mid-1960s, had crippling effects on their dramatic plots and acting performances. They thought and spoke, with few exceptions, in clichés or (in Roland Barthes' terminology) myths. 'Speech of pioneers, of woodcutters, is of a transitive type, it is quasi-unable to lie, lying is a richness, a lie presupposes property, truths and forms to spare. This essential bareness produces rare, threadbare myths ... by their very being, they label themselves as myths, and point to their masks'.[3] Thinking in clichés necessarily impoverishes the language. In the realm of filmmaking, it impoverishes its stylistic and expressive capacities. Plots are solved arbitrarily, acting becomes explanatory and stagy, dialogue literary and artificial, cinematography decorative, music pompous, and editing at its best covers up for the flaws of the rest.

The artistic poverty of the Israeli cinema has been well reflected in its studies. First, by their non-existence. Then, when by the late 20th century cinema could not be ignored in cultural studies anymore, by a flood of sociologically oriented publications which followed Ella Shohat's 1989 seminal *Israeli Cinema: East/West and the Politics of Representation*, probably the most influential study of Israeli cinema to date. For these studies the lack of stylistic qualities, the totally 'transparent' mode of representation, made mediocre films prone to, not to say easy for, analysis of contemporary ideologies. Works like *Kazablan*, *Hill 24 Doesn't Answer*, and *B'Ein Moledet* (to be discussed at length below), whether ragingly successful or ignored and forgotten, staged their underlying ideological fantasies at their purest and most naked form, relieving the sociologically minded critic of the task of interpreting. Kitsch always interprets itself. Bad or mediocre films – like speeches of second-rate politicians, dime novels, supermarket music or flea market paintings – supply knowledge and experience of what one already knows and has experienced.

The leveling of theoretical attention to the mediocre as well as to the artistically accomplished ends by supporting and publicizing the mediocre at the expense of the accomplished. In Shohat's canonical *Israeli Cinema: East/West and the Politics of Representation*, the work of David Perlov, one of the most important and influential filmmakers in Israel between the early 1960s to 2005, is mentioned in one footnote while dozens of pages are devoted to second and third-rate filmmakers like Alexander Ramati whose work carries the obvious stamp of Western imperialist ideology or to Hollywood blockbusters like *Exodus*. This is as if one discussed Israeli literature and ignored Shai Agnon or Amos Oz but devoted dozens of pages to Leon Uris.

Perlov's films, from his early *In Jerusalem* (1963) till *My Stills* (2002) completed shortly before his death, are inspired by an almost obsessive questioning of 'I'm in the East and my heart is in the West' and of Yehuda Halevi's obverse which had inspired the Zionist movement from its beginnings and Perlov's immigration from Brazil in the late 1950s. *My Stills*, an experimental documentary, in many respects Perlov's cinematic legacy, ends with shots of prosperous, Northern, predominantly Ashkenazi streets of Tel Aviv with passing glimpses of foreign, Arab and Oriental workers. These images are accompanied by Yair Dalal's highly complex, modernistic and yet clearly Oriental arrangement of a classic Hebrew folk tune written by a composer of Ashkenazi origin. (Dalal is a composer of Iraqi origin, exponent of classical and modern Arab music, an accomplished violin, canoon and oud player.) If one accepts (as I do) that music is the soul or the subconscious of a film, then the heart of Perlov's oeuvre is neither in the East nor in the West, but rather in both. And considering the ambivalent clash between the predominantly Oriental music and the hegemonic Occidental visuals,[4] one could also interpret the sequence as a heart's refusal to be committed to either, or as an ironic comment on 'my heart is in the East'. Such ambiguity is problematic for a critic interested in clear social messages. Films' emphases on stylistic qualities, often condemned as formalism, tend to blur and obscure their 'messages' while the totally 'transparent' mode of representation makes aesthetically mediocre films prone to, not to say easy for, analysis of contemporary ideologies. The resulting studies, which replicate films' most obvious representations and messages, necessarily become clichés in their own right. Though the sociological and aesthetic approaches may overlap, influence, motivate one another and can rarely be completely separate, a discussion of a work of art that ignores its aesthetic value necessarily becomes, as Theodor Adorno pointed out, thoughtless and 'mushy'.[5] Probably against the intentions of its sociologically orientated authors, it plays into the hands of the commercially minded exponents of culture as entertainment, whose vested interest is to present film as an exclusively popular art.

While it would be difficult twenty years ago to discuss the issue of 'I am in the East but my heart is in the West' as reflected in artistically accomplished films – they were too few – the amazing wealth of fresh and unexpected visual, narrative and stylistic approaches generated in the recent decade by Israeli feature, documentary and experimental films justifies a study from an aesthetic perspective. When related to cinema (or any art), the cultural choice implied by 'I am in the East but my heart is in the West' has both a social and aesthetic significance. This paper will emphasize the aesthetic, while discussing sequences and scenes that expressly or implicitly yearn and search for their cultural roots either in the East or West or beyond them.

A brief history (1911–1956)

The hearts of the first films produced in Israel were obviously in the East, though the films were produced by Zionist organizations of the West, directed by filmmakers who came from the West. The appropriately titled *The First Film of Palestine*[6] (the original title lost, this one was given by the S. Spielberg film archive in Jerusalem), made in 1911, directed by Murray Rosenberg and sponsored by the British Zionist Organization, and the recently discovered *Life of the Jews in the Land of Israel*[7] (1913) directed by Noah Sokolovsky and sponsored by the Ezra Association in Odessa, show idyllic vistas of the Holy Land: Oriental exotics with Biblical connotations, Arabs gathering round a well and galloping on horseback, Yemenites cutting stones in a quarry, Jews praying at the Wailing Wall, Zionist pioneers toiling the land and reaping the harvest. This 'heart in the East' sentiment pervades Zionist and Israeli dramas and documentaries till the mid-1960s. Arab-Jewish conflicts were either ignored or solved (like in Alexander Ford's *Tsabar* made in 1934) by bringing modernity and its prosperity into the Middle East. Later, following the Independence War, cinema's main theme became the heroic struggle against Arab aggression. Cultural and economical differences and conflicts between Western and Eastern Jews were ignored – the colorful, laborious, singing and dancing representatives of the Jewish Orient in early films were almost exclusively Yemenites. When toiling the land like in *The First Film of Palestine* they would be titled 'Yemenites' while European Jews doing similar jobs would deserve the title of 'Pioneers'. *B'Ein Moledet* (*Hope*, 1956) by Nuri Habib, the first Israeli filmmaker of Oriental origin (born in Baghdad and trained in Iraq and Egypt), also chose the Yemenite community to show the vicissitudes of the Oriental Diaspora. A belly-dancer of Jewish origin (acted by Shoshana Damari), kidnapped in her youth and raised as a Muslim, discovers her roots and joins the Jewish exodus to the Land of Israel. Chased and attacked by Arab horsemen, she and other refugees are saved by brave fighters dressed in khaki who arrive from Israel (probably members of Hagana – the action of the film takes place in the 1920s). This slow-paced, stagy and rather uneventful film, in the style of popular Oriental melodramas, filmed mostly in long-shots like amateur still photographs, created little interest in its time, though it was the first and for years to come the only attempt to dramatically present the plight of an Oriental Diaspora. Cinematically, Nuri Habib's heart was in the East, though his story leads its characters to the geographical West (relatively to Yemen or Iraq).

By the time it was made, the mainstream of Israeli cinema dealt almost exclusively with Holocaust refugees. Oriental Jews were shown in newsreels and documentaries as speechless elements of montage: ethnic types yearning for their homeland but with no speech, accent or individual traits of their own. As late as 1962 in *Dimona* (by Natan Gross), a documentary about a developing town in the Negev, its narrator, a new immigrant from Morocco, delivers his lines with a pronounced Yiddish accent, probably hoping that this would endear him to the audience. In fact the narration was read by German-born Arik Lavi.

Israeli's national epic of the 1950s, Thorold Dickinson's *Hill 24 Doesn't Answer* (1955), follows the events of the Israeli Independence War of 1948. The only Arabs in it are disciplined and well-trained soldiers of the Jordanian Arab Legion, friendly Druses, Muslim oil magnates, and German Nazis who serve them. There are no Palestinians. In its concluding episode a brave, blond Israeli Palmach fighter (an Israeli predecessor to Leon Uris' Ari Ben Canaan) captures an Egyptian prisoner in the Negev. He soon learns that his captive, Artur von Riebenhoff, was an Obersturmfuhrer in the Waffen SS. The Nazi dies of his wounds, shouting in delirium 'Heil Hitler' to the sounds of Horst-Wessel-Lied. The sequence abounds in endless explanatory dialogue, obvious and trivial visuals like the shadow of the outstretched arm in a Nazi salute, and over-acting as if the actors were frantically and desperately trying to convey a truth or hide a lie. On the overloaded soundtrack the Horst-Wessel-Lied fades into a Palmach tune as tanks bring relief and airplanes bomb Egyptian outposts (although a few moments earlier we were assured that the impoverished Israeli forces are short of artillery and ammunition).

In terms of this paper, one could say that while the heart of *Hill 24 Doesn't Answer* pretends to be in the East, it really remains in the West, deeply anchored in its culture, prejudices, traumas and political aspirations. In order to cover up for this it has to clarify, visualize and verbalize its unequivocal messages. Kitsch, 'the evil element of art' in Herman Broch's famous definition,[8] is always transparent, unambiguous and at its bluntest in the art – or lack of art – of film. It follows Zionism's bad conscience like a shadow (as it does all the nationalisms and ideologies of the 20th century). Produced just before the Sinai Campaign, *Hill 24* was inspired by an urgent need to explain and justify itself.

Yehuda Amichai's poem 'I Want to Die in My Own Bed', written more or less at the same time, had no need for that:

> All night the army came up from Gilgal
> To get to the killing field of slaughter.
> In the ground, warf and woof, lay the dead.
> I want to die in my own bed.[9]

It took almost 30 years for the Israeli cinema to catch up with Amichai's ironic distancing from heroism (and kitsch).

Film and folklore (1963–1986)

W.H. Auden once made a fruitful distinction between music as folklore and music as art, the latter 'having come to a conscious realization of its true nature'. Folkloristic proto-music 'bears the same relation to music that magical verbal formulas bear to the art of poetry. A primitive magic spell may be poetry but it does not know what it is, nor intends to be. ... In primitive proto-music, the percussion instruments which best imitate recurrent rhythms and, being incapable of melody, can least imitate novelty, play the greatest role'.[10] This distinction between proto-music, uncritical, unaware of itself and unable to reflect changes and novelties, and music as art – aware of itself and open to novelties – well applies to Israeli cinema. Its proto-films were capable of reproducing reality as determined by ideological clichés. This reproducing capacity was cinema's percussion.

David Perlov's 33-minute documentary *In Jerusalem* (1963) is one of the first Israeli films to demonstrate 'a conscious realization of its "true nature"' beyond seemingly mechanical but ideologically determined reproduction. To the rhythm of the same pompous Palmach tune used in *Hill 24 Doesn't Answer*, now played during a deadly serious military parade on the main street of Jerusalem, we see a turkey happily rocking on a broken branch. The film's protagonists, Eastern or Western, are no longer anonymous ethnic types, raw material for sociological or anthropological montages, but highly individualized and very self-conscious and camera-conscious characters. An old street cleaner in the Bukhara Quarter (at that time populated mostly by Oriental Jews) makes funny faces and puts up a show with his broom and bucket, entertaining both the filmmaker and the kids gathered around him. He is obviously as conscious of the camera as the camera is conscious of him. The surrounding kids yell 'Titztalem oti', which in jargonized faulty Hebrew means 'film me'. It seems to me that the heart of *In Jerusalem* is neither in the East nor in the West, not even in Jerusalem, but in the people who are filmed and in the very act of filmmaking. In this respect *In Jerusalem* anticipates developments in Israeli cinema which were to take place almost half a century later.

One of the first feature films conscious or at least attempting to be conscious of East/West cultural differences and conflicts inside the Israeli society was *Sallah Shabati* (Efraim Kishon, 1964), probably the first Israeli feature film to combine commercial and artistic achievement. It ridiculed the local political establishment and its bureaucracy, kibbutz hypocrisy, echoed the resentment of new immigrants detained for years in the misery of transit camps. Its hero, Sallah Shabati, a new immigrant from an undefined Oriental state, is quite incapable of counting his own children. He plays backgammon with an Ashkenazi friend fond of coo-coo clocks and when drunk sings songs to the Messiah, pleading for help out of his misery. His notion of culture is revealed when he is scorned by a kibbutz member: 'You must forget all the barbaric customs you brought with you'. To which he replies: 'You want us to forget all that is useless for you...' He sings a popular Oriental tune and comments: 'That's bad. But Symphony in F-minor played all day on the radio till it drives you nuts – that's good'. It seems that for Efraim Kishon Western culture was epitomized by F-minor symphonies and coo-coo clocks, as Eastern was by songs to the Messiah, backgammon games and ignorance of basic arithmetic.

As the spirit of the time moved away from Soviet-like heroism to Western-like individualism, films' purposes and justifications, formerly ideological, became commercial. They had to make money. A state with a population of 5 million people (in the 1960s) speaking an esoteric language has to support its film industry if it wants it to survive: the more tickets that were sold, the greater the bonus the film got from the government. Discussions of culture or rather cultures (and subcultures) and their differences became relevant and legitimate as film subjects only as long as they could be profitable. Culture became characterized mainly by ethnic food, flea markets and folklore. As a result, the film industry became abundant with ethnic comedies and melodramas, sometimes sexy, sometimes patriotic, usually both, most often copies of Hollywood successes – like Menahem Golan's *Kazablan* (1972). It transfers *West Side Story* to the slums of Jaffo. In a colorful flea market the people sing as they buy and sell: 'We're all Jews, so nice too/ Jews 100 percent, whether from Orient or Occident/ We all have the same father/ From Romania, Algiers or Kfar Sava/ And when there's trouble and pain/ We understand one another/ And all of Israel are friends'. Its hero (acted by Yoram Gaon), a golden-hearted hoodlum of Moroccan origin, but in the past a brave IDF officer, falls in love with an Ashkenazi girl who tames him, civilizes and finally marries him to the dismay of her family, but to the applause of audiences who were served a solution to ethnic conflicts with an assurance that: 'all of Israel are friends'.

Reflections on culture (1986–2011)

I find it significant that one of the most poignant filmic reactions to the tradition of Israeli kitsch started as a (commercially) disinterested 20-minute student film made in the mid-eighties for the Film Department of the Tel Aviv University. It gradually developed into a full-length feature film: *Avanti Popolo* (Rafi

Bukai, 1986). Its story takes place in the Sinai Desert during the 6 Days War of 1967. Two Egyptian soldiers, lost in the desert without water, discover in a UN abandoned jeep two bottles of whiskey, which they drink to survive. Khaled (Salim Daw) is an aspiring actor in a Cairo fringe theater. He would love to act in Hamlet but instead has been the given the part of Shylock, the Jew, in Shakespeare's *The Merchant of Venice*. As the two wander, thirsty and drunk in the desert, they run into an Israeli patrol. Khaled stuns them as he desperately quotes Shakespeare tinged with an Arab accent 'I am a Jew! Has a Jew not eyes? Hath not a Jew hands, organs, dimensions, senses, affections, passions, fed with the same food…'

What strikes me about this film, besides its obvious, perhaps even too obvious, humanist message, is its longing for culture. For high culture, disinterested and universal – for Shakespeare – capable of transcending Israeli/Egyptian differences and conflicts. *Avanti Popolo* seems to me another (after *In Jerusalem* and *Salakh Shabati*) pregnant moment in the history of Israeli cinema which has since activated dozens of Israeli movies, whether of Oriental or Occidental origin.

Eran Kolirin's *The Band's Visit* (2007) closes a circle of Israeli-Egyptian relations opened by *Hill 24 Doesn't Answer* and continued in *Avanti Popolo*. The Alexandria Police Symphonic Orchestra arrives in Israel to celebrate the opening of an Arab cultural center in Petah Tikva. A few minutes after their arrival they take a group photograph and look for their destination. Khaled, the orchestra's trumpet player, makes a pass at a girl behind the information desk and tries to discuss with her his favorite jazz trumpeter, Chet Baker, who she has never heard of. The music of Chet Baker, Gershwin and a beautiful Oriental tune by Habib Shehada Hana played from a jukebox unite, like Shakespeare 20 years earlier, Jewish and Arab women and men of different ethnicities and civilizations.

Like *Avanti Popolo*, this is not a record of reality, nor a mirror to life. It is sheer utopia. In reality an Arab cultural center could be established in Nazareth, Haifa, even Tel Aviv; never in Petah Tikva with its numerous orthodox inhabitants. One could imagine a visit from an Alexandria Police band, but it would be surrounded by cordons of police and Mossad agents. Not to mention Egyptian secret agents. But Kolirin's film, like the best works of the last decade, does not copy reality – it questions it. A question that transcends the issue of the geographical or ethnic-cultural location of the heart.

So does *Atash (Thirst)* made in 2004 by the Arab director Tawfik Abu Wa'el. Its story, while not less symbolical, is much more plausible: Abu Shukry, a tyrannical father, forces his family to live in an abandoned military camp. His elder daughter Jamila has brought disgrace on the family ten years ago – she had a secret love affair with a man. There is a sexual tension, almost incest, between the father and his daughter. While her young sister plays with bullet cartridges, and her brother tries to repair a radio transistor which may enable some contact with the outside world, Jamila reads a piece of poetry (or philosophy) she loves: 'The world's beauty is fading and vanishing. I heard this truth from a mute'.

Similarly the teenaged Rachel in *Shkhoor* (Shmuel Hasfari & Hanna Azoulai, 1994) watches classical ballet on TV with zeal in a godforsaken, impoverished developing town. The dreamlike elegance of the dancers on the screen seems to her an antithesis to the dreary suburban lifestyle and to the Moroccan black magic practised by her sister and her mother. The film itself is ambivalent about the possible superiority of Western classical dance and TV over the North African charms and superstitions. Rachel makes a career and ends up being an unhappy TV broadcaster (not a classical dancer) with a retarded daughter. The only person capable of communicating with her child is her demented sister who still practises black magic. The film rejects both European and Moroccan popular cultures, suggesting a different culture that could contain elements of both.

Benny Torati's *Desperado Square* (2001) expresses longing for Oriental music and art that is (or could be) as universal as Westerns – but rooted in the East. An Oriental, poverty-stricken neighborhood outside Tel Aviv rises to life when the old theater, closed for three decades by its now deceased owner, is to be opened by his sons to honor their father's memory. They screen what they remember to be the greatest Indian movie of all times: *Sangam* with Raj Kapoor. The upcoming screening stirs conflicting emotions, by those who adore the film and by those who feel that the movie may have dangerous implications. Especially for the widowed wife of the owner who was in love with Avi, his brother. Now, after his brother's death and more than 20 years after their love affair, Avi comes back to watch the movie. So does Sultana.

This is a film about love for cinema, for Oriental music, for simple people and for their culture, often despised by the Westernized cultural establishment. This establishment, however, is never shown or mentioned (as it often had been in popular ethnic comedies and melodramas[11]). Torati cares more for his characters and for what happens to them than for an outspoken social critique for which his film, intentionally or not, supplies rich materials. The insightful article by Shoshana Madmoni[12] draws our attention to the fact that the casting of Mohammad Bakhry, a well-known Arab actor, for the part of Avi, carries a message of solidarity between the oppressed Mizrachi Jews and Arabs. Torati told me in a conversation that he never had such intentions – he chose Bakhry exclusively for the quality of his acting (which in no way contradicts the political significance of his choice, whether intentional or not).

Despite their different styles, themes and fields of interest, all these films share an obvious human warmth, are capable of asking questions, being critical and skeptical of the reality they represent, and – what is least obvious and most important in the context of this paper – they question the existing Israeli cultures (often non-cultures) and express a passionate desire for a universal culture, for a share in the intellectual life of the world. This is outspoken in the Shakespearean monologue *Avanti Popolo*, in Khaled's admiration for Chet Baker and Dina's for an Oriental tune in *The Band's Visit*, in Jamila's readings of poetry and philosophy in *Thirst*, in the longing for Raj Kapoor's cinema in *Desperado Square*. The need for universal high culture, the desire to open up to the world rather than cuddle and cower in an Oriental or Occidental cultural ghetto, has become a recurrent theme in recent Israeli cinema. It echoes the lines of the great Hebrew poet Saul Tshernichovsky, who wrote in 1899 in 'Facing the Statue of Apollo':

Youth-God, sublime and free, the acme of beauty...
I came to you – do you recognize me?
I am a Jew – your eternal adversary...
... I bow, I kneel to the good and the sublime,
To what is worshipped in the fullness of life
To what is splendid in all creation.
I bow to life and courage and beauty
I bow to all the treasures robbed
by human corpses and the rotten seed of man,
rebels against life created by God,
God, Lord of the wondrous deserts,
God, Lord of the conquerors of Canaan by storm—
And they bound him in straps of phylactery.[13]

Tshernichovsky's attack on the rabbinical 'rotten seed of man' has for many generations become an act of defiance in the civil war of culture, which still rages on today. His heart is in the West, with Apollo, but to realize its desire he had to turn East and join 'the conquerors of Canaan'. Shakespeare, Raj Kapoor, Chet Baker, an Oriental tune, classical ballet are to *Avanti Popolo*, *Desperado Square*, *Band's Visit* and *Shkhoor* what the statue of Apollo was to Tshernichovsky – objects of desire, Western or Eastern, through which they can sense the world, face it on equal terms and hold a dialogue with it.

On freedom of interpretation – concluding remarks.

How is the cultural choice implied by 'I'm in the East and my heart is in the West' reflected in Israeli cinema? It is easy to locate the heart of Ze'ev Revach's *Tipat Mazal* (*A Bit of Luck,* 1992) in the East – with its outspoken nostalgia for the happy and prosperous days in Morocco before the exodus to the Ashkenazi dominated Israel; while the heart of Menahem Golan's *Fortuna* (1966) is obviously located in the West with its gentle, cultured and Westernized characters who redeem or attempt to redeem its heroine from the clutches of her Oriental, primitive and brutal father and brothers. Baruch Dinar's *They Were Ten* (1960), with the friendship evolving between the French-speaking Arab sheikh and a kind-hearted Jewish pioneer, could probably be located in David Ohana's Mediterranean option which implies a mixing of both East and Western cultures. Their sympathies are apparent on their very surfaces – in their obvious stories, images and acting.

It is much more difficult to locate the hearts of Ze'ev Revach's *Today Only* (1966) with its sympathetic characterization of both Mizrahi and Ashkenazi protagonists; Efraim Kishon's *Sallah Shabati* (1964), which seems to patronize and detest both East and West cultures alike; Shmuel Hasfari and Hanah Azulai's *Shkhoor* (1994), its complexities so eloquently discussed in *Identity Politics* by Yosefa Loshitzky;[14] Benny Torati's *Desperado Square* (2000); Dover Koshashvili's *Late Marriage* (2001), in which sex and love defy ethnic obligations and finally, unhappily, fail to defeat them; Tawfik Abu Wa'el's

Atash (*Thirst*, 2004); or more recently, *Seven Days* (2008) by Shlomo and Ronit Elkabetz, in which a quarrel among members of a Moroccan family over the need to observe traditional mourning rituals turns out to be really a fight over family money – a truly universal theme; the Israeli-Arab co-production *Ajami* (2009) by Scandar Copti and Yaron Shani, in which the cultures (or rather subcultures) of both Jewish and Arab communities make life unbearable; the anti-war *Waltz with Bashir* (2007) by Arik Fulman; and *Lebanon* (2009) by Shmulik Maoz, which were both shocked to realize that cultural differences become meaningless when faced with the horrors of war; or Dover Koshashvili's *Hitganvut Yehidim* (*Heart Murmur*, 2010), in which friendship and enmity between army recruits transcend their ethnic commitments. The complexities, subtleties and skepticisms of these films deliver quite equivocal representations of their respective cultures. The same could be said of the Palestinian *Divine Intervention* (2002) by Elia Suleiman, with its ironic representation of the Arab community in Nazareth and Jerusalem. Earlier Palestinian films like Michel Khleifi's *Wedding in the Galilee* (1987) deliver crude portrayals of perfidious Israelis brutally abusing the peaceful, kind-hearted and soil-toiling Palestinians, just as *Hill 24 Doesn't Answer* ignored the Palestinians and presented the Arabs as Nazi accomplices.

Recent Israeli and Palestinian films, when at their best, are much more complex, ambiguous and opaque; they prefer to ask questions rather then provide answers. Cultural choices that excite sociologists, ethnologists, political scientists and culture studies critics become secondary to what Milan Kundera defined as the sole purpose of literature: 'a revealing observation of human nature'.[15] This 'revealing observation' necessarily takes place in contexts of Occidental, Oriental, or mixed cultures, ethnicities, political realities. Films can – and do, intentionally or not – illuminate these contexts and realities. But in their quest for self-awareness, they transcend issues like 'I am in the East and my heart is in the West', asking instead: 'Which, out of East and West, is best for my work?'.

Good films are more interested in human beings than in issues – whoever is interested in issues has to proceed with his or her own (not the film's) interpretation and evaluation of what was shown in the film. *The Band's Visit*, one of my favorite films of the recent decade, was severely criticized as condescending, artificial and flattering Western tastes at the expense of the oppressed Oriental communities of the peripheries. The titles of these reprimands summarize their contents: *How to Sell the Middle-East*,[16] *Stereotypes in The Band's Visit*.[17] And though I disagree with these interpretations, I have to admit that they are just as legitimate as mine. This is the great privilege which good films bequeath to their spectators: the freedom to interpret. When films refute this freedom by raising issues and solving them by themselves as they did in the past, they condemn themselves to kitsch and their spectators to stupor.

My conclusion from watching Israeli films that have to do with East/West conflicts (most of them do) is that the real issue behind the conflicts is economical and political interests (a conclusion I've probably reached before watching the films – but the films, intentionally or unintentionally, seem to confirm it[18]). The claim that these conflicts are cultural in their nature, that the location of the heart in the East or in the West determines one's consciousness and existence, is an ideological manipulation which plays into the hands of the economical and political establishment. It is easier to support folkloristic events like Mimona festivities or careers of ethnically correct politicians or even to teach the Ashkenazis Arabic than to supply higher wages and better education for what is called 'periphery'. But even this Marxist conclusion would be undermined by at least one of the (good) films discussed in this paper – *Shkhoor*. Its heroine has moved from the impoverished, superstitious East to the prosperous and enlightened West, but is still unhappy. As I said: good films do not supply answers – they undermine them. That is because their hearts are neither in the East nor in the West but with their characters and with their cinema: Eastern, Western or both.

Notes

1 The titles speak for themselves: *Sexuality, Masculinity and Ethnicity in Israeli Cinema* by Yosef Raz (2010), *Cinema in Service of the Zionist Ideology* by Ariel L. Feldstein (2009), *Identity Politics on the Israeli Screen* by Yosefa Loshitzky (2001), *Nostalgia, Groups, and Collective Identity in Israeli Cinema*, Miri Talmon, (2001), *Mythical Expressions of Siege in Israeli Films* by Nitzan Ben Shaul (1997), *Israeli Cinema: East/West and the Politics of Representation* by Ella Shohat (1989) – to mention just few. My own *Face as Battlefield* (1990) is also strongly biased by sociological and ideological interpretations. Other studies like *The Israeli Film: Social and Cultural Influences 1912–1973* by Jacob Arzooni, Ora Gloria (1983), Hillel Tryster's *Israel Before Israel: Silent Cinema in the Holy Land* (1995), *Hebrew Film* by Nathan and Yaakov Gross (1991), Kornish, Amy's *World Cinema: Israel* (1996), Moshe Zimerman's *Signs of Movies, History of Israeli Cinema in the years 1896–1948* (2001) and *Hole in the Camera, Gazes in Israeli Cinema* (2003), Ariel Schweitzer's *Le Cinéma Israélien de la Modernité* (2003) and Nurit Gertz and George Khleifi's study on Palestinian Cinema *Landscape in Mist* (2006) and Yosef Halachmi's *Fresh Wind* (2009) avoid value judgments, concentrating instead on historical accounts with ideological digressions. The only writings with which I am familiar, and which come close to an aesthetic discussion of Israeli cinema, are works by Prof. Nurit Gertz: *Motion Fiction – Israeli Fiction on Film* (1993), *Myths in Israeli Culture* (2000), and parts of the anthology which she co-edited with Orly Lubin and Judd Neeman: *Fictive Looks – On Israeli Cinema* (1998). Dealing mostly with literary adaptations, they touch on issues of film aesthetics under the auspices of literature – legitimized long ago as 'high art'.
2 D. Shalit, Projecting Power, Tel Aviv, Resling, 2005, p. 15.
3 R. Barth, Mythologies, London, Granada Publishing, 1979, p. 181.
4 For Jean Luc Godard, visuals in film represent the hegemonic 'first world' while the sounds that support and serve the picture represent the oppressed 'third world'. He elaborates this in *Ici et ailleurs* (1974).
5 T. Adorno, Aesthetic Theory, London & New York: Routledge & Kegan Paul, 1984, p. 76.
6 There are rumors of the existence of some earlier films but no copies have been found.
7 Its copy was discovered in 1997 in the archives of the National Cinema Center CNC in Paris.
8 H. Broch, Notes on the Problem of Kitsch in Gillo Dorfles (ed.), Kitsch, London, Studio Vista, 1970 p. 63.
9 Y. Amichai, 'I Want to Die in My own Bed'. Translated by Barbara and Benjamin Harshav, in A Life of Poetry: 1948–1994, Harper Collins, 1994.

10 W.H. Auden, Notes on Music and Opera in The Dyer's Hand, London, Faber & Faber, 1975, p. 366.
11 Like Kishon's *Sallach Shabati*, Menachem Golan's *Fortuna* or *999 Aliza Mizrahi*, George Ovadiah's *Ariana*, Ze'ev Revach's *Bouba* and *A Bit of Luck* – to mention just a few.
12 S. Madmoni-Gerber, Kikar Ha-Halomot, in Gonul Dohmez-Colin (ed.), The Cinema of the North Africa and the Middle East, London: Wallflower, 2007.
13 Translated by D. Kuselewitz, 1978. Quoted in T. Mayer, Gender Ironies of Nationalism: Sexing the Nation, Routledge 2000, p. 297.
14 Y. Loshitzky, Identity Politics on the Israeli Screen, Austin, TX, University of Texas, 2001, pp. 72–89.
15 M. Kundera, Hamasakh (Le Rideau), Or Yehuda, Zmora-Bitan, 2006, p. 15.
16 K. Cohen, How to Sell the Middle East, Ha'Aretz, October 26, 2007.
17 M. Shmueloff, Stereotypes in *The Band's Visit*, Maaravon vol. 3–4, Spring 2009, pp. 12–18.
18 *Seven Days* (2008) by Shlomo and Ronit Alkabetz is quite outspoken about it. This outspokenness is probably the film's main aesthetic flaw.

Bibliography

Adorno, Theodor, *Aesthetic Theory*, London & New York: Routledge & Kegan Paul, 1984.
Amihai, Yehuda, 'I Want to Die in My Own Bed', translated by Barbara and Benjamin Harshav, in *A Life of Poetry: 1948–1994*, London: HarperCollins, 1994.
Auden, W.H., 'Notes on Music and Opera' in *The Dyer's Hand*, London: Faber & Faber, 1975.
Barthes, Roland, *Mythologies*, London: Granada Publishing, 1979.
Broch, Hermann, 'Notes on the Problem of Kitsch' in Gillo Dorfles *Kitsch*, London: Studio Vista, 1970.
Bursztyn, Igal, *Face as Battlefield*, Tel Aviv: Hakibbutz Hameuchad, 1989 (Hebrew).
Cohen, Kfir, *How to Sell the Middle East*, Ha'Aretz, October 26, 2007 (Hebrew).
Kundera, Milan, *Hamasakh* (*Le Rideau*), Or Yehuda: Zmora-Bitan, 2006 (Hebrew).
Loshitzky, Yosefa, *Identity Politics on the Israeli Screen*, Austin, TX: University of Texas, 2001.
Madmoni-Gerber, Shoshana, Kikar, Ha-Halomot, in Gonul Dohmez-Colin (ed.), *The Cinema of the North Africa and the Middle East*, London: Wallflower, 2007.
Shalit, David, *Projecting Power*, Tel Aviv: Resling, 2005 (Hebrew).
Shmueloff, Mati, 'Stereotypes in The Band's Visit', *Maaravon* vol. 3–4, Spring 2009 (Hebrew).
Shohat, Ella, *Israeli Cinema: East/West and the Politics of Representation*, Austin, TX: Texas University Press 1989.
Tshernichovsky, Saul, 'Facing the Statue of Apollo' in Tamar Mayer, *Gender Ironies of Nationalism: Sexing the Nation*, New York: Routledge, 2000.

Filmography

The First Film of Palestine, Murray Rosenberg (1911)
Life of the Jews in the Land of Israel, Noah Sokolovsky (1913)
Tsabar, Alexander Ford (1934)
B'Ein Moledet (*Hope*), Nuri Habib (1956)
Hill 24 Doesn't Answer, Thorold Dickinson (1955)

They Were Ten, Baruch Dinar (1960)
Dimona, Natan Gross (1962)
In Jerusalem, David Perlov (1963)
Sallah Shabati, Efraim Kishon (1964)
Fortuna, Menahem Golan (1966)
Today Only, Ze'ev Revach (1966)
Kazablan, Menahem Golan (1972)
Avanti Popolo, Rafi Bukai (1986)
Wedding in the Galilee, Michel Khleifi (1987)
Tipat Mazal (*A Bit of Luck*), Ze'ev Revach (1992)
Shkhoor, Shmuel Hasfari and Hanah Azulai (1994)
Late Marriage, Dover Koshashvili (2001)
Desperado Square, Benny Torati (2001)
Divine Intervention, Elia Suleiman (2002)
My Stills, David Perlov (2002)
Atash (*Thirst*), Tawfik Abu Wa'el 2004
Waltz with Bashir, Arik Fulman (2007)
The Band's Visit, Eran Kolirin (2007)
Seven Days, Shlomo and Ronit Elkabetz (2008)
Ajami, Scandar Copti and Yaron Shani (2009)
Lebanon, Shmulik Maoz (2009)
Hitganvut Yehidim (*Heart Murmur*), Dover Koshashvili (2010)

12 Visions of East and West in contemporary Israeli cinema and television

Paul Kubicek

Given a binary choice between 'East' and 'West', Israeli identity eludes simple classification. In fundamental ways, Israel is a 'Western' country. Its founding ideology, Zionism, was developed in Central Europe, and early Zionists sought to be 'ambassadors of Europe in the Levant'.[1] European Jews (Ashkenazim) have dominated its political, economic, and cultural life. Its democratic government and high level of economic development distinguish it from its Arab neighbors, and geopolitically its closest partner is the United States. Culturally, Ella Shohat observes that 'the dominant Israeli imaginary constantly inclines toward the West'.[2] Yet at the same time, Israel is also (Middle) 'Eastern'. Obviously this is true in a geographic sense, but one can also observe it in fault lines both in Jewish-Israeli society (e.g. Ashkenazi vs. Sephardic or Mizrahi Jews), but, perhaps more significantly, between Jews and Arabs; the latter of which include those who are citizens of the state of Israel as well as those who live in the occupied territories and in the states that are Israel's immediate neighbors.[3] Culturally – with an ethos whose genesis is in Palestine, the centrality of that particular land in their identity, in music and cuisine[4] – Israelis can also find a common idiom with Arabs. The links between the two peoples even have a basis in Scripture, as both claim the lineage of Abraham. Whether all of this can lead to political accommodation and perhaps the rise of a new, synthetic Israeli identity remains to be seen.

This paper will explore how Israeli identity plays out in the socio-cultural sphere, specifically in contemporary cinema and television.[5] Its focus will be on the relationship – in interpersonal more than political terms – between Israelis and Arabs. Representations on the screen both reflect aspects of reality and create larger cultural imaginaries that ask viewers to transcend politics and long-held notions of identity. It will examine elements of East/West representation and Israel's 'Eastern-ness' through the interplay of Jewish-Israeli and Arab characters and portrayals of cross-cultural divisions and parallelisms.

Before proceeding, a couple of justifications/caveats may be in order. First, although one could examine culture and identity in a number of mediums, cinema and television are wholly appropriate. 'Identity politics' has a long history of playing out on the Israeli screen,[6] and Israeli cinema, described by one scholar as 'necessarily and intensely political',[7] has been used didactically as a reflection of ideology, a 'source of mythic narratives' that 'displays an intensive mutual relationship with its political reality'.⁸ Moreover, the predominant discourse in Israeli cinema has varied over time, allowing one to see how representations of self and 'the Other' have evolved. Second, if for no other reason than space, studies of films must be selective about the material. This paper makes no claim to include all Israeli films or to present a 'random' sample, and one should also acknowledge that Israeli filmmakers tend to come from the more cosmopolitan left than the nationalist right. That said, this paper focuses on presentations that touch most explicitly on notions of East/West identity, with the more recent productions that are subjected to extended analysis (*Lemon Tree*, *For My Father*, *Arab Labor*) selected in part because they generated controversy and/or received accolades within Israel and abroad.⁹

Portrayals of Israeli identity and the East: A brief historical digression

Before jumping into consideration of productions from the 2000s, it might be useful to note how Israeli cinema has, in the past, treated issues of identity, particularly those that fall into the East/West paradigm. Following other scholars, one can divide Israeli cinematic history into different periods.[10]

The earliest Israeli films, some of which pre-date the foundation of the state, were largely in a heroic-nationalist genre that served the Zionist enterprise. Films such as *Sabra* (1933) and *This is the Land* (1934) celebrated both the land and the commitment of the early Jewish pioneers who staked a claim to it. After World War II, English-speaking films such as *My Father's House* (1948) and *Faithful City* (1952) were designed to elicit Western support and highlighted the rebirth of Holocaust survivors (typically children or adolescents) who lose their old identities and become 'Hebrew' among dedicated kibbutzim in Palestine. Other films such as *He Walked in the Fields* (1967) and *Hill 24 Doesn't Answer* (1955) paid homage to Jewish fighters in the War of Independence and trumpeted Israel's creation as a new beginning for the Jewish people. Several films after 1948, including the Hollywood epic *Exodus* (1960), also highlighted the positive role played by Westerners who embraced the Zionist project. Overall, the message of these films is quite straightforward: Jews (as settlers and/or Holocaust survivors) progress from 'dust-people to proud *Sabras*', from 'death to resurrection', and from 'desert to flowering garden', represented on-screen by images of the land itself.[11]

Arabs, not surprisingly, were bit players in this narrative, as they could not be, as Holocaust survivors could, transformed into heroic Israelis. They were, in Homi Bhabha's terms, exiled as a threat and as a fringe identity to the desirable, more homogeneous national narrative.[12] They played several roles in these films: the enemy of the heroic settlers; an existential threat to the state; residents of a dead land (and hence 'dead' themselves) that Jews have come to revive; or, at times, wild, primitive or backwards people who welcomed Zionists as bringers of material and civilizational progress. They were typically not developed on-screen as characters and we rarely saw developments from their point of view. At best, perhaps, Arabs served as facilitators for the transformation of the Jewish people: either by helping Jews discover their military courage or by helping them reach their land and home.[13]

In the 1960s and early 1970s the heroic-nationalist genre waned in favor of European-style films (such as those by Bergman and Godard) focused more on the private life of the individual. Nationalistic concerns were pushed to the side. Issues of collective identity were explored in the carnivalesque, comic, and often critically panned '*boureka*' films such as *Sallah Shabatti* (1964) and *Kazablan* (1974), which played up stereotypic ethnic and class differences between the Ashkenazim and Mizrahim (the 'internal Other') and revolved around misunderstandings between the two groups.[14] The Arab question remained, perhaps, an 'unspoken presence'[15] off-screen, while the endings of these films, typically a wedding joining together an Ashkenazi and Mizrahi family, argued in favor of the essential unity of the Israeli (Jewish) people.[16]

The rise of the Likud Party in 1977, together with the war in Lebanon in 1982 and increasing difficulties related to the occupied territories, sparked new developments in Israeli cinema. These were produced by figures on the political-cultural left and were offered as a critique both of contemporary government policy and of the previous heroic-nationalist genre. In films such as *Paratroopers, Wooden Gun, Silver Platter, Beyond the Walls, Smile of the Lamb*, and *Avanti Popolo*, the military was no longer glamorized and the Israeli state was seen as an agent of persecution, not of liberation. More significantly for this paper, in several films Arab and Palestinian issues came to the fore, often with a sympathetic presentation.

Among the ground-breaking films in the 'Palestinian wave' were *My Michael* (1975), *Hamsin* (1982), *A Very Narrow Bridge* (1985), and *Fictitious Marriage* (1989), all of which aroused controversy in Israel. *My Michael*, adapted from a novel by Amos Oz, tells the story of Hana, an Israeli woman who has sexual fantasies about Arab twins with whom she grew up. The twins, however, are not developed as characters in their own right; they are shot mainly from the back; and signify sexual excess, a taboo, an image generated by Hana's imagination and repressed impulses that could be lifted straight from the pages of Edward Said's *Orientalism*. Although novel in many ways, Arabs clearly constitute the exotic and foreign 'Other' in *My Michael*.

Hamsin, which also uses cross-cultural sexual relations as a central element of the plot, paints a fuller and different picture of Arabs. The film is set in Galilee and has parallels with the classic 'Western', centering on the relationships among a Jewish pioneer rancher (Gedalia), his sister (Hava), and Gedalia's Arab worker (Khalid). Gedalia comes across as well-meaning: he offers to buy land from Arabs before the government confiscates it and befriends Khalid. Khalid is also politically moderate, refusing to participate in actions against land confiscation. However, he is attracted to Hava, who has returned from study in Jerusalem. They have an affair, which is viewed as a betrayal by Gedalia, who unleashes a bull which gores Khalid to death. While the film is in many ways sympathetic to the Arabs, Khalid is still subordinated – in his economic position and in the storyline

– to Gedalia, so that audiences still have a 'view of the external other through the perspective of the Ashkenazi Israeli'.[17] As for the eroticism that ties the land to the physical body (e.g. both subject to 'conquest') and even borders on becoming a love-triangle, to the extent that the romance between Hava and Khalid constitutes an allegory of Jewish and Arab attempts at dialogue and reconciliation, the ending of the story indicates 'that there are some borders that still cannot be crossed even by ostensibly liberal Israelis'.[18]

A doomed love affair is also the primary plot element in *A Very Narrow Bridge*, the first film to be shot in the West Bank. The main characters are Benny, who is serving his reserve duty as a prosecutor for the civilian administration in the West Bank, and Leila, the widowed daughter-in-law of a leading Christian-Arab resident of Ramallah. Benny's attraction for Leila grows amid political tensions (the *intifada* broke out two years after this film was released).[19] For Benny, this causes a rift both within his family and at work. Leila is dismissed from her job and threatened for shaming her in-laws. The story of the making of the film carries interest as well, as its makers faced hostility from the Israeli Defense Forces and the lead actress, an Israeli Arab, had to be protected by Israelis because of threats she received from Arab extremists. In the end, however, their romance is doomed, as Leila is forced to cross into Jordan, promising to return but unsure if she will be able to do so. The question of identity is taken up in two ways in this film. For Benny, a Mizrahi Jew, his romance with Leila is a 'story of love for a repressed Orient, a discovery of lost roots' that forces him to abandon his artificial, Ashkenazified identity.[20] On the broader Arab-Israeli question, it is clear that Benny and Leila's relationship serves as a symbol, with 'enlightened' individuals struggling to overcome the intolerance and extremism that prevents a solution to the conflict. Still, as Ilan Pappe suggested, use of a 'sexual or romantic bridge as a way to understand the other side' has limits, as it tends to 'avoid and evade rational recognition of the arguments and feelings of the other side.'[21]

The main story in *Fictitious Marriage* revolves around Eldi, an Israeli who is mistakenly taken as a *yored* (Israeli émigré), which is the first of a series of identities he concocts to 'pass' into new environments. One of these is as an Arab construction worker, facilitated by his knowledge of classical Arabic. Dressed up like an Arab by an older co-worker, he has sex with an Israeli woman, who is excited by the idea of violating a taboo against interethnic sex. Ultimately, Eldi reveals his Jewish identity by (mistakenly) accusing his co-workers of planting a bomb. Despite the humor in the film and the engagement with taboos, the film suggests the limits of 'passing' or of permeable or multiple identities. The Arabs are not only falsely accused of terrorism (for which Eldi does not apologize) but are the butt of the joke at Eldi's passing, and, of course, no sexual taboos were in fact violated. Thus, while the film deals with questions of identity and Arab-Jewish relations more generally, it does less to subvert and more to reinforce existing racial boundaries.[22] Interestingly, however, the film ends with Eldi's son crouching down in a position like that assumed by the Arab workers; a position that Eldi could not successfully assume. The idea, therefore, may be that in the next generation perhaps Jews and Arabs will be more comfortable together.[23]

While the 'Eastern' question was treated in these films in a more sophisticated manner than it had been previously, critics suggested that this was, at best, an incomplete breakthrough. Commenting in general on the 'political films' of the 1970s and 1980s, Ilan Avisar suggested that while they targeted the 'holy cows' of the earlier Zionist period, they were 'failed films', essentially nihilistic and not suggesting a constructive vision or alternative ideology, which gave way to more personal-oriented films in the 1990s.[24] Shohat offered a different critique, arguing that the inclusion of Arabs remains limited. The story in most of these films is still focalized through Israeli protagonists, typically noble *Sabras* who try to be compassionate and understand the Arabs. At the same time, however, there are proscribed limits to Jewish-Arab interaction and emotional 'libidinal anxieties' are favored over a rational critique of power structures.[25] By continuing to pose Arabs as an exotic if not erotic 'Other', they do little to take up the idea that Israeli identity itself needs to become more inclusive or that the 'otherness' of the Arabs can somehow be removed or overcome.

Arabs, Jews, and East/West representations in contemporary film and television

The preceding section helps make it clear that issues of East/West identity, and, in particular, Israelis' relationship with Arabs, is nothing new in Israeli cinema. We'll now turn to three more recent productions – *Lemon Tree*, *For My Father*, and the television show *Arab Labor* – that build upon that prior foundation.[26] While some issues (e.g. cross-cultural romance, Arab resentment of Israeli policies) in these productions have played on Israeli screens before, I would contend these newer works make some important breaks with the past. The normative points – that Israeli Jews and Arabs should try to understand each other and that individual Arabs and Jews, as humans living in the midst of an intractable political conflict, have much in common with each other – come into very sharp focus. The Arab is less an eroticized or exotic Other and more a neighbor, an everyman or everywoman who Israelis should both want and try to understand. While hot-button political issues (the separation barrier and suicide bombings, respectively) drive much of the plot in *Lemon Tree* and *For My Father*, and *Arab Labor* comically deals with political issues and cultural stereotypes with political incorrectness, these productions are in certain ways apolitical, with their characters trying to transcend politics and their creators implicitly asking viewers to imagine an Israel that has made peace with its neighbors and its multiethnic character. However, like the films in the 1980s, none present happy endings. The common theme that emerges is that even if there is a will to overcome the past, look beyond civilizational divides and perhaps forge some sort of an Arab-Jewish or East-West synthesis, simple goodwill may not be enough, as long-standing biases and ignorance, not to mention real political differences, continue to frustrate both sides' efforts to reach accommodation and reconciliation. In other words, political divisions still remain too deep to be resolved by appeals to a common humanity.

Lemon Tree

Lemon Tree is on one level a very political film, taking up the issue of the separation barrier (which is shown in several shots) between Israel and the West Bank. The main setting is on the Green Line between the two sides. On one side is a large house occupied by Israel's Defense Minister, Israel Navon, and his wife, Mira. On the other side is the house and lemon grove of Salma Zidane, a Palestinian widow who inherited the orchard from her father. The plot revolves around the Israelis' attempt to uproot the trees, claiming that their presence is a security threat to the Defense Minister. Salma sues in Israeli courts to stop this action.

The film, however, is also about human relationships, identity, and what it means to be a good neighbor. Mira disagrees with her husband about cutting down the trees, as she finds the orchard 'charming', and even admits she too would sue to protect her home. We see that she and Salma are similar in various ways: both are lonely, both have children in the US, and both feel estranged from their larger national communities. Mira claims, unconvincingly, that she has much in common with army wives, but during the course of the film she is drawn toward Salma out of pity and curiosity and she desperately wants to make a connection to her. Their eyes meet across the fence dividing their property, and later they cross paths at the courtroom. Mira apologizes to Salma when Israeli soldiers, without Salma's permission, go into the grove to pick lemons for a party at the Navons'. At one point Mira even climbs the fence, looks in through a window of Salma's house and sees Salma crying, and goes to knock on the door to speak with her. She is stopped before she knocks, however, by an Israeli solider, who escorts her home. The viewer is left wondering what she possibly could have said that would have enabled her to make a real connection to Salma, who does not speak Hebrew and probably has no interest in getting to know her. Ultimately, Mira is unable to realize her stated aim to 'be a better neighbor to her … a normal neighbor.' Salma's trees are pruned to the ground (albeit not uprooted; a Pyrrhic victory), and what looks to be a ten-meter high wall comes to separate their properties. As Mira predicted, the desire to be good neighbors 'is a bit too much to hope for; there's too much blood and too much politics.'

Politics is thus condemned in the film for (literally) coming between people and preventing Arabs and Jews from finding common ground and being good neighbors. There are hollow efforts at accommodation: 'Arab' food, albeit kosher, is served at the Navons' party and music by the famous Arab singer Farid el-Atrash is played, but Arabs are not invited and the crowd ends up singing a Zionist paean. The Israelis continue – literally as the Navons' property rests above Salma's – to look down on Arabs, in this case to a fenced-in Palestinian woman, who, in this regard, resembles an animal in a zoo. Both of the Navons assert that Salma seems like a nice woman, but they do not know her, nor perhaps could they. There are too many barriers between them. Defense Minister Navon intones early in the film that 'goals are achieved only if you draw boundaries', but by the end of the film, with the wall with his neighbor in place, he is a destroyed man: his wife has left him and his political future is in doubt. Salma's orchard is also in ruins. No one is happy. Earlier in the film, Mira accuses her husband of 'ignoring reality' with his plans to destroy the orchard, suggesting that the 'reality' is that Salma has lived there a long time, has rights, and that Arabs and Jews must work to get along. The true 'reality', as depicted here, is that politics cannot be overcome and that Israel's superior power allows it to do what it wants. Several characters, including Israel Navon himself, make the point that 'trees are like people', that they have 'souls and feelings'. With the trees destroyed in the end, the message of the film is clear.

For My Father

For My Father tries to pull off an incredible feat – presenting a sympathetic picture of a suicide bomber. Tarek, the lead character, has been recruited to blow himself up in a market place in Tel Aviv. However, when he pushes the detonator, it fails to go off and he cannot get a replacement for two days because of the Shabbat holiday. In the interim, he spends time with the eccentric Katz, a Jewish shop keeper, and befriends Keren, a young Israeli woman who is estranged from her family.

The premise in some ways is darkly comedic – what will a frustrated suicide bomber do while the replacement detonator is on order and how will he escape detection? – but the movie functions as a drama. Gradually we learn more about each of the main characters, and what is striking is how parallel currents run through their back stories. Katz's son died because of forced dehydration during his military training, and Katz takes a fatherly interest in Tarek. Keren disgraced her family by becoming pregnant and is hounded by thuggish Orthodox boys from her neighborhood to atone for her sins and give up her more independent, libertine ways. Katz's wife tries to kill herself. Tarek is a reluctant suicide bomber, driven to this act to clear the name of his father, who is suspected of collaborating with Israeli occupation authorities so that he and Tarek could regularly cross into Israel for Tarek to play soccer for a club in Nazareth. His father has been threatened with death by Palestinian terrorists, but if Tarek carries out his mission, he will be spared, hence the title of the film. While biding his time in Tel Aviv, Tarek helps Katz with home repairs and protects Keren from her tormentors, helping spark an attraction between them.

Parallelisms run throughout the film, which work to minimize cultural distance between the characters and, by extension, Israeli and Arab societies. Both Tarek and Keren are preyed upon by religious extremists and are 'more at odds with their own culture than with each other's'.[27] Their mothers, both of whom are briefly on-camera, wear a similar head covering and are greatly concerned about their children.[28] Both the Katzes and Tarek's family, by the end of the film, lose their sons in needless deaths driven by overzealous militarism. Even the Tel Aviv neighborhood depicted in the film, with its sandy hues, crumbling buildings, open air markets, and narrow streets, recalls more an Arab *casbah* than a modern, Western metropolis.

While the viewer senses the attraction between Keren and Tarek, it is never physically consummated, perhaps because he is, after all, trying to hide the fact he has a bomb wrapped around his body. However, it is Keren, not the Arab

Tarek, who is more sexualized and, presumably, sexually experienced. There is little sense, from their point of view, that their relationship is taboo – it naturally evolves from Tarek's kindness toward her and Keren even introduces him to her mother. Katz also sees Tarek in human terms, not as a threatening Other. Even when he discovers Tarek's mission, he does not betray him to the authorities; rather, he tries to appeal to him, as a father who lost a son, to not go through with it. In the end, Tarek's bomb does go off – whether he pushes the button or it goes off as a result of him being shot by the police is unclear – but he has taken out the shrapnel, making him the only fatality of his operation and, perhaps, strangely honorable. His father is saved, but is, as we see, overwhelmed by grief.

If things were different, Tarek and Keren could be happy, but, like the lovers in *Hamsin* and *A Very Narrow Bridge*, they are star-crossed, victims of political circumstances which, for Tarek in particular, cannot be overcome. Again, politics and the ways in which it distorts otherwise simple, pure, human relationships, is to blame.

Arab Labor

The television show *Arab Labor* deals with many of the same themes discussed in the two dramatic films, albeit in a very different manner. The genre is comedy, often with a nihilistic bent reminiscent of *Seinfeld*. The principal characters are Israeli Arabs, who speak fluent Hebrew and in some respects are well integrated into Israeli society. Indeed, Amjad, the main character and a writer for an Israeli paper, is totally unlike most previous portrayals of Arabs on Israeli screens; he wants nothing more than to fit in, to become completely Israeli. He wants a car and clothes like an Israeli so he can 'pass' (literally, through checkpoints), is delighted to be invited to an Ashkenazi Israeli Seder dinner (where he makes an awkward toast), becomes a bit of a sell-out on television when he downplays Palestinian criticism of Israel, is confused about how to define 'your side' and 'our side', and even tries to enroll his daughter in a Hebrew school, where the director does not want to take in an Arab student. His efforts, however, are often in vain: his daughter is not admitted to school, he is pigeonholed in his job to work on 'Arab' stories, he is shown to be a bit of a buffoon, and at times he is frustrated by his family, particularly his father, who, in a sort of role reversal, often plays the 'Shylock'. After Amjad interviews a Jewish backer of a Jewish-Arab separation plan, who greatly disturbs him by asking 'Who needs these [dirty, criminal] Arabs?', he goes to an analyst to try to discover 'who' or 'what' he is.

While touching upon political issues, many characters would prefer not to be bothered with politics. Amjad's best friend, his colleague Meir, is meant to represent a typical, if somewhat naïve, Jewish Israeli. He has only the vaguest notion of politics. He is attracted to Amal, an Arab-Israeli, but their relationship is often problematic: she is very political and identifies herself as a Palestinian, whereas he fears Arabs and brags to her of his activities in the army reserves in Gaza. Although Meir may not fully recognize it, their relationship remains a bit of a taboo: when he tells her parents that his girlfriend is an Arab, his mother says 'there's no reason to call her names.' Interestingly, however, when Meir thinks he is being 'kidnapped' by Arabs, it is his Arab friend Amjad that he calls to help 'rescue' him. For Meir, the personal, not the political, is paramount. He even expresses a desire to learn Arabic, which Amjad characteristically dismisses, 'Why would you want to do that?'.

The show, co-created by Arab-Israeli Sayed Kashua and Daniel Paran, an Orthodox Jew, takes shots at both Arabs and Jews, and one can argue who comes off the worse. By explicitly invoking stereotypes – its very title refers to one[29] – the aim, one assumes, is to compel viewers to look at them more critically. As a comedy show, it does not point to a wide-reaching political solution for Arab-Jewish conflict, and one might suggest that it transforms interethnic tensions into discrete moments of pleasure instead of fostering serious discussion. However, unlike the *bourekas*, where the comedy allowed for the bypass or overcoming of ethnic conflict,[30] *Arab Labor* presents – at least in Season 1[31] – no comforting resolution. Awkwardness, at best, remains the norm. The larger point is that Arab-Israelis cannot be ignored; that some want and deserve a place in Israeli society; and that what it means to be Israeli must therefore be transformed. It can no longer, as it did in Israel's early history, rest on dichotomies and exclusion. By putting Arab and Israeli characters together in comic storylines and pointing to the foibles of each, it plays up differences between them while diminishing the importance of those differences. In this respect, then, it can be viewed as a call for tolerance and diversity.

Conclusion

Writing at the end of the 1980s, Ella Shohat concluded that Israeli cinema remained 'Eurotropic' as opposed to 'polyphonic', as it 'spurned any authentic dialogue with the East' and showed 'ambivalence toward its status as a country "in" the East but determined not to be "of" it.'[32] This paper suggests that a good deal has changed since then. Films such as *Lemon Tree* and *For My Father*, as well as the show *Arab Labor*, articulate the desires of the Arab/Palestinian 'Other', focalizing on Arab characters. At the same time, their similarities to Jewish characters, or, in the case of *Arab Labor*, the desire by some to become 'Israeli', are highlighted. The point is not simply a banal one that Arabs are part of a common humanity, but that Israelis and Arabs could, if politics did not intrude, potentially find deep bonds with each other. In other words, they are not so different, which implicitly asks whether the identity of 'Jewish' or 'Israeli' or even 'Western' or 'Eastern' should be that important. The issues in *Arab Labor*, although comically portrayed, are perhaps even more provocative, in that the show confronts the issue of whether Arabs, in particular Arab-Israelis, can be not only good neighbors (e.g. the issue in *Lemon Tree*) but literally a part of the Israeli 'us'. In this sense, it directly tackles the issue of what is Israeli identity and how far it can be stretched to include those that in no way embrace the Zionist version of Israeli history.

These explorations, however, still remain limited in scope. Presentations frequently remain focused on individuals in very particular situations, not a broader, more general collective struggle.[33] Indeed, the primary Arab characters in all the productions discussed above – Salma in *Lemon Tree*, Tarek in *For My*

Father, and Ajmad in *Arab Labor* – are divorced in various ways from the broader Arab/Palestinian struggle and are, to a certain extent, outcasts. Their goals are wholly individual in nature. In this way, one could contend that the critique of the existing social structure is underdeveloped, asking viewers not so much to envision how long-standing conflicts can be solved through political means but instead simply to imagine a world where the conflict did not exist and politics can be transcended. *Lemon Tree*, for example, suggests that the world would be a better place if there was no wall separating Palestinians and Israelis, but it also would be naïve to believe that years of separation, resentment, and fear can so easily be overcome. One still wonders what Salma and Mira could say to each other or if they could really be 'good neighbors' to each other. *For My Father* harkens back to earlier films with notions of a 'taboo' romance, but its presentation points more to the human tragedy of the ongoing conflict than to how thorny political issues can be addressed. The comedic genre of *Arab Labor* invites viewers to laugh at or transcend politics, but it is also, in many respects, a double-edged sword. While at times the viewer is laughing at the prejudices of Israeli (Jewish) society, at other times – arguably more frequently – she is laughing at the Arabs, and even though one might sympathize with Amjad's predicament, his quest to become 'Israeli' often makes him look ridiculous. Whether the show in subsequent seasons will offer any resolution or East-West synthesis remains to be seen, although its rather nihilistic *Seinfeld* or even *Simpsons*-like style augurs against it. In short, these creations recognize an East-West boundary within Israeli society and that hard definitions of 'us' and 'them' are both inaccurate and self-defeating, but they stop short of showing how these divisions, on a large scale, can be overcome.

Notes

1. D. Naaman, 'Orientalism as Alterity in Israeli Cinema', *Cinema Journal* 40. Summer 2001, p. 36.
2. E. Shohat, *Israeli Cinema: East/West and the Politics of Representation*, Austin, TX: University of Texas Press, 1989 p. 1.
3. Most estimates place the number of Israeli Arabs at around 20 percent of Israel's population. Counting the population of the West Bank and Gaza Strip, Jewish and Arab populations are roughly equal in the total area of the former mandate of Palestine.
4. Arabs and Israelis may dispute who makes the better hummus, but according to reports, in the late 1990s Syrians and Israelis negotiating in the United States, while failing to reach a political agreement, did concur that the hummus served by the Americans was horrid. See 'Rivalry over hummus: An emotive issue', *The Economist*, 12 November 12, 2009.
5. Identity is a complex subject, and many aspects of Israeli identity (e.g. Ashkenazim/Mizrahim divisions, the transformation of Holocaust survivors into Israelis, gender issues, attitudes toward homosexuality) have been shown on Israeli screens. This paper touches on some of these in passing. For more extended treatment, see N. Gertz, 'From Jew to Hebrew: The Zionist 'Narrative' in the Israeli Cinema of the 1940s and 1950s', *Israel Affairs* 4, Spring 1998, 175–200; O. Lubin, 'Body and Territory: Women in Israeli Cinema', *Israel Studies* 4, Summer 1999, 175–187; Naaman op. cit., 36–54; and R. Yosef, *Beyond Flesh: Queer Masculinities and Nationalism in Israeli Cinema*, New Brunswick, NJ: Rutgers University Press, 2004.

6 Y. Loshitzky, *Identity Politics on the Israeli Screen*. Austin, TX: University of Texas Press, 2001.
7 Shohat op. cit., p. 6.
8 I. Avisar, 'Israeli Cinema and the Ending of Zionist Ideology', in F. Lazin and G. Mahler, eds. *Israel in the Nineties: Development and Conflict*, Gainesville, FL: University Press of Florida, 1996, p. 153, p. 154.
9 *Lemon Tree* was nominated for seven Israeli Academy Awards, winning for Best Actress, and received the Audience Prize from the Berlin Film Festival. *For My Father* was nominated for seven Israeli awards and won the audience award at the Moscow Film Festival. Both have been screened widely at international festivals.
10 The categories borrow most explicitly from Shohat op. cit. and Avisar op. cit. and I. Avisar, 'The National and the Popular in Israeli Cinema', *Shofar: An Interdisciplinary Journal of Jewish Studies* 24, Fall 2005, 125–143. The best source for descriptions of the films discussed in this section is A. Kornish, *World Cinema: Israel*. Madison, NJ: Fairleigh Dickinson University Press, 1996.
11 Gertz, op. cit., p. 177.
12 H. Bhabha, *Nation and Narration*. London: Routledge, 1990, p. 80.
13 Gertz, op. cit., p. 178.
14 Naaman, op. cit.
15 Shohat, op. cit., p. 238.
16 Shohat, op. cit. argues that the existential threat of the Arab is used by the establishment to downplay specific Mizrahim issues and maintain the social hierarchical status quo that favors Ashkenazim.
17 Naaman, op. cit., p. 48.
18 Loshitzky, op. cit., p. 177.
19 *Torn Apart* (1989) has characters of the same name who also fall into a doomed romance, despite the fact that they were childhood friends and brought up by liberal parents who believed in coexistence. The basis for *A Very Narrow Bridge* is the Arabic folktale, 'Kays and Leila', which some speculate inspired *Romeo and Juliet*. See Loshitzky, op. cit., p. 127.
20 Loskitzky, op. cit., pp. 130–131.
21 Quoted in Loshitzky, op. cit., pp. 112–113.
22 Naaman, op. cit., p. 51.
23 Kornish, op. cit., p. 127.
24 Aviar 2005, op. cit., p. 138.
25 Shohat, op. cit., pp. 253–254.
26 One could discuss some other films as well, including *Cup Final* (1992), *Syrian Bride* (2004), *The Band's Visit* (2007), and *Ajami* (2009). Perhaps the best-known Israeli film in the 2000s, at least to foreign audiences, is *Waltz with Bashir*, which won the Golden Globe for Best Foreign Film in 2009 and was nominated for the Best Foreign Film Oscar. It features a novel animation style and critically probes issues related to the Israeli invasion of Lebanon in 1982, but does not take up issues of Israeli identity vis-à-vis Arabs as systematically as the productions discussed in this paper.
27 J. Catsoulis, 'Tale of a Terrorist', *New York Times*, 29 January 2010.
28 Contrast Tarek's mother in this film with the far less sympathetic mother of a real suicide bomber in the documentary film, *To Die in Jerusalem* (2007). This raises the issue of whether cinema represents reality or its creators' wishes or perceptions of reality, an issue not taken up in this paper.
29 'Arab Labor' is used to describe something done in a shoddy manner.
30 Naaman, op. cit., p. 41.
31 At the time of writing this paper, the author has only viewed the first season.
32 Shohat, op. cit., p. 272.
33 Shohat, op. cit., p. 266 makes the same point with respect to earlier films.

13 MediterEastern blues

New discourses of locality in Israeli cinema

Miri Talmon

Prologue: 'Homeland' 101: Home, land, and discourses of place in Hebrew-Israeli culture

First scene: A picture on the wall. In it the farmer is ploughing the soil. Cypress trees in the background, a pale summertime sky. The farmer will grow bread for us so that we grow up. This scene is quoted from a song titled: 'Homeland Class', whose lyrics were created by Israeli songwriter Eli Mohar and its melody by musician Efraim Shamir. It is also quoted from my own memory of my own homeland, Israel. My memory of lush green fields, orange groves and cypress trees bordering them. I am not quite certain if I can separate the real cypress trees bordering our farm in the Israeli village I was born and grew up in from the ones in JNF posters Mohar's song alludes to: JNF posters, in which small white houses with red roofs, neatly ordered ploughed fields bordered by cypress trees, establish the iconography of place associated with the revived and becoming 'Israel'. These images, which Israeli visual and cultural texts connote as the emblems of the young national-cultural-geographical entity 'Israel', were created to replace the displacement of the old wandering Jew and locate him within a new geo-cultural and historic scene. Images of the weary, wandering, homeless old man were transformed in propaganda films into a young Israeli female soldier, holding a 'Jaffa' orange, smiling, her whole life yet ahead of her. Whether these scenes are real biographic memories, or a cultural invention captured in old *hasbara* or propaganda posters and films, does not really matter when it comes to how culture works. Ann Swidler[1] discusses culture at work as a repertory of images, songs, memories, and practices, which inevitably become part of a toolkit for its members to understand the world they live in, relate to it and describe it. The farmer, the plough, the field and the cypress tree are items in the Israeli cultural toolkit that designate the Israeli place as experienced and remembered, as communicated by Israelis among themselves, to the next generations and to the outer world. These iconographies of place, however, change over time. New images that permeate visual Israeli culture and the Israeli songbook replace the nostalgic, rustic fecund landscape from Mohar's song. Bold, romantic gestures on a deep blue evening, or a romantic scene in sun-washed landscapes under the Mediterranean skies, replace the green agricultural landscapes and articulate new senses of place. These new cultural iconographies of the Israeli place as articulated in Israeli cinema are the subject of this article. The discussion starts with 1930s Zionist-Hebrew cinema, and proceeds to Israeli films from the first decade of the second millennium by the Israeli author Shemi Zarhin. The core argument of this discussion is that the ideologically invested Orientalist Zionist perceptions of the 'East' as an alternative to the exilic Western-Jewish decadent environment have transformed into the current position in Israeli culture, wherein the Middle Eastern Mediterranean becomes a sensually lived cultural experience. Rather than a fabricated allegorical South from a Bialik song ['El Hatzipor': 'To the Bird'], which articulates the subject position of an exiled Jew in the cold North yearning to go to the sunny shores of the Mediterranean, current popular Israeli songs or commercial advertisements recreate the Israeli everyday visually and sonically as if experienced in a 'taverna' in Greece or in a loud and colorful Italian neighborhood. Rather than representing the land of Israel as a symbolic site of national revival, as early Zionist-Hebrew cinema did, current Israeli cinema represents the Israeli everyday in its Mediterranean Middle Eastern environment, which becomes a taken-for-granted, natural background for the familial and individual dramas that take place within it in the foreground.

'This is the Land' [1934]: The 'East' as a symbolic site of national revival

Second scene: A stretch of virgin land. A farmer – or more precisely, 'a pioneer' – is ploughing the land. The horse seems to be making an effort to progress in the resisting soil. The man is sweating and his face is in agony. The man collapses, sick with malaria. '*Kadima*', he exclaims [literally: 'to the East' or 'forward' in Hebrew], in a last effort to complete his mission. He then falls down and merges with the soil. Another farmer comes running, replacing the fallen pioneer. The pioneer is now holding the plough and keeps conquering the resisting soil. In a technique used by Soviet filmmakers of the early twentieth century, Sergei Eisenstein and Vsevolod Pudovkin, the dead pioneer's image, returning to earth and becoming one with it, is merged by superimposition with the new living one, who keeps ploughing. So that we can have bread coming from the soil, as the song in the first scene tells us, and in order for a new life to blossom in the land of Israel, which is the ultimate ideological objective of this spectacular masculine effort.[2] This scene is quoted from the first Hebrew-speaking blockbuster in Palestine – Baruch Agadati's 1934 film '*This is the Land*'. It represents the idea of the ancient land of Israel as a new and upcoming homeland for the Jewish people. As Haim Nahman Bialik's allegorical poem 'In the Field' described it, the return of the Jews to the land was to be a return to nature,[3] to physical work of cultivating the soil, a sensual bonding with it.[4] Reinventing the people meant reinventing the land and the people's relation to it.[5] The abstract, grand narrative of the place lost to the Jewish people, or the 'big' place as Aran and Gurevitch define it,[6] which had become a textual entity captured in the bible, the prayers and the Jewish rituals commemorating Zion and practising the yearning to return, was to become the real, concrete 'small' place again, which one can remember as an authentically lived sensual experience of a concrete place.[7] Indeed, the Zionist cultural production in the land of Israel, including Agadati's cinema or the dance scenes he created, as well as festivities created in the self-consciously evolving culture,[8] or invented and staged at Hebrew schools and settlements,[9] underscored the affiliation of the emerging old-new Hebrew nation to the soil, to the land, the return to its longed-for place. These early Hebrew cultural texts and practices, from the first *aliyot* and into the 1930s, underscored the land as the ancient, desolate cradle of the nation, upon which the ancient biblical forefathers trod as shepherds and farmers, waiting to be redeemed by manual, physical manly labor. The land was to be repossessed and owned through the endeavor of pioneers, who, as articulated in the oxymoronic superimposition quoted from Agadati's film, will be willing to die and merge with the soil in order for new life to bloom. This oxymoronic fusion of living and ruin, the idea of new national life emerging from the desolate homeland in ruins and the sacrifice of the dead underlies the myth of Tel-Hai – literally meaning: a living grave or ruins.

Hebrew cinema was a major site of cultural production for the emerging Hebrew-Israeli culture, no less than literature, music, and folk Hebrew culture including festivities, textbooks for early education and other cultural practices which constructed the imagined revived nation. It is telling, however, that in the scene discussed here from '*Zot Hee Ha'aretz*' by Agadati, the exclamation of the fallen pioneer is '*Kadima*'. This yearning for the East in early Zionist discourses is not to be underestimated. This yearning for the land of Israel in the East from the European West is described by Shohat as an Orientalist fabrication of a European colonialist endeavor to appropriate a foreign territory.[10] David Ohana describes the Israeli attitude to the Mediterranean East as ambivalent.[11] As far as cinema as a cultural text can attest to it, and based on other evidence from studies of literature,[12] the 'East' is constructed in the early Hebrew national imagination as a yearned-for attribute of place and culture which would revive the decadent Western existence of the Jews in the Diaspora and return them to the cradle of their national culture. This return to the East and to a masculine, hard-working agrarian 'normal' national existence, as depicted in Agadati's film, is represented and retold in a later film paying homage to the first settlers' endeavor – Baruch Dienar's *They Were Ten* [1960]. As this film constructs it[13] and as captured in Zionist-Hebrew literature[14] [Peleg, 2005], the birth of the young nation or the rebirth of the ancient one involves its masculinization through manly manual labor, horse riding and other Middle Eastern, Arab rituals of masculinity. Hence, the plough, the drill, the horse and the rifle become in early Hebrew cinema phallic extensions by which the New Hebrew male appropriates the forsaken land, and tames the wild eastern frontier. In that process, as represented in both cinematic and literary texts, the Arab male and peasant of the Middle Eastern exotic Orient is a model for the Hebrew pioneer. He represents an authentic living in the territory as well as capturing the ancient agricultural practices of the biblical forefathers. Accordingly the pioneer says to his comrade in the 1960 film *They Were Ten*, yearningly gazing at a wooden Palestinian plough, 'this is what our forefather Abraham must have used'.

Cinematic senses of place and the Mediterranean

The complex affiliation to land, or place, stood at the heart of my discussion of a seminal and telling scene from the 1934 film *This Is the Land*. This notion of cultural affiliation to place and the cultural construction of place on film shall underlie my discussion of Israeli cinema, as a crucial site for the negotiation of Israelis' sense of place. Cinema is a major site for the articulation of discourses of place because as a medium and an art it captures place in mimetic and reflexive modes. In other words, whether shot on location or recreated and fabricated in a studio, films reproduce, recreate places and idioms of place as an inevitable aspect of their storytelling and functionality as a visual, narrative medium. We expect cinematic places to be accurate and authentic reproductions of their origin in reality. Does this mean that the nocturnal claustrophobic city in Hollywood's post WWII film noir or the American frontier in American Westerns are accurate reflections of real places? The answer is no, not at all. They are mythic reproductions of imagined places in the collective American unconscious, mythologized through generic conventions and expressing further unique meanings the individual talent and idiosyncratic expression of filmmakers infused in them. Are Mediterranean landscapes in the Taviani brothers' films genuine, authentic reflections of the Mediterranean? In what ways are other Italian, Greek, Tunisian or Egyptian films, whether popular, commercialized products or unique artistic instances products of their place of production, or expressions thereof?

This discussion of discourses of place, and of the Mediterranean and Middle Eastern context and place as a relevant cultural presence in Israeli films, does not aim for big generalizations about the place of place in films. It does adopt the basic theoretical assumption that 'place' is always a culturally produced construction, always invested in meanings not inherent in it by 'essence', or nature.[15] Likewise, 'The Mediterranean', whether discussed by Fernand Braudel, Albert Memi, Jaqueline Kahanoff, Irad Malkin, Yaacov Shavit, David Ohana, or Alexandra Nocke, is a name or a tag for a range of cultural and historic phenomena, which construct discourses or narratives about this 'place' – as a geo-political, cultural, historic or ethnic site of expression, action and interaction.

When it comes to the Mediterranean in the Israeli context, I'd like to second Nocke's approach in her study of 'The Place of the Mediterranean in Modern Israeli Identity'[16] that the discourse and cultural practices associated with the 'Mediterranean' in Israel in the recent decade pertain to and are a symptom of the discourse of contested and negotiated Israeli identity. It is a particular case, one of many, of the negotiation of 'Israeliness' and 'Israel' as a national, cultural, ethnic, historic, geographic entity by Israelis themselves. In my longitudinal study of Israeli culture and cinema I have consistently learned that all cultural phenomena and mythic contradictions in the culture have to do with the constant flux, disagreement, contradiction, self-conscious collective negotiation and open-ended becoming of this identity. Not surprisingly, since the very notions 'Israel' and 'Zion' are linguistic denotations of 'place', the contradictions and conflicts around Israeli and Zionist discourses of identity are focused on place. In addition, the contested existence and legitimacy of Israel is again inextricably bound with notions of affiliation to place, occupation of territory, delineation of borders. Post-Zionist discourses question the very notion of Jewish-Israeli affiliation to Israel as a place; in fact the authentic affiliation of Jews to any particular place, while affirming the natural, authentic affiliation of Palestinians to 'Palestine' as an authentic place.

Discussions of the 'Mediterranean option', the Mediterranean as a sort of 'third way' of discussing Israel in its regional geo-political and geo-cultural context, seem to offer a solution to each one of two approaches. One is a post-colonial, anti-Orientalist approach, which views Zionism and later Israel as an ephemeral, colonial crusader, Western-oriented entity, foreign and inauthentic in the region, which threatens some kind of stable cultural balance and will eventually have to disappear, just as it appeared, and leaving no actual traces. This vision of the Israelis as crusaders, haunting – as both Ohana [2008] and Feige [2008][17] have observed – Israeli discourse as well, is one way of de-legitimizing Israeli history as an instance of immigrant culture, emerging in a traumatic historic Jewish context, a pragmatic solution adopted at the time by immigrants to America, Australia, Argentina and other places by Jews in Europe, as well as non-Jews in Poland, Ireland, or Italy.

The second extreme is the neo-Jewish diasporic discourse, represented by Daniel Boyarin, David Myers, Amnon Raz Krakotzkin and others, who maintain that the Jews have always been more at home in exile, that their moral and ethical vocation is to be distributed among the nations and serve as a model for moral and intellectual values rather than earthly national ones, that the normal Jewish situation is the abnormal dispersion among the nations and around the globe. Both these approaches in a way imply that the Jews are an exceptional ethnic group, and deny the idea that like any other ethnic group they have an equal right to a natural, native, non-problematic affiliation to place. Within this discourse, the Mediterranean option is conceived of as a solution, or a 'third way', in the sense that it represents a hybrid of East and West – hence resolving the post-colonial anti-Orientalist critic of Zionism. The conceptualization of Mediterraneanism Ohana (following Kahanoff) proposes, as a multicultural and multilingual mentality and lifestyle, a tolerance for a vibrant exchange of commodities and cultural capital, resolves the contradiction of Jews and place by equating the Mediterranean and Cosmopolitan Jewish man of the world. Hence, the multilingual, multicultural Mediterranean openness actually reflects the Jewish cosmopolitanism and the hybrid openness of the Jewish minority according to a Deleuzian understanding of Kafka's discussion of minor literature. This elaboration of the Mediterranean idea, as David Ohana discusses it, evades the problematic conceptualization of Israeli identity in relation to place, in my view. It actually reproduces both the neo-Jewish diasporic discourse of place, and the post-colonialist discourse, by legitimizing Israel's place in the region and its self-image only as an indeterminate, open-ended entity, always open to influences and exchanges, rather than evolving as a unique cultural Mediterranean and Middle Eastern concrete instance, offering its own idiosyncratic cultural contribution and variant, which evolves in the actual living in the Mediterranean and in the Middle East.

In an article titled: 'The concept of "Homeland" and the Jewish ethos: Chronicles of a Dissonance',[18] Hagai Dagan rereads the biblical stories of our forefather Abraham and Exodus – the constituting myths of the Israelite-Hebrew-Jewish people and its contested affiliations to a stable homeland. The idea that dominates post-Zionist and neo-Jewish discourses, that Zionism in a deeply substantial way contradicts the soul of Judaism, is being examined by Dagan in reference to Israelis' sense of place. Dagan, much in the spirit of Gurevitch's cultural-anthropological study of Israeli discourses of place, regards the yearning for the land of Israel – rather than the actual living in it – as a crucial constitutive foundation of the Jewish people. Dagan proposes that it is this abstract notion of the 'promised land', of Israel as a spiritual, holy, yearned-for entity, that actually underlies Zionist texts. This ethos of the return to the promised land as an act of redemption for the persecuted and displaced Jewish people is epitomized in the 1947 film *My Father's House* (Meyer Levin screenplay, directed by Robert Kline and Joseph Leijtes), in which the newly found house for the Holocaust orphan survivor David is 'the house of my father Israel', namely the ancient and symbolic house of the forefathers. Coming back to Dagan's argument, however, he maintains that for most Israelis Israel is a concrete, personal and private home rather than a symbolic, national one. Not an abstract yearned-for entity, but a real sensual aggregate of everyday practices, fragrances, tastes and colors.

Israel, or 'Ha-Aretz' – THE land, as Israelis call it- is a home, a personal private memory and place of residence, rather than a national house -'Bayit Leumi' – as it was defined in the Balfur declaration. It is this concrete, sensual, not ideologically committed but personally and privately experienced domestic context that dominates current cultural Israeli film and television production and the new ideologies of place they articulate. This Mediterranean, Middle Eastern, local vernacular of Israeliness, which is intimately rooted in the local territory as homeland, dominates the visual and artistic cultural discourses of place. Nevertheless, at the same time, and in no contradiction whatsoever with the '*Gola*' or '*Galut*' [exile, Diaspora] as an idea and material cultural resource – current Israeli culture is completely at ease with its non-Hebrew, Jewish and exilic traditions, heritages, and imports. They no longer threaten a culture completely and authentically in place, at home.

In the following cultural analysis of two Israeli films by Shemi Zarhin, I'd like to establish my claim that Israeli cinema attests to the observation that Israelis are indeed open to multicultural negotiations, and keep debating the dosages of Eastern-ness and Western-ness in the culture – while at the same time constantly moving eastward towards the local and the regional, as far as the cultural production and tastes go. Israeli culture in its mundane popular and grassroots expressions is merging into the Mediterranean, Middle Eastern culture and lifestyle of the region, as Nocke so persuasively demonstrated in examining several cultural practices such as cuisine, music and architecture. As I hope to show, Israeli cinema attests to these very same trends.

While Nocke conducted interviews with self-reflexive Israelis about the place of the Mediterranean in their life or as an ideological option, and examined objective material phenomena in everyday Israeli life, my observations are based on textual, visual and sonic phenomena in Israeli cinema, which materialize the subtle ways in which the two films I discuss, *Bonjour Monsieur Shlomi* [2003] and *Aviva My Love* [2006], articulate new Israeli senses of place and locality.

A window to the Mediterranean: Senses and scenes of Israeli place in Shemi Zarhin's films

First scene: A window. A white lace curtain. The camera gazes through the window at a blurred horizon in blue, the Sea of Galilee decorated with mountains. It then moderately pans right through a series of objects. Light green walls. A 'Hamsa' on the wall. Several jars. Salted seeds of watermelon, a typical Middle Eastern snack, in one of them. The camera finally lands on Aviva's puzzled eyes. Aviva, as it turns out later, is the protagonist of this eponymous film. It is her point of view, as the author Shemi Zarhin explains in an interview with Pablo Utin,[19] that is oblivious to the beautiful landscape outside – and is preoccupied with the interiors of a dentist's clinic. Aviva is a hard-working mother of three, a hotel cook who is the breadwinner for her family, and wife of an unemployed mechanic. She is also a talented author, who turns the oppressing trivia of her everyday life into inspirational prose fiction. Aviva lives with her family in smalltown Israel, Tiberias. Tiberias is an ancient town at the shores of the Sea of Galilee, with a longstanding history. The director, Shemi Zarhin, who grew up in Tiberias, depicts it in all of its Mediterranean-Israeli sensuality. The film about Aviva and her family, her special relationship with her sister and mother, the hardships and beauty of her mundane life, is the story of the Israelis, as Israeli cinema has learned to tell it: devoid of pathos and heroism of the great national myths, focusing on the edgy, nervous, sticky everyday of a small and crowded place with no parking, no air condition, unemployment, and the constant threat of terror and war. Current Israeli cinema visualizes and narrativizes the 'normal' life of ordinary people, which becomes poetry in director Shemi Zarhin's well-accomplished cinematic art. The film was first screened in the summer of 2006 in a shelter in Tiberias, during the second Lebanon war, and was the most successful Israeli film of that year.

Aviva's dysfunctional, low-class Israeli family of Mizrahi heritage is typical of Zarhin's cinematic-poetic world, as he explains in an interview with Doni Inbar on the eve of the screening of the film at the San Francisco Jewish Film Festival. His choice to focus on these lower-class Israelis of Mizrahi heritage socio-economic milieu was manifested in his 2003 *Bonjour Monsieur Shlomi* as well. This artistic choice stems from Zarhin's commitment to capture Israeli reality in his film art and his artistic credo that this reality has its own visual character.[20] Every detail in the mise-en-scene, preferably not studio created, should play a crucial part in this ode to the Israeli everyday: the colors, the décor, the walls, the props. The Hamsa, a prevalent prop in Israeli houses both in Israel and in Florida, USA, the watermelon seeds in a jar, the local herbs – rosemary, thyme, basil- used for cooking in *Bonjour Monsieur Shlomi*, The '*Shakshuka*'- a Middle Eastern dish made of tomatoes and eggs which Aviva cooks, the *Ma'amul* cookies – again, a Middle Eastern pastry Aviva's father bakes, the hanging of laundry on the roof – a typical scene in Tunisian, Lebanese, Egyptian and Palestinian films – these details in the visual reality of the film stand for Israeli reality as Zarhin sees it in his art's eye, and yet they reverberate with visuals typical and prevalent in Middle Eastern and Mediterranean cinema. Zarhin insists that in making films he tries to re-construct his own experience, in his case his Israeli experience, or, if you will, and I am quoting him here, his Tiberias experience: 'This experience is first and foremost sensual: there's fragrances, tastes, colors, texture in it, far more than prototypes, stereotypes, attitudes, opinions and ethnicities' (Hebrew: *edot*, my translation, MTB, in Utin, 2008: 291).

When insisting upon an authentic, concrete, sensual reproduction of Israeli reality, representing his own experience as an Israeli from Tiberias, Zarhin's art materializes what I propose to characterize as 'the discourse of authenticity' in current Israeli cinema. The insistence upon representing an autobiographically lived experience rather than a collectivized one, the refusal to recreate stereotypes, ethnic types, attitudes and opinions, stands in sharp opposition to the kind of allegoric, ideological bias Israeli cinema was characterized with and criticized for. Ella Shohat, in her groundbreaking study of Israeli cinema [1989] focused on its Orientalist discourses and political Zionist allegories. She discussed Israeli cinema, in particular the personal-political cinema, as articulating a claustrophobic sense of place, the sense of Western, European Israeli alienation in the Middle Eastern space. Scenes taking place particularly on the beach in some 1970s-1980s films are interpreted by Shohat as articulating the anxiety of Israelis, yearning to flee by sea from the besieging Middle Eastern Orient. Contrary to this argument, I would argue that the beach, the shore of the Mediterranean, is a mythic cinematic site for the articulation and negotiation of an authentic Israeli identity, particularly in the films '*Peeping Toms*' [Hebrew: *Metzizim*, Uri Zohar, 1972] and *Late Summer Blues* [Hebrew: *Bluz la-khofesh Ha-gadol*, Renen Schorr, 1987]. The very liminality of the beach as a spatial edge as well as the 'edginess' of the infantile males refusing or unable to come of age in *Peeping Toms* captures an Israeli myth not yet obsolete. More important, however, is the kind of aesthetics Uri Zohar films created, his attitude to Israeli reality, which was discussed by Renen Schorr in an 1978 essay as epitomizing the 'Sabra' experience in its directness, documentary-like spontaneous and even improvised rendering of dramatic exchanges, colloquial Israeli Hebrew, use of non-actors and shooting with a handheld camera on location.

Although the 'Sabra' metaphor for native-born Israelis is no longer politically correct, and the Israeli experience is now located within complex multiethnic heritages and histories rather than the past free 'Sabra' myth, Zohar's cinematic idiom of Israeliness is the one Zarhin inherited. While Zohar chose the shore of the Mediterranean and the mythic lustful Sabra male gang as an expressive cinematic site of authentic Israeliness, Zarhin addresses a new site of authentic Israeliness, current in Israeli culture – the family.

The opening scene of *Aviva My Love* epitomizes Zarhin's artistic manifesto as well as the aesthetic discourse of Israeli films that pertain to a new trend, for which the appropriate title is: 'Films from Here'. [Hebrew: *Sratim Mikan*]. The project, initiated by the Israeli cable TV producer HOT [the Israeli version of HBO] supports Israeli filmmaking, and hosts those films in the stages of production, providing budgets, providing professionals in the film industry with jobs and a site for self-expression, as well as in the stages of public exposure, screening them to Israeli audiences on the cable television screen.

The 'Films from Here' enterprise is part of a more comprehensive and tremendously significant trend in Israeli culture. The last decade of the twentieth century witnessed dramatic changes in Israeli consciousness and culture. In the mid 1990s it seemed as if peace could actually materialize and transform Israelis' daily existence and collective agenda. The disposition towards peace brought about a turning point long due in the culture; it legitimized what I suggest to characterize as a feminization of the culture: the private sphere, personal priorities, the family and relationships became less marginal with regard to the national agenda and collective concerns. The home replaced communal spaces and collective forms of entertainment. The media, which dominated the domestic space, turned the home and the family into Israelis' most significant space for socialization and socializing. Television, the video cassette recorder and player, the personal computer and the internet, the DVD player and the home theater filled the domestic space with forms of entertainment and contents they used to consume in collective, public forums. The national holidays were now passively and intimately experienced opposite the television screen, with family and close friends, rather than in the public spaces that used to contain and celebrate such national, collective events. The traditional military marches of Independence Day, the last of which was symbolically transmitted on the first experimental broadcast of Israeli national television in 1968,[21] were an example of the way Israeli Independence Day was experienced as a collective event that expressed Israelis' pride in their army and their confidence in its power to defend their very existence. Since the late 1980s collective festivities have become secondary to family and close friends' picnics and backyard barbecues on Independence Day. The Home Depot has become one of Israel's favorite shopping spaces, as their homes have become their favorite castle. Homemaking as well as parenting is at the top of many Israelis' agenda. The family became the central site of identification and resource of identity rather than the nation, and other social institutions such as school or informal education frameworks like the youth movement.

In a society as collective-oriented as Israeli society, this trend is no less than a revolution. The supremacy of peers and the cohesive Israeli collective on the national as well as personal agenda was relinquished in favor of family trips abroad, romantic relationships and individual success and happiness as the ultimate Israeli Utopia.

Shemi Zarhin's films represent this trend in focusing the drama within the confines of the family and the domestic sphere, as well as in working within a traditionally feminine genre such as the family drama. Yet his films capture the unique sensuality of the Mediterranean in their consistent visual palette of blues, greens and azures, ever-present in the mise-en-scene of both *Bonjour Monsieur*

Shlomi and *Aviva My Love:* in the former, not one single scene misses a prop or a general shade of blue, and it is the predominant color in the latter as well. Zarhin accounts for this aesthetic choice (and I am quoting again in reported speech); these blue colors seem to him more suitable to the Mediterranean climate he was trying to get in touch with, not in a way that would imply a political or social commentary, but something completely experiential. He goes on and adds that the greens and the blues are also more respectful of the kind of Israeli light the way he likes it and tried to capture – a blazing white Israeli light [reminding me of the blazing azure light Israeli author Amos Oz chose as a title for a collection of essays about his own Israeli experience], and the kind of blues and greens that seem to have soaked a lot of this sunlight into them.[22]

The 'Mediterranean' visual idiom in Zarhin's films, as he explicitly accounts for it and grounds it in his own authentic experience of Israeli reality, as lived on a daily and biographic basis, as well as his insistence upon not grounding it in any ideological or political framework, reflect my own view of the way Israeli cinema in particular and the culture at large have come to deal with the Mediterranean and Middle Eastern as an inevitable, natural, taken-for-granted, non-apologetic, needing no justification – for better and for worse – aspect of life.

Another example of that visual, cinematic idiom is the dynamics of human interaction located in semi-public, liminal spaces such as balconies, stairwells, the dynamics of human exchange from balcony to balcony, from window to window, from a flat upstairs to the street downstairs, which predominantly characterized Zarhin's cinematic fictional world. This very exchange between Aviva upstairs and her sister downstairs, Aviva in the street and her mother about to jump from the window, the neighbor demanding from her window at Aviva's window that her vacuum cleaner be returned to her, Shlomi's father peering inside the house through the window outside, a family feud taking place through windows and doors with a ping-pong-like exchange which challenges the distinction between private and public/collective/communal space, and exposes all the family scandals to the ever-present control of the community's gaze and gossip.

This vibrant, edgy inter-human dynamic reverberates with the sensual world of the domestic sphere, in which Ella Shohat recognizes the distinctly Middle Eastern aesthetics and discourse of the mundane, as articulated in Moshe Mizrahi's 1973 film *The House on Chelouche Street*.[23] It lives its vibrant life on the patio, the site of solidarity, cooperation and colorful communal life of neighbors, in a setting and architecture that allow for a constant human exchange and interaction; it is in such semi-public interactive communal spaces that family life is always exposed to the community's public surveillance. It is this 'theater of the everyday' against the sensual, colorful Middle Eastern backdrop that Gabriel Ben-Simchon[24] identifies the positive, vital heritage of Moroccan Jewry; according to Shohat, it is the loss of this way of life, which is at one with its Middle Eastern spatial-cultural context and symbiotic with the Arab population and culture, that contributes to the identity crisis of Sephardic Jews in Israel. In this context of alienation to cultural spaces and traditions, Shohat claims, *Mizrahim* are doomed to live in an alien Europeanized space, and regard their own culture as the Arab enemy's culture, to suppress their own origins of identity and turn against their own former community in their countries of origin.[25]

Shemi Zarhin seems to articulate in his films not a return to his lost heritage anchored in a traumatically lost past or heritage, but an authentic cultural affiliation to a spatial reality, to a locality that is distinctly Israeli, yet self-consciously Mediterranean, according to his own testimony. As Yonatan Bar-Giora describes the process of creating the musical score for Zarhin's films, in close collaboration throughout the creative process, he tried to bring Zarhin home – to the Mediterranean, and brought him and the music and the film home safely by fusing Western melodies with Middle Eastern instruments. The unique Mediterranean hybrid of East and West, as discussed by Ohana and lived by Kahanoff, are not a theoretical option in Zarhin's films and Bar-Giora's unique musical idiom. It is a lived, sensual experience of light, color, sound and human exchange, transformed into art and a cultural idiom – distinctly Israeli, yet authentically MediterEastern.

In closing, I'd like to quote the Israeli rappers' 'Subliminal and the Shadow', concluding with another insight into 'homeland 101', going full circle from the Zionist enterprise of re-appropriating place to just being in one's place:

Who am I? What am I?
I know my roots and where I came from
I am from here and from here I arrived
Hadi Ardi Huna Biladi
[Arabic: This is my land, here is my homeland][26]

© Miri Talmon, March 7, 2011

Notes

1 Swidler, 2003.
2 For a discussion of representations of space and masculinity in Zionist Hebrew cinema, see Talmon, 2001, a, b.
3 Shavit, 1997.
4 Neuman, 2009.
5 Berlovitch, 1996.
6 See a later version of their discussion titled 'About the Place: an Israeli Anthropology' [*Al Hamakom: Antropolgia Israelit*], which appeared originally under this title in 1991 in Alpayim, number 4, p. 9–44 in Gurevitch, 2007: 22–73. This essay was published in English under the title: 'The Land of Israel: Myth and Phenomenon' in *Studies in Contemporary Jewry, Vol X*. 1994: 195–210.
7 Ibid.
8 Zerubavel, 1995 and Berlovitch, 1996.
9 Shavit and Siton, 2004.
10 Shohat, 1991.
11 David Ohana describes it as such; see Ohana, 2008.
12 Peleg, 2005.
13 Talmon, 2001a, b and Gertz, 1993.
14 Peleg, ibid.
15 Edward Soja in During, 1999.
16 Nocke, 2009.

17 Feige, 2008 and Ohana, 2008.
18 Dagan, 1999.
19 Utin, 2008: 292.
20 Ibid: 290.
21 Caspi Dan, and Limor, Yekhiel: 117.
22 Zarhin quoted in Utin, 2008: 290–291.
23 Shohat, 1991: 168–169.
24 Quoted in Shohat, ibid.
25 Shohat, ibid.
26 Subliminal 'Biladi' lyrics quoted from: http://www.shiron.net/artist?type=lyrics&lang=1&prfid=1118&wrkid=3862 (my translation).

Bibliography

Berlovitch, Yaffa. 1996. *Inventing a People, Inventing a Land. [Lehamtzi Eretz, Lehamtzie Am]* Tel Aviv: Hakibbutz Hameuchad [Hebrew].

Caspi, Dan and Limor, Yekhiel. 1986. *The Mediators: The Mass Media in Israel 1948–1990 [Hametavkhim: Emtzaei Hatikshoret BeIsrael 1948–1990]*. Tel Aviv: Am Oved. Jerusalem: The Hebrew University, Eshkol Institute.

Dagan, Hagai. 'The concept of "Homeland" and the Jewish ethos: Chronicles of a Dissonance'. In: *Alpayim, Number 18*. Tel Aviv: Am Oved Publishers, 1999, pages 9–23 [Hebrew].

Feige, Michael. 2008. 'The Crusader Myth: Fear and Anxiety in Zionist Negative Mythology' An essay presented at the 24th annual conference of the Association for Israel Studies, New York University, May 2008.

Gertz, Nurith. 1993. *Motion Fiction: Israeli Prose Fiction on Film. [Sipur Mehasratim: Siporet Israelit Ve'ibudeiha Lekolno'a]* Tel Aviv: Open University of Israel [Hebrew].

Gurevitch, Zali. 2007. *About the Place [Al Hamakom]*. Tel Aviv: Am Oved [Hebrew].

Neuman, Boaz. 2009. *Land and Desire in Early Zionism* [Tshukat Hakhalutzim] Tel Aviv: Am Oved and Sapir Academic College.

Nocke, Alexandra. 2009. *The Place of the Mediterranean in Modern Israeli Identity*. Leiden and Boston, MA: Brill.

Ohana, David. 2008. *Nor Cana'anites, Nor Crusaders: The Origins of Israeli Mythology*. Shalom Hartman Institute, Faculty of Law-Bar Ilan University, Keter Books [Hebrew].

Peleg, Yaron. 2005. *Orientalism and the Hebrew Imagination*. Ithaca and London: Cornell University Press.

Shavit, Yaacov. 1997. *Athens in Jerusalem: Classical Antiquity and Hellenism in the Making of the Modern Secular Jew*. London and New York: Oxford University Press.

Shavit, Yaacov and Siton, Shoshana. 2004. *Staging and Stagers in Modern Jewish Palestine: The Creation of Festive Lore in a New Culture 1882–1948*. Detroit, MI: Wayne State University Press.

Shohat, Ella. 1991 (1989). Trans: Anat Glickmann. *Israeli Cinema: East, West and the Politics of Representation. [Hakolno'a Haisraeli: Historia Veideologia]* Tel Aviv: Brerot. English edition: Austin, TX: Texas University Press.

Soja, Edward. 1999 (1993). History: Geography: Modernity. In Simon During, ed. *The Cultural Studies Reader*. London: Routledge (2nd edition): 113–125.

Swidler, Anne. (1986) 2003. 'Culture in Action' ['Tarbut Bife'ula']. Trans: Orit Friedland. In: Liebes Tamar and Talmon, Miri, eds. *Communication as Culture-Reader, Vol. 1*.: 53–78. Ramat Aviv: The Open University of Israel. *American Sociological Review*, 51, (April, 1986): 273–286.

Talmon, Miri. 2001a. *Israeli Graffiti: Nostalgia, Groups, and Collective Identity in Israeli Cinema* Haifa: University of Haifa Press and Tel Aviv: Open University Press [Hebrew].

Talmon, Miri. 2001b. *Here, There, and Nowhere: Representations of Space and the Negotiation of Identity in Israeli Cinema and Television of the 1990s.*

Utin, Pablo. Ed. 2008. *The New Israeli Cinema: Conversations with Filmmakers*. Tel Aviv: Resling [Hebrew].

Zerubavel, Yael. 1995. *Recovered Roots: Collective Memory and the Making of Israeli National Tradition.* Chicago, IL and London: Chicago University Press.

Part IV
Arabs and Jews

14 Israeli-Palestinian conflict

The psychosocial and identity impact on Arab and Jewish adolescents in Israel

Alean Al-Krenawi

Political violence is an ongoing threat to human well-being amongst all members of Israeli society.[1] Exposure to political violence is related to post-traumatic stress disorder (PTSD), depression, anxiety, and behavioral problems.[2] But it may also be associated with such positive outcomes as pro-social behavior and positive self-esteem.[3] The present paper is among the first to compare Jewish and Palestinian-Israeli adolescent respondents to political violence within Israel. Results show high levels of problems in both populations. In contrast to previous scholarship,[4] the paper finds that Palestinian-Israeli peoples had less exposure to political violence, but experienced higher impacts; one of the major factors for this differential experience being socioeconomic status (SES). By focusing on both populations living in the state of Israel, greater insight can be had into similar and divergent subjective experiences of political violence, and consequently the nature of the required medical and allied disciplinary responses to political violence can be tailored to suit these needs.

Political violence in Israel

War has been part of the Middle East prior to the 1948 creation of the state of Israel, and on an ongoing basis since that date.[5] There has been a profound impact on all peoples who have experienced political violence on both sides of the pre-1967 Israeli border, and on both sides of the Israeli-Gaza/West Bank green line. Since September 2000, upwards of 1000 Israelis have been killed and over 4000 injured, with numbers in the West Bank and Gaza estimated to be higher.[6] People from throughout the region are directly vulnerable to political violence, and experience it daily and vicariously through the experiences of those with whom they are close.[7]

Today, Israel is home to approximately 7,410,000 million people. Of these, about 1.3 million or 19.4 percent are Palestinian-Israeli. Eighty-two percent of the country's Palestinian-Israeli population is Muslim, 9 percent are Christian, and 9 percent are Druze.[8] Similar to other places in the Arab world, the majority of Muslims are Sunnis.[9] Prior to 1948, Palestinian-Israelis made up the majority of inhabitants of Palestine, but subsequent to the establishment of the state of Israel, 84 percent of the Palestinian population was exiled and became refugees.[10] Those who were left became a minority. About a quarter of those who remained were displaced from their homes to other locations, thus becoming internal refugees.[11]

The Palestinian-Israeli minority is considered to be a society in transition, caught between Eastern and Western cultures due to the process of Westernization within Israel.[12] The minority has significantly higher rates of poverty, unemployment, infant mortality and school attrition than the Jewish majority.[13] Many Palestinian Arabs in Israel live under a military regime and may experience social exclusion, leaving them in a conflict of dual identity as both Israeli and Palestinian. Although they live in the state of Israel, their Palestinian-Israeli identification has been shown to be more nationally and emotionally connected with being Palestinian and with the Palestinians in the Occupied Territories.[14] Furthermore, it has been postulated that the Israeli component of the Arabs' collective identity does not include a sense of belonging to the state, identifying with it, and developing a sense of attachment because the antinational superstructure excludes their identity.[15]

Since its inception, the very definition of Israel as a Jewish state has cast Arab national identity and social status into ambiguity.[16] Social identity is thought to be the means through which individuals understand themselves in their social context. Moreover, understanding the processes of identity formation in the context of intergroup conflict is particularly important, since social identity is critical to understanding how people act. When groups are in conflict, their members are placed under great pressure to completely conform to the values and practices of the in-group.[17] With regard to the Jewish-Israeli perspective, Kelman states that inherent to Jewish-Israeli identity is the negation of the Palestinian 'other' and the portrayal of this other as 'the enemy'.[18] Palestinian-Israelis experience a double trauma of exposure to political violence leading to negative social and psychological responses; furthermore, this study raises questions about the identity of Arab youth in Israel. Previous studies on Arab communities in Israel reveal strong identifications towards Palestinian national heritage and negative attitudes towards Israeli policies of Palestinian citizens. Scientific literature categorizes the Arab minority in Israel as significant, non-assimilating (differing from the majority in language, religion, nation, culture and ethnic descent), dissident (rejecting the State's official ideology of Zionism) and hostile (viewed by the Jewish majority as untrustworthy).[19] Nonetheless, Smooha asserts that presently a hybrid identity is emerging that may be referred to as 'Palestinians in Israel' and that 'conveys the primacy of Palestinian affiliation and orientations, without renouncing Israeli connections'.[20] In addition, Amara and Schnell's empirical study found that Arabs in Israel feel strongly attached to at least three identities.[21] The identity of Muslim adolescents in Israel reflects the components of identity of the adult Muslim population in Israel outlined here. Furthermore, the identity of Muslim adolescents in Israel is an amalgamation of identity formation during adolescence, the reality of belonging to a traditional culture in a Western nation and the unique manifestations of the Israeli context, in which Muslim adolescents are viewed as part of a 'hostile' non-assimilating minority. In fact, one recent study has documented that the identity of Muslim adolescents in Israel may change with the political situation evident in a specific moment in time.[22] A more recent study that asked Muslim adolescents in Israel to categorize themselves as either Muslim, Arab or Palestinian found that those whose major identity was Muslim had relatively low collective self-esteem.[23] Furthermore, the group that chose to characterize themselves as Muslim expressed little interest in acculturating into Israeli society. Thus, the findings of the present study pointed out that the Arab youth in the Israeli context are living in a multi-traumatic environment; the exposure to political events, and living in the margin of the Israeli society, resulting in having identity problems while living in two different worlds simultaneously.

The Jewish population in Israel is highly diverse. Being a country of immigrants, the majority remain Sephardim (European origins), with the remainder Ashkenazi (from other parts of the world). Most places on the globe are represented; recent places of migration include Russia, the former Eastern Bloc countries, and Ethiopia. The post-1967 context has seen considerable Jewish settlements constructed in the West Bank and Gaza Strip, although now only those in the West Bank remain. Recent estimations hold that upwards of 300,000 settlers are in the West Bank.[24] There are tremendous variances in socioeconomic status and most other well-being indicators throughout the Jewish sector of Israel. It is vital to emphasize the heterogeneity of this population. Palestinian-Israelis and Jewish-Israelis often live in separate cities, although there are major centres that mix the two backgrounds, including: Jaffa, Tel Aviv, Haifa, and Akko.

Methodology

The sample consisted of male and female school-attending adolescents aged 14–18 from Israel (442 Jewish and 475 Palestinian-Israelis). Cluster sampling proceeded as follows: geographically, the sample was recruited from three Israeli urban centres. Tel-Aviv-Jaffa and Haifa are district cities with heterogeneous populations in culture, religion and class, and Ariel is a West Bank settlement and is more homogeneous. All three cities were subject to suicide bombings and other politically violent events since the outbreak of the Intifada in September 2000. While Ariel suffered from less major terror attacks, its location within the West Bank may promote exposure to a greater number of minor political violence events. To ensure comparable internal diversity, the Palestinian-Israeli sample was recruited from Palestinian-Israeli villages, cities and mixed cities where Palestinian-Israeli and Jewish peoples live. The sample was taken across Israel: the Galilee in the north, the 'Triangle' in the centre, and the Negev in the south.

We applied the questionnaire randomly to schools and then randomly selected co-educational grades (grades 8–12). Graduate and undergraduate students were trained to coordinate questionnaire distribution and to answer any respondent queries. Respondents were gender-matched with research assistants, and Jewish populations were interviewed by Jewish students, and the Palestinian population by their Palestinian-Israeli counterparts.

We used seven instruments:

1   Background sociodemographic questionnaire – Thirteen items probed the socioeconomic status of participants' family, their parents' education, and included questions regarding gender, age, family structure and dwellings.
2   Political violence – This instrument aimed to capture the level of exposure to violence resulting from political acts. In order to assess political violence the researchers created an eighteen-item Traumatic Event Questionnaire[25] tailored to each community's language (Hebrew or Arabic), and to their respective modes of exposure to political violence (for example, the questionnaire asked about bomb or missile attacks). Nominal scale questions self-reported individual and friend/relative exposure. A total score was computed by summing all positive answers (range of scale 0–18), and thus a high score indicated more exposure to political violence. The internal reliability of the questionnaire was adequate among both the Jewish adolescents (Cronbach's alpha = 0.71) and among Palestinian-Israeli adolescents (Cronbach's alpha = 0.82).
3   Mental health – Mental health was assessed by clinically relevant psychological symptoms in adolescents. For this aim, we used the Brief Symptom Inventory (BSI).[26] This measure consists of 53 self-reported items covering nine symptom dimensions: somatization, obsession-compulsion, interpersonal sensitivity, depression, anxiety, hostility, phobic anxiety, paranoid ideation, psychoticism; and a composite measure of General Severity Index (GSI). A mean score was computed for each sub-scale and it ranged from 0–4 with a higher score indicating more mental health problems (scores of 2.52 and above indicate positive clinical diagnosis). The internal reliability of the nine odd-scales is adequate (Cronbach's alpha = 0.71–0.81) and the test-retest reliability is satisfactory (r= 0.60–0.90). The measure also has a moderate level of validity, which was measured by comparison to the MMPI. Norms and scores among youth populations in Israel and the United States are available for comparison. The internal reliability of the current measure in general, and of its sub-scales, was measured in a Jewish research population[27] with reasonable results (Cronbach's alphas ranged from 0.62 to 0.90). In the current study the reliability of the sub-scales among the Jewish adolescents was Cronbach's alpha 0.61–0.82 and 0.96 for the GSI, and among the Palestinian-Israeli adolescents 0.61–0.80 for the sub-scales and 0.95 for the GSI.
4   PTSD – Post-traumatic stress disorder was measured by the PTSD Symptom Scale: The PSS-I.[28] This measure is a 17-item instrument in which each symptom is rated on a 4-point scale. Sub-scale scores are calculated by summing items in each of the PTSD symptom clusters: re-experiencing, avoidance and arousal. A mean score was computed for each sub-scale and total scale with results ranging from 1–4, with a higher score indicating more PTSD. The scale has high internal consistency (Cronbach's alpha = 0.85) and moderate to high correlations with other measures of psychopathology. The

PSS-I has high test-retest reliability (r = 0.80) and inter-rater reliability (k = 0.91). In the current study the reliability of the total score was Cronbach's alpha 0.89 and sub-scales ranged from 0.75–0.78 among the Jewish adolescents and 0.89 for total score and 0.73–0.78 for the sub-scales among the Palestinian-Israeli participants.

5   Social functioning – To assess the social functioning of the adolescent participants we used the Peer Relations questionnaire, which is a standard measure for assessing peer group relationships.[29] The questionnaire, consisting of 25 questions, is suitable for respondents aged 12 and older. The sum score of the instrument was computed (ranging from 0–100), with a higher score indicating more problems in relationships with friends. The measure has a cut-off point at 35 points: individuals who score below 35 are categorized as being within the norm and those who score above 35 are categorized as having problems. The measure has high internal reliability (Cronbach's alpha = 0.94) and a low standard measure error (4.44). The peer group measure also has high validity and is able to discriminate between clinical and normal populations. Based on prior research, the internal reliability of the measure has been found to be high in an Israeli study of Jewish adolescents[30] (Cronbach's alpha = 0.93, N=146), and in studies among Bedouin-Arab adolescents (Cronbach's alpha = 0.89, N=256).[31] The reliability of the scales among the Jewish adolescents in the current study was Cronbach's alpha 0.94 and 0.91 among the Palestinian-Israeli adolescents.

6   Aggression – In order to assess adolescents' aggressive responses and their ability to channel those responses in a safe, constructive manner, we used the Aggression Questionnaire (AQ). This 34-item instrument[32] assesses adolescents' aggression on four sub-scales: physical aggression, verbal aggression, anger and hostility. A mean score was computed for each sub-scale and total scale. Each scale ranges from 1–5 with a higher score indicating more aggressive behaviors. The internal consistency of the AQ is relatively high (Cronbach's alpha = 0.89). The AQ is a stable instrument with good test-retest correlations of 0.80. Scores on the AQ sub-scales were moderately correlated with each other. However, when the variance in the correlations due to the anger score was partialled out, correlations were not significant. This supports the theoretical validity of the AQ in that the associations between physical aggression, verbal aggression, and hostility are due to their connection with anger. Scores also had good concurrent validity.[33] In the current study the reliability among the Jewish participants was Cronbach's alpha 0.89 for the total scale and 0.72–0.85 for the sub-scales, and among the Palestinian-Israeli participants 0.89 for the total scale and 0.65–0.84 for the sub-scales.

7   Family functioning – In order to assess the overall health and pathology of participants' family functioning we used The McMaster Family Assessment Device (FAD).[34] The FAD describes structural and organizational properties of the family group and the patterns of transactions among family members which have been found to distinguish between healthy and unhealthy families. This instrument includes 60 items on six dimensions of family functioning

and one general functioning scale. All sub-scales range from 1–4, with a higher score indicating more problems in a family's functioning. Cut-off points discriminating between 'clinical' and 'normal' families in American populations are available, though there are none for Israeli families. The scale has satisfactory reliability (Cronbach's alpha = 0.72–0.92), good test-retest reliability (r = 0.66) and high validity, as indicated by comparing the scale's scores to other measures of the same matters.[35] At this stage we analyzed only the 12 items that assess the family's general functioning. A recent study[36] found that these 12 items give a satisfactory picture of the family's general functioning, and as a result there is no need to use all 60 questions. In the current study the reliability among the Jewish participants was Cronbach's alpha 0.82 and 0.71 among the participants from Gaza Strip.

Data analysis is in four parts. First is a t-test and Chi-square analysis of demographic, socioeconomic status, and other differences between the two sample groups. Next is an analysis of the association between ethnicity and participant exposure to traumatic events, psychosocial, family functioning, PTSD and aggression. Third, we deploy Pearson correlations to analyze the association between political violence and dependent variables. Finally, we deployed multiple regressions to assess how political violence and ethnicity might predict the dependent variables.

Results

Table 14.1 shows the results of Chi-square tests and independent sample t-tests. Jewish parents had higher education, higher socioeconomic status, and lower unemployment than their Palestinian-Israeli counterparts.

Table 14.2's t-tests indicate that Jewish participants reported more exposure to political violence. No systematic results were found regarding mental health symptoms using the general severity index. Palestinian-Israeli participants reported more phobic anxiety psychoticism, PTSD, family and social problems, and aggression (physical); while Jewish participants reported more paranoid ideation and aggression (verbal).

Table 14.3's multiple regression shows that political violence was a positive significant correlation for Jewish participants regarding the general severity index and the PTSD index and aggression; but not for family or social functioning. For Palestinian-Israeli participants, political violence was found to correlate with mental health symptoms, aggression, family and social functioning.

When controlling for socioeconomic status, parents' education, gender, and religiosity, multiple regression analysis shows that exposure to political violence is a major significant predictor. As summarized in Table 14.4, respondents exposed to greater political violence reported higher levels of various mental health symptoms (somatization, obsession-compulsion, depression, anxiety, hostility, phobic anxiety, paranoid ideation, psychoticism, GSI), and more PTSD symptoms. In addition, exposure to political violence was found to be a significant predictor of problems in family functioning, social functioning and aggression.

Table 14.1 Nationality differences on sociodemographic variables

	Jewish (n=442)	Palestinian-Israelis (n=475)	Significant test
Gender, %			
Male	44.9	37.9	$\chi^2 =4.59^*$
Female	55.1	62.1	
Age, mean (SD)	15.35 (0.66)	15.53 (1.02)	$t=3.03^{**}$
Religiosity, %			
Very religious	4.8	4.5	$\chi^2 =23.65^{***}$
Religious	34.2	36.3	
Traditional	51.4	40.6	
Not religious	9.6	18.6	
No. of siblings, mean (SD)	2.00 (1.14)	3.66 (1.83)	$t=16.31^{***}$
Father's education			
Less than 8 years	2.4	10.5	$\chi^2=47.09^{***}$
8–9 years	8.1	15.5	
10–11 years	14.0	12.0	
12 years	39.2	24.9	
13 years or more	36.3	37.1	
Mother's education			
Less than 8 years	1.6	8.6	$\chi^2 =60.85^{***}$
8–9 years	4.0	14.2	
10–11 years	8.4	10.3	
12 years	45.9	30.5	
13 years or more	40.0	36.5	
Father's employment status			
Works	87.7	75.8	$\chi^2 =21.24^{***}$
Does not work	12.3	24.2	
Mother's employment status			
Works	80.4	61.9	$\chi^2 =166.91^{***}$
Does not work	19.6	38.1	
Parents' marital status			
Married	83.8	90.4	$\chi^2 =8.95^{**}$
Unmarried	16.2	9.6	
Family's economic status			
Low	4.1	5.5	$\chi^2=30.74^{***}$
Average	55.4	37.0	
High	40.5	57.4	

* $p<0.05$; ** $p<0.01$; *** $p<0.001$

Table 14.2 A comparison of Jewish and Palestinian-Israeli participants on political violence and psychological functioning

	Israel-Jews (n = 442)		Palestinian-Israelis (n=475)		t-value
	Mean	SD	Mean	SD	
Political Violence					
Traumatic Events Questionnaire	3.11	(2.61)	2.21	(2.78)	5.05***
Mental Health Symptoms (BSI)					
Somatization	0.81	(0.71)	0.84	(.66)	0.85
Obsession-Compulsion	1.16	(0.80)	1.19	(.64)	0.53
Interpersonal Sensitivity	1.01	(0.90)	0.99	(.79)	0.21
Depression	0.96	(0.76)	0.95	(.77)	0.25
Anxiety	1.13	(0.77)	1.06	(.65)	1.52
Hostility	1.11	(0.93)	1.12	(.77)	0.09
Phobic Anxiety	0.56	(0.60)	0.82	(.67)	6.11***
Paranoid Ideation	1.36	(0.87)	1.14	(.75)	4.04***
Psychoticism	0.77	(0.75)	0.85	(.67)	1.74*
General Severity Index	0.99	(0.64)	1.00	(.56)	0.30
Post-traumatic stress disorder (PTSD)					
PTSD Symptom Scale	1.19	(0.39)	1.52	(.48)	7.97***
Re-Experiencing	1.23	(0.44)	1.53	(.56)	7.44***
Avoidance	1.24	(0.39)	1.47	(.53)	7.38***
Arousal	1.37	(0.52)	1.59	(.58)	6.00***
Family Functioning					
Family Assessment Device	1.81	(0.51)	1.91	(0.46)	3.07**
Social Functioning					
Index of Peer Relations	17.79	(14.49)	19.24	(15.58)	1.45
Aggression					
Buss-Perry Aggression Questionnaire	1.99	(0.58)	2.12	(.60)	3.40***
Physical Aggression	1.83	(0.78)	2.03	(.85)	4.72***
Verbal Aggression	2.57	(0.82)	2.46	(.78)	2.01*
Anger	1.79	(0.67)	2.11	(.70)	7.05**
Hostility	1.97	(0.67)	1.96	(.69)	0.14

PTSD – Post-traumatic stress disorder; BSI - Brief symptom inventory
*p<05 **p<.01 ***p<.001

Table 14.3 Pearson product moment correlation coefficients between the research variables: Jewish participants above the diagonal, Palestinian-Israeli participants below the diagonal

	1	2	3	4	5	6
1. Political violence		.20***	.27***	.07	.06	.17***
2. General Severity Index (GSI)	.20***		.47***	.39***	.38***	.54***
3. Post-traumatic stress disorder (PTSD)	.31***	.58***		.25***	.23***	.29***
4. Family Assessment Device (FAD)	.18***	.40***	.36***		.42***	2.9***
5. Index of Peer Relations (IPR)	.17***	.42***	.37***	.38***		.25***
6. Aggression	.21***	.39***	.40***	.14***	.24***	

* p <.05; **p<.01; *** p<.001

Ethnicity was also found to be a major predictor. Palestinian-Israelis had more symptoms of somatization, phobic anxiety, psychoticism and less paranoid ideation; plus more PTSD symptoms, family functioning problems and aggression (specifically, physical aggression and anger). Regression results did not indicate a significant interaction for any of the dependent variables; thus they are not reported in Table 14.4. Findings show that exposure to political violence has a detrimental effect on social and mental health for both Jewish and Palestinian-Israeli participants.

Several sociodemographic factors are significant predictors of social and mental functioning. Participants with higher socioeconomic status have less mental health symptoms, PTSD symptoms, less family and social functioning problems and less anger. Parents' education likewise predicts family functioning. Girls tend to have more mental health symptoms and PTSD symptoms, and boys tend to have more problems with peers and more aggression. Religiosity does not predict any of the dependent variables.

Discussion

Seven points bear emphasis. First, political violence is a major predictor of psychosocial functioning. This was true for both Jewish and Palestinian-Israeli respondents, and it is highly consistent with findings in previous scholarship. Exposure to war can lead to such major problems as PTSD responses and anxiety attacks.[37] Like exposure to domestic and community violence (among victims and witnesses), it can produce psychological trauma; cognitive, emotional, and behavioral problems;[38] and other maladaptive strategies for coping with violent behavior.[39] Children exposed to violence are more likely to develop violent behavior leading to juvenile delinquency [40] and are more likely to display aggression and to legitimate violence.[41] Previous research on Palestinians in the West Bank shows well-established connections between political violence, domestic violence, community violence, and school violence;[42] among Israeli adolescents exposed to war there is comparable evidence of self-perceived problems in psychological growth and mild-to-severe PTSD.[43]

Table 14.4 Political violence, nationality, and sociodemographic variables as predictors of psychosocial functioning: standardized coefficients, β; unstandardized coefficients, b; and 95% confidence intervals of multiple regressions

	Political violence	Nationality	Socioeconomic status	Parents' education	Gender	Religion	R^2	F value
Mental health symptoms (BSI)								
Somatization								
β	.16***	.07*	-.18***	.04	.19***	-.03	.10	15.21**
b	.04	.10	-.12	.02	.26	-.03		
95% CI	.02 to .05	.01 to .19	-.16 to -.08	-.02 to .07	.17 to .35	-.09 to .03		
Obsession–compulsion								
β	.15***	.04	-.20***	-.01		.02	.09	13.76**
b	.04	.06	-.14	-.01	.19	.02		
95% CI	.02 to .06	-.03 to .16	-.18 to -.09	-.06 to .04	.09 to .28	-.04 to .08		
Interpersonal sensitivity								
β	.13***	.04	-.25***	.03	.20***	.04	.13	20.69**
b	.04	.07	-.20	.02	.44	.05		
95% CI	.02 to .06	-.04 to .18	-.25 to -.15	-.03 to .07	.23 to .45	-.02 to .12		
Depression								
β	.18***	.04	-.25***	-.01	.14***	-.03	.12	20.08**
b	.05	.07	-.18	-.01	.22	-.03		
95% CI	.03 to .07	-.04 to .17	-.23 to -.13	-.05 to .04	.13 to .32	-.10 to .03		
Anxiety								
β	.15***	-.02	-.17***	-.01	.20***	.06	.11	17.37**
b	.04	-.03	-.11	-.01	.29	.05		
95% CI	.02 to .06	-.13 to .06	-.16 to -.07	-.05 to .03	.20 to .39	-.01 to .11		
Hostility								
β	.17***	.05	.12***	.01	-.01	.02	.05	7.13***

	Political violence	Nationality	Socioeconomic status	Parents' education	Gender	Religion	R^2	F value
b	.05	.08	−.10	.01	−.01	−.01	.03	
95% CI	.03 to .07	−.03 to .20	−.185 to −.05	−.05 to .06	−.13 to .10	−.05 to .10		
Phobic anxiety								
β	.11**	.22***	−.19***	.05	.19***	.02	.14	22.56***
b	.03	.28	−.12	−.03	.25	.02		
95% CI	.01 to .04	.19 to .36	−.16 to −.08	−.07 to .01	.17 to .33	−.04 to .07		
Paranoid ideation								
β	.17***	−.10**	.16***	.02	.12***	.03	.09	14.07***
b	.05	−.16	−.12	.01	.19	.03		
95% CI	.03 to .07	−.27 to −.05	−.17 to −.07	−.04 to .07	.09 to .30	−.04 to .10		
Psychoticism								
β	.18***	.10**	−.24***	−.03	.12***	−.02	.12	19.03
b	.05	.15	−.16	−.02	.18	−.02		
95% CI	.03 to .06	−.01 to .15	−.17 to −.10	−.04 to .04	.14 to .29	−.04 to .06		
General Severity Index								
β	.20***	.06	−.24***	−.01	.18***	.01	.14	22.80***
b	.04	.07	−.14	−.01	.22	.01		
95% CI	.03 to .06	−.01 to .15	−.17 to −.10	−.04 to .04	.14 to .29	−.04 to .06		
Post-traumatic stress disorder (PTSD)								
PTSD								
β	.30***	.31***	−.14***	−.02	.10**	−.01	.18	31.63***
b	.05	.27	−.06	−.01	.09	−.01		
95% CI	.04 to .06	.21 to .23	−.08 to −.03	−.03 to .02	.03 to .14	−.04 to .04		

Continued....

Table 14.4 continued...

	Political violence	Nationality	Socioeconomic status	Parents' education	Gender	Religion	R^2	F value
Re-experiencing								
β	.26***	.29***	-.13***	-.02	.11**	.02	.16	26.54***
b	.05	.29	-.06	-.01	.11	.02		
95% CI	.04 to .06	.22 to .36	-.09 to -.03	-.04 to .02	.05 to .18	-.03 to .06		
Avoidance								
β	.26***	.28***	-.14***	-.02	.06	.01	.14	23.88***
b	.04	.26	-.06	-.01	.06	.01		
95% CI	.03 to .06	.20 to .32	-.09 to .03	-.04 to .02	-.01 to .12	-.04 to .04		
Arousal								
β	.26***	.24***	-.10***	.01	.10**	-.02	.12	19.54***
b	.05	.27	-.05	.01	.11	-.02		
95% CI	.04 to .07	.19 to .34	-.08 to -.02	-.04 to .04	.04 to .18	-.06 to .03		
Family functioning								
Family assessment device								
β	.13***		.14***	-.09*	-.06	-.10**	.09	14.01***
b	.02	.14	-.09	-.04	-.06	-.06		
95% CI	.01 to .04	.07 to .20	-.11 to .06	-.07 to -.01	-.13 to .01	-.10 to -.02		
Social functioning								
Index of peer relations								
β	.12***	.05	.20****	-.01	-.07*	-.04	.06	9.70***
b	.02	.06	-.10	-.01	-.08	-.03		
95% CI	.01 to .04	-.02 to .13	-.14 to -.07	-.04 to .03	-.15 to -.01	-.08 to .02		
Aggression								
Buss-Perry aggression questionnaire								

	Political violence	Nationality	Socioeconomic status	Parents' education	Gender	Religion	R^2	F value
β	.18***	.14***	-.05	-.03	-.13***	-.01	.06	9.76***
b	.04	.17	-.03	-.02	-.16	.01		
95% CI	.02 to .05	.09 to .25	-.07 to .01	-.05 to .02	-.24 to -.08	-.05 to .06		
Physical aggression								
β	.14***	.19***	-.02	-.05	-.32***	.01	.14	23.77***
b	.04	.31	-.02	-.04	-.53	.01		
95% CI	.02 to .06	.21 to .42	-.07 to .03	-.09 to .02	-.64 to -.43	-.06 to .08		
Verbal aggression								
β	.09*	-.05	-.01	.01	.02	-.02	.01	1.73
b	.03	-.09	.01	.01	.04	-.02		
95% CI	.01 to .05	-.20 to .03	-.05 to .05	-.05 to .05	-.08 to .15	-.09 to .05		
Anger								
β	.17***	.24***	-.03	-.04	-.04	-.02	.08	12.32***
b	.05	.35	-.02	-.03	-.07	-.02		
95% CI	.03 to .06	.25 to .44	-.06 to .02	-.07 to .02	-.16 to .03	-.08 to .04		
Hostility								
β	.15***	.02	.11**	.01	.01	.04	.04	6.01***
b	.04	.03	-.07	.01	.01	.04		
95% CI	.02 to .06	-.07 to .12	-.11 to .03	-.04 to .05	-.08 to .11	-.02 to .10		

* $p<.05$, ** $p<.01$; *** $p<.001$#
Nationality: 0=Jewish, 1=Palestinian-Israeli, Gender: 0=male, 1=female

The second point: our data finds important differential responses to political violence. Our sample's female respondents had more mental health symptoms and PTSD symptoms and boys had more problems with peers and more aggression. But other demographic factors are not as significant. Religiosity does not predict any of the dependent variables. Jewish participants, on the other hand, were more exposed to political violence than their Palestinian-Israeli counterparts. But for both sample groups, and indeed for anyone, exposure to violence can be a major influence on adolescent development.[44] Adolescence itself is already a critical period, characterized by major changes in biological, psychological and social systems[45] as well as by major social and situational challenges.[46] Moreover, adolescents have reached a stage of cognitive development and awareness[47] wherein consequences of exposure to violence may include PTSD reactions, dropping out of school, behavior problems, delinquency, lack of security and dissolution of social structures, and perceived threats to physical, emotional and social development.[48] Previous research shows that responses to living in a context of violence and trauma are not universal in nature and can manifest in a range of mild-to-severe psychological disorders,[49] or no disorder at all. Indeed, there is no universal response to highly stressful events, and many of those exposed to the excesses of war heal within the community, as personal recovery is deeply rooted in social recovery.[50]

The third related point: Palestinian-Israeli respondents have more mental health problems, PTSD symptoms, family and social problems, and more aggression. The preceding discussion outlines the negative impact on a precarious period of human development – adolescence. But one needs to read these findings in the context of the already existent stresses on the Palestinian-Israeli families because of pressure to survive economically and other ways. Almost 60 percent of non-Jewish children in Israel live in poverty; this is 2.5 times higher than the Jewish population poverty rates.[51]

In the Jewish sector, 15 percent of children have unemployed parents, compared with 23 percent of Palestinian-Israeli children.[52]

Families are already weakened; and therefore people might need to seek outside support services. Yet research confirms lack of services and lower service usage rates for relevant services, youth in particular.[53] Also, funding for social and allied services for the Palestinian-Israeli sector is markedly lower than that for their Jewish counterparts. There are long-term implications that bear emphasis. The youth demographics are particularly profound; those who are 15 years old and under constitute about 41 percent of the Palestinian-Israeli community in Israel; those under age 20 are a little under 50 percent of the Palestinian-Israeli sector.[54] For both populations, there are great issues of risk, given the proportions of youth who are exposed to political violence. Yet the Palestinian-Israelis experience a double trauma: like their Jewish counterparts, they are exposed to political violence; but their population has higher unemployment, lower socioeconomic status, and lower funding for educational, health, and social services.[55]

There are likewise implications to family structures. The impact on the family unit – in Palestinian-Israeli and Jewish sectors – bears emphasis. Various studies have shown that exposure to political violence leads to a multitude of significant changes in the structure and everyday actions of the family unit.[56] The family unit, when subjected to political violence, becomes highly vulnerable to various stress-related factors.[57] Familial relations become overburdened by conflict as traditional normative understandings that define the family unit, structure and hierarchy are challenged; parents may lose employment, and gender and age roles may be challenged.[58]

The fourth major point relates strongly to the above notion of a double trauma: it is expected that the group that was exposed to more political violence (Jewish) will show more mental health symptoms; but the reverse is true. Palestinian-Israelis experience more symptoms of social and family problems. One wonders why this is. In part, it may be because Palestinian-Israeli communities receive less money for professional caring services; are less inclined to seek outside services; and are the clients of service systems that are already underfunded.[59] Then there is the social significance of death – which needs to be understood in its immediate impact on those who are associated with the dead, as well as a wider community and political symbol of ongoing war-related trauma. Traumatic events such as the death of friends, community members, and relatives require culturally specific, and clinically particular, services.[60] Particularly with high context communities in which community linkages are vital, bereavement responses need to be situated collectively, and such community responses may be an impetus for consciousness development and community learning, as we discuss below.

Fifth, and also related to the double trauma, the socioeconomic status of the Palestinian-Israeli in Israel is lower than his Jewish counterpart; and this has implications for all areas of life, including responses to trauma and health. Economic status and level of education are known to be associated with the psychological well- being of families and individuals. Previous scholarship correlates low levels of education and unemployment with high risk factors for poor mental health.[61] Indeed, chronic poverty has a deleterious impact on many life domains, including basic needs, family and social relations, leisure, and self-esteem.[62] According to Tolman and Wang,[63] domestic violence is associated with various forms of material deprivation, as well as increased welfare dependence and decreased work reliance. Other studies have linked job loss to domestic violence.[64] Low educational attainment has also been found to be associated with domestic violence.[65] Domestic violence, in turn, has been linked to increased rates of mental health problems, including depression, suicidal ideation and PTSD.[66] Moreover, since the education system is a part of the broader society, there is reason to believe that there is a relationship between an environment of political violence and high rates of school violence.[67]

The sixth point deals with the impact of political violence on the identity formation of Palestinian-Israeli adolescents. This study demonstrates evident differences between Palestinian-Israeli adolescents and their Jewish counterparts in the degree of exposure to political violence; whereas the Jewish adolescents experienced more exposure to acts of political violence, the Palestinian-Israelis experienced higher social and emotional consequences. In addition, it has been shown that Palestinian-Israeli adolescents' ability to cope with their complex reality is harder than that of their Jewish counterparts, due to lower educational levels, unemployment, domestic violence, and social and economic discrimination and deprivation. According to Slone,[68] the adolescent period is a developmental one – with its predominance of identity-seeking characteristics, the quest for autonomy, and the facility of emotionality – while in the midst of a volatile external situation. It has been noted that the overall issue of Arab-Israeli identity has become even more complex against the background of the Israeli-Palestinian conflict.[69] These multiple aspects of the Palestinian-Israeli adolescent's reality raise questions as to their implications on that individual's social and personal identity as s/he grows into adulthood. The period of adolescence is a critical time, in which individuals search to secure a stable and consistent identity.[70] Following one study's assertion that under constructivist assumptions, one's identity is not eternally fixed but can be shaped by external events and the attempts of ethnic entrepreneurs to mobilize constituencies,[71] there is a need to examine the identity construction of adolescent Palestinian-Israelis in the context of both their immediate environment and Israeli society as a whole.

Finally, there are myriad implications for human service and teaching professionals, policy makers, and political actors. Psychoeducational and psychotherapeutic models of intervention need to be developed for Palestinian-Israeli and Jewish populations that are culturally sensitive and relevant.[72] Services could take into account distinctive characteristics within populations; there is profound diversity in Jewish and Palestinian-Israeli communities in terms of geographic and other forms of identity. Leverage may be made to encourage Palestinian-Israeli families who might be reluctant to receive services, and one such leverage is the well-being of children – a priority around which all community members may rally.[73] Sufficient funding and sufficient relevance need to occur; then all community stakeholders can be usefully brought together to ensure collaboration and the maximized targeting of needs with services.

Likewise, popular psychoeducational campaigns can be aptly deployed in schools and community milieu, in order to bring about awareness and to provide support and access to services. Strategies of poverty reduction and community economic development could likely reduce the double trauma of Palestinian-Israeli life. And throughout, there are linkages between all aforementioned systems; political actors, policy people, service administrators and providers, as well as the communities they serve, need to work collaboratively and the insights from each constituency need to be reciprocally shared.[74]

Conclusion

The present study is necessarily limited in sample size and in sampling methods. Yet it provides compelling evidence that while political violence and behavioral and emotional problems were high among all respondents, they were particularly high among Palestinian youth. Any increase in mental health services directed towards youth and their families would be beneficial to either population, but especially those who are vulnerable to various trauma-related health problems. The researchers were surprised by the extent of the relationship between low socioeconomic status and problematic responses to trauma, as well as by the impact of the Palestinian-Israeli double trauma. The findings provide evidence that Palestinian- Israelis, particularly those in poverty, suffer significantly, raising questions about the long-term health of this sector of society, their feelings of social exclusion, and hence the peace process. Investments in jobs, funding for municipal, health, and social services, and other means of increasing social inclusion and raising socioeconomic status are all worthy goals for reducing gaps between Jewish and Palestinian-Israeli populations in Israel. This double trauma that Palestinian-Israelis face is central to our analysis. The fates of the Palestinian-Israeli and Jewish populations are mutually reciprocal. Thus, for the long-term sake of the region, investments in the entire community, Palestinian-Israeli included, are worthwhile. In the end, helping those vulnerable Israelis who are exposed to trauma is a viable objective for service providers, scholars, and, perhaps most important of all, policy makers and political actors.

Notes

1 A. Al-Krenawi & J.R. Graham, 'Somatization among Bedouin-Arab women: Differentiated by marital status', Journal of Divorce and Remarriage 42, 2004, 131–143. M. Cohen & J. Eid, 'The effect of constant threat of terror on Israeli Jewish and Arab adolescents', Anxiety, Stress, and Coping 20, 2007, 47–60.
2 E. Durakovic-Belko, A. Kulenovic, & R.Dapic, 'Determinants of posttraumatic adjustment in adolescents from Sarajevo who experienced war', Journal of Clinical Psychology 59, 2003, 27–40 F. A. Hadi, 'Predicting psychological distress in children', Journal of the Social Sciences 27, 1999, 73–87. V. Vizek-Vidovic, G. Kutervac-Jagodic, & L. Arambasic, 'Posttraumatic symptomatology in children exposed to war', Scandinavian Journal of Psychology 41, 2000, 297–306.
3 A. Laufer, Y. Raz-Hamama, S.Z. Levine, & Z. Solomon, 'Posttraumatic growth in adolescence: The role of religiosity, distress and forgiveness', Journal of Social and Clinical Psychology 28, 2009, 862–880
4 ; M. Cohen & J. Eid, 'The effect of constant threat of terror on Israeli Jewish and Arab adolescents', Anxiety, Stress, and Coping 20, 2007, 47–60.
5 T. Lavi & Z. Solomon, 'Palestinian youth of the Intifada: PTSD and future Orientation', Journal of the American Academy of Child Adolescent Psychiatry 44, 2005, 1176–1183.
6 M. Cohen & J. Eid, 'The effect of constant threat of terror on Israeli Jewish and Arab adolescents', Anxiety, Stress, and Coping 40, 2007, 47–60.
7 T. Lavi & Z. Solomon, 'Palestinian youth of the Intifada: PTSD and future Orientation', Journal of the American Academy of Child Adolescent Psychiatry, 44, 2005, 1176–1183.
8 O. Nir, 'Israel's Arab minority, policy brief: Middle East Institute', retrieved September 29, 2008, from www.mideasti.org/articles/doc22.html.
9 A. Al-Krenawi & J.R. Graham, 'Culturally sensitive social work practice with Arab clients in mental health settings', Health and Social Work, 25, 2000, 9–22.
10 S. Kanaana, Still on vacation! The eviction of the Palestinians in 1948, Ramallah and Jerusalem: Shamal-Palestinian Diaspora and Refugee Centre, 1992.
11 Arab Association for Human Rights, More house demolitions in the Negev, Weekly Review of the Arab Press in Israel 26. Retrieved August 1, 2003, from http://www.

arabhra.org. W. Wakim, The National Committee for the Defence of the Rights of the Uprooted in Israel, presented at the first Conference for Human Rights in Arab Society, held in Nazareth, 1994.

12. M. Al-Haj, 'Social research on family lifestyles among Arabs in Israel', Journal of Comparative Family Studies, 20, 1989, 175–95.

13. Sikkuy, Sikkuy Report 2004, Retrieved September 14, 2009, from http://www.sikkuy.org.il/english/reports.html.

14. A. Ganim & S. Smooha, 'Attitudes of the Arabs to the State of Israel'. Haviva Institute of Peace Research, Retrieved September 14, 2009, from http://66.155.17.109/peace/publications.

15. M. Slone, 'The Nazareth Riots: Arab and Jewish Israeli Adolescents Pay a Different Psychological Price for Participation', The Journal of Conflict Resolution, 47, 2003, 817–836.

16. M. Slone, 'The Nazareth Riots: Arab and Jewish Israeli Adolescents Pay a Different Psychological Price for Participation', The Journal of Conflict Resolution, 47, 2003, 817–836.

17. S. Elbedour, D.T. Bastien, & B.A. Center, 'Identity Formation in the Shadow of Conflict: Projective Drawings by Palestinian and Israeli Arab Children from the West Bank and Gaza', Journal of Peace Research, 34, 1997, 217–231.

18. H.C. Kelman, 'The Political Psychology of the Israeli-Palestinian Conflict', Political Psychology, 8, 1987, 347–63

19. S. Smooha, 'The status quo option', In: S. Ozacky-Lazar, A. Ghanem, & I. Pappe (Eds.) Seven roads: Theoretical options for the status of the Arabs in Israel, Geva'at Haviva, Israel: Peace Research Institute, pp. 23–28.

20. S. Smooha, 'Arab-Jewish relations in Israel as a deeply divided society', In: A. Shapira (Ed.) Israeli Identity in Transition, New York: Praeger, pp. 31–67.

21. M. Amara & I. Schnell, 'Identity repertoires among Arabs in Israel', Journal of Ethnic and Migration Studies, 3, 2003, 175–193.

22. M. Hujierat, The collective identity of Arab-Israeli students: Identity complexity and collective self esteem. PhD dissertation, Beer-Sheva, Israel: Ben-Gurion University of the Negev, 2005.

23. M. Hujierat, The collective identity of Arab-Israeli students: Identity complexity and collective self esteem. PhD dissertation, Beer-Sheva, Israel: Ben-Gurion University of the Negev, 2005.

24. D. Kraft, (2009, July 28). 'Number of settlers in West Bank has doubled', The Independent, retrieved September 14, 2009, from http://www.independent.ie/world-news/middle-east/number-of-settlers-in-west-bank-has-doubled-1843605.html.

25. A. Al-Krenawi, J.R. Graham, & Y. Kanat-Maymon (in press), 'Analysis of trauma Exposure, symptomatology and functioning in Jewish Israeli and Palestinian Adolescents', British Journal of Psychiatry, 195, 427–432.

26. L. Canetti, A.Y. Shalev, & A. De-Nour-Kaplan, 'Israeli adolescents norms of the Brief Symptom Inventory (BSI)', Israel Journal of Psychiatry and Related Sciences, 31, 1994, 13–18.

27. V. Slonim-Nevo, & Y. Shraga, 'Psychological and social adjustment of Russian-born and Israeli-born Jewish adolescents', Child and Social Work Journal, 17, 2000, 455–75.

28. E.B. Foa, D. Riggs, C.V. Dancu, & B.O. Rothbaum, 'Reliability and validity of a brief instrument for assessing posttraumatic stress disorder', Journal of Traumatic Stress, 6, 1993, 459–73.

29. W.W. Hudson, The Clinical Measurement Package: A field manual, Chicago, IL: Dorsey Press, 1982.

30. V. Slonim-Nevo & Y. Shraga, 'Psychological and social adjustment of Russian-born and Israeli-born Jewish adolescents', Child and Social Work Journal, 17, 2000, 455–75.

31 A. Al-Krenawi & V. Slonim-Nevo, 'Mental health aspects of Arab-Israeli adolescents from polygamous versus monogamous families', The Journal of Social Psychology, 142, 2002, 446–60.
32 A.H. Buss & M. Perry, 'The aggression questionnaire', Journal of Personality and Social Psychology, 63, 2002, 452–59.
33 K. Corcoran & J. Fischer, Measures for clinical practice, New York: Free Press, 2000.
34 N.B. Epstein, L.M. Baldwin, & D.S. Bishop, 'The McMaster Family Assessment Device: Reliability and validity', Journal of Marital and Family Therapy, 9, 1983, 171–180.
35 N.B. Epstein, L.M. Baldwin, & D.S. Bishop, 'The McMaster Family Assessment Device: Reliability and validity', Journal of Marital and Family Therapy, 9, 1983, 171–180.
36 T.A. Ridenour, J.G. Daley, & W. Reich, 'Factor analysis of the family assessment device', Family Process, 38, 1999, 103–129.
37 B.K. Barber, 'Political violence, family relations, and Palestinian youth functioning', Journal of Adolescent Research, 14, 1999, 206–230 ; A.B.M. Thabet & P. Vostanis, 'Child mental health problems in the Gaza Strip', Israel Journal of Psychiatry, 42, 2005, 84–87. A.B.M. Thabet & P. Vostanis, 'Child mental health problems in the Gaza Strip', Israel Journal of Psychiatry, 42, 2005, 84–87. R.H. Gurwitch, M. Kees, & S.M. Becker, 'In the face of tragedy: Placing children's reactions to trauma in a new context', Cognitive and Behavioral Practice, 9, 2002, 286–295.
38 T.L. Kuther, 'A developmental -contextual perspective on youth covictimization by violence', Adolescence, 34, 1999, 669–714.
39 D. Flannery, M. Singer, & K. Wester, 'Violence exposure, psychological trauma, and suicide risk in a community sample of dangerously violent adolescents', Journal of the Academy of Child and Adolescent Psychiatry, 40, 2001, 435–444 . D. Flannery, K. Wester, & M. Singer, 'Impact of violence exposure at school on child mental health and violent behaviour', Journal of Community Psychology, 32, 2004, 559–574. S. Overstreet & S. Braun, 'Exposure to community violence and post-traumatic stress symptoms: Mediating factors', American Journal of Orthopsychiatry, 70, 2000, 263–271.
40 J.D. Osofsky, Young children and trauma: Intervention and treatment, New York: The Guilford Press, 2004. M.T. Zingraff, J. Leiter, K.A. Myers, & M.C. Johnson, 'Child maltreatment and youthful problem behavior', Criminology 31, 1993, 173–202.
41 A. Bandura, Mechanisms of moral disengagement, In W. Reich (Ed.) Origins of terrorism: Psychologies, ideologies, theologies and state of mind, Washington DC: Woodrow Wilson Center Press, pp. 161–191. K.M. Fitzpatrick, 'Fighting among America's youth: A risk and protective factors approach', Journal of Health and Social Behavior, 38, 1997, 131–148.
42 A. Al-Krenawi, R. Lev-Wiesel, & M. Sehwail, 'Psychological symptomatology among Palestinian male and female adolescents living under political violence 2004–2005', Community Mental Health Journal, 43, 2007, 49–56.
43 A. Laufer & Z. Solomon, 'Posttraumatic Symptoms and Posttraumatic Growth among Israeli Youth Exposed to Terror Incidents', Journal of Social and Clinical Psychology, 25, 2006, 429–447.
44 A. Al-Krenawi & J.R. Graham, 'A comparison of family functioning, life and marital satisfaction, and mental health of women in polygamous and monogamous marriages', International Journal of Social Psychiatry, 52, 2006, 5–17.
45 S. Feldman & G. Elliott (Eds.), At the threshold: The developing adolescent, Cambridge, MA: Harvard University Press, 1990. L.P. Spear, 'The adolescent brain and age-related behavioral manifestations', Neuroscience & Biobehavioral Reviews, 24, 2000, 417–463.
46 D. Cicchetti & F. A. Rogosch, 'A developmental psychopathology perspective on adolescence', Journal of Consulting and Clinical Psychology, 70, 2002, 6–20.

47 J.D. Osofsky, Young children and trauma: Intervention and treatment, New York: The Guilford Press, 2004.
48 Cicchetti & Rogosch, 'A developmental psychopathology', 6–20 ; Flannery, Wester, & Singer, 'Impact of violence exposure at school', 559–574. J.H. Osofsky & J.D. Osofsky, 'Violent and aggressive behaviors in youth: A mental health and prevention perspective', Psychiatry: Interpersonal & Biological Processes 64, 2001, 285–295. T. Yurtbay, B. Alyana, O. Abali, N. Kaynak, & M. Durukan, 'The psychological effects of forced emigration on Muslim Albanian children and adolescents', Community Mental Health Journal, 39, 2003, 203–212.
49 A.M. Baker & N. Shalhoub-Kevorkian, 'The effects of political and military trauma on children: The Palestinian case', Clinical Psychology Review, 19, 1999, 930–950.
50 D. Summerfield, 'War and mental health: A brief overview', British Medical Journal, 321, 2000, 232–235.
51 Israeli Central Bureau of Statistics, Statistical Abstract of Israel 2009 No. 60, Retrieved September 14, 2009, from http://cbs.gov.il/reader.
52 Israeli Central Bureau of Statistics, Statistical Abstract of Israel 2009 No. 60, Retrieved September 14, 2009, from http://cbs.gov.il/reader.
53 R. Savaya, 'The under-use of psychological services by Israeli Arabs: An examination of the roles of negative attitudes and the use of alternative sources of help', International Social Work 41, 1998, 195–209. R. Savaya, 'Attitudes towards family and marital counseling among Israeli Arab women', Journal of Social Service Research, 21, 1995, 35–51.
54 Israeli Central Bureau of Statistics, Statistical Abstract of Israel 2009 No. 60, Retrieved September 14, 2009, from http://cbs.gov.il/reader.
55 R. Boudreaux, 'Israel: Digital gap between Arabs and Jews', Los Angeles Times. Retrieved September 14, 2009, from http://latimesblogs.latimes.com/babylonbeyond/2008/02/israel-digital.html.
56 P.T. Joshi, D.A. O'Donnell, L.M. Cullins, & S.M. Lewin, 'Children exposed to war and terrorism', In M.M. Feerick and G.B. Silverman (Eds.) Children exposed to violence, Baltimore, MD: Paul H. Brookes Publishing, pp. 53–84. S. Weine, N. Muzurovi, Y. Kulauzovic, S. Besic, A. Lezic, A. Mujagic, J. Muzurovic, D. Spahovic, S. Feetham, N. Ware, K. Knafl, & I. Pavkovic, 'Family consequences of refugee trauma', Family Process, 43, 2004, 60–147.
57 A. Al-Krenawi, J.R. Graham, & M. Sehwail, 'Mental health and violence/trauma in Palestine: Implications for helping professional practice', Journal of Contemporary Family Studies, 35, 2004, 185–210. V. Khamis, 'Posttraumatic stress disorder among school age Palestinians Children', Child Abuse & Neglect 29, 2005, 81–95. R. W. Srour, 'Children living under a multi traumatic environment', Israel Journal of Psychiatry, 42, 2005, 88–95.
58 J. Suad, 'Conceiving family relationships in post-war Lebanon', Journal of Comparative Family Studies, 35, 2004, 271–293.
59 A. Al-Krenawi & J.R. Graham, 'A comparison of family functioning, life and marital satisfaction, and mental health of women in polygamous and monogamous marriages', International Journal of Social Psychiatry, 52, 2006, 5–17. A. Al-Krenawi & J.R. Graham, 'The provision and use of social services among the Bedouin-Arab indigenous population in Israel', Social Development Issues, 29, 2007, 100–118.
60 A. Al-Krenawi, J.R. Graham, & M. Sehwail, 'Bereavement responses among Palestinian widows, daughters, and sons following the Hebron massacre', Omega: Journal of Death and Dying, 2002 44, 241–255. A. Al-Krenawi, J.R. Graham, & M. Sehwail, 'Mental health and violence/trauma in Palestine: Implications for helping professional practice', Journal of Contemporary Family Studies, 35, 2004, 185–210.
61 T. Harpham, E. Grant, & C. Rodriguez, 'Mental health and social capital in Cali, Colombia', Social Science & Medicine, 58, 2004, 2267–2277.

62 R. Wilton, 'Putting policy into practice? Poverty and people with serious mental illness', Social Science and Medicine, 58, 2004, 25–39.
63 R.M. Tolman & H.C. Wang, 'Domestic violence and women's employment: Fixed effects models of three waves of women's employment study data', American Journal of Community Psychology 36, 2005, 147–158.
64 R.M. Tolman & H.C. Wang, 'Domestic violence and women's employment: Fixed effects models of three waves of women's employment study data', American Journal of Community Psychology 36, 2005, 147–158.
65 J.R. Vest, T.K. Catlin, J.J. Chen, & R.C. Brownson, 'Multistate analysis of factors associated with intimate partner violence', American Journal of Preventive Medicine, 22, 2002, 156–164.
66 R.M. Tolman & H.C. Wang, 'Domestic violence and women's employment: Fixed effects models of three waves of women's employment study data', American Journal of Community Psychology 36, 2005, 147–158.
67 A. Al-Krenawi, R. Lev-Wiesel, & M. Sehwail, 'Psychological symptomatology among Palestinian male and female adolescents living under political violence 2004–2005', Community Mental Health Journal, 43, 2007, 49–56.
68 M. Slone, 'The Nazareth Riots: Arab and Jewish Israeli Adolescents Pay a Different Psychological Price for Participation', The Journal of Conflict Resolution, 47, 2003, 817–836.
69 M. Slone, 'The Nazareth Riots: Arab and Jewish Israeli Adolescents Pay a Different Psychological Price for Participation', The Journal of Conflict Resolution, 47, 2003, 817–836.
70 A. Tsou, 'Understanding the influence of ethnic identity and acculturation on psychological adjustment among Chinese American adolescents', PhD dissertation, Berkeley, CA: California School of Professional Psychology, 2002.
71 S. Lowrance, 'Being Palestinian in Israel: Identity, protest, and political Exclusion', Comparative Studies of South Asia, Africa and the Middle East, 25, 2005, 487–499.
72 A. Al-Krenawi & J.R. Graham, 'Culturally sensitive social work practice with Arab clients in mental health settings', Health and Social Work, 25, 2000, 9–22. A. Al-Krenawi & J.R. Graham, 'Somatization among Bedouin-Arab women: Differentiated by marital status', Journal of Divorce and Remarriage, 42, 2004, 131–143.
73 A. Al-Krenawi, J.R. Graham, & S. Al-Krenawi, 'Social work practice with polygamous families', Child and Adolescent Social Work Journal, 14, 1997, 444–458.
74 J. Graham & K. Barter, 'Collaboration: A social work practice method', Families in Society: The Journal of Contemporary Human Services, 80, 1999, 6–13.

References

Al-Haj, M. (1989). Social research on family lifestyles among Arabs in Israel. *Journal of Comparative Family Studies*, *20*(2), 175–95.

Al-Krenawi, A., & Graham, J.R. (2000). Culturally sensitive social work practice with Arab clients in mental health settings. *Health and Social Work*, *25*(1), 9–22.

Al-Krenawi, A., & Graham, J.R. (2004). Somatization among Bedouin-Arab women: Differentiated by marital status. *Journal of Divorce and Remarriage*, *42*(1/2), 131–143.

Al-Krenawi, A., & Graham, J.R. (2006). A comparison of family functioning, life and marital satisfaction, and mental health of women in polygamous and monogamous marriages. *International Journal of Social Psychiatry*, *52*(1), 5–17.

Al-Krenawi, A., & Graham, J.R. (2007). The provision and use of social services among the Bedouin-Arab indigenous population in Israel. *Social Development Issues*, *29*(1), 100–118.

Al-Krenawi, A., Graham, J.R. & Al-Krenawi, S. (1997). Social work practice with polygamous families. *Child and Adolescent Social Work Journal*, *14*(6), 444–458.

Al-Krenawi, A., Graham, J.R., & Kanat-Maymon, Y. (in press). Analysis of trauma exposure, symptomatology and functioning in Jewish Israeli and Palestinian adolescents. *British Journal of Psychiatry*, 197, 425–432.

Al-Krenawi, A., Graham, J.R., & Sehwail, M. (2002). Bereavement responses among Palestinian widows, daughters, and sons following the Hebron massacre. *Omega: Journal of Death and Dying*, 44(3), 241–255.

Al-Krenawi, A., Graham, J.R., & Sehwail, M. (2004). Mental health and violence/trauma in Palestine: Implications for helping professional practice. *Journal of Contemporary Family Studies*, 35(2), 185–210.

Al-Krenawi, A., Lev-Wiesel, R., & Sehwail, M. (2007). Psychological symptomatology among Palestinian male and female adolescents living under political violence 2004–2005. *Community Mental Health Journal*, 43(1), 49–56.

Al-Krenawi, A., & Slonim-Nevo, V. (2002). Mental health aspects of Arab-Israeli adolescents from polygamous versus monogamous families. *The Journal of Social Psychology*, 142(4), 446–60.

Amara, M., & Schnell, I. (2003). Identity repertoires among Arabs in Israel. *Journal of Ethnic and Migration Studies*, 3(1), 175–193

Arab Association for Human Rights, The. (15–22 July, 2003). More house demolitions in the Negev. *Weekly Review of the Arab Press in Israel*, 126. Retrieved August 1, 2003, from http://www.arabhra.org.

Baker, A.M. & Shalhoub-Kevorkian, N. (1999). The effects of political and military trauma on children: The Palestinian case. *Clinical Psychology Review*, 19, 935–950.

Bandura, A. (1998). Mechanisms of moral disengagement. In W. Reich (Ed.), *Origins of terrorism: Psychologies, ideologies, theologies and state of mind* (pp. 161–191). Washington DC: Woodrow Wilson Center Press.

Barber, B.K. (1999). Political violence, family relations, and Palestinian youth functioning. *Journal of Adolescent Research*, 14, 206–230.

Buss, A.H., & Perry, M. (2002). The aggression questionnaire. *Journal of Personality and Social Psychology*, 63(3), 452–59.

Boudreaux, R. (2008, February 26). Israel: Digital gap between Arabs and Jews. *Los Angeles Times*. Retrieved September 14, 2009, from http://latimesblogs.latimes.com/babylonbeyond/2008/02/israel-digital.html.

Canetti, L., Shalev, A.Y., & De-Nour-Kaplan, A. (1994). Israeli adolescents' norms of the Brief Symptom Inventory (BSI). *Israel Journal of Psychiatry and Related Sciences*, 31(1), 13–18.

Cicchetti, D., & Rogosch, F.A. (2002). A developmental psychopathology perspective on adolescence. *Journal of Consulting and Clinical Psychology*, 70, 6–20.

Cohen, M., & Eid, J. (2007). The effect of constant threat of terror on Israeli Jewish and Arab adolescents. *Anxiety, Stress, and Coping*, 20(1), 47–60.

Corcoran, K., & Fischer, J. (2000). *Measures for clinical practice*. New York: Free Press.

Derogatis, L., & Spencer, P. (1982). *The brief symptom inventory (BSI): Administration, scoring and procedures, Manual I*. Baltimore, MD: Johns Hopkins.

Durakovic-Belko, E., Kulenovic, A., & Dapic, R. (2003). Determinants of posttraumatic adjustment in adolescents from Sarajevo who experienced war. *Journal of Clinical Psychology*, 59, 27–40.

Elbedour, S., Bastien, D.T., & Center, B.A. (1997). Identity Formation in the Shadow of Conflict: Projective Drawings by Palestinian and Israeli Arab Children from the West Bank and Gaza. *Journal of Peace Research*, 34(2), 217–231.

Epstein, N.B., Baldwin, L.M., & Bishop, D.S. (1983). The McMaster Family Assessment Device: Reliability and validity. *Journal of Marital and Family Therapy*, 9(2), 171–180.

Feldman, S., & Elliott, G. (Eds.). (1990). *At the threshold: The developing adolescent.* Cambridge, MA: Harvard University Press.

Fitzpatrick, K.M. (1997). Fighting among America's youth: A risk and protective factors approach. *Journal of Health and Social Behavior, 38*, 131–148.

Flannery, D., Singer, M., & Wester, K. (2001). Violence exposure, psychological trauma, and suicide risk in a community sample of dangerously violent adolescents. *Journal of the Academy of Child and Adolescent Psychiatry, 40*(4), 435–444.

Flannery, D., Wester, K., & Singer, M. (2004). Impact of violence exposure at school on child mental health and violent behaviour. *Journal of Community Psychology, 32*(5), 559–574.

Foa, E.B., Riggs, D., Dancu, C.V., & Rothbaum, B.O. (1993). Reliability and validity of a brief instrument for assessing posttraumatic stress disorder. *Journal of Traumatic Stress, 6*, 459–73.

Ganim, A., & Smooha, S. (2001). *Attitudes of the Arabs to the State of Israel.* Haviva Institute of Peace Research. Retrieved September 14, 2009, from http://66.155.17.109/peace/publications.

Graham, J., & Barter, K. (1999). Collaboration: A social work practice method. *Families in Society: The Journal of Contemporary Human Services, 80*(1), 6–13.

Gurwitch, R.H., Kees, M., & Becker, S.M. (2002). In the face of tragedy: Placing children's reactions to trauma in a new context. *Cognitive and Behavioral Practice, 9*(4), 286–295.

Hadi, F.A. (1999). Predicting psychological distress in children. *Journal of the Social Sciences, 27*(1), 73–87.

Harpham, T., Grant, E., & Rodriguez, C. (2004). Mental health and social capital in Cali, Colombia. *Social Science & Medicine, 58*(11), 2267–2277.

Hudson, W.W. (1982). *The Clinical Measurement Package: A field manual.* Chicago, IL: Dorsey Press.

Hujierat, M. (2005). *The collective identity of Arab-Israeli students: Identity complexity and collective self esteem.* PhD dissertation, Beer-Sheva, Israel: Ben-Gurion University of the Negev.

Israeli Central Bureau of Statistics. (2009). *Statistical Abstract of Israel 2009 No. 60.* Retrieved September 14, 2009, from http://cbs.gov.il/reader.

Joshi, P.T., O'Donnell, D.A., Cullins, L.M., & Lewin, S.M. (2006). Children exposed to war and terrorism. In M.M. Feerick and G.B. Silverman (Eds.), *Children exposed to violence* (pp. 53–84). Baltimore, MD: Paul H. Brookes Publishing.

Kanaana, S. (1992). *Still on vacation! The eviction of the Palestinians in 1948.* Ramallah and Jerusalem: Shamal-Palestinian Diaspora and Refugee Centre.

Kelman, H.C. (1987). The Political Psychology of the Israeli-Palestinian Conflict. *Political Psychology, 8*, 347–63.

Khamis, V. (2005). Posttraumatic stress disorder among school age Palestinians children. *Child Abuse & Neglect, 29*(1), 81–95.

Kraft, D. (2009, July 28). Number of settlers in West Bank has doubled. *The Independent.* Retrieved September 14, 2009, from http://www.independent.ie/world-news/middle-east/number-of-settlers-in- west-bank-has-doubled-1843605.html.

Kuther, T.L. (1999). A developmental-contextual perspective on youth covictimization by violence. *Adolescence, 34*, 669–714.

Laufer, A., Raz-Hamama, Y., Levine, S.Z., & Solomon, Z. (2009). Posttraumatic growth in adolescence: The role of religiosity, distress and forgiveness. *Journal of Social and Clinical Psychology, 28*, 862–880.

Laufer, A & Solomon, Z. (2006). Posttraumatic Symptoms and Posttraumatic Growth among Israeli Youth Exposed to Terror Incidents. *Journal of Social and Clinical Psychology, 25*(4), 429–447.

Lavi, T., & Solomon, Z. (2005). Palestinian youth of the Intifada: PTSD and future orientation. *Journal of the American Academy of Child Adolescent Psychiatry, 44,* 1176–1183.

Lowrance, S. (2005). Being Palestinian in Israel: Identity, protest, and political exclusion. *Comparative Studies of South Asia, Africa and the Middle East, 25*(2), 487–499.

Miller, I.W., Epstein, N.B., Bishop, D.S., & Keitner, G.I. (1985). The McMaster Family Assessment Device: Reliability and validity. *Journal of Marital and Family Therapy, 11*(4), 345–356.

Nir, O. (2003). *Israel's Arab minority, policy brief: Middle East Institute.* Retrieved September 29, 2008, from www.mideasti.org/articles/doc22.html.

Osofsky, J.D. (2004). *Young children and trauma: Intervention and treatment.* New York: The Guilford Press.

Osofsky, H.J., & Osofsky, J.D. (2001). Violent and aggressive behaviors in youth: A mental health and prevention perspective. *Psychiatry: Interpersonal & Biological Processes, 64*(4), 285–295.

Overstreet, S., & Braun, S. (2000). Exposure to community violence and post-traumatic stress symptoms: Mediating factors. *American Journal of Orthopsychiatry, 70,* 263–271.

Ridenour, T.A., Daley, J.G., & Reich, W. (1999). Factor analysis of the family assessment device. *Family Process, 38*(4), 103–129.

Savaya, R. (1995). Attitudes towards family and marital counseling among Israeli Arab women. *Journal of Social Service Research, 21*(1), 35–51.

Savaya, R. (1998). The under-use of psychological services by Israeli Arabs: An examination of the roles of negative attitudes and the use of alternative sources of help. *International Social Work, 41,* 195–209.

Sikkuy. (2004). *Sikkuy Report 2004.* Retrieved September 14, 2009, from http://www.sikkuy.org.il/english/reports.html.

Slone, M. (2003). The Nazareth Riots: Arab and Jewish Israeli Adolescents Pay a Different Psychological Price for Participation. *The Journal of Conflict Resolution, 47*(6), 817–836.

Slonim-Nevo, V., & Shraga, Y. (2000). Psychological and social adjustment of Russian-born and Israeli-born Jewish adolescents. *Child and Social Work Journal, 17*(6), 455–75.

Smooha, S. (1999). The status quo option. In: S. Ozacky-Lazar, A. Ghanem, & I. Pappe (Eds.), *Seven roads: Theoretical options for the status of the Arabs in Israel* (pp. 23–28). Geva'at Haviva, Israel: Peace Research Institute.

Smooha, S. (2004). Arab-Jewish relations in Israel as a deeply divided society. In: A. Shapira (Ed.), *Israeli Identity in Transition* (pp. 31–67). New York: Praeger.

Spear, L.P. (2000). The adolescent brain and age-related behavioral manifestations. *Neuroscience & Biobehavioral Reviews, 24,* 417–463.

Srour, R.W. (2005). Children living under a multi traumatic environment. *Israel Journal of Psychiatry, 42*(2), 88–95.

Suad, J. (2004). Conceiving family relationships in post-war Lebanon. *Journal of Comparative Family Studies, 35*(2), 271–293.

Summerfield, D. (2000). War and mental health: A brief overview. *British Medical Journal, 321,* 232–235.

Thabet, A.B.M., Abed, A.M., & Vostanis P. (2002). Emotional problems in Palestinian children living in a war zone: A cross-sectional study. *Lancet, 359*(9320), 1801–1805.

Thabet, A.B.M., & Vostanis, P. (2004). Comorbidity of PTSD and depression among refugee children during war conflict. *Journal of Child Psychology and Psychiatry, 45*(3), 533–542.

Thabet, A.B.M., & Vostanis, P. (2005). Child mental health problems in the Gaza strip. *Israel Journal of Psychiatry, 42*(2), 84–87.

Tolman, R.M., & Wang, H.C. (2005). Domestic violence and women's employment: Fixed effects models of three waves of women's employment study data. *American Journal of Community Psychology, 36*, 147–158.

Tsou, A. (2002). *Understanding the influence of ethnic identity and acculturation on psychological adjustment among Chinese American adolescents.* PhD dissertation, Berkeley, CA: California School of Professional Psychology.

Vest, J.R., Catlin, T.K., Chen, J.J., & Brownson, R.C. (2002). Multistate analysis of factors associated with intimate partner violence. *American Journal of Preventive Medicine, 22*(3), 156–164.

Vizek-Vidovic, V., Kutervac-Jagodic, G. & Arambasic, L. (2000). Posttraumatic symptomatology in children exposed to war. *Scandinavian Journal of Psychology, 41*, 297–306.

Wakim, W. (1994). The National Committee for the Defence of the Rights of the Uprooted in Israel, presented at the first *Conference for Human Rights in Arab Society*, held in Nazareth.

Weine, S., Muzurovic, N., Kulauzovic, Y., Besic, S., Lezic, A., Mujagic, A., Muzurovic, J., Spahovic, D., Feetham, S., Ware, N., Knafl, K., & Pavkovic, I. (2004). Family consequences of refugee trauma. *Family Process, 43*(2), 147–60.

Wilton, R. (2004). Putting policy into practice? Poverty and people with serious mental illness. *Social Science and Medicine, 58*, 25–39.

Yurtbay, T., Alyanak, B., Abali, O., Kaynak, N., & Durukan, M. (2003). The psychological effects of forced emigration on Muslim Albanian children and adolescents. *Community Mental Health Journal, 39*, 203–212.

Zingraff, M.T., Leiter, J., Myers, K.A., & Johnson, M.C. (1993). Child maltreatment and youthful problem behavior. *Criminology, 31*, 173–202.

15 Paradoxes of identity

Jewish/Muslim interpenetration in Almog Behar and Sayed Kashua

Ranen Omer-Sherman

In the summer of 2009, Ariel Atias, Israel's housing minister, declared that it was a national responsibility to curtail the Arab population in the state. He stipulated that the proximity of Jewish and Arab populations (especially in the Galilee, a region of many Arab-Israeli communities) was highly undesirable: 'Populations that should not mix are spreading there. I don't think that it is appropriate [for them] to live together.' Though it is hard to imagine a more incendiary statement (nor one more likely to be painful for those who would defend Zionism from the charge of racism), such rhetorical efforts to undermine the prospects for healthy civic attitudes toward Israel's multicultural complexity were uttered with increasing frequency in subsequent months by members of Benjamin Netanyahu's rightwing ruling coalition. Yet, even at a time when members of Israel's minority have good cause to feel dangerously alienated from the state, a careful examination of cultural and intellectual trends suggests that a more hopeful multicultural ethos based on an expansive sense of regional belonging (that transcends national identity) continues to find vibrant expression. In a pair of twenty-first century magical-realist stories of transformation, the Israeli writers Almog Behar and Sayed Kashua, a Jew and a Muslim respectively, each interrogate the notion of 'Arab' and 'Jewish' identity as exclusive, impermeable categories by considering both the permutations of the historical past and the contemporary fluidity of Israeli society. Most significantly, each of their narratives of identity confusion, published just a year apart from one another, is provocatively set in the eternally troubled and contested city of Jerusalem. Both writers respond to the segregations, divisions and separations that govern the lives of the 'reunited' city's Jewish and Arab citizens.[1] In disparate narrative modes, each recovers the buried promise of the philosophical and religious discussions that were once a part of the traditional Middle Eastern world, opening worlds of dialogue and debate that are so distant from our presently polarized realities. And intrinsically, each explores the beckoning premise formulated by James Clifford: 'once the representational challenge is seen to be the portrayal and understanding of local/global historical encounters, co-productions, dominations, and resistances, one needs to focus on hybrid cosmopolitan experiences as much as on rooted, native ones.'[2] Yet given the currently polarized nature of Israeli society, few would deny the increasingly inauspicious prospects for applying such creative investigations of identity to the fraught and divisive reality of contemporary Jerusalem.

In Vered Vinitzky-Seroussi's compelling essay, '"Jerusalem Assassinated Rabin and Tel Aviv Commemorated him": Rabin Memorials and the Discourse of National Identity in Israel', she builds on the foundation of anthropologist Chaim Chazan's assertion that 'in Jerusalem, the boundaries between mythological time and terrestrial time are blurred ... while Tel Aviv is a place of one time—local, palpable' (Vinitzky-Seroussi, 186) to investigate Israeli society in the aftermath of Prime Minister Yitzhak Rabin's murder by his Israeli rightwing fanatic who sought to undermine the peace process.[3] For Vinitzky-Seroussi, and a number of influential journalists and cultural figures she consults, 'Jerusalem' has come to signify 'fundamentalism, militarism, uncompromising politics, ethnocentrism, and a Jewish ghetto' whereas 'Tel Aviv' represents 'universalism, secularism, pragmatic politics' (186). The author, who is currently a professor at the Hebrew University, Jerusalem, does not rest on these rhetorical abstractions but instead takes the reader directly into a representative day that demonstrates the binary identities of the two cities:

> On October 19th, 1997, during the Jewish holiday Sukkot, Israeli Prime Minister Benjamin Netanyahu attended a huge gathering of mostly religious Jews following the holiday tradition of pilgrimage to Jerusalem. On the same day, at the Tel Aviv Hilton, former Labor Party leader Shimon Peres inaugurated 'The Peres Center for Peace', an event attended by leaders from thirty countries. The rally in Jerusalem was about looking inward ... in regards to Israeli domestic politics. The opening in Tel Aviv was about disseminating the message of the 'new Middle East', looking for ways to make peace between Israel and its Arab neighbors, keeping in touch with the world, and looking outward. (187)

Aside from providing such exemplars of the indelible ways that 'Jerusalem' and 'Tel Aviv' embody a Janus-faced Israel divided between tribalism and universalism, Vinitzky-Seroussi examines the Jerusalem municipality's troubling reluctance to erect an official monument to Rabin in a genuinely public space; a lapse that Tel Aviv embraced with alacrity. Thus, she argues, 'Tel Aviv expanded its symbolic reach beyond its geographical boundaries. Tel Aviv can be said to compete with and challenge the existing national identity represented by Israel's official capital ... by appropriating Rabin, Tel Aviv gained a measure of legitimacy in claiming to be the real capital of the state of Israel, while Jerusalem by omission, relinquished its symbolic role as one' (198). [4] As I hope to demonstrate in this essay, Behar and Kashua defiantly 'import' the cosmopolitan, leftwing and secular spirit of Tel Aviv into tense and separatist Jerusalem's stony and unyielding 'sacred' space.[5]

For Almog Behar (b. 1978), migrations, journeys, and cultural dislocations are not just past experiences that might form the basis for new understandings but charged catalysts that threaten to disrupt and destabilize the prospect of comfortably static identities defined by others in the present. A remarkable young Israeli writer, educator, and journalist living in Jerusalem, Behar presents a more radical narrative of muddled identities than A.B. Yehoshua. His lyrically written prose fantasy about the transgression of identity and national boundaries, '*Ana min al yahoud*' (I Am One of the Jews), won the Israeli newspaper *Haaretz*'s short story competition in 2005, impressing the jury with its gentle use of 'humor and unexpected changes of direction' – qualities they felt ensured that the work, in spite of its strong political implications, triumphs as art rather than polemic. They further noted that though 'this is a very "local" story, it has a universal message that can apply to any immigrant society.'[6] To this I would add that '*Ana min al yahoud*' is simply one of the boldest, creative examinations of identity and heritage to be published in Hebrew in recent memory. In a fantastical and darkly humorous mode that bears a kinship to Kafka, Behar creates a gripping tale of cultural memory, dispossession, and recovery. At the same time, the story offers an indictment of a society in which Mizrahi writers like Behar himself were too long condescended as *arrivistes*, largely ignored by the cultural establishment. Filled with jarring temporal and linguistic slippages, '*Ana min al yahoud*' is primarily concerned with the almost uncanny capacity of language and culture (even when neglected or repressed) to reclaim the individual with force and vitality, sometimes shattering the walls of nationality.

One day, the story's Jewish-Israeli narrator, who lives in contemporary Jerusalem, discovers that he has somehow lost his ability to speak normative Israeli Hebrew. To his intense discomfiture, his utterances are suddenly possessed by the Arabic accent of his long-deceased grandfather Anwar, an Iraqi-born Jew. In contrast, we learn that in his mother's immigrant childhood, feeling the disapproval of her teacher and fellow students, she labored until she subdued the harsh glottal '*ayyin* that betrayed her roots. Yet now the narrator is helpless as the unwelcome alien sounds erupt from him: 'I tried to soften the pharyngeal fricative *het* … I tried to make the *tsaddi* sound less like an "s" and I tried to get rid of that glottal Iraqi *quf* and pronounce it like "k" but the effort failed'. Like a Kafka protagonist, he finds himself standing accused by 'strangers passing by' and soon he attracts the attention of policemen for his 'tremendous guilt' – he is suspected of being an Arab.

In the following days, the narrator suffers a number of inexplicable incidents that strip him of his safe sense of national belonging. When the police stop him (it doesn't help that his identity card mysteriously vanishes every time he needs to prove his identity), he reassures them that he will immediately contact Ashkenazi friends with 'beautiful' accents – 'Hebrew as Hebrew should be spoken, without any accent' to aid his struggle to restore his civic integrity and secure identity. When these refuse to take his desperate telephone calls, he turns in desperation to a second tier of linguistic hierarchy, friends whose parents immigrated from 'Aleppo or Tripoli or Tunisia' but whose native-born Hebrew will surely satisfy the officials. Yet their speech too 'suddenly … had a heavy Arab accent and they'd be listening to some meandering *oud* in the background … and they'd greet me with "*ahlan bik*" and call me "*ya habibi*" … and take their leave of me with "*salamatek*".'[7] At this point, appearing less an 'Israelite' and more like an 'Ishmaelite', the narrator, already suffering as a hapless conduit for the alien language and culture that erupt through him, is subject to increasingly intrusive

Paradoxes of identity 267

(and surreal) investigations into his true identity and loyalties. The officials apply their most precise instruments to examine his case, but something about the alien identity lurking within eludes their most conscientious efforts and indeed assumes a deeply rooted and defensive position within its host:

> They'd check me slowly, rummaging in my clothes, going over my body with metal detectors, stripping me of words and thoughts in their thorough silence, searching deep in the layers of my skin for a grudge, seeking an explosive belt, an explosive belt in my heart, eager to defuse any suspicious object. And when the policemen presented themselves to me in pairs, the one would say to his companion a few minutes into their examination, look, he's circumcised, he really is a Jew, this Arab, and the other one would say, an Arab is also circumcised, and explosive belts don't care about circumcision, and they would continue their search. And really, during the time when I left my body to them explosive belts began to be born on my heart, swelling and refusing to be defused, thundering and thundering. But as they were not made of steel or gunpowder they succeeded in evading the mechanical detectors.

Set loose in the city, the speaker's unfortunate hybridity seems to infect Jerusalem's very topography – even its temporality. Hebrew street signs vanish and streets, city landmarks, and inhabitants are all Palestinian Arabs and 'not only construction workers, not only street cleaners and renovators.' The city suddenly reappears as it did in the days of the British Mandate: 'as if there had never been a 1948 war.' Here it seems that Behar's Jerusalem is inhabited by its own Levantine memories – which thwart the notion of possession or containment by any people's 'homeland' discourse.[8] As the narrator plunges recklessly into this dangerous counterhistorical space, readers might assume that at last he will have a sense of belonging, but here too his fragmented identity places him at odds with his surroundings:

> I do not succeed in mingling ... because all I have at my disposal is Hebrew with an Arabic accent and my Arabic, which doesn't come from my home but from the army, is suddenly mute, strangled from my throat, cursing itself without uttering a word, hanging in the suffocating air of the refuges of my soul ... all the time, when I tried to speak to them in the small, halting vocabulary of the Arabic I knew, what came out was Hebrew with an Arabic accent, until they thought that I was ridiculing them.

Readers familiar with W. E. B. Du Bois' description of the 'double-consciousness' of black Americans will immediately recognize the fraught nature of this Mizrahi Jew's plight, his lack of legitimacy in any of the disparate linguistic, cultural, and political worlds that surround him at various junctures. At the story's midpoint, the beleaguered narrator discovers that neither of those societies can accommodate the inconvenient complexities of his identity: 'I had lost their language and they didn't know my language and between us remained the distance of the police forces and the generations.' Such darkly lyrical descriptions of the speaker's metamorphosis beautifully convey Behar's underlying insistence, not only that there are real stresses and fractures that invariably undermine any concept of a universal or otherwise absolute form of identity, but that the seemingly deracinated individual contains dormant multitudes within.

Ironically, just as the narrator fails to function as a coherent unit within his defensive society, he becomes more integrated *within*. He no longer embodies a clear rupture between the generations (no longer 'pil[ing] non-memory on memory') and indeed, the more he accepts the alterity within, the more confident and expressive he grows:

> And thus my voice was replaced by my grandfather's voice, and suddenly those streets that had become so accustomed to his death and his disappearance and his absence from them began to hear his voice again. And suddenly that beautiful voice, which had been entirely in my past, started coming out of me and not as a beggar and not asking for crumbs, but truly my voice, my voice strong and clear. And the streets of Jerusalem that had grown accustomed to my silence, to our silence, had a very hard time with the speech, and would silence the voice, gradually telling it careful, telling me careful, telling me I am alien, telling me my silences are enough. And despite my fear, and even though this voice was foreign from the distance of two generations of forgetting, I spoke all my words in that accent, because there was speech in me that wanted to come out and the words would change on me as they came out of the depths of my throat.

One thing leads to another, however, and (to paraphrase A.B. Yehoshua), the narrator's identity chaos spreads like a virus. First, his girlfriend's speech begins to blend her father's Yemenite Arabic with her mother's Ladino accent from Turkey. In the coming days she reports news of 'a small plague' as 'the old accents that were hoped to have vanished' mysteriously reappear. Even the Ashkenazim are affected, though the latter, in one of Behar's gently mocking asides, succumb to the malady more decorously: 'for them, the change would develop more slowly ... because their children were convinced that their parents' accent and their grandparents' accent had originally been American, and they have less concrete memories of their old speech.' Where others have often critiqued the 'Eurocentrism' that they regard as the partial cause for Zionism's failure to ensure that Jewish Israelis have a genuine sense of belonging to the surrounding Arab Middle East, this slyly humorous allusion points to what is often Israel's actual (if unspoken) and ultimately misguided cultural loyalty. Interestingly, at one point Behar identifies the new unclarity as a 'dybbuk'. Whether or not an intentional reference to A.B. Yehoshua's ambivalent use of this motif earlier in *The Liberated Bride* (which seems to waver between a celebratory cultural fusion and a reluctant indictment of a schizophrenic condition), Behar's approach to this haunting is decidedly affirmative, as the previously homogenized culture bursts forth with a cacophony of Polish, Hungarian, Rumanian, German and Ukrainian accents and memories. Unsure of how best to respond to the national emergency of this new Babel and fearing that nobody will be left to 'instruct our children in the secret of the correct accent', the 'security authorities ... reinforce the radio with announcers whose Hebrew is so pure' that everyone else 'will feel alien in our speech.'

As one might already expect from the protagonist's picaresque journey, redemption proves elusive; the generational rift not so easily healed. Rather than gratification at their son's 'discovery' of his heritage, his parents recoil, feeling their hard labor to assimilate shamelessly repudiated: 'my parents stood staunchly against me and against the plague, remembering the years of effort they had invested to acquire their clean accent.' At such moments, the anxieties that seethe throughout Behar's narrative bear a remarkable resemblance to the shifting priorities in America's own epic story of immigration, assimilation, and triumphant reclamation of ethnicity.[9] In Behar's story, as in culture itself, the younger generation prevails and the narrator's parents are 'alone in their non-transformation' while the transgressive dybbuk stirs its reluctant host 'to write my stories in Arabic letters.' At times, the 'important departments' are shocked by this challenge to cultural hegemony while on other occasions they dismiss his activities with condescending laughter: 'Let him write stories that only he can read, his parents or his children will not read them and our children will not fall into the danger ... we will give him all the government prizes for Arabic literature without having read a word in his books.' But the reversal of forgetting seems to take hold on the streets of Jerusalem, and not merely in the unthreatening bastions of art.

The narrative's intergenerational complexity grows as the previous generations' hopes and aspirations for him are given plaintive voice. The grandfather's ghost speaks for the 'generation of the desert'. This ideological term [*Dor HaMidbar*] derives from the wanderings of the ancient Israelites who were ultimately judged to be unworthy of entering and dwelling in the Promised Land and applied by Zionists to those whose modern yearnings of Return they fulfilled. He bemoans the confusion that encroaches on his grandson's hitherto uncomplicated sense of place and identity, the clarity and purpose that the end of diasporic wandering should have ensured: 'why is this history of mine mixed up with yours, how I have come to trouble your life ... you are the generation for which we waited so that there would be no difference between its past and the past of its teachers, because our past was already very painful and we remained in the desert for the birds to eat us for your sake, so that you would not remember.' Traumatized by his strange condition, the narrator finds himself paralyzed ('I am not being, and I am not becoming') and mute, which in turn anguishes his parents who look on helplessly as their material ambitions are defeated by their recalcitrant offspring: 'speak, if you don't speak how will you get a scholarship, how will you continue your studies and what will you do?'. In the end, the narrator's silence is deemed as politically transgressive as his speech – the police take him to jail where his parents stoically await his repentance. Instead he pleads: 'read my story, Mother, Father, read all my stories that I have hidden from you for many years, you too are the same exile, the same silence, the same alienation between heart and body and between thought and speech.' The final sections of the story take on a peculiarly biblical cadence, drawing on Ezekiel's prophecy; a valley of dry bones that are resurrected and invigorated with life once again presents a rich allegory of a return to life for the entire Israelite nation who was stripped of their humanity through the cruelty of oppression (by reading about the valley of dry bones on Passover, Jews celebrate their own rebirth ritualistically). Invoking this fecund imagery, Behar playfully suggests something extraordinary about his own identity, that death is not death, and that what is genuinely vital in this world cannot be silenced forever.

To put Behar's unusual project in some perspective, it is worth pausing to examine a few of the voices that have called for similar reevaluations of the complex claims of history and identity. For example, it seems pertinent to recall an exchange between Sephardic and Mizrahi scholars that took place in a forum several years ago, beginning with the Moroccan-Israeli writer Albert Swissa's charge that the ingathering project of Zionism engendered the woeful condition of what he identifies as 'the smelting pot' of contemporary Israel, in which the ancient communities of the Levant found themselves struggling against deracination and various forms of re-education and institutionalized cultural intolerance, which greatly undermined a more regional and expansive locus of identity.[10] Yet in a more affirmative tone, Ruth Knafo Setton observes that 'in Israel today, Sephardic/Mizrahi aesthetics, customs, cuisine and music have become prominent in the cultural landscape; and in America, people are growing more aware that there are different, equally authentic ways of being Jewish. This gradual appreciation has opened the gates to Sephardic memory, as if giving permission to Sephardim to reclaim, rediscover, and redefine themselves' (Stavans, 27). What seems important to note in these conflicting narratives is the stark necessity of Sephardic memory and alternative Jewish experiences of the modern world. This alternative tradition challenges the essential but all-consuming project of Holocaust and genocide commemoration that too frequently dominates Israel and other 'official' forms of modern Ashkenazi life while sacrificing their voices. In the contemporary Middle East, the combined effects of Zionism and Arab nationalism initiated a historical process that destroyed the old pluralistic Levantine culture. In its place, we often endure the effects of the old dream of mono-ethnic cultures, the rage for purity that has produced so much violence and bloodshed. As Amnon Raz-Krakotzin argues, 'In Israel, Mizrahim became the new Marranos; in this case, however, it was not their religion that had to be concealed, but their culture. People had to hide their Arabic culture, afraid to listen to the music that preserved their contact to a cultural framework considered hostile and primitive. In other words, they had to abandon the culture in whose terms they defined their Jewish identity' (175). Sometimes, it would seem, to be most authentically Jewish actually necessitates a bolder embrace of hybridity or in-between identity. In Raz-Krakotzin's cogent argument, 'It is by resisting the dichotomy Jew/Arab that a Mizrahi perspective can become a 'Jewish' perspective—a restoration of the critical potential of modern Jewish discourse ... this location embodies the perspective of the colonizer and the colonized, as well as the interrelations between them' (178).[11]

Alternatively, Behar imagines a Levantine Israel in which the unpredictable rewards of renewal – and cultural ambivalence – are still possible. In fact, it is tempting to regard Behar's work as fulfilling the kind of radical paradigm shift Hochberg posits: 'Unfolding the imagined space between ... two ends of the spectrum, between, that is, past and future, actuality and potentiality, loss and hope, history and imagination, the Arab Jew "we were" and the Arab Jew "we might become" ... literary texts ... revisit forgotten narratives and figures and missed opportunities as a means for envisioning the future. ... Articulated in terms of a restless movement across borders and in between familiar precincts—Haifa and Beirut, Hebrew and Arabic, the Mellah and the Medina, lover and enemy, Islam and Judaism, the Arab and the Jew—such possibilities of being escape the limits of the separatist imagination' (140).[12] And to a stirring degree, Behar's tale also conjures up something Cynthia Ozick once wrote in a different context: 'To remain Jewish is a process—something which is an ongoing and muscular thing, a progress, or, sometimes, a regression, a constant-self reminding, a caravan of watchfulness always on the move; above all an unsparing *consciousness*' (168; italics original). Here Ozick addresses the need for a spirited and enduring struggle of the Jewish self caught between Jewishness and the West, but it seems to me that her language ('sometimes, a regression') of arduous becoming must ultimately apply to the inherent plurality of Jewish identity, with all its fissures and contradictions, *within* Israel itself. And I can think of no more mindful embodiment of this imperative than Behar's quirky and profound Levantine allegory of creative potency and cultural possession – '*Ana min al yahoud*' – a formulation that gestures urgently to the kinds of cultural bridges that might yet be built in the Middle East.[13] It seems worth noting that once one looks beyond the story's 'surreal' qualities, it is, of course, firmly rooted in historical experience. In Rachel Shabi's remarkable study *We Look Like the Enemy*, after documenting the fact that Jews and Muslims often made pilgrimages to the burial sites of the same prophets, she notes that Jews and Muslims in North Africa (and Iraq) 'would often write different words of prayer over the same music' (149) (a phenomenon that would be nearly unheard of in Christian Europe), a fact that underwrites the blended cultural notes that seize Behar's poetic rendering of how the past might yet speak to the present.[14] Moreover, from a similar theological perspective, prominent historian and cultural critic Meron Benvenisti finds Jewish and Muslim collaboration an altogether unremarkable pairing, given the simple fact that (unlike Christianity) both faiths adhere to 'an uncompromising iconoclastic monotheism (i.e., absolute prohibition against "graven images"), [enabling] Jews and Muslims to venerate the same saints at the very same sites' (280).[15] In significant ways, the story's fantastical elements embody a profound allegory of how the experience of Mizrahi Judaism in the Diaspora might yet contribute an open-ended give and take between disparate worlds: the old and the new; Eurocentric Jews and the Other within; Jews and Arab Muslims.

* * *

Herzl Haliwa, the protagonist of Sayed Kashua's 'Cinderella', is tormented by a similarly mischievous metamorphosis.[16] The juxtaposition of 'Herzl' and 'Haliwa' (which means 'sweetness' in Arabic) is especially ironic given his historical namesake's famous 1896 pamphlet 'The Jewish State' wherein he observes of the Zionist enterprise that 'For Europe we will constitute a bulwark against Asia, serving as guardians of culture against barbarism.'[17]

The genesis of the protagonist's plight stems from the desperate prayer of a hitherto childless woman who at the Western Wall 'begged God for a son, even if he was born half Arab.' Of course, in the perverse tradition of such prayers, hers is answered. Consequentially, his childhood nights are haunted by fearful nightmares of 'expulsion, war, and refugee living', the significance of which he cannot possibly comprehend. Thirty-odd years later, the long-suffering Herzl Haliwa still has a lot of explaining to do, especially to his girlfriend Noga with whom he has never spent a single night in their two-year relationship. Nor does it help that his Jewish half drinks wine at dinner with Noga and the Arab side, 'Haliwa', indulges in heavy Arak drinking after midnight. From that liminal time, the Arab elects to spend his nights in the company of pro-Palestinian European tourists (because 'Arab girls aren't to be found after midnight'). On the verge of losing her forever, Herzl Haliwa can think of no alternative but to spend the entire night together, which Noga endures as 'this idiotic game'. As the night ensues, she experiences the fact that her lover doesn't understand her Hebrew and insists on spending their date in East Jerusalem, 'the Arab sector of the city, which no nice Jewish girl has any business visiting'. Moreover, when a cab stops for them, he curses the driver in English when he recognizes that it belongs to a company that refuses to hire Arab drivers.

As in Behar's story, Kashua's young man encounters Jerusalem as both a Palestinian Arab and a Jewish Israeli. But here the doppelganger motif is even closer to home as Kashua himself is an Arab citizen of Israel who, as a journalist whose personal essays frequently appear in the pages of *Haaretz* (where 'Herzl Disappears at Midnight' first appeared), writes in Hebrew and thus dwells between Israel's Jewish and Arab communities, a life lived in perpetual translation, so to speak. In his early thirties, Kashua was born in the Arab town of Tira not far from Haifa in central Israel. As an adolescent, he won a scholarship to attend the Israel Arts & Sciences Academy, a Jewish boarding school. His experiences there led to an acute sense of occupying a low position in the Jewish school's social hierarchy, which eventually inspired the novel *Dancing Arabs* (2004), following a similar boy's struggle to belong and even leave behind his Arab identity altogether. At certain junctures, he resembles A. B. Yehoshua's Arab adolescent, Na'im, in *The Lover*, who is tempted by the seductive prospect of 'passing' and mimicking Zionist culture to overcome the burden of being part of a minority. Yet it seems important to emphasize that Kashua is hardly the only representative of such a complex minority position in contemporary literature among his generation. Consider the Palestinian-Israeli poet Na'im 'Araydi, who, like Behar, expresses a more hopeful relation to cultural ambivalence, the essence of Levantine openness: 'Until the age of thirteen I studied in our local village school. I learned to ask: "what" and "who". After thirteen, my parents sent me to study in the city, in an Israeli-Jewish school where I learned to ask "why" and "how". Today people keep asking me if I am an "Arab Poet" (*meshorer Aravi*) or a Hebrew poet (*meshorer Ivri*). This question makes little sense to me, but I fear it nevertheless. In order to overcome my fear [of needing to identify myself with one or another position] I had to become very optimistic. This optimism is my Levantinism.'[18]

Of his current work, a humorous and mildly satiric column that appears in the *Haaretz* weekly magazine, Kashua says: 'I hope people identify with the person and forget for a moment that he is an Arab. For me that is the ultimate goal of my column. I learned quickly that it would be pointless to talk to the Israeli public about politics. My goal is to make people laugh and forget it was written by an Arab. Or cry and see that you can cry with an Arab, too.'[19] His second novel, *Let it Be Morning* (2006) also has autobiographical elements, presenting the painful cultural and political dilemmas of its protagonist, an Israeli-Arab journalist who returns with his young family to his home village. Almost immediately alienated from his birthplace, the journalist and his family are trapped by a military curfew that bewilders and enrages the village residents. An astute observation of the enormous daily pressures faced by Israel's minority citizens, it seems to reflect on its author's own palpable lack of at-homeness. Obliquely commenting on the events and tensions portrayed in *Let it Be Morning*, he revealed his anxiety to the journalist Shoshana London Sappir: 'If the state views me as a "demographic problem" ... and a "cancer in the heart of the nation", there is a chance that one day it will try to surgically intervene to rescue the country.' When asked why he doesn't bother to exercise his right to vote, he responds: 'I don't feel like a citizen ... I don't feel like anyone is asking my opinion' ('Profile'). In both narratives, the unnamed narrator is a passive and resentful witness to the divided parties that surround him, discomfited by Israel for its discriminatory practices, by his fellow Arabs for their insularity and lack of compassion for West Bank Palestinians, and equally ill at ease over the fundamentalist ideology of the Islamists. Kashua's two novels have been translated into seven languages to date but the Arab world shows no interest in Arabic translations (though his work has been favorably reviewed in Arabic newspapers such as *A-Nahar* in Beirut).

Michael Romann and Alex Weingrod launch their study, *Living Together Separately: Arabs and Jews in Contemporary Jerusalem*, by examining a single day, in which the Jewish residents celebrate *Yom Yerushalayim* ('Jerusalem Day'), which was established as a triumphal secular holiday following the 1967 war and Israel's assertion of sovereignty over the previously divided city. The Muslim residents observe the religious holiday *al-Isra Wal-Mi'raj*, which commemorates the Prophet Mohammed's night journey between Mecca and Jerusalem, from where he ascended to heaven mounted on the horse al-Burak. In their summary of the separatist dynamics of these celebrations, the authors declare that those lay bare the essential conflict:

> [T]he Jews celebrated Israeli rule over all of Jerusalem at the same moment that the Arabs spoke of defending Jerusalem against her Israeli captors. Set within holy places claimed equally by both sides, these conflicts do not seem to be merely political and national, but ideological and religious as well. The messages were delivered practically simultaneously, but neither side heard or paid much attention to the other. The Israelis were unaware of the Muslim observance, just as the Arabs ignored the Israeli holiday. The Israeli press did not even mention the Muslim celebration, just as the Jerusalem Arab newspapers made no mention of *Yom Yerushalayim*. So close to one another in actual physical space, the two groups seemed to be on different planets. (5)

In the Jerusalem these academics investigated '[r]esidential segregation [was] practically complete. ... In fact, one of the most striking features of the united city is that an Arab or Jewish identity can be and is attributed to all neighborhoods, public functions, commercial establishments, and even basic consumer goods. There is very little that appears to be neutral or that can be given a different label: practically everything is categorized as either "Jewish" or "Arab". ... Crossing over to the "other side" is a highly conscious act that is often avoided, just as manifestations of avoidance and obstruction of intercommunal relationships are widely practiced in many everyday situations' (221). I draw attention to this observation because, unlike Behar's more sanguine allegory of transformative cultural interpenetration, cohabitation, and recovery, the narrator's bifurcation in Kashua's work mirrors the reality of obdurate oppositions as described by Romann and Weingrod, fated to remain alien to one another.[20] The story concludes with the character's Jewish half awakening from a deep slumber. When his beloved Noga tentatively asks what will 'happen with this whole Arab story' his bleak response (with its ironically unexamined Holocaust allusions) assures her that she has got her Jew back: '"If you ask me ... "they can all go up in smoke."' Speaking from a more oppressive political circumstance than Behar, Kashua nonetheless affirms a powerful sense of identity as contingent and adaptive, rather than static or absolute.

In spite of their sharply divergent tones, the two stories are richly creative exemplars of young Israeli artists whose self-conscious sense of play in creating characters, whose alterity may challenge readers' own sense of identity, their insistence that identities are never unequivocal, a subversive refusal to treat the Hebrew language as an exclusively Jewish possession, and a common resistance to the violently reductive narratives that increasingly entrap Jewish Israelis, Palestinians, and the Palestinian citizens of Israel. I see in their visionary and disruptive writing a paradigm of identity that is paradoxically also an 'uprooting', or welcome displacement, in the Jewish philosopher Emmanuel Levinas' sense of recoiling from the violence of nationalism and fetishization of place and origins: 'Every word is an uprooting. Every rational institution is uprooting. The constitution of a true society is uprooting.'[21] In this regard, it must be noted that here remain a number of vigorous intellectual champions of the Middle East's potentiality for coexistence and multiculturalism. In imagining their own vision of a democratic and secular state that would serve Israeli Jews and Palestinian

Christians and Muslims, Omar Barghouti, the Palestinian peace activist and essayist, finds inspiration in the words of Mexican novelist Carlos Fuentes: 'cultures are not isolated, and perish when deprived of contact with what is different and challenging. ... No culture ... retains its identity in isolation; identity is attained in contact, in contrast, in breakthrough' (Barghouti, 4; Fuentes 7–8). Among Israeli and Palestinian writers one increasingly finds a fervent insistence on bridges not merely to overcome political conflict but for the preservation of culture itself. Finally, in Israeli dramatist Yehoshua Sobol's evocative rendering of the rewards of proximity: 'Our mission as Jews is to open ourselves up and develop a dialogue with other cultures. Cultures, like people, oscillate between the erotic and the neurotic. Erotic cultures are interested in intercourse and exchange, in living metabolically, in the exchange of the spiritual and the material. ... The quintessence of Jewish culture is eroticism—a lively contact with others.'[22]

Notes

1. This reality is comprehensively examined in Michael Romann's and Alex Weingrod's aptly titled study *Living Together Separately: Arabs & Jews in Contemporary Jerusalem* (Princeton: Princeton UP, 1991). Almog Behar and Sayed Kashua's stories are available in the Hebrew originals and in translation online. See: Almog Behar, 'Ana min al yahoud,' *Haaretz*. 'Literature and Culture Supplement.' April 22, 2005: pg. 2; and: http://www.haaretz.com/hasen/pages/ShArt.jhtml?itemNo=570226 . Accessed January 12, 2010. Kashua's 2006 story was also originally published in *Haaretz* and translated by Vivian Eden. The English translation is available at *Words Without Borders: The Online Magazine for International Literature*: http://www.wordswithoutborders.org/article.php?lab=Cinderella. Accessed August 17, 2009.
2. See Routes: Travel and Translation in the Late Twentieth Century (Cambridge, MA: Harvard UP, 1997), 24.
3. See Chaim Chazan's essay 'The Way We Were' (Hebrew) in *Tel Aviv-Jaffa Research*, eds. Gila Menachem and David Nachmias (Tel Aviv: Tel Aviv University, 1993): 261–279.
4. For those unfamiliar with the increasingly polarized nature of Israeli society, Vinitzky-Seroussi's elaboration on its urban oppositions may prove greatly clarifying: 'The two cities can be said to appeal to and define two distinct national Israeli Jewish identities. Jerusalem may be seen as representing the mostly religious and right-wing nationalists who are fiercely opposed to Rabin's legacy. Tel Aviv represents the more secular and left-wing segment of Israel's population that supported Rabin's policies, particularly in regard to the conflict with the Palestinians. The difference in commemoration underlines the increasing bifurcation of Israel into (at least) two very distinct kinds of societies with two very different kinds of capitals. The social, political and cultural conflict between religious and secular life, between past and present, between universalism and particularism, between Right and Left, is not only marked, highlighted, reflected and represented by Jerusalem and Tel Aviv. The ways in which each urban center collectively remembers this event has become an arena through which larger social conflicts and identities are constructed and defined' (199). In 'Jerusalem Assassinated Rabin and Tel Aviv Commemorated him': Rabin Memorials and the Discourse of National Identity in Israel', *City & Society* 10 (1998): 183–203.
5. Israelis often note that whereas Jerusalem always bears the full weight of its ancient ruins and sacred sites claimed by the three monotheisms, youthful Tel Aviv, which rose from sand-dunes a little over a century ago, is relatively unburdened by history.

6 The full jury statement presenting its criteria for selecting Behar's story was appended to the story's original publication in the Culture & Literature weekend supplement of *Haaretz* (April 22, 2005), pg. 2 (my discussion cites this version). The English translation by Vivian Eden appeared on April 29th, 2005, pgs. 24–26 and was followed a year later by the Arabic version in the cultural monthly *Al-Hilal* (June 2006), pgs. 117–122.
7 Oud: a musical instrument of the Lute family, native to North Africa and the Middle East; *ahlan bik*: standard response to a friendly greeting; *ya habibi*: my dear, my darling; *salamatek*: to your good health.
8 The kind of vision of a sacred city expressed in Behar's story, one whose preservation truly respects its complex history, is increasingly challenged by those like Israel's Transportation Minister Yisrael Katz, a Likud party member who recently announced his intention to abolish Arabic place names (including Al-Quds for Jerusalem). See Ron Friedman, '"Yerushalayim" or "Jerusalem"?' *Jerusalem Post* (July 13, 2009), 6. The longstanding practice was to honor Israel's three official languages (Hebrew, Arabic, English) as well as the traditional names for locales. Thus 'Jerusalem' is identified as *Yerushalaim* in Hebrew, Jerusalem in English and *Al-Quds* in Arabic. Under Katz's proposed policy the Holy City will only be identified as Yerushalaim in all three languages. Similarly, Nazareth (*Al-Nasra* in Arabic) will be identified as *Natzrat* and Jaffa (Jaffa in Arabic) will appear as *Yafo*. The vexed issue of naming seemed to accelerate in the summer of 2009 on other fronts as well. On July 22, the Israeli Education Ministry announced that it would remove from school textbooks the Arabic term *nakba*, widely used by Palestinians to describe the events of 1948, in which 700,000 Palestinians fled or were expelled from their homes, as a 'catastrophe'. Prime Minister Benjamin Netanyahu had long argued that the word 'nakba' in Israeli Arab schools amounted to disseminating propaganda against Israel. Yet previous Israeli governments embraced the teaching of comparative histories, at least in the Arab sector. It was first introduced into a textbook used by Arab schools in 2007 when Yuli Tamir of the Labor party headed the Education Ministry.
9 Consider Herbert Gans, writing in the 1970s, observing the contrast between second-generation Jewish Americans, for whom ethnicity often carried severe economic and social costs and their children, for whom an ethnic Jewish identity became more desirable while the social stigma associated with it subsided. Gans analyzed the myriad ways in which Jews, like other 'white' Americans, overwhelmingly shifted from religion to 'ethnicity', which has a voluntary, symbolic nature that increasingly eludes the constraints and definitive forms of religion. See his 'Symbolic Ethnicity', *Ethnic and Racial Studies* 2 (1979).
10 Stavans, Ilan. 'The Experts', *The Forward* (January 21, 2005): 23–25. Quotation appears on pg. 24.
11 Amnon Raz-Krakotzkin, 'The Zionist Return to the West and the Mizrahi Jewish Perspective', *In Orientalism and the Jews* edited by Ivan Davidson Kalmar and Derek J. Penslar. (London: UP New England/UP Brandeis, 2005: 162–181).
12 In fact, Behar has recently pursued precisely this kind of inquiry in his journalism where he examines the intricate influences of the Islamic milieu on the development of Sephardic liturgy and musicology and describes their enduring legacy: '[The] phenomenon, in which "Jewish saints" hear Ishmaelite melodies, has been associated since the 16th century with Rabbi Yisrael Najara, a native of Safed and the greatest cantor of his era. Najara was deeply familiar with both the tradition of Hebrew liturgical poems and the doctrine of the Eastern maqam (a kind of musical mode), and was closely acquainted with musical activity present in the society around him – whether in coffee houses or among the Sufi orders. Najara set his liturgical poems to Arab, Turkish and Spanish melodies, and they became extremely popular in every Jewish community. The combination of new and sacred Hebrew texts with beloved melodies drawn from the local surroundings has been accepted ever since by

a majority of the *paytanim* (liturgical poets) living in the Jewish Orient.' In Behar's interview with one such contemporary *paytan*, Moshe Habusha, born in Jerusalem, to a family that immigrated from Baghdad, the latter enthusiastically discusses his disparate sources of inspiration, suggesting a fluid intermingling of Jewish and Muslim forms: In my cantorial singing, and as a singer and oud and violin musician, I introduce authentic music of Abdel Wahab and Umm Kulthum and Daoud Hosni, the late Karaite Jew who wrote many songs translated into Hebrew and also composed songs for Umm Kulthum.' Habusha is convinced that the organic connections Mizrahi Jews and Muslim Jews share is an untapped potential for a more peaceful Middle East: 'If I had a big party at [Syrian President Bashar] Assad's house, and brought in musicians from Aleppo, and we sang in Arabic – we'd make peace within minutes. You don't need [to involve] the whole Ashkenazi state that doesn't know how to speak their language. I want to say one thing to the Arab people: that the government of Israel does not represent us. We Mizrahim can make peace quickly; the government came from Europe. They have another language. We do not have hatred and we can live in peace, and the day will come when that happens. I have a plan to speak with [Sephardic Chief] Rabbi Yosef on this subject – about the fact that the Mizrahim can bring peace.' In Almog Behar, 'Umm Kulthum in the Men's Section: An Interview with Cantor Moshe Habusha', *Haaretz*, October 2, 2009: http://www.haaretz.com/hasen/spages/1118247.html.

13 Most promisingly, the story has been translated into Arabic, and even garnered warm attention in *Al-Hilal*, an immensely popular Egyptian cultural monthly where it was published in its entirety.

14 Rachel Shabi, *We Look Like the Enemy: The Hidden Story of Israel's Jews From Arab Lands* (New York: Walker & Company, 2008).

15 Readers may also find Benvenisti's chapter titled 'Saints, Peasants, and Conquerors' highly instructive. He addresses the complex and often contentious history of Jewish and Muslim sacred burial places in *Palestine in Sacred Landscape*, pgs. 270–306. After considering a number of such sites, he remarks that 'The adoption of Muslim traditions regarding the burial places of the forefathers of the Israelite nation and the transformation of sacred sites that had never been known in the Jewish tradition into pilgrimage places essentially bring events full circle: Jewish traditions were absorbed by Islam, which turned biblical figures (including those of the New Testament) into Muslim saints, made them objects of religious adoration, and identified the sites of their graves. Now the Jews have taken over the Muslims' "sacred geography" and are supposedly returning it to its Jewish origins' (278). He also writes that for Muslims (and I can't think why this wouldn't also apply to the pious Jews attracted to such sites in North Africa or the Middle East) 'saints are mortals whose good deeds have elevated them to a supernatural level and whom the sovereign of heaven has invested with the ability to control supernatural forces, perform miracles, bring luck, heal the sick, enrich the poor, and punish sinners. Belief in saints has assisted the indigenous Arab in times of hardship: during illness or drought, in wartime, in time of famine or natural disaster. And belief in the saints' ability to help was more important to him than religious orthodoxy' (279). See Meron Benvenisti, Palestine *in Sacred Landscape: the Buried History of the Holy Land Since 1948* (Los Angeles, CA: University of California Press, 2002).

16 Originally titled 'Herzl Disappears at Midnight', Kashua's 2006 story was also originally published in *Haaretz* and was translated by Vivian Eden. The English translation is available at *Words Without Borders: The Online Magazine for International Literature*: http://www.wordswithoutborders.org/article.php?lab=Cinderella. Accessed August 17, 2009.

17 Herzl did not harbor any animosity toward Arabs and in his utopian novel *Altneuland* (Old New Land, 1902) a major character is a Haifa engineer, Reshid Bey, who feels indebted toward his immigrant Jewish neighbors for improving the economic

prosperity of Palestine's inhabitants and is optimistic about the prospects for Jewish and Arab coexistence. In this visionary work, the secular writer even portrays a fanatical rabbi's scheme to disenfranchise the non-Jewish citizens, a plot that ultimately fails in the aftermath of an election in which Arabs and Jews both vote and enjoy equal rights.

18 Quoted in Gil Z. Hochberg, *In Spite of Partition: Jews, Arabs, and the Limits of Separatist Imagination* (Princeton, NJ: Princeton UP, 2007), 72. Na'im 'Araydi, 'L-hiyot levantini' [To Be a Levantine]. *Moznayim* 78: 79.

19 By all accounts, he has attracted an enthusiastic following. As one reader observed ironically, 'Sayed Kashua is the only Jewish humorist living among us today. We lost our sense of humor. We do not have the ability to see ourselves as others see us. And we don't have the ability to empathize with the other.' See Shoshana London Sappir, 'Profile: Sayed Kashua', *Hadassah Magazine* 88.2 (October 2006): http://www.hadassah.org/news/content/per_hadassah/archive/2006/06_oct/profile.asp.

20 In one of his more scathing satirical editorials, Kashua revisited the phenomenon of cultural 'passing' through his acerbic account of the *mistarvim* – undercover agents from Israel's security forces trained to 'be Arabs' but whose presence in his neighborhood he claims is all too obvious due to crude cultural gaffes and misapprehensions. See Sayed Kashua, 'How to be an Arab', *Haaretz* (October 23, 2009): http://www.haaretz.com/hasen/spages/1121401.html.

21 Emmanuel Levinas, *Difficile liberté: Essais sur le judaisme* (Paris: Éditions Albin Michel, 1963), 165.

22 Yehoshua Sobol. Address. 'Writing the Jewish Future Conference'. National Foundation for Jewish Culture. San Francisco, CA, February 2, 1998.

16 Democracy and liberal-democratic values in Religious-Zionist discourse

The case of Halakhic Q&A websites

Oren Steinitz

Introduction

Religious-Zionism, also known as 'National-Religious-Zionism', refers to a sector of Israeli Orthodox Jews who see themselves committed to the values of Zionism and generally accept the supremacy of Israeli secular law. While they are often associated with the political right, and especially with the West Bank settlements, as a group they are quite diverse, both politically and in their adherence to Jewish Law.[1] Moreover, they support a wide range of views with regards to accepting or rejecting liberal-democratic values, such as pluralism, universal human rights, equality of different groups, and the treatment of human life as an ultimate value. This sector is often treated as a society in transition. It is depicted in Israeli media and popular culture as a movement that used to be associated with religious moderation and a positive attitude towards modernity and towards the general Israeli society, but has been going through a process of political and religious radicalization ever since the 1967 war.

Over the last few years, internet websites where religious scholars answer surfers' questions related to Jewish Law have become increasingly common in the Jewish world as a whole, and in particular amongst the Israeli Religious-Zionist sector.[2] Although a lot has been written regarding how the web's lack of centralized supervision allows anyone to spread their ideas,[3] radical though they may be, the internet also allows web-surfers access to esteemed spiritual leaders, regardless of their geographical location. In addition, the questioners enjoy relative anonymity, which allows them to present delicate questions that one might not dare to ask a scholar face-to-face, for various reasons; the most common example of such topics are questions related to sexuality and sexual orientation.[4] The respondents, on their part, enjoy an unprecedented opportunity to spread their agenda all over the world, using a medium that is accessible to every web-surfer. Popular websites such as *Kipa*, *Moreshet* and *Yeshiva* feature answers by prominent rabbinic authorities from all across the Religious-Zionist spectrum. These include moderate Modern-Orthodox figures such as Rabbi Yuval Sherlo and Rabbi Shai Piron, as well as more right-wing scholars (both politically and religiously) belonging to the National-*Haredi* stream, such as Rabbi Shumel Eliyahu and Rabbi Moshe 'Amiel.

Internet discourse is often perceived as democracy in action. Some scholars even went as far as claiming that the web may be 'the only form of mass media that has the potential to be genuinely democratic'.[5] Even when discussing Jewish-religious web-based discourse, the democratic and egalitarian nature of the net is often emphasized. For example, in his article 'Mara d'Atara', Azriel Weinstein mentions the fact that differing – and even conflicting – rabbinic views are present on the web, sometimes even on the same website.[6] Even rabbis who generally oppose Halakhic pluralism, he claims, have to reluctantly accept the fact that when participating in a web-based discourse their opinions are often challenged not only by their colleagues, but also by web-surfers whose comments to the rabbis' answers are published side by side with them, even if the surfers challenge the scholars' authority.[7]

While it is evident that the democratic nature of the medium has had its impact on the nature of the online Jewish legal discourse, it is not clear whether this influence has extended to content rather than form. Participants in online Halakhic discussions were quick to adopt the inherent democratic value of free speech, but did other liberal-democratic values penetrate into this discourse as well? In order to answer this question, this paper will look at two case studies: questions and answers regarding the attitude towards the Palestinian population in Israel and the occupied territories; and questions and answers portraying National-Religious response decisions and actions taken by the Israeli government and legal system that the enquirers or responding scholars perceive to be contradictory to Jewish Law. The questions concerning the attitude towards the Palestinian population include issues such as selling and renting properties to Palestinians, the Halakhic status of non-Jewish residents in the Land of Israel, and – perhaps surprisingly – questions regarding strategic military decisions during wartime. The other types of questions deal with issues such as the appropriate responses to the Jerusalem Gay Pride Parade and illegal outposts and settlements in the West Bank.

An examination of both the enquirers' questions and the scholarly answers to them reveals the spectrum of opinions within Religious-Zionist society, not only with regards to the case studies, but also concerning the acceptance of Western liberal-democratic values in this sector. While some responders seem to have absorbed the Western mindset regarding universal human rights and equality, the majority of scholarly opinions found on the web demonstrate that ideas of cultural exclusivity, and even ethnic superiority, still dominate extensive portions of the Religious-Zionist discourse. Moreover, although the websites represent themselves as Halakhic, the answers are quite often based on the scholars' personal opinion without any references to authoritative religious sources.

In addition to the scholarly answers, the questions themselves often reveal how prevalent this mindset is among the population that makes use of such websites. Another aspect that influences the web discourse is the content of surfers' comments to the scholarly answers, which are, as noted, presented side by side with the rabbinic answers. These comments not only express the surfers' opinions, they also help to define the discourse's boundaries, so that if a scholarly answer is perceived to be too deviant from the perceived mainstream, the responders will not spare the scholar from scathing criticism.

Methodological note

The questions and answers reviewed here appeared in three well-known National-Religious websites: *Kipa*, *Moreshet*, and *Moriya*.[8] These websites feature prominent rabbis and scholars from the Religious-Zionist stream, as well as answers from younger Yeshiva students who assist the rabbis by answering some of the questions directed towards them. These websites operate in a different manner than a blog or an open forum; surfers can send their questions through a special forum in which they can choose which Rabbi they wish to answer them. The Rabbi's answer, however, is not only sent directly to the enquirer, it is also posted publicly. While surfers can post their comments to the scholarly answers, they cannot present themselves as one of the responding rabbis. The rabbis have the ability to censor parts of the surfers' questions (or choose not to answer them altogether), and they often do so, but it is not clear whether they can (or do) censor the surfers' comments.

Attitudes towards the Palestinian population on Q&A websites

The first topic that will be reviewed is the general treatment of Palestinians in a time of conflict. A surfer who considers herself a supporter of the 'radical right' submitted a question on the *Kipa* website in which she reported that since the beginning of the second *Intifāḍa*[9] she encountered many people using the slogan 'death to the Arabs', as well as reports of a Jewish Underground that killed an Arab baby, and found it difficult to accept a perception promoting the killing of an entire nation.[10] 'How are we different from them,' she asks, 'if we can take the life of an innocent person?' A Yeshiva student identified only by his first name, Raphael, provided her with a lengthy answer, in which he portrayed his views about required moral standards during a state of war. According to Raphael, while the Torah is very clear in its prohibition on killing, regardless of religion, race or sex, a state of war is a different reality. In this situation, he claims, Jews are commanded to kill as many as possible, and in some case even women and children, although these are very unique circumstances, and usually the killing of innocent people is forbidden even in a state of war.

After a general review of the subject, Raphael continues to a more specific answer, regarding what he refers to as the 'Oslo war'. He states that since it is not the entire Palestinian people that 'seek to destroy us' and most of them are seeking to live peacefully, then 'once we overpower them, we are not to kill them all, heaven forbid.' The question is, he continues, how to overcome the 'terrorist gang' controlling the Palestinians, pushing them to war. The answer, according to him, is that 'security experts agree that only an acute military operation can fight terror' and those claiming that the conflict can be solved by negotiations and 'giving away parts of our country' are wrong and misleading the public. Raphael adds that he intentionally ignores the issue of a Halakhic ban on giving away parts of the Land of Israel, assuming that no one disputes this claim. He summarizes his argument by stating that during a state of war the Israel Defense

Forces (IDF) must not 'occupy itself with differentiating between terrorists and [innocent] women and children' as this may reduce its effectiveness. He ends his response by emphasizing that even though there are situations permitting killing innocent people, this only applies to official state representatives (i.e. the army, etc.), and no individual should take the law into their own hands. If there is a Jewish Underground, he adds, it does not have any Halakhic basis to rely on. It is worth noting that although Raphael is not a Rabbi or any kind of real Halakhic authority, the *Kipa* website presents his response as a scholarly answer in the same format as those written by ordained rabbis. Thus, it appears to be authoritative and can just as effectively influence the web-based discourse as responses from ordained rabbis.

A practically identical question, probably submitted by the same enquirer, was answered several months later by Rabbi Shay Piron,[11] whose answer was short and unambiguous: 'There is absolutely no room for a comprehensive saying like "Death to the Arabs"! There is absolutely no room for sayings based on injustice and a serious moral flaw!'. He adds that anyone promoting such opinions in the name of the Torah is to be 'banished [from religious society] and be prevented from speaking in the name of the Torah, as he desecrates the Name [of the Lord].' Piron emphasizes that while the Jewish people have a long-lasting conflict with the Arab nation, 'who declared war against us and seeks to prevent us from returning to Zion, our homeland', 'we have nothing against individual Arabs living in this Land', who were created in the image of God. Piron ends his answer by urging the enquirer to protest against people using such slogans, so that such 'invalid opinions will not prevail in our camp'.

An interesting recurring topic on the National-Religious websites is the permissibility of businesses dealing with non-Jews in general and with renting or selling houses to non-Jews in the Land of Israel specifically. This is in light of a Maimonidean prohibition stating that while selling lands or houses to non-Jews in the Land of Israel is categorically forbidden, renting out houses to non-Jews is allowed as long as they do not seek to start their own neighborhood.[12] This issue gained public interest in 2004 after Rabbi Shmu'el Eliyahu, the chief Rabbi of Safed and son of the late Chief Rabbi Mordecai Eliyahu, said in a radio interview that Jewish Law forbids renting an apartment to Arabs, a saying that caused him to be charged with promoting racism.[13] Eliyahu's statement provoked a stream of questions sent to the different Jewish-religious websites, and specifically *Moriya* – a religious website managed by Shmu'el Eliyahu himself.

One question, for example, was sent to Rabbi Moshe 'Amiel by an enquirer who 'wanted to understand "what they said on the news" regarding selling a house to an Arab'.[14] The enquirer adds that he does not understand why this is forbidden and why the Arabs should be treated as unworthy, as 'they also have rights in this land.' 'Amiel's lengthy response is unambiguous. Firstly, he states that if the enquirer refers to Eliyahu's saying, then 'this is the Torah's opinion, and this is the law.' The Rabbi explains that the Land of Israel is 'the land of the Lord', which was given to the Jewish people 'not as a free gift for all purposes, but for a clear spiritual purpose in the ways of the Lord'. He adds that it is not permissible to 'transfer, sell, divide, disengage or leave the country' as 'the country does not belong to us, but to the Lord.' After stating his Halakhic opinion, 'Amiel moves on to political reasoning: 'Why deny the clear reality? Our status in this land is a state of war against the Arabs. An obvious life-threatening war, and a hidden war [portrayed] in the cultural sense of acquaintances leading to intermarriage.' Surprisingly, the model 'Amiel wishes to incorporate as far as treating minorities is clearly inspired by Muslim *Dhimma* regulations, which ensure limited rights for minorities while preserving a clear distinction between them and the Muslim population: 'Every Arab country understood it better than the government's [legal] advisor and the rest of the ministers, journalists, etc. Every Arab country ensured the Jews' rights as a somewhat respected minority, in a suitable housing area'.[15]

Apparently, the Rabbi does not consider the Islamic concept calling for the isolation of minorities to be degrading – even if the Jews are the minority in question – but sees it as a way to maintain separate communities, free of intermarriage. 'Amiel emphasizes that most Jews do not understand the importance of separation between the nations and their responsibility towards the status of the people of Israel and the Land of Israel. He protests the use of the term 'Dimocracy [*sic*]' in order to defend the mixing of the nations, and claims that those who do so do not understand the true meaning of the term (he does not, however, explain what the term means to him). He concludes his answer by responding to the enquirer's claim that the Arabs 'also have rights in this land': 'No, Brother. Rights in this land – are for us alone, and we are not to deny this clear historical truth. Rights in this land – are derived from the giving of the Creator. They have the rights of a minority – and their status is not to be blurred.'

Another question was sent through the *Moriya* website to Shmu'el Eliyahu himself by a real-estate agent who wondered whether he is allowed to provide Arabs with information about apartments for rent in Haifa.[16] The enquirer states that he remembers the Rabbi's saying regarding selling Arabs an apartment. Interestingly, Eliyahu's answer does not contain a single Halakhic argument. Instead, he argues that it 'is forbidden. Especially today when every apartment rented by an Arab from Gaza or the Galilee can be a place of hiding for murderers.' He adds that even though not every Arab is a suspect, and some are indeed 'righteous of the world', 'you are not a *Shin Bet*[17] agent, and even they don't know everything.' He concludes his answer by telling the enquirer that 'the Holy One praised be He will find you a good living from another source.' Unfortunately, since *Moriya* does not list the dates in which the answers on the site was given, it is impossible to determine if the answer was posted before or after Eliyahu's indictment.

A recent question on the subject of daily interaction with Palestinians, posted on the *Kipa* website, demonstrates how the questions themselves as well as the web-surfers' comments to the scholarly answer can be indicators of prevalent mindsets among the National-Religious population. The question was sent after a new supermarket was opened close to one of the West Bank settlements (the *Gush* junction), and the inquirer was astonished to find out that 'Arabs shop there as well!'.[18] The enquirer expresses his concerns that 'not only do these Arabs make the supermarket dirty with their faces, they will also make a move on the Jewish girls there!'. He wonders if one is allowed to shop at the supermarket or it is to be boycotted, and ends his message by asking 'how do we make these Gentiles keep away from our stores?'.

Rabbi Baruch Efrati, who responded to the question, appeared to be appalled: 'you can turn to the *Yad v'Shem* [holocaust] archive and find writings by Himmler and Goebbels containing similar expressions to those you used to refer to the Arabs, about us.' After a few more words of scolding, the Rabbi emphasizes that while the Talmudic rabbis enacted a few prohibitions on interaction with non-Jews in order to prevent intermarriage, such as the prohibition on enjoying wine handled by Gentiles, 'adding prohibitions out of your own heart is forbidden. You are not God's deputy.' The scholar continued his reply by asserting that

> the conquering of the land is not exclusively conquering by physical strength. [...] A real conquering [of the land] refers to the application of Israeli culture and law. Thus, when an Arab does his shopping in an Israeli supermarket, it reinforces our entitlement to the land. He is buying from us and not the other way around. We own the land. If one creates a separation – they also create recognition that there are two economic entities.

As a final remark, the Rabbi requested the enquirer to make *t'shuvah*, or show remorse, for his hatred and use of foul language.

This rabbinic answer received quite a lot of attention and quite a few surfers' comments were sent to the website. While a large portion of them praised the Rabbi for his firm reply, a number of surfers who thought that the scholar's answer was peculiar – or at least incompatible with the prevalent discourse among the National-Religious sector – did not spare the Rabbi their opinion. Some of them did so while ignoring Jewish Laws demanding respect for a religious scholar, or even the norms of common curtsey. One commenter, for instance, asked 'why can't we use such expressions to refer to Gentiles who fight the People of Israel? What is the problem here? I want to understand.' Another surfer wrote 'I agree with the inquirer. One might think these Gentiles are from Holland.' One surfer wrote a lengthy reply, explaining that the Rabbi's comparison of the enquirer to Nazi Germany was inappropriate, and that the attitude the enquirer displayed towards the Palestinian population cannot be classified as racist:

> We would be fooling ourselves if we decide that the source of the problem is hatred towards fellow human beings – I have never encountered a Jew who hates a Gentile due to nationalist reasons, I never heard that of hatred among us towards black Africans or slant-eyed Thais [*sic*] – but the explanation to this phenomenon is simple – the Arabs are hostile towards us, wish to see us fail[,] some are actual killers and amongst those that are not[,] most of them support their actions and they should not be blamed [...] we should not expect them to be righteous and oppose the killing of Jews, this is [their] national quality as decided by the Master of the Universe. [...] Despite everything our enemies are still the Lord's creation but without extensive study to say

about our enemies that 'pleasant are those created in the image [of God]' is just as superficial and childish, and of course the comparison to Himmler and Goebbels is completely inappropriate.

Another question demonstrating both the influence of responders on the web-based discourse and the place of fear of sexual contact with non-Jews in general, and Palestinians in particular, can be seen in another answer by Rabbi Efrati.[19] In this instance, a surfer approached the Rabbi, telling him that his ex-girlfriend is now dating a Palestinian Arab and thus 'ignoring social conventions and her parents' will.' The enquirer states that 'it is well known that the girl has had marital relations with the Arab', who is drawing her to the practice of Islam. The Rabbi's answer was short and decisive: 'First of all, cry for this horrible situation, and remember that despite it there is always hope to correct it.' He then suggests that the enquirer approach the *Yad l'Aḥim* organization which specializes in 'rescuing' women who are romantically involved with non-Jews.

The question attracted several responses from very upset responders. One of them, identified by the name Eyal, considered this case to be evidence of the failure of democracy –

> Because of this difficult situation, in which the state finds it difficult to define itself as Jewish and because of it being 'democratic', such cases are possible and no one raises their voice [about it]. Unfortunately, without a severe response innocent girls will keep falling into the hands of the Gentiles trying to seduce them in every way. Who would believe that such a strong assimilation is taking place within the state of Israel, and these cases are only one aspect of this epidemic. We must come together and act against this with full force.

This obviously emotional responder was not clear about what kind of 'severe response' should be conducted, or whether it should be directed against the phenomenon of inter-religious dating, or towards the democratic system which he perceives to be the source of the problem.

Attitudes towards the supremacy of Israeli Law

The tension between Jewish Law and non-Jewish legal systems [*'arka'ot shel goyim*] has been the subject of many scholarly debates and studies, and the case of the Israeli secular legal system, striving to balance between 'Judaism' and 'Democracy', is particularly complicated. On one hand, Israeli judges and legal authorities are for the most part Jewish, but on the other hand they do not accept the superiority of traditional Jewish Law. While different Orthodox figures treat the issue differently,[20] the Religious-Zionist sector is often differentiated from Ultra-Orthodox, or *Ḥaredi*, groups by the fact that it generally accepts (though sometimes grudgingly) the superiority of Israeli secular law on civil issues.[21] Nevertheless, Halakhic Q&A sites reveal that certain groups within this sector, particularly those associated with the settlement movement who were characterized by Charles Liebman and Eliezer Don-Yehiya as 'expansionists',[22] challenge this general acceptance of the supremacy of Israeli democratic decision-making. While these trends were observed before,[23] they were usually limited to issues of foreign policy and the Arab-Israeli conflict. The following examples will demonstrate that National-Religious views that challenge Israeli democracy do not focus exclusively on these issues – although, as will be seen, they still play a major part in the online discourse – but also address other issues, such as homosexuality in the public sphere.

A questioned titled 'The Despicableness Parade' was answered on the *Moreshet* website by Rabbi Ratson 'Arusi – a prominent Religious-Zionist Rabbi.[24] The enquirer expressed his concerns regarding statements issued by rabbis and key figures in the Orthodox world regarding the Pride Parade which was due to take place in Jerusalem in the coming month. 'Rabbis are calling for an uncompromising struggle,' he writes, 'and even for "martyr-like devotion" [*mesirut-nefesh*].' He adds that every time he hears these statements he expects 'to hear, even only a concluding remark, a clear reservation against violent measures as legitimate methods of struggle', but his expectations are never fulfilled. The enquirer states that he is certain that Rabbi 'Arusi, and other prominent rabbis, do not think that violent measures are a legitimate instrument in the struggle against the Parade, but he wonders why they remain silent. He also expresses his concern that an individual would commit a 'Phinehas-like'[25] act, and try and physically harm participants in the Parade.

The Rabbi started his answer – which does not contain a single reference to Jewish legal texts – by stating that while it is obligatory to protest the 'disgrace parade', it is also obligatory to refrain from violent acts, and mentions that the Chief Rabbi of Israel issued a clear statement on the matter. However, he adds, since he shares the enquirer's concerns, he allows himself to write the following statement:

> Democracy is an essential and pretty important [*sic*] and very useful concept but mainly for those who know what democracy is. And know how to use it. If not used properly, it may not only be non-beneficial, but also dangerous. [...] In democracy the risk is [great], as we are dealing with a diverse society. There are crowds that cannot always be controlled when outraged. Thus, in a democracy one should adopt an important rule, don't be right, be smart.

He adds that some minorities abuse the idea of democracy in order to justify 'an abandonment of all values' and that this 'is a sick phenomenon that should be corrected through education.' The Rabbi expresses his regret that the Supreme Court judges do not bear in mind that by allowing events such as the Parade to take place they are creating 'situations in which the majority is deeply offended by a minority's provocative demonstration, in a way that cannot be controlled', and essentially stirs the blame for any future violent act at the Supreme Court. He ends his response by declaring that 'we cannot allow this "democracy" to become an instrument in dismantling the unity and values of our people.'

A completely different rabbinic response, portraying a far more positive attitude towards the Supreme Court (while maintaining an opposition to the Parade itself) was written by Rabbi Yuval Sherlo – a National-Religious Rabbi known for his generally moderate views, especially on issues related to homosexuality – after the July 2005 Pride Parade, in which an Ultra-Orthodox man tried to stab one of the participants.[26] The enquirer, who stressed his objection to 'this parade of blasphemy', wrote the Rabbi that his 'body shivered at the site of this man's zeal that caused him to lose his mind as far as attempting to murder another human being.' Like the previous enquirer, he found a parallel between the stabbing and the story of Phinehas, and as the Torah appears to legitimize Phinehas' deed, he wondered what the difference between the two cases is. The enquirer ended his question by emphasizing that he does not mean to simply be provocative, but was indeed wondering where the line is drawn.

In his short answer, Rabbi's Sherlo admitted that the issue is far from being simple, and that it is indeed quite difficult to draw the line. He refrained from giving an exact definition of when an act of zealotry is permitted, but instead outlined two principles that may 'give a sense of direction'. First, he claims, a 'zealous person must be worthy of this title, must be clean of all other transgressions, and have his intentions directed towards the Heavens.' As it is virtually impossible to prove that a person is free of transgressions, the Rabbi effectively assures that while the biblical concept of zealotry is not compromised, it cannot be practically applied in current times.[27] The second guideline that Sherlo portrays is that an act of zealotry cannot be committed against the public. Jewish laws of zealotry, he claims, as well as the story of Phinehas, relate to an issue that the public prohibits and the leadership fails to deal with. In the case of the Pride Parade, however, 'to our great disgrace, [it] is endorsed by the public, as seen by the decisions of the [Supreme] Court which the public endorses.'

The last answer that will be reviewed here is attributed to the 'Rabbis of Har Brakha Yeshiva', and is related to the issue of settlers re-building illegal outposts in the West Bank after they were previously dismantled by the IDF.[28] This Yeshiva, headed by Rabbi Eliezer Melamed, gained some media attention in 2009–2010 after Minister of Defense Ehud Barak decided to remove the Yeshiva from the *Hesder* arrangement that allows Yeshiva students to take part in a shortened army service in dedicated units. This was after several soldiers who studied in Har Brakha demonstrated against the army's participation in the evacuation of a settlement.[29]

The enquirer wondered if settlers are doing the right thing by re-building outposts that the government declared illegal and were dismantled by the army. 'On one hand,' he says, 'we keep saying how important it is to vote, influence, and participate in political life […] but on the other hand we do not accept the regime, and [do not see ourselves] obligated by a law or two that do not suit us.' He asserts that he knows for certain that the government is wrong, 'that the right is good and the left is evil. However, we must fight for our stand only according to the law and not against the law.'

The Rabbi's lengthy answer starts with a short, unambiguous statement – 'Heaven forbid. I beg your pardon, but your words remind me of idolatry.'

According to the nameless Rabbi, the regime receives its power from the people, and thus if Ariel Sharon was elected according to his promise that Netsarim is as important as Tel Aviv, and later evacuated the Gaza Strip, then 'he does not fulfill the people's will and his immoral crimes are not legally valid anyway.' After maintaining that the evacuation of settlements is not democratic, he reminds the reader that democracy does not guarantee moral behavior, as the Nazis were democratically elected, and asserts:

> The State of Israel is a Jewish state, period. The term Jewish-Democratic is incorrect, as democracy is merely a technicality[.] A type of government that is not as bad as other types, but it is not a supreme value. [...] We should never say [the term] Jewish-Democratic in a manner that hints as if these two values are equal and in practice the Supreme Court disregards the manner of the Jews [sic] and forces the opinions of the domineering secular leftist minority on the traditional religious rightist majority.

As it seems, the Rabbi moves between declaring that democracy is merely a form of government that is superseded by Jewish Law, and protesting that the state of Israel is not democratic enough, as it disregards the majority opinion. This trend is also evident in the rest of the Rabbi's answer, in which he asserts that one should participate in the defense of the country because there is 'a commandment to do so' and not in order to present oneself as more likable to secular-Zionists. 'If you fold too much in order to gain a sense of brotherhood, you end up with no respect and no brotherhood.' He ends his response by stating that 'all of this ties, of course, to the issue of girls in the army', and that the IDF's 'treatment of religious soldiers and the Torah of Israel is disgraceful'.

Conclusions

When reviewing the web-based questions and answers, the treatment of liberal-democratic values and democracy itself both by surfers and responding scholars is revealed. As it seems, many of the scholars and surfers appear to reject the concepts of universal human rights, protection of minorities and equality between human beings. This can be seen in their harsh treatment of inter-religious romantic or sexual relationships; the fact that some of the scholars see no problem in harming civilians during a state of war; the emphasis on the Maimonidean prohibition against selling land to non-Jews in the Land of Israel; the all-encompassing objection to the LGBT's community right to demonstrate; and the suspicious attitudes towards the Supreme Court and the Israeli legal system. Some of these concepts – especially the attitude towards intermarriage – may be perceived as an integral part of Jewish Law, but the treatment of other issues, such as the permissibility of selling of property to non-Jews in the Land of Israel or the attitude towards the secular legal system, often ignores the fact these topics are under Halakhic dispute and aims to incorrectly present Jewish Law as a monolith. This is often done without reference to authoritative Jewish legal sources.

This trend is clearly demonstrated in the answer written by Raphael – the Yeshiva student who chose to use this medium in order to give strategic advice to the IDF and the Israeli government without any authority or qualifications to do so. Not only did Raphael promote a hawkish view of the Arab-Israeli conflict, and claimed that the IDF should not be bothered with the ethical question of harming civilians during a state of war, he also insisted that the Halakhic stance forbidding giving away parts of the land of Israel is indisputable. This attitude contradicts Rabbi Ovadya Yossef, perhaps Israel's most prominent Sephardic Halakhic authority, who supported the Oslo agreements and ruled that the sanctity of human lives is more important than the sanctity of the Land of Israel.[30] While this may be attributed to ignorance on Raphael's side, as he is not an ordained Rabbi, the fact that the *Kipa* website allows Yeshiva students to answer such questions is by itself an indication that the online Halakhic discourse is often influenced by personal opinions rather than actual legal precedents.

A particularly interesting theme is the treatment of democracy itself. Such is Rabbi Moshe 'Amiel's protest against those who, according to him, do not understand the true meaning of democracy and use the term in order to advocate equal rights to all the residents of Israel, Jewish or not. 'Amiel's suggestion to favor the Muslim *Dhimma* model of separation between religious communities rather than the Western democratic model is quite peculiar, especially considering his harsh treatment of the Palestinian population. An even harsher view of democracy was seen in the comments by the surfer 'Eyal', who seems to openly blame the democratic system for what he considers to be the worst ailment of Israeli society – the lack of segregation between Jews and non-Jews which may lead to romantic relationships. The trend is also evident in Rabbi 'Arusi's claim that the Supreme Court's emphasis on democratic values and the rights of minorities cannot be used to sever the nation's unity, and especially in the answer by the nameless Har Brakha Rabbi who alternated between claiming that Israel is not democratic enough as the majority's views are disregarded by the Supreme Court, and arguing that democracy is at best a necessary evil which will always be superseded by Jewish Law.

Strikingly, while some democratic values appear to be shunned by participants in the online National-Religious discourse, one value is wholeheartedly embraced – the freedom of speech. Rabbis and enquirers do not seem to have a problem using a democratic medium such as the web in order to promote non-democratic – or even anti-democratic – outlooks. In a recent column, Rabbi Shmu'el Eliyahu went as far as proposing that websites should not be allowed to screen or censor the surfers' comments to news articles, claiming that these comments are the only way to find out what the public's opinion really is, rather than the picture portrayed in the media.[31] This view is, of course, in line with the view advocated by some of the reviewed rabbis claiming that the majority's voice is under-represented in Israel.

Eliyahu's notion that internet-based discourse is an ideal opportunity to reveal the public's opinion, unbound by the influence of class or status, is compatible with some scholarly views regarding the nature of the internet.[32] It is also, however, quite simplistic. The surfers' ability to respond to rabbinic answers makes it tempting to view religious websites – and the internet in general – as an ideal Habermasian public sphere, encouraging an open and rational debate, free from the constraints of social status or the natural distance between a scholar and the laity. A democratic, rational-critical public sphere, however, is characterized by what Habermas referred to as an 'ideal speech situation' in which the participants in a discussion all attempt to arrive at the truth, without behaving strategically.[33] However, scholars studying the internet have pointed out that this idealized view of the web has very little basis in reality, and that internet discourse is often characterized by group polarization – a tendency to read blogs and websites only if they conform to the readers' own views and beliefs. Readers of online rabbinic answers, as seen in the examples above, are no different.

When Rabbi Efrati's responsum concerning the Arab shoppers at a West Bank supermarket appeared too liberal or 'democratic' for some readers, they used their democratic right to free speech to let the Rabbi know he was stepping outside the boundaries of legitimate discourse. Rabbi Efrati's answer concerning a romantic relationship between a young Jewish woman and her Arab boyfriend may have fit well within the discourse's boundaries, but a surfer nonetheless used the opportunity to preach against the dangers of democracy and called for severe actions against such relationships, and maybe even towards democracy itself.

In short, while Halakhic pluralism and freedom of speech do characterize the web-based National-Religious discourse, other liberal-democratic values are not always present. Surfers and rabbis appear to be eager to use their democratic right to publicly spread their agenda, even if it is anti-democratic. Some participants in the discourse openly oppose democratic ideas; some perceive democracy to be a tool rather than a set of values, while others do not seem to be sure of what democracy even is. Even if the web is indeed the only type of media that has the potential to be genuinely democratic, National-Religious Halakhic websites do not presently live up to this potential.

Notes

1 S. H. Rolef, 'National Religious Party (NRP)', *Encyclopedia Judaica*, Detroit, MI: Macmillan Reference USA, 2007: http://go.galegroup.com/ps/i.do?id=GALE|CX2587514603&v=2.1&u=ucalgary&it=r&p=GVRL&sw=w; C. S. Liebman and E. Don-yehiya, *Civil Religion in Israel: Traditional Judaism and Political Culture in the Jewish State,* Los Angeles: University of California Press, 1983, pp. 185–213.
2 O. Z. Steinitz, 'Responsa 2.0: Are Q&A Websites Creating a New Type of Halachic Discourse?', *Modern Judaism* 31:1, 2011, 85–102; See also A. Weinstein, 'Mara d'Atara: 'Al Posqim v'Psiqot Hilkhatiyot ba'Internet [Heb: On Halakhic Rulings and Rulers on the Internet]' *De'ot* 16, 2003/5763, 8–12.
3 G. B. Rodman, 'The Net Effect: The Public's Fear and the Public Sphere', in *Virtual Publics. Policy and Community in an Electronic Age*, 2003, 18, 27.
4 See Weinstein, 'Mara d'Atara: 'Al Posqim v'Psiqot Hilkhatiyot ba'Internet [Heb: On Halakhic Rulings and Rulers on the Internet]'.
5 Rodman, 'The Net Effect: The Public's Fear and the Public Sphere', 28.

6 Weinstein, 'Mara d'Atara: 'Al Posqim v'Psiqot Hilkhatiyot ba'Internet [Heb: On Halakhic Rulings and Rulers on the Internet]', 9.
7 For a more elaborate discussion on the subject, see Steinitz, 'Responsa 2.0: Are Q&A Websites Creating a New Type of Halachic Discourse?'.
8 *Moriya* recently went offline, for unknown reasons.
9 The Palestinian uprising that began in October 2000.
10 Ḥavreim Maqshivim, 'Musar u'Milḥama, "Mavet la'Aravim"? Maḥteret Yehudit', *Kipa*. 25 Av, 5761. http://www.kipa.co.il/ask/show/537.
11 Piron, Shay, 'Mavet la'Aravim', *Kipa*. 9 Shvat, 5762. http://www.kipa.co.il/ask/show/413.
12 See *Mishneh Torah, Avodah Zarah*, 10:4.
13 See E. Ashkenazi, 2006. 'Yevutal ha'Ishum Neged Raba shel Tsfat 'al Hasata l'Giz'anut', *Haaretz*. 18.6.2006. Later on, Eliyahu's indictment was annulled after Eliyahu declared that he only referred to Arabs who support terrorist acts. The issue recently returned to the center of media attention when Eliyahu was interviewed once again and called for a ban on renting out houses to Arab students in his hometown Safed. Later, 50 municipal rabbis signed a statement of a similar nature. See K. Naḥshoni, 2010. '50 Rabanei 'Arim: Lo l'Haskir Dirot l'Aravim', *yNet*. 7.12.2010. http://www.ynet.co.il/articles/0,7340,L-3995411,00.html.
14 'Amiel, Moshe, 'Ha-Im Limkor Bayit l'Aravi', *Moriya*, Question No. 20339. http://www.moriya.org.il/shut/indexid.asp?id=20339.
15 While 'Amiel is correct in his assumption that the *dhimma* regulations were intended to create a barrier between Muslims and non-Muslims, these regulations never included separate housing or neighborhoods.
16 Eliyahu, Shmu'el, 'Haskarat Dira l'Aravim', *Moriya*, Question No. 2140. http://www.moriya.org.il/shut/indexid.asp?id=2140.
17 *Shin Bet* – Israel's General Security Service, in charge of internal security affairs.
18 Efrati, Baruch, 'Rami Levi Gush Etzyon,' *Kipa*, 3 Av 5770. http://www.kipa.co.il/ask/show/219414.
19 Efrati, Baruch, 'Yehudiya 'Im 'Aravi,' *Kipa*, 10 Sivan 5770. http://www.kipa.co.il/ask/show/214372.
20 One fascinating example is Rabbi 'Ovadia Yossef's attitude towards the Israeli legal system. See chapter 9 in A. Picard, *Mishnato Shel ha-Rav 'Ovadyah Yosef Be-'idan Shel Temurot: Ḥeḳer Ha-halakhah U-viḳoret Tarbut,* Ramat-Gan: Universiṭat Bar-Ilan, 2007. Pages 186–192 deal specifically with Rabbi Yossef's view of multi-cultural liberalism and legal pluralism.
21 For a thorough review of different Orthodox responses towards Zionism, and towards Israeli secular law and culture, see chapter 7 in Liebman and Don-yehiya, *Civil Religion in Israel*, pp. 185–213.
22 Unlike the *Ḥaredim*, Expansionists attribute Divine value to secular-Israeli establishments such as the IDF, and seek to extend the Religious-Zionist influence over the entire Israeli society rather than separate from it completely. See Ibid, 200–206.
23 See C. S. Liebman, 'The Rise of Neo-Traditionalism among Modern-Orthodox Jews in Israel', *Megamot* 27, 1982; E. Don-Yehiya, 'Review Article: Jewish Messianism, Religious Zionism and Israeli Politics: The Impact and Origins of Gush Emunim', *Middle Eastern Studies* 23:2, 1987, pp. 215–234; Y. Meir and S. Rahav-Meir, *Yamim Ketumimha-hitnaḳtut – Ha-ḥeshbon Ṿeha-nefeshm* Tel Aviv: Yedi'ot aḥaronot, Sifre ḥemed, 2006.
24 'Arusi, Ratson, '*Mits'ad HaSh'felut*', *Moreshet*. 5.11.2006. http://www.moreshet.co.il/web/shut/shut2.asp?id=79978.
25 The enquirer is referring to the biblical story of Phinehas the Priest, who stabbed an Israelite man and a Midianite woman fornicating in front of the Tabernacle. See Numbers 25:1–9.

26 Sherlo, Yuval. '*Qana'uto Shel Pinḥas*', *Moreshet*. 3.7.2005. http://www.moreshet.co.il/web/shut/shut2.asp?id=57087.
27 This is a standard Halakhic technique for dealing with inapplicable biblical concepts and commandments. The most common example of it is the Talmudic treatment of the 'Rebellious Son' mentioned in Deuteronomy 21:18–22. See Bavli Sanhedrin 70:2 and Mishna Sanhedrin 88:4.
28 Rabbis of Har Brakha Yeshiva. '*Demokratya*', *Kipa*, 17 Sivan 5769. http://www.kipa.co.il/ask/show/182900.
29 C. Levinson, '*Sar HaBitaḥon, Ehud Barak, Horah l'Hotsi et Yeshivat Har B'rakha m'HaHasder 'im Tsahal*,' *Haaretz*. 13.12.2009. http://www.haaretz.co.il/hasite/spages/1134733.html.
30 Y. Meital, *Peace in Tatters: Israel, Palestine, and the Middle East*, Boulder, CO: Lynne Rienner Publishers, 2006, p. 66.
31 Eliyahu, Shmu'el. '*Eḥad sh'yode'a:Yyeshudrag Ma'amad HaTalkbackim*', *NRG*. 20.12.2010. http://www.nrg.co.il/online/1/ART2/191/202.html.
32 See Rodman, 'The Net Effect: The Public's Fear and the Public Sphere'.
33 C. R. Sunstein, 'Neither Hayek nor Habermas', *Public Choice* 134:1, 2008, p. 91.

Index

'Abduh, M. 5
Abuhatzeira, Y. (Baba Sali) 97
Abu Wa'el, T. 205, 207–8
acculturation 1, 13
Adler, L. 8, 118–34; and archaeology 129–30; biographical details 119–22; buildings in Tel-Aviv 123–5; influences 130–2; and orientation 126–30; theory 120–2; and Zionism 132–4
Adorno, T. 201
Agadati, B. 224–5
Agamben, G. 145, 153
Agassi, Y. 92
Agnon, S. 199–200
Ahmadinejad, M. 47
Aizman, M. 18
Almond, G. 66
Al-Qurayẓiyya, S. 141
Althusser, L.P. 141–2
Amara, M. 240
Amichai, Y. 203
'Amiel, M. 279, 282–3, 289
Amir, A. 93–4
Amir, Y. 110
Anderson, B. 90
Arab-Israeli conflict: and adolescents 239–255; and architecture 118, 125; and cinema 201–3; and foreign policy orientation 26–7, 35–6, 38; and orientation 10, 15, 17, 18–24, 26–8, 33, 35–40, 44–50, 51, 58, 62, 94–5, 101, 147–52, 182, 199, 212–21
Arad, U. 33
architecture: and Arab-Israeli conflict 118, 125; biblical influences 130–4; classical roots 126, 128–34; and orientation 8, 118–34, 228, 232; and socialism 129–30, 133–4; and Zionism 118–20, 128, 131–4

Arendt, H. 91
Arian, A. 66
Ariel 241
'Araydi, N. 272
'Arusi, R. 286, 289
Ashkar, M. al– 110, 112
Ashkelon 110–11
Ashkenazi Jews: attempts to define Israeli culture 6–7, 51–2, 100, 118–34, 141, 149–55, 199, 201–9, 266; attempts to define Mizrahi culture 1, 107, 145, 149, 204–9, 266; and Ottoman Empire 17; and the United States 166
Atias, A. 264
Atrash, F. el 217
Auden, W.H. 203
Avineri, S. 33
Avisar, I. 216
Avnery, U. 51, 89
Avnon, D. 66
Aznar, J.M. 39
Azoulai, H. 205–7

Baerwald, A. 118
Baker, C. 205–7
Bakhry, M. 206
Balass, S. 51, 154
Balbūl, Y. 148
Banai, E. 109
Barak, E. 38, 287
Barash, A. 199
Barghouti, O. 275
Bar-Giora, Y. 233
Bar Kochba 91
Barnes, S. 66
Barnett, M. 67
Barthes, R. 199
Bataille, G. 140, 155

Bauman, Z. 142–3, 145
Beck, U. 144
Be'er Sheva 106, 112
Behar, A. 264–72
Beit Alpha 130
Ben-Avi, I. 85–6
Ben-Gurion, D. 5–6, 34, 47, 71, 85–6, 199
Ben-Simchon, G. 232
Ben Sira, Y. 130
Benvenisti, M. 271
Ben-Yehuda, E. 21–2
Ben, Z. 106–15
Ben-Zvi, Y. 22, 85
Berger, D. 111
Bergman, I. 214
Bergman, S.H. 89
Berlin, J. 118
Bialik, H.N. 224
Bienstock, Y. 19
Biesecker, B. 147
Bilu group 17, 20
Blum, S.S. 124
Bos, R. ten 145
Boyarin, D. 91, 227
Boyarin, J. 91
Bram, C. 150–1
Braudel, F. 100, 132, 226
Brenner, H. 199
Broch, H. 202
Buber, M. 85
Bukai, R. 204–5
Burke, K. 146

Canaanites movement 51, 81, 88–91, 97; and Crusader analogy 93–5; and Gush Emunim 93, 96; post-Zionism and 92–3, 98–9
Carr, E.H. 153
Chazan, C. 265
Cherner, M. 123
Chetrit, S.S. 153
Cieri, M. 109
Cixous, H. 155
Choucri, N. 179
Clifford, J. 264
Cohen, H. 91
Copti, S. 208
Crusader analogy 16–17, 48, 85–8, 90, 92–9, 227

Dagan, H. 228
Dalal, Y. 200
Damari, S. 202

Darwīsh, S. 148
Davis, D. 155
Dinar, B. 207, 225
Don-Yehiya, E. 286
Dubnow, V. 17
Du Bois, W.E.B. 267
Duverger, M. 66, 68

Eban, A. 28, 47
Efrati, B. 284–5, 290
Ehteshami, A. 45
Ein Harod 123
Eisenstein, S. 224
Elam, Y. 92
Eliade, M. 96
Eliasi, Y. (the Shadow) 233
Eliyahu, M. 282
Eliyahu, S. 279, 282–3, 289
Elkabetz, R. 208
Elkabetz, S. 208
Epstein, Y. 23–4
Erdoğan, R.T. 47
Ethiopian Jews 2, 178, 186, 241

Feierberg, M.Z. 85–6
Feige, M. 94, 227
Feki, M. 48
Ford, A. 201
Fuentes, C. 275
Fulman, A. 208

Gaon, Y. 204
Gaza Strip: Hamas and 36, 41; Israeli policy 27, 29, 219; settlements in 241, 288; violence in 239, 244
Geddes, P. 118, 133
Gefen, A. 110–12, 114
Gefen, Y. 107
Gelblum, A. 150
Gencebey, O. 106
General Zionists 70
Gershwin, G. 205
Gilory, P. 154
Ginsberg, A. (Ahad Ha'am) 20, 22–4, 91, 118
Godard, J.L. 214
Goethe, J.W. 131
Golan, M. 204, 207
Goldberg, H.E. 150–1
Gorny, Y. 22
Gross, N. 202
Guri, H. 90, 92
Gurevitch, Z. 224, 228
Gush Emunim 93, 96

Guttman, E. 66

Habermas, J. 290
Habib, N. 202
Ḥaddād, E. 148
Haifa 112, 122, 205, 241, 271–2, 283
Halacha 11, 178, 182, 279–90
Hamas *see* West Bank, Gaza
Haskalah 17–19
Halevi, R. 1
Halevi, Y. 50, 200
Hall, S. 142
Hana, H.S. 205
Hanson, V. 3
Hasfari, S. 205–7
Hazan, R. 66
Hazaz, H. 199
Herzfeld, M. 111
Herzl, T. 22, 86, 118, 188, 272
Heine, H. 131
Hirshfeld, Y. 128
Hisin. H. 20
Hochberg, G. 271
Hourani, A.H. 148
Humboldt, A. 131
Huntington, S. 30, 95
Ḥuṣrī, S. al–, 147

Imber, N.H. 114
immigration: absorption of 8, 87, 126, 191; cultural orientation 1, 7, 15–24, 87, 90, 146, 149–53, 266, 269; and demography 187; from Israel to the United States 8, 115, 161–73; Israeli policy on 180; migrant workers 177–193
Inbar, D. 229
interpellation 140–2, 145–51, 154
Iraqi Jews 1–2, 9, 140–1, 145–55, 200, 266, 271
Israeli Arabs 264, 272–5; and orientation 1–2, 5, 7, 43, 60–2, 177–8, 212, 219–20, 239–55, 264; in relation to Palestinians 219, 273
Israeli cinema: and Arab-Israeli conflict 212–19, 220–1; and orientation 8–10, 199–209, 212–19, 220–1, 223–33; Palestinians in 202, 213–15
Israeli foreign policy: alliance of the periphery 34–5, 42; and the "Arab spring" 27, 35, 40, 48–9; and diaspora Jews 32–3; and domestic politics 47; European orientation 33–4, 39; one great power doctrine 31–3; and orientation 26–50; and peace process 29, 35–6, 38–40, 49; unilateralism 29–30, 35–6; and the United Nations 30, 32; relations with Jordan 35, 41–3; relations with the United States 31–2, 39
Israeli identity: collectivism versus individualism 44, 86, 88–90, 94, 101, 188, 192, 204, 214, 230–2; and democracy 2, 65–78, 99, 177–8, 187, 212, 283, 285, 288; exile and diaspora 33, 85, 88–99, 130, 172, 183, 187, 202, 224–5, 227–8, 269–71; and family 148–9, 161–73, 230–1; and food 43, 51, 188, 217; and the holocaust 95, 213, 228, 270, 274, 284; and minorities 182–93, 216, 220, 264–75; and the sabra concept 90, 92, 188, 213–14, 216, 223, 230; territorial conception 88–9, 91, 97, 192, 227–8
Israeli literature: and the conscience of Zionism 97–8, 203; and orientation 24, 38, 98, 199–200, 225, 264–75
Israeli music: and cultural orientation 8, 10, 24, 38, 43, 105–15, 170–1, 199–201, 205–6, 212, 217, 223, 225, 228, 233, 270–1; and peace process 108–9
Israeli party-system: and Ashkenazi–Mizrahi divide 70; fragmentation of 67–8, 72, 74–6, 78; and proportional representation (PR), 68–71; 78; and religious parties 68; stability of 77–8; Zionist roots of 68–9
Israeli television: and Arab-Israeli conflict 10, 231–2; and orientation 10, 212, 216, 219–220, 228, 231

Jabès, E. 91
Jabotinsky, Z. 85
Jaffa 19, 21, 70, 241
Jarbawi, A. al– 48–9
Jeanneret-Gris, C.E. (Le Corbusier) 127, 132
Jerusalem 17, 147; architecture in 118; in film 203, 208, 214; as a symbol of conservatism 264–75, 280, 286
JNF 223

Kadima 77
Kafka, J. 227, 266
Kahanoff, J. 99–100, 226, 233
Kapoor, R. 206–7
Kashua, S. 220, 264–5, 272–4

Kelman, H.C. 240
Khalidi, Y. al– 22
Khalifa, S.K.A al– 48
Khleifi, M. 208
Khouri, R. 44
Kipling, R. 107
Kiryat Shemoneh 111
Kishon, E. 204, 207
Klausner, J. 20, 86
Kolirin, E. 205
Kook, H. 92
Koshashvili, D. 207–8
Kracauer, S. 148–50
Krakotzkin, A.R. 227
Krier, L. 129
Krier, R. 129
Krois, S. 130
Kulthum, U. 108–10, 112–14, 277
Kundera, M. 208
Kurzweil, B. 89

Laakso, M. 72
Laufer, E. 109–12
Labour Party 59, 69, 77, 110, 265
Landshut, S. 148
Lavi, A. 202
Lazare, B. 91
Levantinisation 97, 100
Levinas, E. 274
Lévi-Strauss, C. 94
Levontin, Z. 18, 20
Lieberman, A. 34
Liebman, C. 286
Lifton, R.J. 142
Likud (political party) 77, 110–11, 214
Lilienblum, M. 18, 85
Livni, T. 77
Loshitzky, Y. 207
Luebbert, G. 66
Luttwak, E. 38

Madmoni, S. 206
Maimonides, M. 282
Malkin, I. 226
Malul, N. 18
Manuel, P. 114
Maoz, S. 208
Mashal, K. 47
Mediterranean option: as culture 10, 99–101, 118–20, 126–7, as policy 49–50, 207; as solution 8, 85–7, 95, 99–101, 227
Melamed, E. 287
Melucci, A. 144

Memi, A. 226
Mendelsohn, E. 120
Meretz 59, 110–11
Michael, S. 151–2, 154
Middleton, R. 114
migrant workers *see* immigration
Miller, A.D. 38
Miller, C. 146–7
Mizrahi Jews: and Arab culture 1–2, 8, 10, 59–60, 108–9, 146–8, 215, 278–, 232–3, 265–71; attempts to define Israeli culture 51–2, 202, 205–9, 231–3; attempts to define own culture 6–7, 9–10, 52, 105–15, 140–1, 146–54, 202, 205–9, 231– 3, 266–71; in film 229; and Ottoman Empire 18; and political parties 70, 110; and religion 97, 289; immigration to the United States 166; and Zionism 147
Mizrahi, M. 232
Modernism 11, 85; in architecture 123, 126–7, 133; Islamic response 3–6
Mohammed 273
Mohar, E. 223
Moroccan Jews 106, 109–12, 114, 202, 204, 206–8, 232, 270
Moshe, H. 113–14
Muller, W.C. 72, 75
Mumford, L. 133
Musil, R. 145
Myers, D. 227

Nasser, A. 34, 113
National-Religious-Zionism 11, 279–86; and democracy 285; and homosexuality 286–7; and the internet, attitudes towards Palestinians 281–5; and settlements 93, 281–3, 286–7
Nazareth 205, 208, 218
Nehama, Z. 108
Netanyahu. B. 33–4, 77, 110–11, 264–5
Netsarim 288
Nocke, A. 226, 228–9
Nordau, M. 118

Occidentalism 2–6, 11
Ohad, M. 107
Ohana, D. 207, 225–7, 233
Olmert, E. 183
Orientalism 2–3, 45, 86, 214,
Ottoman Empire 5, 15–7, 20
Oz, A. 97, 200, 214, 232
Ozick, C. 271

Palestinians: adolescents 10, 239–55; conflict with Israel 8, 36, 40, 47–8, 51, 56, 98–101; in Israeli cinema 202, 208; in Israeli literature 275; and orientation 62, 87, 94, 96–7, 101, 110, 112, 212, 240; labor relations 182–3; and peace process 33, 35–6, 38, 58, 60, 110; in relation to Israeli-Arabs 273; and the United Nations 27
Pappe, I. 215
Paran, D. 220
parenting 161–73, 269
Parmenides 146
Pavlides, E. 134
Peres, S. 37, 46, 77, 110–2, 265
Perlov, D. 200, 203
Petah Tikva 20, 205
Pinkerfeld, Y. 120, 129
Piron, S. 279, 282
public opinion: and age 56–7, 59; Arab-Israeli 60–1; and ethnic origin 54–55; and orientation 47, 51–6; and political orientation 58–9; and religion 57–8
Pudovkin, V. 224
Pukhachewsky, N. 24

Qadhafi, M. 47

Rabin, L. 112
Rabin, Y. 106, 110–12, 265
Radding, A. 122
Radler-Feldman, Y. 22
Rahat, G. 66
Raijman, R. 187
Ramati, A. 200
Ratosh, Y. 51, 89–92
Ratzel, F. 132
Rav-Hai, D.B. 71
Ravitsky, A. 96
Raz-Krakotzin, A. 270
regional integration: cultural 2, 7, 22–4, 27, 51–61, 63, 118, 134; economic 45–6, 51–61, 63; political 7, 26–7, 29, 63
Rejwan, N. 154
Revach, Z. 207
Ritter, C. 131–2
Romann, M. 273–4
Rosh Pina 23
Rosenberg, M. 201
Rosenzweig, F. 91
Rossi, A. 129
Rotblitt, Y. 110–11, 114

Rudofsky, B. 129
Russian Jews 2, 16–17, 34, 56, 90, 178, 241

Sa'ada, A. 90
Said, E. 86, 95, 214
Sappir, S.L. 273
Sartori, G. 67–8
Schatz, B. 118
Schinkel, K.F 131
Schnell, I. 240
Schorr, R. 230
Semyonov, M. 187
Sharon, A. 288
Shā'ul, A. 148
Sherlo, Y. 279, 287
secularism 3–5, 85, 101, 265
Semper, G. 120
Senor, D. 38
Sephardi Jews *see* Mizrahi Jews
Serlin, Y. 71
Setton, R. K. 270
settlers *see* National-Religious-Zionism, West Bank, Gaza
Shabi, R. 271
Shakespeare, W. 205–7
Shamir, E. 223
Shani, Y. 208
Shavit, Y. 226
Shenhav, Y. 1, 10, 153
Shiloah, A. 114
Shimoni, Y. (Subliminal) 233
Shohat, E.: film criticism 200, 216, 220, 230, 232–3; on Israeli identity 212, 225; and Mizrahi identity 1, 10, 153
Shoshan, D. 106
Singer, S. 38
Smilansky, I. 199
Smilansky, M. 22, 199
Smooha, S. 2, 240
Sobol, Y. 92, 275
Sokolov, N. 85–6
Sokolovsky, N. 201
Somekh, S. 154
Soviet Jews *see* Russian Jews
Steiner, G. 91
Strom, K. 72
Suleiman, E. 208
Swidler, A. 223
Swissa, A. 270
Sznaider, N. 144

Taagepera, R. 72
Taviani, P. 226

Taviani, V. 226
Tavori, S. 170–1
Tel Aviv 34, 185, 218, 288; architecture,118–34, 185; and orientation 8, 106–7, 200, 205–6, 241, 265, 288
television: and cultural orientation 9, 169, 212, 216, 219–20, 228, 231
Temple, H.J. (Lord Palmerston) 48
Tiberias 229–30
Tira 272
Torati, B. 206–7
Tshernichovsky, S. 206–7
Tsror, R. 106

ultra-orthodox *see* ultra-religious
ultra-religious 2, 7, 55–7, 70, 285, 287
Uris, L. 200, 202

Vinitzky-Seroussi, V. 265

Wehebe, H. 110
Weingrod, A. 273–4
Weinstein, A. 280
West Bank: in cinema 215, 217; economy of 43; Hamas and 36, 41; Israeli policy in 27; settlements in 241,279–80, 283, 287, 290; violence in 239, 247
Wilson, A. T. 147

Xenophon 3

Yalan, E. 123
Yehoshua, A.B. 91, 97, 265, 268, 272
Yemenite Jews 70, 110, 113, 201–2, 268
Yishuv: architecture 8; migrant labor 182–3; orientation 1, 6, 8, 15–24, 85–93; security issues 16; Separatism vs. integration debate 22–4; political parties 68–71
Yossef, O. 289

Zalmona, Y. 86
Zarhin, S. 224, 228–33
Zionism 88–90, 95–7, 101; and Arabs 21–4, 28, 36–9, 42, 48, 52, 86, 225; and architecture 132–4; and cinema 199–203, 213; and Crusader analogy 85–8, 90, 92–8; mythology of 85–9, 93–4, 96, 101, 114, 182, 188, 212–13, 224–6, 228–30; and orientation 17–24, 40, 51, 85–7, 100, 118–20, 123–34, 146–50, 212, 270; and the Ottoman Empire 16–17, 20; post-Zionism 92–3, 97; and the United Nations 30
Zionist Congress 42, 65, 69, 85
Zizek, S. 97
Zohar, U. 230
Zücker, P. 120–1

www.routledge.com/middleeaststudies

Also available...

Routledge Handbook of Modern Israel

Edited by Alain Dieckhoff

Israel is a country made up of contradictions. A lively democracy in a multicultural society but within a state promoting a strong national identity; a thriving economy in an unequal society; a culture open to modern trends but drawing on the Hebrew past and preoccupied with the Holocaust and the Arab-Israeli conflict; a sovereign member in the international arena, whose existence is still contested in the Middle East.
The Routledge Handbook of Modern Israel provides a comprehensive profile of the intricacies of contemporary Israel, offering a unique, in-depth survey of the country.

Organized thematically, a full range of topics are discussed, including:
- Politics and international relations
- The foundation of the Israeli state
- The birth and development of the Israeli economy
- Israeli culture
- Israel's role in the Middle East

Bringing together more than thirty notable contributors from across the globe, this *Handbook* sheds light on the multifaceted reality of modern Israel in order to better understand, beyond clichés, this complex society.

February 2013: 234x156: 358pp // **Hb:** 978-0-415-57392-4
http://www.routledge.com/books/details/9780415573924/

Available from all good bookshops

www.routledge.com/middleeaststudies

Also available...

The War in Darfur:
Reclaiming Sudanese History

By Anders Hastrup

Series: Routledge Studies in Middle Eastern Society

No other crisis in Africa has received as much attention in the West during the past 10 years as the war in Darfur, yet the underlying complexities of the war and the background to the crisis remains poorly understood by scholars, activists and aid workers.

This anthropological study of the war in Darfur explores the personal experience of war from the perspective of those refugess who have fled from it and puts forward potential solutions to the conflict. Drawing on ethnographic research carried out in the refugee camps of neighboring eastern Chad, *The War in Darfur: Reclaiming Sudanese History* gives a voice to people who to date have had little opportunity to articulate their experiences.

Through facilitating the telling of the refugees' tale, examining what happened and how, this book will be an interesting contribution to the areas of refugee studies, anthropology and history.

December 2012: 234x156: 166pp // Hb: 978-0-415-52487-2 // Eb: 978-0-203-07538-8

http://www.routledge.com/books/details/9780415524872/

Available from all good bookshops

www.routledge.com/middleeaststudies

Also available...

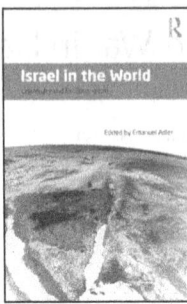

Israel in the World
Legitimacy and Exceptionalism

Edited by Emanuel Adler

Since independence, Israel has lived with a paradox, needing and seeking legitimacy, understanding, and empathy from the world community while simultaneously also discounting the world. This volume reflects upon Israel's troubled attempts to balance its desire to be different from a world that it simultaneously genuinely needs and that it also wants to be a legitimate member of.

Gathering distinguished scholars and public figures, this timely book discusses the causes and consequences of Israel's unsettled relations with the world. With essays ranging from an account of Israel's exile mentality and the cosmopolitanism of suffering to a fragmenting international legal order and whether an authentic religious process can transform religion into a powerful lever for peace, the book's innovative analysis will spark both academic and public debate.

Israel in the World: Legitimacy and Exceptionalism will appeal to scholars and students with broad ranging research interests including Middle East Studies, Israeli Studies and international relations more generally.

November 2012: 234x156: 150pp // Hb: 978-0-415-62415-2 // Pb: 978-0-415-63099-3

http://www.routledge.com/books/details/9780415630993/

Available from all good bookshops